T0284046

"THERE ARE NO HISPANIC STARS!"

GABRIEL NAVARRO

"THERE ARE NO HISPANIC STARS!"

COLLECTED WRITINGS OF A LATINO FILM CRITIC IN HOLLYWOOD, 1921–1939

EDITED & TRANSLATED BY
COLIN GUNCKEL & LAURA ISABEL SERNA

UCLA CHICANO STUDIES RESEARCH CENTER PRESS
LOS ANGELES
2023

CSRC Director: Veronica Terriquez
Project Director: Chon A. Noriega
Senior Editor: Rebecca Frazier
Copyeditor: Catherine A. Sunshine
Production: William Morosi

UCLA Chicano Studies Research Center
193 Haines Hall
Los Angeles, California 90095-1544
www.chicano.ucla.edu

UNIVERSITY OF
WASHINGTON PRESS
Seattle uwapress.uw.edu

Distributed by the University of
Washington Press
PO Box 50096
Seattle, Washington 98145-5096
www.washington.edu/uwpress

Cover: Gabriel Navarro at his typewriter, ca. 1925, while working for the Spanish-language newspaper *El Hispano Americano* in San Diego. The photograph near him on the left is of film star Dolores Del Rio. Photographer unknown. Image courtesy of Mike Navarro.

Library of Congress Cataloging-in-Publication Data
Names: Navarro, Gabriel, active 1926-1938, author. | Gunckel, Colin, 1975-
    editor. | Serna, Laura Isabel, 1971- editor.
Title: "There are no Hispanic stars!" : collected writings of a Latino film
    critic in Hollywood, 1921-1939 / Gabriel Navarro; [edited by Colin
    Gunckel, Laura Isabel Serna].
Description: Los Angeles : UCLA Chicano Studies Research Center Press,
    2023. | Includes bibliographical references and index. | Summary: "First
    English translations of three works of short fiction and a selection of
    articles from the 1920s and 1930s by Los Angeles cultural critic Gabriel
    Navarro. Navarro's columns, published in regional Spanish-language
    newspapers, focus primarily on the film industry"-- Provided by
    publisher.
Identifiers: LCCN 2023031650 (print) | LCCN 2023031651 (ebook) | ISBN
    9780895512048 (paperback) | ISBN 9780895512055 (ebook)
Subjects: LCSH: Navarro, Gabriel, active 1926-1938--Translations into
    English. | LCGFT: Film criticism. | Short stories.
Classification: LCC PN1998.3.N3817 A25 2023 (print) | LCC PN1998.3.N3817
    (ebook) | DDC 791.4309721--dc23/eng/20230724
LC record available at https://lccn.loc.gov/2023031650
LC ebook record available at https://lccn.loc.gov/2023031651

CONTENTS

Acknowledgments

This project took much longer than we had anticipated. That is not unusual for an academic project, but this book came to fruition, slowly, during a global pandemic. Both of us were dealing with the transition to online teaching and managing children suddenly learning at home. That said, it has been a joy to work together on this volume of translations. We have known each other for over a decade and each of us has seen our scholarship extended and complemented by the other's, so it was a delight to put our heads together to write about a figure we had both encountered during our respective research.

We would like to thank Chon Noriega for supporting this project. Garrison Sposito, Professor Emeritus of Environmental Engineering at the University of California, Berkeley, also deserves special recognition. His inquiry into our scholarship about his grandfather, Gabriel Navarro, ignited this project, and he patiently answered our questions, connected us with documents and photographs that we would not have had access to otherwise, and expressed enthusiasm as we made progress. We thank Aida Bautista for securing archival materials in Mexico and Eileen DiPofi for compiling the bibliography. Finally, we are grateful to the many colleagues, friends, and family who extended words of support and encouragement throughout this process.

ABOUT THE TRANSLATION

Gabriel Navarro wrote in a style typical of the time for Spanish-language authors. In practice this means long sentences, liberal use of semicolons, and a flowery vocabulary. We've made an effort to preserve the colorful, striking aspects of his prose while making the text accessible to modern English-language readers. We added endnotes to guide the reader through Navarro's references to literary figures, visual culture, and Mexican geography and culture that would have been familiar to his readers in the 1920s and 1930s. (There are also two original notes that Navarro himself included as footnotes on his writing; these are indicated as such.) Names of real persons that were misspelled in the original texts have been silently corrected.

In order to preserve Navarro's language, we have left certain words, such as *Cinema* capitalized for emphasis when they appear that way in the original texts. There are other words, such as *colonia*, that we opted not to translate from Spanish either because they are historically significant or because a satisfactory equivalent in English may not exist. We have also retained the various pan-ethnic identifiers Navarro used as they originally appeared: *Hispano American*, *Latino*, and *Hispano*, among others. However, for the sake of clarity, we have opted to use the umbrella term *Latina/o* in our introduction to refer to US-based people of Latin American descent. While it was a less common term in the 1920s and 1930s, our usage of *Latina/o* allows us to place Navarro's writing in conversation with other historical phenomena and contemporary issues in media studies, ethnic studies, and beyond.

INTRODUCTION

COLIN GUNCKEL AND LAURA ISABEL SERNA

Gabriel Navarro (1894–1950) was the most prolific Spanish-language film critic working in the United States during the 1920s and 1930s. He did not merely report on film news for his Spanish-speaking readers; he critically analyzed the relationship between mass culture and Mexican audiences in the United States. Over the course of his career, he confronted the racial hierarchies that structured Hollywood's practices of labor and representation, first in the silent film era and then during the industry's foray into Spanish-language film production. Throughout the 1930s, he also wrote extensively about a newly invigorated Mexican cinema. During this period he became one of the most prominent voices for Spanish-speaking audiences in the United States, always insisting that they deserved dignified representation on the silver screen. A playwright and musician himself, he firmly supported the immigrant cultural scene in Los Angeles as a site of self-determination and community formation.

Navarro wrote for a range of publications based in San Antonio, San Diego, and Los Angeles. His career is deeply intertwined with the mass migration of Mexicans to the United States in the wake of the Mexican Revolution (1910–17), the subsequent expansion of Spanish-language press culture in the United States, and the emergence of Hollywood as a global force. Despite his extensive body of work, which includes reams of cultural criticism, a number of theatrical works, several film scripts, and at least three pieces of long-form fiction, he is almost unknown today beyond a core of specialists working in Spanish-language literature, theater, or film in the United States. This volume, which makes a broad selection of his work available in English for the first time, seeks to remove the barriers of language and archival access that have obscured both Navarro's work and the place of Latina/os in US film history.

Beyond correcting a historical oversight, we aim to illuminate the vibrant migrant culturescape of early twentieth-century Los Angeles, "culturescape" being our term for the intertwined complex of popular literature, film, theater, and live musical performance, along with the immigrant press that documented and promoted them. Part of an alternative, cross-border public sphere, this migrant culturescape and its institutions both thrived on and contended with the influence of cinema made in both Hollywood and Mexico. Navarro's work grappled with all of these cultural forms and their varied impacts, compelling us to rethink this period in film history as fundamentally transnational and intermedial. The concept of migrant culturescape offers a framework through which other marginalized film histories might be studied, challenging the categories and boundaries that have left them in the shadows for too long. This extensive introduction sheds light on the significance of Navarro's work for US film history and histories of the Spanish-language press; provides a sketch of Navarro's life and career in the context of Mexican Los Angeles; discusses the major themes that animate his writing across forms and genres; and traces the contours of his media advocacy and its connections to contemporary efforts to claim a place for Latina/os in American media.

Immigrant Los Angeles and US Film History

Navarro's work challenges assumptions about the boundaries between cultural formations and the frames that have been placed around cinema as an object of study. It also illuminates the role of culture in navigating the tensions between immigrants' ties to Mexico—whether cultural, political, or affective—and their simultaneous engagement with American mass culture, a tension that has long preoccupied scholars. When historians set out to document the formation of ethnic Mexican communities in early twentieth-century Los Angeles, they often focused on how migrants' sense of self, daily lives, and political sensibilities were transformed by the racism and discrimination they experienced in the United States.[1] They also explored the cultural institutions that gave migrants refuge amid this hostility, created space for community building, and reinforced links between migrants and their home countries.[2] Chief among those institutions was the Spanish-language press, which expanded in scope and reach in the early twentieth century, and a vibrant Spanish-language live theater network that extended across the Southwest.[3] Cinema was a more problematic form of media, characterized sometimes as an agent of acculturation, if not outright assimilation, and at other times as the site of audience agency.[4]

As both of us have explored in our scholarship, despite skepticism regarding the influence of US mass culture, ethnic Mexican cinema culture prospered across the Southwest and the US-Mexico border region in the early twentieth century.[5] Ethnic Mexican audiences—composed of US-born and migrants alike—in border towns and urban immigrant enclaves were served by entrepreneurs who regularly screened films produced in the United States alongside live entertainment and community events, integrating Hollywood films into ethnic Mexican life.[6] The creation of these theaters was largely a response to segregation that frequently relegated Mexican patrons to specific sections of motion picture venues or excluded them entirely. With the introduction of sound technology in the late 1920s, these venues adapted to make Spanish-language films, whether produced in Hollywood or elsewhere, a significant share of their offerings. By the 1930s, Los Angeles alone had nearly a dozen movie theaters that screened Spanish-language films; between the late 1920s and the 1960s, an astounding seventy venues in the city were dedicated to Spanish-language cinema at some point in time.[7] From the 1930s onward, these theaters showed nearly every feature film produced by Mexico, in addition to films from Argentina, Spain, and Cuba.[8] On a national level, such theaters were spread across the Southwest and other localities where Spanish-speaking migrants settled, from Detroit to New York.[9] Navarro's criticism primarily addressed the audiences that frequented these spaces.

Even a cursory glance at Mexican Los Angeles during the early twentieth century troubles the boundaries and assumptions that have typically shaped the writing of film history. Theaters presented Hollywood silent films for Mexican immigrant audiences alongside Spanish-language musical performances and live theater; performers regularly moved throughout the Southwest and across the US-Mexico border; Mexican films shared local screens with "Poverty Row" B movies and Argentine features; and critics like Navarro wrote for an audience of fellow immigrants in the borderlands and beyond. These phenomena elude both the text-centric approaches of Mexican film studies and accounts of early twentieth-century film cultures in the United States, a body of work that relies largely on English-language sources or materials produced by the Hollywood film industry.

A rigorous, more inclusive historical understanding of American film history requires accounting for this film culture, along with others that emerged as a by-product of racial discrimination and residential segregation. A historical narrative that embraces this complexity and integrates US film history *and* ethnic Mexican cultural life requires that we acknowledge whiteness as being at the center of prevailing histories of classic Hollywood, as some scholars have already done.[10] It also requires the painstaking work of recovering other means of participating in film culture beyond on-screen representation and developing analytic frameworks that decenter the nation as a primary lens for thinking about how film fit into migrant cultural life in early twentieth-century Los Angeles.

Film studies, like the study of media more broadly, has historically adopted the nation and national cinemas as historiographic and analytic frameworks. Discrete national cinemas, demarcated most frequently by language and geography, have often been placed in opposition to Hollywood, posited as alternative, competing, or minor cinemas. While generating a wealth of scholarship that continues to enhance our understanding of film history, conventional categories like the nation can obscure as much as they reveal. Indeed, phenomena that fall between national frames or outside of them (like migrant film cultures) are often treated as outliers and exceptions within much of the literature on national cinemas. These limitations are exacerbated by a scholarly tendency to understand these cinemas as a procession of films, rather than as a multifaceted cultural and social experience.

In part to address the limitations of nationally bound analyses, transnational frameworks have gained purchase in cinema and media studies over the past two decades. Globalization, the growing interdependence of economies, and the social and cultural impacts of neoliberal policies became the catalyst for scholarly analysis of the transnational dimensions of cinema. Topics include the circulation of cinema across national borders, regional cinemas, the themes generated by unevenly distributed forms of global mobility, and the movement of creative personnel across borders.[11] This conceptual shift also led to scholarly inquiry into the transnational dimensions of film's circulation in the past and allowed scholars to foreground regional dynamics, opening up new ways of studying national cinemas as the product of local debates about what films and film culture count as national, rather than as predetermined categories.[12]

We would venture to say that the history of Latina/os and cinema has always been transnational. The transnational nature of this history is undeniably specific; nonetheless, it is part of a more capacious, expansive understanding of US film history that disrupts the equation of "American film" with Hollywood and white audiences by examining the film production and film cultures of communities relegated to the margins of Hollywood.[13]

Rather than merely including marginalized communities, such scholarship asks us to reframe a film history that has been shaped by industry and archival practice, public discourse, academic theory, and historiography. Mexicans were never outside Hollywood looking in, with aspirations to belong, but were always already deeply enmeshed in the industry, broadly conceived, and in the cultural formations that emerged out of production, distribution, and reception of Hollywood films. Reconstructing that history entails not only "looking past the screen" but also looking beyond the English-language US film industry and its films, stars, publicity materials, and trade press.[14]

Indeed, beyond a transnational framework that examines "a realm of interdependence or relation that, by definition, supersedes national sovereignty and boundaries," we might productively view this local, immigrant film culture through the lens of entanglement.[15] *Histoire croisée*, which translates roughly as entangled histories, is an approach that seeks to explore connections, interrelations, and mutual influences that emerge between social groups that very often possess asymmetrical levels of power but whose histories are deeply connected.[16] Scholars in the field of Atlantic history, for example, have mobilized the notion of entangled histories to help us understand the relationships between imperial powers in the Americas.[17] Other scholars have used the conceptual framework of entanglement to explore the production of religious, ethnic, or regional identities in diverse geographic and temporal contexts ranging from medieval Europe to Manchuria.[18] In contrast to comparative history, which seeks to demonstrate similarities and differences, or even transnational histories, which presuppose the existence of the national as a discrete entity, entangled histories refocus on interconnections at the local, regional, and supraregional levels as mutually constitutive. Media history scholars have begun to apply this frame to global media histories in scholarship that focuses on the relationship between media forms and across national boundaries.[19] Indeed, shuttling between media and across borders, Navarro's writing—as both historical document and critical intervention—presents us with a cultural milieu that was thoroughly intermedial and transnational. In this context local immigrant film culture was deeply entangled with Hollywood *and* Mexican cinema, as well as with other dimensions of migrant cultural life. As Michele Hilmes has argued, tracing the multidimensional career of a "cultural translator" like Navarro can expand film and media studies by challenging the primacy of national boundaries and the scholarly tendency to focus on a single medium.[20]

Navarro's life and work shifts our understanding of the relationship between Latina/os and Hollywood in several important ways. Examining his criticism and his literary works in tandem presents a fuller picture of the role of the author/journalist in the formation of a Mexican immigrant film culture. His writing bridged the divide between fiction, nonfiction, criticism, and cultural commentary, suggesting the diverse ways in which both film culture and the Spanish-language press permeated Mexican immigrant life. What's more, it demonstrates the way that journalism and authorship were used as tools of community building, activism, advocacy, cultural retention, and identity formation. Navarro, like many of his generation, imagined his readers as belonging to communities at multiple levels, from the local Mexican colonia in Los Angeles to the Spanish-speaking United States to a broader "Hispano American" public. As such, his writing gestures toward emerging hemispheric and pan-ethnic identities and the role of media in fostering them. While G. Cristina Mora has demonstrated how multiple constituencies, including media industries and advertisers, had invested in the concept of a pan-ethnic "Hispanic" population by the early 1970s, Navarro's work reveals that an analogous array of media interests, journalists, and community advocates began proposing similar formulations nearly five decades earlier.[21]

Just as important, Navarro's work allows us to more fully appreciate that Mexican immigrants, and Latina/os more broadly, spoke back to cinema in complex and often ambivalent ways. For the most part, scholarship on Latina/os and cinema in the 1920s and 1930s focuses either on the analysis of on-screen representation and narrative function or on the careers of prominent Latina/o stars of the period like Dolores Del Rio and Ramon Navarro.[22] As valuable and necessary as such scholarship may be, it does not account for the myriad ways that Mexican immigrants during the period experienced, engaged with, and participated in film culture and multiple film industries. In shifting our analysis to sources in Spanish-language publications, including film reviews, interviews, cultural commentary, and novels, scholars are able to gauge the various uses and meanings of cinema as it circulated through specific geographic or cultural contexts. Navarro's writing is but one prominent example of the critical reception of Hollywood films by Mexican immigrant audiences. It also provides tantalizing glimpses of other dimensions of the historical relationship between cinema and Latina/o audiences, from the plight of Mexican extras who labored anonymously at the studios to the formation of amateur film clubs.

This is not to say that Latina/os did not produce (or want to produce) their own cinematic representations. If we search for independent Latina/o film production during the period, it most certainly existed. A handful of filmmakers such as Guillermo Calles, Romualdo Tirado, and Jaime del Amo produced independent films by, about, and for Latina/os between the 1920s and 1930s (although prints of most of them no longer exist).[23] There were also a number of very short-lived studio ventures.[24] But in general, a marginalized and economically distressed population could not support or sustain an alternative film industry. And, as is more widely known, Latina/os struggled to find a foothold in the Hollywood film industry. On-screen roles were largely limited to stereotypical depictions or background work. Off-screen opportunities were even more limited, particularly before the studios' experiments in Spanish-language production briefly opened up the possibility of consulting, directing, translating, and screenwriting work.

But when we look beyond the screen, we discover a rich media and performance culture in Mexican Los Angeles that responded to, built on, criticized, or otherwise engaged with the popularity of cinema among Mexican immigrants. The pages of *La Prensa* (San Antonio) and *La Opinión* (Los Angeles) provide evidence of a broad readership of Spanish-speaking movie fans across the borderlands and beyond to whom Navarro addressed his work. Navarro also wrote dramatic theater, vaudeville-style revistas, fiction, biography, and film criticism. Like film magazines, these various dramatic and literary genres can be understood as intermedial points of connection between the Hollywood film industry (mostly) and other dimensions of Mexican immigrant cultural life.[25] Adopting this vantage point, exploring these connections, and fully engaging such sources in Spanish allow us to approach the history of Latina/os and media on different terms. We take seriously the challenge posed by recent work in film history that proposes an expansive conception of cinema, connects film culture to social processes, places cinema within a broader cultural ecology, and upends conventional distinctions between text and context.[26] What's more, translating their work allows figures like Navarro to be written into broader histories of film criticism and reception in the United States. The present volume constitutes the most extensive translation of Spanish-language film criticism published in this country to date.[27]

If Navarro's career and published work prompts us to think differently about film history and film criticism, it also allows us to think in new ways about the history of Mexican print culture in the United States. Navarro's work troubles the linguistic and national boundaries of existing literary canons, especially those concerned with nonfiction. Spanish-language literature produced in the United States has been largely excluded from accounts of both national and regional literature. This exclusion has played out in terms of both language and genre.[28] The research, preservation, and digitization efforts of Arte Público Press in its Recovering the US Hispanic Literary Heritage project have done much to provide access to this over-looked body of Spanish-language work, as have the translated volumes that Arte Público has published.[29] Such efforts challenge conventional accounts of American literary history, but work like Navarro's, written and published by Mexicans living in the United States, also offers crucial glimpses into immigrant experiences and attitudes in the early twentieth century, helping us sketch a more complete picture of migrant culturescapes.

In the early decades of the twentieth century, newspapers were central components of Mexican immigrant cultural life, especially in large cities like Los Angeles and San Antonio. If, as literary scholars Sean Latham and Robert Scholes assert, the historical study of periodicals reveals "often surprising and even bewildering points of contact between disparate areas of human activity," Spanish-language newspapers, where Navarro found his profes-sional home, served as a nexus where local businesses, entertainment venues, literature, politics, and community advocacy groups like mutual aid societies met and intertwined.[30] As Kirsten Silva Gruesz contends, these newspapers were part of networks of circulation that made a wide range of literature, including religious texts, instruction manuals, translated classics, and popular fiction, as well as news and advertisements, available to Spanish-language readers across the Southwest.[31] The study of Spanish-language newspapers thus allows scholars to trace the contours of the commercial, cultural, and political life of Mexican Los Angeles.

Finally, while scholars have identified early examples of media activism during the silent period, sustained critique of on-screen representation is a phenomenon more closely associated with the civil rights movements of the 1960s and 1970s.[32] Navarro's multilayered engagement with Hollywood's representational and labor practices represents an early, unappreciated chap-ter in the history of criticism and advocacy by communities the industry has historically marginalized. Arcelia Gutiérrez has argued that activism has largely been overlooked as a factor that informs decisions within the indus-try, potentially impacting on-screen representation.[33] Exploring Navarro's role as an advocate for Mexican immigrant audiences and as an intermediary between his readership and Hollywood demonstrates how his efforts worked to shape the industry's early approach to both Latina/o audiences in the United States and the Latin American market, not to mention the overlap between them. Navarro's efforts require us to revise existing histories of Latina/o media activism, extending them further into the past. They also gesture toward histories yet to be excavated, materials and accounts that might further transform the history of Latina/os and the media.

MEXICAN LOS ANGELES

While clearly exceptional, Navarro's career is inextricable from the larger history of Mexican immigration to Los Angeles in the early twentieth century. After the 1848 Treaty of Guadalupe Hidalgo, California's residents of Mexican descent were automatically granted US citizenship, though their access to the rights and benefits of citizenship was tenuous and subject to the whims of the state's Anglo settlers.[34] Throughout the remainder of the nineteenth century, this population was supplemented by those migrating to the Southwest to find work in agriculture, mining, or railroad construction. This phenomenon accelerated by the turn of the century as the result of multiple factors. While Mexico experienced unprecedented economic growth under the dictatorship of Porfirio Díaz, this was propelled in part by foreign investment and came at the expense of the rural poor. At the same time, California's agricultural economy was booming. Transcontinental railroad connections and refrigerated train cars allowed the state to supply the country with citrus and other produce, facilitating the expansion of industrial agriculture and the need for labor along with it.[35] Widespread industrialization and electrification also spurred a copper-mining boom that drew Mexicans across what was still a relatively porous border; mining towns in New Mexico and Arizona became stopping points for migrants who would eventually make their way to Southern California.[36] With restrictive, xenophobic immigration measures cutting off the influx of workers from East Asia, Mexican immigrants emerged as the preferred source of cheap labor.

These factors set the stage for what would become a mass exodus of Mexican nationals in the first decades of the twentieth century. In 1910 simmering unrest exploded into a full-blown revolution with the removal of Porfirio Díaz and the installation of the moderate reformer Francisco I. Madero as president. Over the next decade Mexico descended into a bloody civil war, with multiple factions in various parts of the country vying for control of the nation. This violent conflict generated economic precarity and fostered political persecution of the supporters of various factions as they lost power or fell out of favor. Out of a population of 15 million, approximately 350,000 to 400,000 people crossed the US-Mexico border, some as political refugees but many more as economic refugees.[37] An almost equal number migrated to the United States in the 1920s, though most scholars agree that the real figures are likely higher given the inability of state sources to account for unofficial migration. As a result, the growing US agriculture and railroad industries had a steady supply of workers.

During this second wave of Mexican immigration to the United States, many more immigrants came to California. Los Angeles, along with cities such as Denver, El Paso, and San Antonio, became home to what some at the time referred to as readily available "reservoirs of labor."[38] As George Sánchez notes, Los Angeles was a particularly attractive destination to migrants. After working in seasonal agriculture or other temporary positions in the region, laborers would often spend winters in Los Angeles; before long, many settled there permanently.[39] By 1930 the population of Los Angeles, which had transformed into a bustling metropolis, exceeded a million people; about 10 percent of this (likely undercounted) population was of Mexican descent.

Mexican immigrants contributed to the explosive economic growth of the city and of the greater Southern California region. Their presence led to the formation of a commercial, social, and civic infrastructure that catered to their needs for access to consumer goods, leisure opportunities, and support in their new surroundings. Among the most important of these organizations were mutual aid societies such as the Liga Protectora Latina, which was founded in 1914 and had branches in California, New Mexico, and Arizona. Mutual aid societies provided death benefits and other forms of social assistance to their members as well as taking up issues of employment discrimination and civil rights for Mexican immigrants.[40] They also worked to sustain and celebrate a sense of Mexican culture, language, and community in an often-hostile environment by, for example, holding public celebrations of Mexican holidays or organizing in support of community members in need. Other community groups were more ephemeral, arising in response to specific issues or incidents.[41] Alongside civic organizations, businesses like small department stores, pharmacies, photo studios, record stores, and offices offering medical and legal services opened in or around downtown and in other barrios to cater to the Spanish-speaking population.

Coincident with the rapid expansion of commercialized leisure in the early twentieth century, Mexican immigrants in Los Angeles also participated in a rich cultural world, mostly in Spanish, that generated its own perspectives and visions of Mexican life in Los Angeles. Record stores like Mauricio Calderón's Repertorio Musical Mexicana sold phonographs and records, as independent and major labels alike aspired to capitalize on "ethnic" markets.[42] As cinema and vaudeville theaters proliferated throughout downtown, a number of venues opened that catered to an immigrant demographic, including Teatro Estela, the Plaza Theater, and Teatro Hidalgo. These theaters hosted a diverse and ever-changing array of entertainment, including musical performances, cinema, touring theatrical troupes from Mexico, local theater productions, variety shows, and radio broadcasts. By the early 1930s, in fact, cultural brokers like Pedro J. González were purchasing airtime for their Spanish-language radio programs—often broadcasting live from local theaters—and finding an enthusiastic and receptive audience.[43] The Spanish-language press served as a clearinghouse of information about services and entertainment in Los Angeles, highlighting local businesses and events in their coverage and offering advertisements directly aimed at the ethnic Mexican community. Editors of these papers maintained close connections with civic organizations and other community-based efforts. A young Gabriel Navarro entered this vibrant cultural milieu in the late teens. His professional life became intimately intertwined with both the Spanish-language press and the Mexican community's entertainment and leisure culture.

GABRIEL NAVARRO

Navarro was among the diverse group of Mexican immigrants that came to Los Angeles in the early twentieth century. In broad strokes, his life followed a trajectory common to many of his compatriots. He was born in 1894 in Talpa de Allende, a small silver-mining town in the highlands of the western Mexican state of Jalisco which would become the site of intense revolutionary activity in 1913. At some point during the revolution, he joined the forces of the constitutionalist general Venustiano Carranza, and after the military phase of the conflict ended, he made his way to Southern California sometime between 1918 and 1919.[44] Though his precise route across the border is unknown, by 1919 he was in Los Angeles with his then wife, Leonor Díaz, who was about to give birth to their third and only surviving child, Gabriel.[45]

Like other Mexican immigrants, Navarro sought opportunities to establish himself in his new home. Unlike others, he possessed some distinctive skills. He was a musician—he had, one publication asserted, served as the director of Carranza's National Military Band—and he was literate.[46] He used these two forms of cultural capital to carve out a space for himself in elite circles of the Los Angeles Mexican immigrant community. In May 1920, the Los Angeles newspaper *El Heraldo de México* noted that a promising young musician named Gabriel Navarro was employed in the orchestra at Tally's Theatre (also known during the 1920s as Tally's Broadway Theatre).[47] The young musician was also busy composing his own music.

Around this time Navarro's byline began to appear in *El Heraldo de México*, at first as the author of a series of published editorials commenting on Mexico's political situation during the ill-fated provisional presidency of Adolfo de la Huerta, who, along with Alvaro Obregón, had helped overthrow the more conservative Carranza. In those editorials Navarro expressed his dismay at the state of affairs in Mexico.[48] That Navarro would be skeptical if not critical of the radical turn the revolution seemed to take is not surprising. During the late teens and early 1920s, the Mexican immigrant community was ideologically diverse, as it is today; it included many who had fought for competing revolutionary factions and held distinct views on Mexico's future.[49] In addition to the series of editorials published in the summer of 1920, Navarro also tried his hand at penning poetic historical accounts such as his reflection on the Mexican War of Independence, "Los mártires," as well as romantic poems, short stories, and reviews of musical concerts.[50]

During this period Navarro integrated himself into the life of the Mexican immigrant community in Los Angeles. He joined Liga Protectora Latina and became an active member, speaking at meetings, which frequently combined light musical entertainment with the group's business agenda, and serving as master of ceremonies for Liga cultural events. He actively fundraised for the celebration of Mexico's centenary in 1921.[51] Navarro also participated in the life of the migrant community's elite, attending society events and receiving mentions in *El Heraldo*'s social pages.[52] Navarro offers a fictionalized account of one such event in his 1925 novella *La Señorita Estela (Historia de un amor)* (Señorita Estela [A Love Story]) (fig. 1).

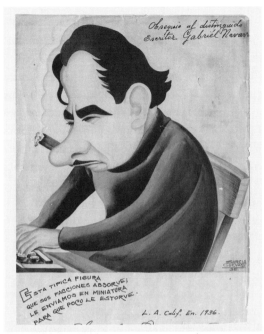

FIGURE 1. Caricature of Gabriel Navarro by García Cuevas, 1936. The inscription reads, "A gift to the distinguished writer Gabriel Navarro" and "This typical figure shows your features. We send it to you in miniature so it won't get in your way. Los Angeles, CA, 1936." Image courtesy of Mike Navarro.

As Navarro made inroads in the Spanish-language press as a journalist and later an editor, his marriage to Leonor dissolved. In 1924 he met María de la Luz Flores Aceves, a young Mexican singer better known as Lucha Reyes, who had come to Los Angeles to perform and study music.[53] Their relationship has been described in biographical accounts of Reyes as turbulent, perhaps even violent, and short-lived.[54] After his split from Reyes, who returned to Mexico, Navarro left Los Angeles for San Diego, where he served as editor of the newspaper *El Hispano Americano*. During this time he wrote *La Señorita Estela (Historia de un amor)*, which was published by the Sociedad Editora Mexicana, a publishing concern associated with the newspaper. He contributed film-related content to *La Prensa*, a widely circulating daily Spanish-language newspaper based in San Antonio. He also became a regular contributor to and entertainment section editor of *La Prensa*'s sister publication in Los Angeles, *La Opinión*, upon its founding in 1926. At some point, likely in the late 1920s or early 1930s, he created a radio program, "La Hora de Hollywood," which would have brought his commentary on the industry to Southern California's Spanish-language radio waves.[55] During the American film industry's transition to sound, he became both an invested observer and occasional dialogue consultant for films set in "Latin" locales and for Hollywood Spanish-language productions. In 1929, after a brief second marriage, he met his third wife, Clara María Flores, on the set of the Warner Bros. technicolor musical *Under a Texas Moon* (1930, dir. Michael Curtiz), reportedly the first sound film to be shot completely outdoors.[56] They had two children, Francisco Daniel (Dan) and James Raul (Mike), and remained married until Navarro's death in 1950 (fig. 2).[57] In the 1940s Navarro edited *El Pueblo*, a Los Angeles–area Spanish-language periodical, no copies of which survive.[58]

While some accounts suggest that Navarro turned to journalism when his prospects in the theater seemed dim, the consistency with which his journalism, activities as a playwright, and cultural criticism overlapped suggests that Navarro himself saw them as complementary, if not intertwined. In 1922 he wrote a revista, *Los Angeles al día*, with another playwright, Eduardo A. Carrillo (a revista was a popular theatrical form in France, Spain, and Latin America that combined music, dance, and brief, often humorous theatrical sketches). This was followed by *Malditos sean los hombres* in

FIGURE 2. Navarro with his three sons, Francisco Daniel (Dan), Gabriel Jr. (Hap), and James Raul (Mike), 1943. The photograph was taken by Josephine Lucero, who married Gabriel Jr. five years later. Image courtesy of Mike Navarro.

1924. This play was an adaptation of a 1920 novel sometimes attributed to Spanish writer Manuel Ibo Alfaro but now known to have been written by Catalan author José Lezcano Comendador in 1904 and published under Comendador's own imprint.[59] In 1925 Navarro mounted a production in San Diego based on his novella *La Señorita Estela*.

The years 1927 and 1928 were particularly fertile for him. Another theatrical piece, *La ciudad de irás y no volverás* (The City of No Return), premiered in the fall of 1927 and was subsequently published as a serialized novel in the pages of *La Prensa*. Three other plays, *La tragedia del zorro* (The Tragedy of the Fox), *Los emigrados* (The Emigrants), and *La sentencia* (The Sentence), all premiered in Los Angeles in the first half of 1928. These productions, as Colin Gunckel has pointed out, were widely discussed in the press and made important contributions to the entertainment culture of immigrant Los Angeles.[60] What's more, Navarro's activities as a playwright built on his activities as a journalist and author. Two of his theatrical works were based on his books or other published fiction, and many of his works drew on the film culture in which he had immersed himself as a critic and columnist.

While it was never his primary vocation, Navarro occasionally became involved in film production after the introduction of sound technology. He wrote and voiced the Spanish-language commentary for the nationalist travelogue *Pro-Patria*, produced and directed by Mexican actor Guillermo Calles in 1932.[61] And when Hollywood began to produce Spanish-language films, Navarro not only wrote about these productions and the opportunities they presented for Mexican and other Latin American creative talent but also tried his own hand at writing dialogue. In 1938 he was listed with Enrique Uthoff as among the screenwriters for the Tito Guízar vehicle *Papá soltero* (1939, dir. Richard Harlan), which would be distributed by Paramount Pictures. He also wrote the dialogue for *El trovador de la radio*, a Paramount-Dario production (fig. 3).[62]

Over the course of his life, Navarro remained active in community affairs. As noted above, this initially took the form of involvement in the activities of the Liga Protectora and working to raise funds for celebrations mounted by the Mexican immigrant community in Los Angeles. In the 1920s he was also active in the Sociedad Filarmónica Mutualista, a mutual aid society for musicians in Los Angeles.[63] During this period he used his connections to the film industry to organize benefits for various causes. For example, in 1933 he was master of ceremonies and artistic director

FIGURE 3. Gabriel Navarro with Mexican singer and actor Tito Guízar, 1930s–1940s. Navarro worked with Guízar on four films released by Paramount Pictures in the late 1930s. Photographer unknown. Image courtesy of Mike Navarro.

of an event featuring Ramon Novarro, Dolores Del Rio, and Conchita Montenegro that was to benefit victims of a severe hurricane that had made landfall in Tampico.[64] During the 1940s he could be found at various civic and cultural events: celebrating the opening of a cultural center in East Los Angeles, appearing on the program of annual events honoring Mexican independence, or serving as guest conductor for musical programs that drew on a Mexican repertoire (fig. 4).[65]

FIGURE 4. Gabriel Navarro with actor Adolphe Menjou, likely on the set of *The Trumpet Blows* (1934, directed by Stephen Raft). Photographer unknown. Image courtesy of Mike Navarro.

In the 1940s Navarro was drawn to causes that brought him out of both the Mexican immigrant community and Hollywood and into the politics of multiracial Los Angeles. For Navarro, the boundaries between racially and linguistically segmented communities in Los Angeles were as porous as the boundaries between entertainment and politics. In addition to continuing his practice of organizing and appearing at civic events, he became more engaged in overtly political causes. He was a member of the Sleepy Lagoon Defense Committee, which had formed in the wake of the arrests, with little evidence, of seventeen young Mexican American men and their deeply problematic trial for a 1942 murder.[66] The Defense Committee, which was made up of activists and sympathetic public figures including Orson Welles and Rita Hayworth, supported the young Mexicans accused in the case and was labeled a communist front by the California state legislature's Joint Fact-Finding Committee on Un-American Activities in California.[67] In

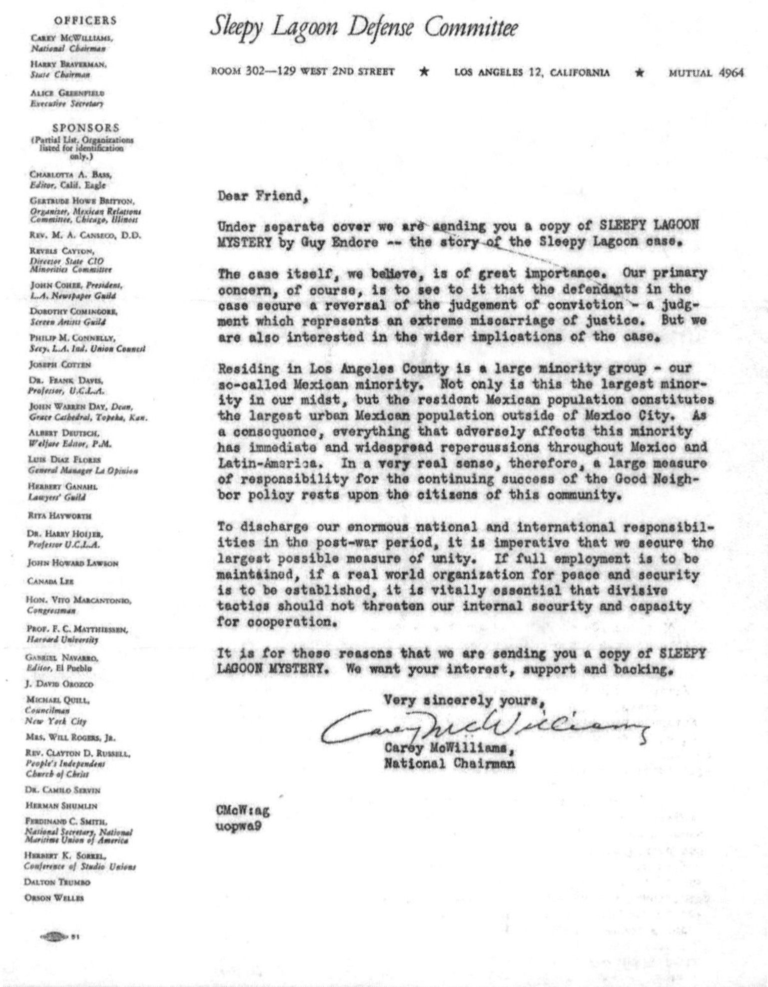

OFFICERS

Carey McWilliams, *National Chairman*

Harry Braverman, *State Chairman*

Alice Greenfield *Executive Secretary*

SPONSORS
(Partial List. Organizations listed for identification only.)

Charlotta A. Bass, *Editor*, Calif. Eagle

Gertrude Howe Britton, *Organizer, Mexican Relations Committee, Chicago, Illinois*

Rev. M. A. Canseco, D.D.

Revels Cayton, *Director State CIO Minorities Committee*

John Cohee, *President, L.A. Newspaper Guild*

Dorothy Comingore, *Screen Artists Guild*

Philip M. Connelly, *Secy. L.A. Ind. Union Council*

Joseph Cotten

Dr. Frank Davis, *Professor, U.C.L.A.*

John Warren Day, *Dean, Grace Cathedral, Topeka, Kan.*

Albert Deutsch, *Welfare Editor, P.M.*

Luis Diaz Flores *General Manager La Opinion*

Herbert Ganahl *Lawyers' Guild*

Rita Hayworth

Dr. Harry Hoijer, *Professor U.C.L.A.*

John Howard Lawson

Canada Lee

Hon. Vito Marcantonio, *Congressman*

Prof. F. C. Matthiessen, *Harvard University*

Gabriel Navarro, *Editor*, El Pueblo

J. David Orozco

Michael Quill, *Councilman New York City*

Mrs. Will Rogers, Jr.

Rev. Clayton D. Russell, *People's Independent Church of Christ*

Dr. Camilo Servin

Herman Shumlin

Ferdinand C. Smith, *National Secretary, National Maritime Union of America*

Herbert K. Sorrel, *Conference of Studio Unions*

Dalton Trumbo

Orson Welles

51

Sleepy Lagoon Defense Committee

ROOM 302—129 WEST 2ND STREET ★ LOS ANGELES 12, CALIFORNIA ★ MUTUAL 4964

Dear Friend,

Under separate cover we are sending you a copy of SLEEPY LAGOON MYSTERY by Guy Endore -- the story of the Sleepy Lagoon case.

The case itself, we believe, is of great importance. Our primary concern, of course, is to see to it that the defendants in the case secure a reversal of the judgement of conviction - a judgment which represents an extreme miscarriage of justice. But we are also interested in the wider implications of the case.

Residing in Los Angeles County is a large minority group - our so-called Mexican minority. Not only is this the largest minority in our midst, but the resident Mexican population constitutes the largest urban Mexican population outside of Mexico City. As a consequence, everything that adversely affects this minority has immediate and widespread repercussions throughout Mexico and Latin-America. In a very real sense, therefore, a large measure of responsibility for the continuing success of the Good Neighbor policy rests upon the citizens of this community.

To discharge our enormous national and international responsibilities in the post-war period, it is imperative that we secure the largest possible measure of unity. If full employment is to be maintained, if a real world organization for peace and security is to be established, it is vitally essential that divisive tactics should not threaten our internal security and capacity for cooperation.

It is for these reasons that we are sending you a copy of SLEEPY LAGOON MYSTERY. We want your interest, support and backing.

Very sincerely yours,

Carey McWilliams

Carey McWilliams,
National Chairman

CMcW:ag
uopwa9

FIGURE 5. Fundraising letter from Carey McWilliams, national chairman of the Sleepy Lagoon Defense Council, listing Gabriel Navarro, then publisher-editor of *El Pueblo*, as a sponsor of the council's efforts, 1944. UCLA Library Special Collections, Charles E. Young Research Library.

the wake of that activism, Navarro became a member of the Los Angeles Council for Civic Unity, a civil rights organization founded in 1943 that brought together labor activists, religious organizations, and other community groups to work against prejudice and discrimination (figs. 5, 6).[68]

Navarro died in December 1950 at the age of fifty-six. We do not have access to the obituaries that must have been printed in *La Opinión* and *La Prensa*, but scattered evidence suggests how he might have been remembered. Just four days after his death, the City of Los Angeles adopted a memorial resolution, sponsored by first-term councilman Edward

FIGURE 6. Navarro with Orson Welles, with whom he worked on the Sleepy Lagoon Defense Committee, 1944. Photographer unknown. Image courtesy of Mike Navarro.

FIGURE 7. The Los Angeles City Council resolution in honor of Gabriel Navarro, adopted shortly after his death in December 1950. Image courtesy of Mike Navarro.

Roybal.[69] The resolution highlighted Navarro's multifaceted career as a "newspaperman, musician, dramatist, poet, historian and lecturer" and drew attention to his contributions to the cultural life of the city and the fact that he had "devoted many years of his life to community affairs" (fig. 7).[70] On December 21 the Mayan Theater, reopened by Spanish-language film and live entertainment entrepreneur Frank Fouce in 1949 as the "Nuevo Teatro Máximo de la Raza Home of Mexican Film," held a benefit for the Navarro family.[71] The function included a performance of two songs written by Navarro, sung for the occasion by tenor Rodolfo Hoyos, a mainstay of Spanish-language theater and radio in Los Angeles since the 1930s.[72] The details of that benefit were surely covered in La Opinión but only warranted a cursory mention in an ad for independent theaters in the Los Angeles Times. Early the following year, the Spanish-language newspaper El Sol (Phoenix, Arizona) reported that Mexican officials were considering renaming one of the streets in Ciudad Miguel Alemán (formerly San Pedro de Roma, in the state of Tamaulipas) after Navarro, someone who "knew how to gallantly sustain pride in being Mexican, [who] lived dedicated to rendering admiration for the grand elements of his native land."[73]

These acknowledgments—as limited as our knowledge about some of them might be—speak to Navarro's central role in a dynamic, cross-border, Spanish-language migrant culturescape. By contrast, a short, unsigned obituary in the Los Angeles Times mentioned his role as the "Latin-American" founder of El Pueblo and a "top correspondent in Los Angeles for Mexico City newspapers during the days when Lupe Velez was at the height of her career" before briefly gesturing toward his "association" with La Opinión.[74]

In one short paragraph, the *Los Angeles Times* erased Mexican migrant Los Angeles, replacing it with a vaguely hemispheric context ("Latin-American") and making Navarro relevant only as a one-way conduit between two cosmopolitan centers, Los Angeles and Mexico City. Our account of Mexican Los Angeles's early film culture, which places Navarro at the center, seeks to counter this erasure and displacement, restoring the complexity and richness of both his experience as a writer, critic, and advocate and the experiences of his readers immersed in a migrant culturescape that included Hollywood, Mexico, and Mexican Los Angeles (fig. 8).

FIGURE 8. The last known photograph taken of Gabriel Navarro, 1950. Photographer unknown. Image courtesy of Mike Navarro.

THE SPANISH-LANGUAGE PRESS

As this brief account suggests, Navarro's professional trajectory was intimately linked with the flourishing of a new generation of Spanish-language publications that emerged in the early twentieth century. Serving primarily a working-class readership, the newspapers and other publishing operations were generally owned and staffed by an educated expatriate elite or middle class, many of them entrepreneurs who fled Mexico to avoid political persecution during the revolution. More exiles than immigrants, many of them remained deeply invested in Mexico, which is reflected in the amount of coverage their publications devoted to Mexico's economy and politics.[75] Among the most prominent of these figures was Ignacio Lozano. After establishing *La Prensa* in San Antonio in 1913, he began publishing the Los Angeles–based *La Opinión* in 1926, now the longest-running Spanish-language newspaper in the United States. He also owned Casa Editorial Lozano, a publishing house that specialized in books about Mexican politics, history, and culture, many of them penned by journalists working for his papers, including Navarro. The company also sold books from Mexico, Spanish-language versions of literary classics, business and household guides, and religious texts.[76]

As political exiles, Lozano and many of the journalists who wrote for his newspapers were generally critical of the revolution or supported more conservative factions within Mexico. These newspapers initially focused on keeping immigrants abreast of news from the homeland, under the assumption that Mexican nationals would return home once the conflict subsided. As more Mexicans continued to settle in the United States, however, such publications gradually shifted focus to helping immigrants navigate their new surroundings through a combination of news, sports coverage, entertainment pages, classified ads, and editorials.

Both of these functions point to the role of the Spanish-language press in offering a space for immigrants to discuss issues that affected their lives. Indeed, Nicolás Kanellos argues that newspapers like *La Prensa* and *La Opinión* were "community leadership institutions, often serving as forums for intellectuals, writers and politicians, and often spearheading political and social movements."[77] This aligns with Evelyn Brooks Higginbotham's observations that during the same period the Black press "functioned as a discursive, critical arena—a public sphere in which values and issues were aired, debated, and disseminated throughout the larger black community."[78]

Indeed, in Los Angeles the Spanish-language press functioned as one cornerstone of what Nancy Fraser calls a "subaltern counterpublic," an intertwined network that connected local businesses, civic organizations, the Mexican Consulate, radio, and Spanish-language entertainment like theater to enable the city's ethnic Mexicans to "formulate oppositional interpretations of their identities, interests, and needs."[79]

This counterpublic sphere was, however, also internally stratified, with educated or elite Mexican journalists often adopting a somewhat patronizing version of community guardianship toward their working-class readership. Although this "revolutionary generation" of migrants was politically diverse, as John H. Flores has shown, this class-based attitude of guardianship was a key component of the major daily newspapers from Los Angeles to San Antonio and Chicago.[80] As an educated class, publishers and journalists regarded it as their mission to guide and instruct their working-class compatriots by encouraging the maintenance of Catholic religious practice, the Spanish language, Mexican customs, and traditional gender norms. By safeguarding their Mexicanidad (or Mexicanness) while abroad, immigrants could avoid assimilating or succumbing to the supposedly corrupting influence of US culture as they awaited their eventual return home.[81] Across varied content and with this project of cultural maintenance in mind, newspapers promoted the notion of the Mexican immigrant community as "México de afuera," Mexico abroad, part of a nation that exceeded geopolitical borders and bound migrants to their homeland.[82] This ideology was fundamental to how Navarro viewed the cultural world of Mexican Los Angeles, animating his fiction and even his media criticism.

Central to this ideology were class-based ideas about traditional gender roles. For many of the Mexican immigrant elite, the American woman, often personified by the flapper, was by turns scandalous and intriguing, even titillating. But Mexican women, especially poor or working-class women, who copied the flapper's style and behavior were perceived as a threat to men and male privilege. As historian Vicki Ruiz notes, the flapper type was frequently satirized in popular culture such as corridos.[83] Perhaps paradigmatic in this respect was the writing of Julio G. Arce, a journalist and the publisher of *Hispano-America* in San Francisco. His Crónicas diabólicas (Diabolic Chronicles), a widely syndicated column, provided a picture of working-class immigrant life that frequently excoriated working-class women's desire to participate in American consumer culture, adopt new gender norms that included sexual freedom, and even marry outside of the immigrant community. This same set of concerns, and a pervasive dismissal of American and Americanized women as sexually promiscuous gold diggers, animated the fiction produced by Mexican and Mexican immigrant writers alike, including Navarro.[84]

POPULAR ROMANTIC FICTIONS

Navarro engaged in two distinct types of writing: long-form popular fiction that including a fictionalized star biography, and journalism that included regular columns, criticism, and editorials. Both types of writing grappled with the themes of national identity, cultural retention, and gender. Navarro's known long-form fiction includes the tragic romance *La Señorita Estela* (1925), a cautionary tale about a Mexican immigrant navigating the hypocrisy and deception of Los Angeles; *Barbara La Marr: Una historia de placer y dolor* (Barbara La Marr: A Story of Pleasure and Pain), a fictionalized biography of the silent film star (1926); and the incomplete serialized novel *La ciudad de irás y no volverás* (1926–27), which follows a young Mexican woman trying and failing to make her way in silent-era Hollywood. Each of these projects offered Navarro the opportunity to elaborate on the distinctions between Mexican and Anglo-American culture, critique modern gender norms, and forge connections between Mexican migrants and Hollywood film culture.

Across these works there is an abiding focus on Mexican womanhood and the intersection between gender, migration, national identity, and class. In this respect, his writings offer a window onto the concerns of the elite strata of the Mexican immigrant community in Los Angeles. They also offer tantalizing glimpses of Los Angeles in the 1920s, from the Mexican theaters on Main Street to chic celebrity haunts and Hollywood studios, tracing the Los Angeles that Navarro ostensibly traversed as a Mexican-born film critic. What's more, many of Navarro's observations in these longer works—about celebrity, aspiring actors, romantic love, and the perils of Hollywood—are echoed in his film criticism of the 1920s and 1930s.

In addition, Navarro's body of work maps the class hierarchies within the Mexican community of Los Angeles, from the respectable yet "pretentious" families of the West Side to what the narrator of *La ciudad de irás y no volverás* calls the "little repulsive theaters" on Main Street that served a working-class clientele.[85] But he also places Mexicans within a stratified, multiracial Los Angeles. His writing thus offers unique insight into the fraught relationships between marginalized populations as they navigated the racial hierarchies of

Los Angeles and Hollywood alike. In his criticism, Navarro noted the expectations that the film industry placed on both Asians and Latina/os to signal ethnic and racial difference so as to deliver some form of exotic appeal to US audiences.[86] At other moments, as he does in *Barbara La Marr*, he seemingly reproduces Hollywood's exotifying gaze, casting Asians as caricatures that could have walked off the silver screen. This reliance on stereotypes implicitly lends comparative humanity and complexity to the Mexican characters of his fictional works, just as his characters use racial differences to bolster class status. For instance, while Navarro (as author and critic) and his fictional avatar, Fidel Murillo, seem to move freely among Mexican Los Angeles and Hollywood nightspots, anonymous Asian characters are relegated to spaces like Chinese restaurants, serving as an exotic backdrop to the narrative's action. Navarro likewise makes it apparent that the Black population of Los Angeles occupied the bottom of the city's racial hierarchy, especially in terms of the labor market.[87] Skewering the veneer of respectability adopted by the Mexican "aristocracy" of Los Angeles in *La Señorita Estela*, one of Estela's so-called society friends actually works "like a black woman in an overalls factory." While hardly a thorough analysis of Los Angeles's racial landscape, his work offers a provocative portrait of a city and industry in which marginalized groups jockeyed for position relative both to white power structures and to one another.

Notably, romantic love is at the center of each of Navarro's longer works. Rather than heterosexual union signaling narrative closure, however, Navarro focuses on love forestalled or interrupted by either social norms or fate. While each text's narrative conflict springs from the disruption of a romantic coupling or domestic stability, a common trope in popular literature and film of the period, it is the transformative, corrupting power of Hollywood and, in the case of *La Señorita Estela*, Los Angeles that emerges as the ultimate villain. The donning of new identities required by the film industry or by the migration to Los Angeles is portrayed by Navarro as a disruption of gender norms, class status, racial identity, or all three at once.

Such a skeptical stance toward Hollywood channeled anxieties about modern life, the mass media, and the consumer economy. As Joan Shelley Rubin has explained, many cultural critics in the early twentieth century feared a societal shift from the unified integrity of "character" to interchangeable, fickle notions of "personality" enabled by consumer culture and fashion.[88] Part and parcel of this transformation was the advent of the star system and "picture personalities," which, as Richard deCordova argues, relied on the production of knowledge about the personal lives and predilections of cinema performers.[89] While star systems existed before cinema, notably in theater, scholars agree that the emergence of mass media in the early twentieth century led to an amplification of stardom as a cultural force that inspired emulation, not only in terms of personal style but also in terms of professional and sexual fulfillment.

In Navarro's case, these broader societal dilemmas were overlaid with concerns about national belonging, morality, and cultural preservation. His writing, rather than offering moral or cultural certainty, conveyed the complexity of the time, particularly in relation to gender. For example, in *La Señorita Estela*, which echoes warnings about the dangers of migration found in much Mexican immigrant literature of the period, domestic stability is disrupted by the appearance of a young, sexually liberated immigrant woman. And, although the dilemma she represents for the protagonist, a Mexican immigrant journalist named Fidel Murillo, is resolved through the restoration of his domestic unit and their return to Mexico, that resolution is contradictory and ambivalent.

Briefly, the novella introduces readers to a Mexican Los Angeles that is heterogeneous in its social composition, characterized as much by internal tension as by common ground. Murillo, who fought in the Mexican Revolution, has relocated to Los Angeles to try his luck as a journalist. His foray into Mexican Los Angeles reveals a pompous, self-obsessed, self-identified elite clinging to the traditions and symbols of their homeland. Venturing beyond that sphere, however, thrusts him into a world of moral uncertainty even as it reveals the hypocrisy lying just beneath the Mexican expatriate community's facade of respectability. In this context, he becomes infatuated with Señorita Estela, a beautiful and talented member of the Mexican immigrant community who composes poetic verse and has the voice of an angel. Murillo imagines that he has met his soulmate, whose artistic inclinations are a striking contrast to the monotony of middle-class domesticity that he finds with his wife, María Luz. As the reader will discover, Estela's respectability is the Janus face of her participation in casual sex work. Rather than repelling Murillo, his discovery of her secret identity draws him into a passionate affair that only ends after a surprising plot twist that restores Estela to respectability, leaving him the outcast and motivating his return to Mexico with his wife and young son.

That this story resonates with the romantic dramas being churned out by Hollywood studios with morally compromised protagonists, shocking revelations, and neat resolution is not surprising. What is surprising is that this romance takes place almost entirely in Mexican Los Angeles and its key players are Mexican migrants. Throughout the 1930s the name Fidel Murillo could be found in the byline of articles that appeared in the entertainment section of *La Opinión* during Navarro's tenure as the section's managing editor. The name appears again as a character in Navarro's fictionalized biography of silent film star Barbara La Marr, as discussed below. Although we don't have definitive proof, it's highly likely that Fidel Murillo was a pseudonym used by Navarro and, in the context of Navarro's fiction, a sort of stand-in or avatar for the author. Are the events of the novella a coded version of Navarro's reportedly tumultuous relationship with soon-to-be-famous Mexican singer Lucha Reyes, which ended shortly before the book's publication? Perhaps. Regardless of these intriguing ties to Navarro's biography, at the very least we can suppose that Murillo stands in for Navarro's cohort of educated exiles—journalists, civic leaders, and entrepreneurs—who found themselves navigating a new life in Los Angeles shot through with conflicts over national identity, gender, and class.

Estela, Murillo's love interest, is neither a virginal debutante nor a malicious femme fatale. Rather, as portrayed by Navarro, her fear of social censure prevents her from eloping with Murillo. Like him, she is caught between the expectations of two cultures, a dilemma that many young Mexican women faced as they tried to navigate the social norms of the immigrant community and the contradictory norms promoted by American mass culture and nurtured by a growing modern metropolis like Los Angeles. Estela, as the reader discovers, moves through two spaces: the respectable social circles of Mexican immigrant civic groups and the tawdry shadow world of casual sex work associated with American social and cultural norms. It is Estela's inability to reconcile this dichotomy that drives the plot, but that inability also means that Estela eludes easy definition and cannot be reduced to a simple archetype.

Although women's behavior and morality form the crux of the plot, the novella is also deeply invested in teasing apart the effects of migration on men. Murillo functions as one version of Mexican masculinity in the text; his childhood friend and confidant Pepe Calles is another. While the two share similar experiences, Calles is portrayed as having been in the United States longer. Well versed in gender and sexual norms, he knows where to find pleasure, including in alcohol (during Prohibition) and female companionship. Although he is also welcome in elite Mexican immigrant society, he works as a dishwasher, as did many immigrants confronting a racialized labor market. Calles moves deftly between social and cultural worlds and seems to have adjusted to bilingual, bicultural life in the United States. If Murillo's return to Mexico represents one potential resolution of the tensions between US and Mexican culture, Calles's cultural dexterity represents another.

This meditation on gender—however ambivalent and complex—was also at the center of Navarro's focus on Hollywood. His two other longer fictional works explore gender relations while highlighting what Richard Abel and Amy Rodgers describe as "the tangled web that bound motion pictures with popular print culture."[90] Navarro wrote his fictionalized biography of Barbara La Marr shortly after the star's tragic death from tuberculosis in January 1926 at the age of twenty-nine. He was not alone in capitalizing on her life story. Another biography, *Barbara Lja-Mar*, appeared in Moscow that same year. Yet another, by Austrian playwright and director Arnolt Bronnen, was published in German in 1928 and subsequently translated into French and Spanish. A testament to La Marr's international celebrity, these biographies were part of a cottage industry in star profiles that fed Hollywood's celebrity machine with embellishments, half-truths, and apocryphal stories. They were designed to capitalize on the public's interest in motion picture stars and, as it was portrayed in the press, the sensational and often lurid world of Hollywood (fig. 9).

FIGURE 9. Advertisement for Navarro's book *Barbara La Marr: Una historia de placer y de dolor*. *La Prensa*, March 28, 1926, 12.

BARBARA LA MARR

UNA HISTORIA DE PLACER Y DE DOLOR
(POR GABRIEL NAVARRO.)

No hay, entre las artistas del mundo cinematográfico, una cuyo nombre haya sonado tanto en los últimos tiempos como Bárbara La Marr. Su muerte, ocurrida hace apenas unos cuantos días, vino a poner de relieve la importancia que en el arte mudo tenía esta mujer excepcional, de cuyo agitado vivir se seguirá hablando todavía durante mucho tiempo. Desaparecida en plena juventud y en plena gloria, Bárbara La Marr continuará dando motivo a miles de comentarios de parte de sus admiradores y de todas aquellas personas que gustan de observar el desenvolvimiento del cine, que se apasionan por sus personajes y saborean el anecdotario de todos los artistas que a diario se exhiben en la pantalla frente a millones de seres.

Gabriel Navarro, el fino cronista de asuntos cinematográficos de "La Prensa", acaba de escribir un bello libro sobre Bárbara La Marr. Lo subtitula "Una historia de placer y de dolor" y podemos asegurar que es algo más que eso: es un poema que rebosa sentimiento y que llegando a todos los corazones servirá para hacer justicia a la personalidad incomprendida de la bellísima Bárbara.

El lector encontrará en este libro a muchos personajes que resultarán antiguos conocidos suyos, entre ellos el mexicano Ramón Navarro, que con Bárbara La Marr filmó dos de sus mejores películas:

ORQUIDEAS NEGRAS
Y
TU NOMBRE ES MUJER

La obra, tras un prólogo que el autor pone a manera de EXPLICACION, está dividida en once interesantísimos capítulos, a saber:

I.—El Kaleidoscopio de la Vida.
II.—Jack Daugherty.
III.—Una Noche del Montmartre.
IV.—Sobre las Hojas de su Diario.
V.—Cuando el Amor renace.
VI.—"Don't be too sure."
VII.—Rumbo a las playas americanas.
VIII.—La Falena.
IX.—Sol que Declina.
X.—Una Noche de Angustia.
XI.—Como una Lámpara Votiva.

No solamente las personas que gustan del cinematógrafo, sino todos, leerán con agrado

Bárbara La Marr
Una historia de placer y de dolor

pues se trata de un libro de lectura fascinante, de páginas conmovedoras; es una de esas obras que dejan honda huella en el espíritu por narrar hechos que hemos tenido casi a la vista, de personas a las cuales podemos decir que conocemos.

Forma un bonito volumen con carátula a colores, llevando un magnífico retrato de la protagonista.

VALE **40** CENTAVOS

Pídase a la

CASA EDITORIAL LOZANO
118 N. Santa Rosa Ave.—San Antonio, Tex.

A los pedidos de fuera de los Estados Unidos deben agregarse quince centavos, también en moneda americana, para la certificación del paquete.

La Marr was a notorious alcoholic and bon vivant whose health was broken by her hard living and by the film industry's demands. She had no fewer than four husbands, and Navarro narrates her brief life as one of perpetual failure to find true love. His account also paints a portrait of a woman struggling to reconcile her public image with her private life. As a star, he writes, La Marr "folded up her real personality, her ordinary self, into the depths of her soul" to become the "seductive and malevolent" vamp required by film roles and publicity.[91] While she ached for love and acceptance, Navarro suggests, this desire seems to have been perpetually forestalled by a public persona distanced from a true self. At the same time, she found herself constrained by the expectations of men who desired a partner to somehow be a "seductive siren and housewife at the same time."[92] Sympathetically, Navarro places the blame for her premature death on Hollywood, its publicity machinery, and the cost of fame.

Navarro's biography reproduces many long-standing misperceptions about La Marr, many of them part of her public persona during the period. The actress's "secret" Italian heritage was a fabrication of her own making, for instance, one in keeping with a silent film industry that trafficked in exotic sensuality and ethnic masquerade.[93] Her notoriously steadfast refusal to accept prescribed roles or notions of feminine propriety is most certainly echoed in Navarro's own description of La Marr. Some of the information that he presents is drawn from accounts of the actress's life circulating in the press at the time, some of which she supposedly authored. These articles and Navarro's biography were certainly influenced by La Marr's roles in films like the comedy-drama *Souls for Sale* (1923, dir. Rupert Hughes), which itself was set in Hollywood. Mirroring Navarro's own ambivalent coverage of silent Hollywood, the film paints a damning portrait of the industry's underside and the perils of stardom, all while trading on the glamour and notoriety of its star. As Navarro recounts her life, we see La Marr fall victim to the production of her public self across a dizzying array of cultural products, falsifications, and, in Navarro's words, the "malevolent spider of publicity."[94]

His biography of La Marr is, however, deceptively straightforward. Throughout the text Navarro offers details that, while obviously fictional or more suggestive than declarative, bring his immigrant readership in closer proximity to Hollywood. Most markedly, Navarro leaves La Marr's ethnic identity murky—following the actress's own insinuation that she was of Italian heritage—in a manner that might have allowed his readers to identify more closely with her. This claim is bolstered in the narrative by Navarro's description of La Marr's dark hair and passionate temperament, traits he claims Mexican women share. Navarro himself makes a brief appearance in the novel as a Mexican immigrant journalist named Fidel Murillo, who not only moves in the same heady circles as the star and her husband but also plays a key role in one of the narrative's romantic threads. In this way, Navarro's presence in the novel as both author and character reframes the perspective from which such star biographies were typically narrated. As an intermediary, he placed Mexican immigrants within the narrative, opening opportunities for his readers to imagine themselves as active participants, if not protagonists, in Hollywood, with intimate access to all its scandal, glamour, and alluring tragedies. More than yet another biography of a tragic figure, the novel is bound up with Navarro's broader efforts to claim for his readers a space of belonging so often denied them by the industry.

The relationship between ethnic Mexican audiences and Hollywood is further cemented in the book's afterword, "Fame," written by Mexican journalist Teodoro Torres Jr., former editor of *La Prensa*. In flowery prose, Torres meditates on fame and the power of cinema to make the dead come to life. But he also offers a window onto Mexican and Mexican immigrant moviegoing practices as he imagines "the girls who lived for nothing else but to make themselves beautiful and then go to see their 'flapper' figures reproduced on screen . . . as they were getting ready to go to their *colonia*'s respective cinema" on the night of La Marr's death.[95]

The subtle subtext of *Barbara La Marr* was directed at a community of readers who were regularly marginalized by English-language fan magazines even as Hollywood worked to attract them as potential audience members. Navarro converted this community of readers into protagonists in his serialized novel, *La ciudad de irás y no volverás*. *La ciudad* is unique in the larger body of popular serial literature that emerged with the cinema. It was initially published weekly, with summaries of the action described in the previous week's installment. Readers would have encountered this example of Spanish-language motion picture fiction on the entertainment page of *La Prensa*, alongside news about local entertainment culture, advertisements for local movie theaters serving San Antonio's ethnic Mexican community, and original or reprinted articles about Hollywood cinema. While many serialized narratives from this period expanded on or connected to their filmed counterparts, such as those related to popular serials like *The Perils of Pauline*, Navarro's serial offers readers a Hollywood inhabited and protagonized by Mexican immigrants (figs. 10, 11).

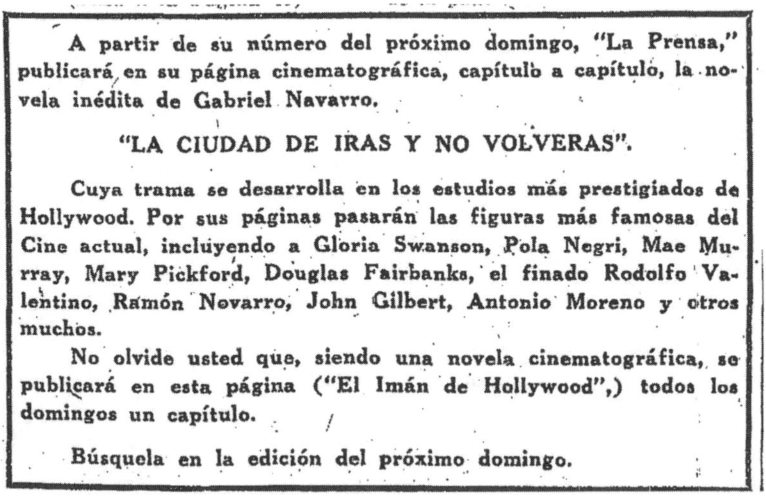

A partir de su número del próximo domingo, "La Prensa," publicará en su página cinematográfica, capítulo a capítulo, la novela inédita de Gabriel Navarro.

"LA CIUDAD DE IRAS Y NO VOLVERAS".

Cuya trama se desarrolla en los estudios más prestigiados de Hollywood. Por sus páginas pasarán las figuras más famosas del Cine actual, incluyendo a Gloria Swanson, Pola Negri, Mae Murray, Mary Pickford, Douglas Fairbanks, el finado Rodolfo Valentino, Ramón Novarro, John Gilbert, Antonio Moreno y otros muchos.

No olvide usted que, siendo una novela cinematográfica, se publicará en esta página ("El Imán de Hollywood",) todos los domingos un capítulo.

Búsquela en la edición del próximo domingo.

FIGURE 10. Advertisement announcing the imminent publication of Navarro's serialized novel, *La ciudad de irás y no volverás* (The City of No Return). *La Prensa*, December 12, 1926, 16.

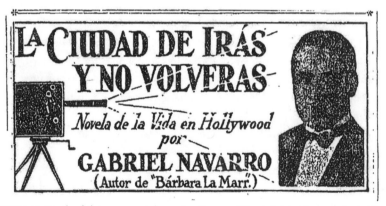

FIGURE 11. Masthead that accompanied most installments of *La ciudad de irás y no volverás* (The City of No Return). *La Prensa*, January 30, 1927, 12.

Laura Cañedo, the novel's protagonist, arrives in Los Angeles in search of stardom; she finds sacrifices, deprivation, dishonor, and arrest. If the resolution of *La Señorita Estela* was ambiguous, here the moral is clear: Hollywood, and by proxy the United States, is a dangerous place for women in general and for Mexican women in particular. Proper Mexican (middle-class) femininity is portrayed as fundamentally incompatible with stardom and modern urban life in the United States. Certainly the didactic tone of the narrative participates in a broader, alarmist discourse in the English-language US and Mexican press, but Navarro might also have been motivated by genuine, practical concern for his readers. In the 1920s, as Denise McKenna notes, the public fretted about the "movie-struck girls who descended on Los Angeles in ever-increasing numbers."[96] What's more, by 1926 Hollywood had become synonymous with sex scandals; the "casting couch" had found its way into public discourse as shorthand for women's ascension to stardom through sexual favors, causing consternation on the part of the film industry, city officials, and reformers alike.[97] While many men also worked as extras, the studios paid women substantially less, making it difficult for them to support themselves on extra work alone.[98] Navarro's admonitions certainly parallel a broader concern about women migrating to Hollywood. He was acutely aware that Mexicans in particular faced irregular and uncertain employment prospects and even lower pay (to say nothing of demeaning roles), which likely motivated this cautionary tale.[99]

Despite its ultimately bleak message, *La ciudad* presents a captivating, sensational portrait of Hollywood and Los Angeles from a Mexican vantage point, from casting calls at major studios to the Mexican theaters of Main Street. Like other accounts of Hollywood, it frames deception as the industry's modus operandi. Once in Hollywood, for instance, Laura Cañedo is "reborn" as Linda Celli, adopting a persona that obscures her true identity and ever so slightly shifts her ethnic identity from Mexican to Italian (taking a page, no doubt, from Barbara La Marr). Indeed, *La ciudad* posits ethnic masquerade as central to Hollywood's logic. Extras are hired to play various national and ethnic types regardless of their own identities, with the Mexican actors' ethnic ambiguity allowing them to play a range of characters. This sort of transformation and deception is posited as a prerequisite to stardom.

Not surprisingly, Navarro suggests that for Mexican women, this process also entails casting aside gender and sexual norms depicted in the narrative as traditionally Mexican. Laura/Linda is lured into what she thinks will be the glamorous world of Hollywood, only to encounter deception and exploitation. As the reader learns, her encounters first with novels and then with films and Hollywood lead her down a familiar road to ruin. By contrast, the narrative supports men's forays into cinema. Raymundo Nava, Laura's masculine counterpart and romantic interest in *La ciudad*, works his way up from extra to movie stardom, an heir apparent to silent film star Ramon Novarro. While the narrative ends with his fate seemingly secure,

Laura's remains less certain. The novel's ending does not seem to have been published, leaving the reader in medias res. In some ways the lack of resolution, whether intentional or not, seems appropriate. Laura departs Los Angeles for the border, where she has secured work as a taxi dancer in Tijuana. Unlike Fidel Murillo in *La Señorita Estela*, this is not a comfortable return to one's homeland but rather one of further marginalization, somewhere between Los Angeles and Guadalajara, between Hollywood and homeland, but located in neither.

Navarro's fictional account aligns with his advice to readers in his regular column in *La Prensa*, El cristal encantado. His articles during the silent period regularly dissuaded young Mexican women from migrating to Hollywood in search of fame, citing many of the pitfalls and hurdles described in *La ciudad*, while being somewhat more encouraging toward young Mexican men anxious to seek their fortunes in Hollywood. This is just one example of the resonance between the themes and narratives found in Navarro's fiction writing and the criticism and regular columns he published in *La Prensa* and *La Opinión*. His prolific body of journalism advocated for the immigrant community's right to work in the industry, to see themselves represented on screen as characters beyond stereotypes, and to participate in the fan culture that was so essential to Hollywood's success.

NAVARRO AS MEDIA ACTIVIST

A general orientation toward community stewardship and the overarching principle of "México de afuera" guided Navarro's contributions to Latino media activism in the United States. While a new generation of scholarship has attended to media activism within the framework of industry studies, most of this research at least implicitly locates its origins in the civil rights struggles of the 1960s and 1970s.[100] But the first decades of the twentieth century also saw the Spanish-language press function as a critical site for defending and advocating for Mexican immigrants as audiences for popular entertainment. The rise and consolidation of Hollywood as a major industry depended on the proliferation of stereotypes that characterized Mexicans as greasers or bandidos. The Spanish-language press, consular officials, and spectators on both sides of the border vehemently condemned what they referred to as denigrating images. In the early 1920s, outrage on the part of members of the Mexican consular corps culminated in Mexico's unprecedented boycott of multiple Hollywood studios.[101] Though not organized around a specific film, these responses resonate with African American media activism targeting racist depictions before World War II, including a nationwide coordinated response to *The Birth of a Nation* (1915, dir. D. W. Griffith).[102]

Navarro's media activism stemmed from his conviction that Mexican audiences, as fans of Hollywood, deserved to be treated respectfully. By the time he became a cultural critic in the mid-1920s, Mexico's boycott of US film companies had already served as a reminder to an increasingly global industry that its most neglected audiences also possessed a degree of leverage. Although this incident motivated studios to self-regulate their representations of Mexican or Latin characters in the interest of avoiding further international offense (and potential losses of box office revenue), a larger problem remained: Mexicans, and Latina/os in general, continued to be depicted by Hollywood as perpetual others, outsiders distanced from whiteness, respectability, and claims to civic or cultural citizenship. As the US Mexican population continued to grow and Hollywood consolidated into a vertically integrated oligopoly, these dynamics were exacerbated. It was in this environment that Navarro emerged as a critical voice, using his position as a journalist to advocate for change at multiple levels. While he continued to condemn stereotypes and encouraged his readers to retain ties to Mexican culture, he also addressed both the US and Mexican film industries, speaking on behalf of his readers, advocating for local Latina/o talent, and lauding the enterprises that employed them.

He became one of the most prominent Mexican cultural critics living in the United States, and his career serves as a point of departure from which to construct a longer, more capacious history of Latina/o media activism. In her book *Asian American Media Activism*, Lori Kido Lopez defines media activists as those whose "goal is to make meaningful, long-term change in the media landscape—whether that means changing the images that have been created, the structures that produce those images, or the way that images are understood by viewers."[103] Navarro worked across all of these registers during his time as a critic. He was involved in multiple aspects of Los Angeles's migrant culturescape during the 1920s and 1930s: music, theater, radio, cinema, and the press. These cultural formations fostered community, offered immigrants a sense of belonging, and supported the careers of Latina/o talent in substantive ways, remedying the representational exclusions of the film industry. But rather than attending only to this alternative sphere, Navarro also sought to create substantive structural change in Hollywood as a means of making mainstream entertainment more inclusive of and responsive to his readership.

As a journalist and advocate, however, Navarro never adopted a uniform or singular attitude toward the media industries. Acting as an intermediary of sorts, he helped readers negotiate their relationships with Hollywood, just as his columns offered studio executives advice about attracting that very same Spanish-language or immigrant audience. For him, these two missions seemed inseparable: he wanted his readership to see their lives reflected on screen, just as he argued for a more inclusive and responsive industry that would conceivably make this possible. Embracing the power and allure of mass media rather than rejecting it, Navarro modeled a realpolitik that acknowledged yet pushed against the power differential between Hollywood and its Spanish-speaking audience. His body of work encouraged a critical, multifaceted engagement with popular culture that encompassed pleasure, critique, fandom, community advocacy, and the production of culture itself. His writing on media, even in lighter forms such as question-and-answer columns, gestures toward the various ways that Mexican immigrants and critics were positioned by and responded to the film industry.

Above all, he proposed an ambivalent and negotiated engagement with mass culture, positioning his readers as active viewers and potential creators. Like many film critics of his generation, Navarro believed in the power of Hollywood to facilitate assimilation or otherwise erode Mexican cultural values. He and others writing for *La Opinión*, for instance, worried about Mexican American youth, whose enthusiasm for US popular culture might endanger the retention of their parents' language and culture. Alongside Americanization programs that encouraged immigrants to assimilate, popular culture served as a central agent of "de-Mexicanization" in the eyes of many Mexican critics working in the United States.[104] Aside from occasionally lamenting the cultural influence of jazz, however, Navarro never spent his time on the censorship battles or moral panics that occupied many reformers, for instance, nor did he unconditionally paint the culture industries as a pernicious influence. Far from sounding the alarm about mass culture, he implicitly encouraged the consumption of film, equipping his readers with a range of critical perspectives and strategies in the process. For Navarro, the question was not whether to engage mass culture at all, but on what terms to engage it. Rather than proposing that Mexican immigrants somehow escape from or surrender to the inevitable dominance of US popular culture, he instead hoped to fundamentally transform the nature of the relationship between his readership and Hollywood.

Navarro's prolific output of criticism occurred in the face of a dizzying array of cultural and industrial transformations between the 1920s and the start of World War II: the global dominance of a consolidated Hollywood, the upheaval of the transition to sound, the rise of Mexican cinema, and Hollywood's ever-changing approach to the Latin American market at home and abroad. In his capacity as a journalist, author, critic, and advocate, Navarro worked to intervene in these circumstances at multiple, intersecting levels. Most notably, he guided readers' engagement with Hollywood, pressed for increased Latina/o representation and presence in the film industry, advocated for Latina/o talent, encouraged readers to patronize Spanish-language entertainment in Los Angeles, and proposed that readers participate in the creation of culture. While all of these tendencies were a fixture of his criticism over the years, some become more prominent at certain moments. All of them were facets of the same overall strategy: to secure a meaningful, ongoing place for Latina/os in the world of modern entertainment, whether as producers, consumers, or critical viewers.

During the silent period, Navarro's writing for *La Prensa* focused primarily on shaping his readers' relationship and engagement with cinema. As moviegoers and fans, however, Navarro and his readership faced a conundrum. By the mid-1920s, Hollywood was a vertically integrated, consolidated cultural force with global reach. The popularity of its products, both films and stars alike, was undeniable. Just as reformers and cultural authorities in the United States were wringing their hands about the moral implications of this development, analogous entities in other countries worried about its Americanizing impact, particularly as Hollywood's dominance foreclosed possibilities for national or alternative cinemas. Mexico, as it continued to emerge from the upheaval of revolution during the 1920s, was in no position to develop or sustain a viable film industry. So while Mexicans in Los Angeles and elsewhere were just as drawn to cinema as anyone else, there was practically no Mexican cinema with which they might identify until the early 1930s. There was consequently no way of escaping or denying the cultural force of Hollywood. But that industry had an unfortunate track record during the silent period, from the production of "greaser" films to the general exclusion of Latinos from the ranks of above-the-line talent.

Lamenting the lack of any Mexican alternative to Hollywood films and stars during the silent era, Navarro formulated a uniquely *Mexican* positionality for his audience as spectators and fans of the dominant industry. Perhaps counterintuitively, he conceived this mode of fandom as forestalling the Americanization of his young readers. This "Mexicanizing" of Hollywood took multiple forms. First, by following the careers and personal lives of Mexican actors like Ramon Novarro and Dolores Del Rio, Navarro encouraged identification with such figures as fellow Mexicans, offering privileged insight into their careers and personal lives (in Spanish).[105] This provided readers with a culturally specific entry point into Hollywood, allowing them to admire and root for their compatriots as they navigated a fickle and discriminatory industry. The studios' practice of recruiting talent from around the globe enabled Navarro to remain critical of Hollywood just as he retained a degree of optimism about the improving prospects for Latina/o talent within that system. This position allowed his readers to participate in the construction of a Latina/o Hollywood, just as it allowed Navarro to name and leverage this audience as he pushed studios to move toward inclusivity.

As this suggests, Navarro's role as a self-appointed middleman facilitated the creation of an incipient "Hispanic" or "Latino" market as an identifiable entity. He did so in several ways. First, he provided the information and material necessary to foster and sustain fandom among his readership. In columns like El cristal encantado, he answered readers' queries by supplying "insider" knowledge about stars, including height, hair color, marital status, and biographical details. Given the nature of the publication, many of these questions centered on the perceived nationality of various stars and whether or not certain actors were Mexican or would answer fan mail in Spanish. He also offered readers photos of their favorite stars. The geographic scope of the letters—primarily from across the United States and northern Mexico—is indicative of the surprisingly wide distribution of *La Prensa*. But it also attests to this audience's thirst for information in Spanish and their desire to participate in a specifically Mexican brand of fandom encouraged by Navarro. From the late silent period through the transition to sound, Navarro also penned lengthy profiles and interviews with Latina/o actors that focused primarily on their often-circuitous route to Hollywood and the hardships they endured along the road to stardom.

As much as Navarro facilitated these relationships between Hollywood's various products and Mexican fans, however, he also used this intermediary role to offer more pessimistic or cautionary perspectives about the place of Latina/os in 1920s Hollywood. In this respect, his cinema columns in *La Prensa* made clear distinctions between the potential dangers of consuming popular culture and the perils of laboring in the culture industries (or at least aspiring to do so).[106] Both his enthusiasm for Hollywood and his caution were rooted in his status as a privileged insider, an educated Mexican living in close proximity to the studios, with connections to talent and regular access to at least some stars. This intimate working knowledge, which also extended to the city's Spanish-language entertainment scene, allowed Navarro to counsel his readers about their own ambitions. In short, many of them aspired to migrate to Los Angeles in search of stardom and fame. While Navarro could be seen as fueling these dreams by persistently fostering Mexican fandom, he also routinely emphasized the near impossibility of forging a career in Hollywood and discouraged his readers from making the journey. Such warnings were often couched within a seemingly practical understanding of labor in Hollywood: the challenges of working as an extra, the unlikely probability of ascending from extra to star, the training and sacrifice necessary to achieve stardom, and the perils awaiting the naive in Los Angeles. Not surprisingly, his strongest admonitions were aimed at young Mexican women whose career ambitions might compel them to violate the gender norms and sexual decorum expected of them. The serialized novel *La ciudad de irás y no volverás* represents the epitome of these sorts of cautions.

While one could easily characterize Navarro's stance on stardom as somewhat contradictory or hypocritical (he was, after all, a Mexican who had forged a relatively successful career in Hollywood's orbit), we may also understand his approach on different terms. The feeding of fandom, the supplying of information, and the celebration of Latina/o talent in Hollywood, rather than encouraging unrealistic ambitions, was likely intended to provide intimate access at a distance, allowing fans to acquire inside information without placing themselves at risk. Navarro's success as a journalist arguably hinged on his ability to protect or guide his audience while fueling their fantasies, a nimbleness that allowed him to reconcile the often patronizing ideology of "México de afuera" with the undeniable pleasures and promise that Hollywood offered to both him and his readership.

Navarro's writing also engaged and reframed the racial politics of Los Angeles and Hollywood in the 1920s and 1930s. His work for *La Prensa*, including *La ciudad de irás y no volverás*, crafted a portrait of a film industry structured around racial difference that engaged in discriminatory labor practices and prioritized whiteness even as it trafficked in the "exotic." Particularly in the 1920s, Navarro grappled with the dissonance between Hollywood's embrace of the "Latin lover" (embodied by Mexican actors such as Ramon Novarro, Dolores Del Rio, and Gilbert Roland) and the industry's systemic mistreatment of Mexicans, both on screen and as a labor force. Although Navarro, like other Mexican journalists, celebrated actors like Novarro and Del Rio as cinematic ambassadors for Mexico, their star personas allowed them to project exotic sensuality while still maintaining a safe proximity to whiteness. As phenotypically white Mexicans, these actors rarely portrayed Mexican characters. The list of roles Del Rio played in the silent period is indicative of this dynamic: a Russian peasant, a Romani bear trainer, a French barmaid, a French Canadian migrant, and a young Jewish girl.[107] Meanwhile, as Navarro's pointed critiques make apparent, Hollywood continued to populate its westerns, historical dramas set in the Southwest, and adventure films set in Latin America with stereotypical Mexican characters, whether played by ethnic Mexican performers or white actors in brownface.[108]

Navarro was keenly aware of the value ascribed to Latina/os' perceived ethnic malleability, and as an intermediary between Mexican immigrant readers and the industry, he prided himself on demystifying Hollywood's perpetual game of ethnic masquerade. For example, in *La ciudad de irás y no volverás*, he describes casting agents searching for "ambiguous types that could pass for Spaniards, South-Americans, or primitive inhabitants of the South Sea Islands."[109] Raymundo, one of the novel's main characters, explains that as an extra he has portrayed a range of ethnicities and nationalities, including Chinese, Black, and Indigenous characters. As for his love interest, Linda Celli, her first job as an extra at MGM required her to portray a French "prostitute of the slums." In his regular columns, Navarro clarified that Pola Negri was Polish, not Spanish or Mexican; Latin lover Ricardo Cortez was an Austrian Jew, not of Spanish descent.[110]

Immersed in the world of Hollywood, however, Navarro himself was not immune to the lure of ethnic masquerade. At times he perpetuated the kind of deceit he otherwise condemned, waxing poetic, for instance, about Barbara La Marr's "Italian blood" that supposedly made her part of the "Latin race," a fanciful heritage concocted by studio publicity.[111] Nonetheless, Navarro clearly recognized the considerable difference between Hollywood's vision of the exotic and the prospects for actual Latina/o labor in the industry. While Hollywood might elevate a few light-skinned Mexicans of Spanish descent to the rarefied echelons of stardom, Navarro made clear that the prospects for most Latinos, including extras, were relatively bleak.[112] And finding employment was a double-edged sword if it meant perpetuating stereotypes.

Navarro never denied the logic of racial difference per se, as is evident in many of his writings; rather, he strove to reframe it, reversing a racial hierarchy that insisted on the inferiority of Mexicans and other Latina/os. For instance, he routinely dismissed US culture and society as "cold," "mechanical," "logical in its artificiality," and fixated on industrial progress, while characterizing what he referred to as the "Hispano American race" as inherently spiritual, sentimental, artistically inclined, and morally sound.[113] Racial essentialism aside, we might understand these distinctions, which were not unique to Navarro, as rhetorical attempts to puncture reigning notions of Anglo-Saxon superiority, the bedrock of white supremacist thinking in the early twentieth century.

This dimension of Navarro's writing comes into focus most clearly during the early years of sound cinema, as he repeatedly compared Hollywood's Spanish-language films to films made in Latin America that he felt embodied a Latino or Hispano American sensibility. Navarro mobilizes the concept of "racial distinctiveness" in an early attempt to define and valorize a pan-ethnic Latina/o or pan-hemispheric audience.[114] The early sound period was certainly fertile ground for formulating these distinctions. Hollywood's Spanish-language productions, as the first concerted effort to target a Latin American audience, relied heavily on light-skinned characters placed in nondescript or European environments with Spanish-speaking actors merely replacing their more famous English-language counterparts.[115] Critics and filmmakers alike could point to those discrepancies as an opportunity to reach and represent an audience that Hollywood at best routinely neglected.

IMAGINING AND ADVOCATING FOR HIS AUDIENCE

When directing his energy toward Hollywood itself, Navarro worked tirelessly to convince producers that a lucrative but underserved Spanish-language, or "Hispano," market existed and mattered. Defining and advocating for this audience was central to his extensive practice of "talking back" to Hollywood from the columns of La Opinión. While América Rodríguez has credited early Spanish-language radio broadcasting with the creation of an identifiable

"Hispanic audience" beginning in the 1930s, Navarro's parallel efforts imagined a transnational, hemisphere-wide "Hispano American" audience united by sensibility, history, language, and a considerable enthusiasm for cinema.[116] Defining this audience in these terms was at least partially a strategy linked to his position as a journalist. This formulation of a "Hispano" market overlapped significantly with the ostensible readership and circulation of La Opinión; serving and giving voice to that constituency in many ways defined Navarro's professional reputation. Using this audience and its economic potential as leverage to alter representation and create opportunity within the industry was also clearly one of his primary objectives. It was not, however, his only objective. Rather, in keeping with the intermedial, transnational, and multiscalar entanglements that characterized his career, Navarro understood that decisions made by a globally dominant industry had immediate local impact. Sound technology could threaten the viability of Spanish-language theatrical companies. Marginalizing or excluding Latina/o talent meant exacerbating the economic distress of the Depression among Mexican immigrants. A lack of Spanish-language films adversely affected local theaters. In short, Hollywood's neglect of this larger market had an economic and cultural impact beyond the screen. To Navarro, imagining a "Hispano American" market meant advocating for Mexican Los Angeles, and vice versa.

Often addressing hypothetical industry insiders, Navarro advocated on behalf of this audience by arguing for more culturally sensitive representation, for the increased hiring of Mexican or Latina/o talent, and for placing Spanish-speaking individuals in decision-making capacities at the studios. When Will Hays, director of the Motion Picture Producers and Distributors of America, promised in 1931 that studios would "continue" to respect Latin America and its people, Navarro cynically replied with a laundry list of stereotypes and distortions that had pervaded Hollywood's treatment of Latina/os since its inception, directly challenging those claims.[117]

Navarro's efforts in this area resonate with the issues addressed by media activists in the twenty-first century. Navarro clearly indicated that he served marginalized people who had relatively little power to create structural change but who wanted to meaningfully participate in and enjoy an industry that seemed oblivious to their tastes and concerns. He also grappled with the possibilities and limitations of an alternative Spanish-language media. That these issues still resonate today demonstrates how little the industry has changed in this respect over the last century despite considerable cultural, technological, and industrial shifts.[118] Navarro remained optimistic about the industry's ability to change with the times and the technology, just as he remained realistic about its apparent unwillingness to budge when it came to either the humanity or the profitability of the Latina/o audience. As Navarro once lamented, "Whether we like it or not, we will always be second class" in Hollywood's eyes.[119]

Perhaps his most extensive campaign directed at studios originated with the transition of sound and Hollywood's short-lived production of Spanish-language films in the early 1930s. As multiple scholars have documented, this practice was initiated as a way for the studios to retain their valuable international markets despite the language barrier that suddenly emerged with spoken dialogue.[120] Although largely abandoned by 1932, these productions led to the unprecedented hiring of Spanish-speaking talent from around the world. Navarro initially regarded the opening of this "golden door" as a critical opportunity for Latina/o talent and a chance for the industry to fully appreciate the Spanish-language market.[121] But he ultimately criticized the studios for how they managed such productions, using his columns to voice concern about the overall lack of Latina/o directors or screenwriters, the industry's embrace of Castilian pronunciation over Latin American Spanish, the unequal treatment of Latina/o actors relative to their English-language counterparts, the studios' reluctance to contract local Mexican American talent, and the cultural and linguistic foibles that made these films the object of critical disdain.[122]

As with other areas of his media activism, here he adopted a negotiated stance that combined enthusiastic optimism with the understanding that there remained plenty of work to do. Even his reviews during this period, rather than focusing exclusively on the potential experience of the spectator, were directed at least implicitly at the studios, offering constructive advice (and admonitions) about cultural insensitivity, miscasting, the lack of a Spanish-language star system, and the studios' overall misunderstanding of Spanish-speaking audiences and their tastes.[123] And when studios began suspending Spanish-language production in 1932, Navarro openly pleaded with their representatives, both in print and in person, to instead continue improving their offerings to Latin American audiences.[124] While pushing to improve Latina/o representation on screen, he also recognized that these films provided crucial support to Latina/o talent and that local Mexican movie houses had come to rely on them.

Within this broader effort, however, Navarro was mindful to remind all producers, whether working in Hollywood or Mexico, that his readership deserved quality entertainment, formal innovation, and culturally relevant films. In this respect, his rather flexible formulation of "Hispano" or "Hispano American" cinema acknowledged that suitable Spanish-language product could hypothetically originate from anywhere: from the Hollywood studios, independent producers, or, by the mid-1930s, Latin America. While advocating and promoting all of these at various moments over the course of two decades, he maintained relatively consistent criteria for a culturally responsive and enriching cinema. Proposing "Hispanic production, by and for Hispanics, without preference for accents or geographic origin," he envisioned this cinema employing Latina/o talent, offering audiences culturally relevant entertainment, and, in the process, sustaining independent Spanish-language theaters and related businesses.[125] More than aiding in the construction of a "Hispano American" or Latina/o market, he characterized their collective tastes, sensibilities, and interests, an effort that foreshadowed the rise and expansion of Hispanic marketing in the 1970s and 1980s.[126] He repeatedly insisted, for instance, that his readership wanted "cinema to touch their souls, cinema that interests them, that reflects their own lives, and that serves as spiritual nourishment for their own sensibility."[127] This formulation allowed him to make a distinction between truly "Hispano" cinema and the bulk of Hollywood's Spanish-language output, which he disparaged as "Hispano cinema with a Saxon perspective."[128] In this respect, Navarro's work coincided with nationalist evaluations of Hispano cinema that placed it in direct opposition to homegrown productions from Latin America.[129]

For this reason, he routinely promoted and celebrated films from diverse origins, including homegrown independent productions by those involved in the Los Angeles Spanish-language theater scene, such as actor and impresario Romualdo Tirado.[130] Indeed, as late as 1939, when Mexico was producing enough cinema to sustain both downtown theaters and smaller neighborhood venues, Navarro expressed enthusiasm for rumors of new production activity arising in Tijuana.[131] And while some lamented Hollywood's recruitment of Mexican talent in the late 1930s as a blow to that nation's industry, Navarro saw it as a means of improving the quality of "Hispano" cinema overall.[132] By the same token, no producer or director, regardless of where they worked, or no film, regardless of where it was made, remained immune from constructive critique in the service of creating an aesthetically accomplished and culturally relevant cinema that resonated with the sensibilities, tastes, and "ideological line of the Latino spirit" (to use Navarro's turn of phrase).[133]

Navarro's formulation of a true "Hispano" cinema violates the geographic boundaries typically used to understand and historicize cinema. By grouping together Mexican cinema, Spanish-language Hollywood productions, features from Argentina, and independent efforts, Navarro implicitly acknowledged the consumption habits of his readers. What's more, this formulation resonated with the experiences of Latina/o talent and audiences alike who moved across borders, navigating multiple cultures. The very idea of a Hispano cinema gestures toward an early formulation of a community that would be both pan-ethnic and pan-American before the adoption of categories such as Hispanic or Latino. If, as Lisa Jarvinen argues, Hollywood's Spanish-language film production "was an important precursor of Latino media" in the United States, Navarro also has an important role in that story. [134] He drew lines of connection and affinity across national boundaries, but he also understood his readership as being part of a migrant culturescape that did the same.

But again, this focus on the industry was inextricable from yet another aspect of Navarro's writing: his dedicated advocacy on behalf of Latina/o talent and entertainment enterprises in Los Angeles. In concert with fostering Mexican fandom of Hollywood, Navarro regularly showcased and promoted Latina/o actors, whether major stars like Ramon Novarro and Dolores Del Rio or largely forgotten figures like Nelly Fernández and Conchita Montenegro. [135] If Hollywood's attitude toward and representation of Latina/os were to improve, Navarro recognized the necessity of increasing their ranks at every level of the industry. If his articles and columns helped build a uniquely Mexican identification with Hollywood, these readers might also then constitute a fan base that could propel or sustain the careers of Latina/o talent. This mattered to Navarro because he was convinced that increased media visibility had the capacity to change discriminatory attitudes toward Mexicans. When he lauded Del Rio, Novarro, Mona Rico, or Lupe Velez for rendering a service to their nation, he was crediting them with helping to reverse decades of stereotypes that portrayed Mexico as backward, uncivilized, racially problematic, and violent.

Once again, however, this advocacy was hardly straightforward or uncomplicated. As has been the case in parallel contexts, marginalized communities often admired a successful actor while remaining critical of the demeaning roles he or she was compelled to accept. [136] But even during the heyday of Spanish-language production, Navarro repeatedly noted that Hollywood had failed to produce any Spanish-language stars who could draw audiences into theaters. [137] Here again, he remained adamant that the problem resided in the industry and its practices rather than with Latina/o talent or audiences. So while celebrating and amplifying the successes of Latina/o actors, he also routinely criticized the studios for neglecting, miscasting, or otherwise mistreating them.[138] He likewise complained about the treatment of extras and the notoriously exploitative practices of casting directors.[139] He lamented the fickle and competitive nature of labor in Hollywood that found Latina/os alternately in vogue, underutilized, relegated to stereotypical roles, or chronically underemployed.[140] Despite his admonitions to readers, for instance, he noted that thousands of Mexicans had flocked to Hollywood in pursuit of stardom by the late 1920s, with "their heads full of daydreams and their pockets completely empty."[141] He recognized the importance of ongoing community support for Latina/o actors, at one point proposing the foundation of a Casa del Artista that would house and support those unemployed or struggling as a combined result of the Depression, repatriations, and the decline in Hollywood Spanish-language production.[142]

Regardless of how critical he may have been of the studios, he saw that compelling them to change would provide opportunities for underappreciated writers, actors, and other talent. Again, his attitude toward the industry was hardly adversarial; his criticism acknowledged the fact that one of his key constituencies relied on the industry for its livelihood. On more than one occasion, Navarro would provide lists of available talent for the benefit of Hollywood producers and local theater owners alike.[143] And in at least one case, this approach appeared to produce concrete results. Responding directly to one of Navarro's articles in La Opinión, Fox initiated the "New Faces" campaign in 1933 to search for local talent to work in its Spanish-language productions starring popular Mexican tenor José Mojica, leading to auditions for four women "who came either from our theater stages or our society pages."[144] For Navarro, this effort would achieve multiple goals: it would benefit aspiring local talent, improve the quality of Fox's productions, and sustain a local market for these productions. Of the four actresses who tested for Fox, Anita Campillo was chosen to star opposite Mojica in La cruz y la espada (1934, dir. Frank R. Strayer and Miguel de Zárraga), one of the few Spanish-language features produced from an original script rather than as a version of an English-language film. This was indeed the start of Campillo's cinematic career, which would continue through the 1930s in both the United States and Mexico. Not only did Navarro's efforts bear tangible fruit, but they revealed producers' interest in improving studios' standing with Spanish-language audiences. Even as a publicity stunt, the

New Faces campaign was an implicit acknowledgment of the local Spanish-language press and the readership it represented.

But as this episode indicates, Navarro's ultimate constituency was not Hollywood executives, despite the address implicit in many of his columns; he remained focused on the Mexican immigrant community in Los Angeles and, perhaps to a lesser extent, in the rest of the United States. He understood that they participated in a complex migrant culturescape that included cultural formations ranging from the local to the transnational. Navarro saw a place for Latina/os in all of these endeavors and worked to create, sustain, and improve their prospects across the board. Even the articles dispensing advice to studio insiders helped readers understand the industrial practices and logics that hindered Spanish-language cinema and shaped Hollywood's approach to Latin America, ultimately allowing them to more fully appreciate the conditions that made Latina/o talent "an eternally neglected class" in his estimation.[145]

But perhaps Navarro's most sustained strategy was to encourage his readership to patronize local Spanish-language entertainment and the movie theaters that served the immigrant population of Los Angeles. By the late teens, Los Angeles was home to a vibrant Spanish-language theatrical scene propelled by expatriate playwrights and touring talent from Mexico. Navarro himself was one of these playwrights. In addition to staging a version of *La ciudad de irás y no volverás*, he wrote a number of original plays and even at times conducted orchestras. As editor of the entertainment pages for *La Prensa* and *La Opinión*, he closely covered theatrical developments, promoted new works, encouraged readers to attend functions, and offered constructive criticism to impresarios, playwrights, and talent.

If the financial barriers to producing cinema were prohibitive and the influence of Latina/os at the studios was negligible, theatrical production provided an alternative arena where Mexican perspectives, characters, experiences, and music could flourish. Not only did such theaters narrow the distance between cultural creators and their intended audience, but the theaters themselves often served as multipurpose community centers that hosted benefits, provided entertainment, and sustained symbiotic relationships with local businesses and organizations serving the Mexican immigrant community. Located at key intersections and in sections of downtown frequented by a Spanish-speaking population, these venues were a vital part of the migrant culturescape in Mexican Los Angeles.

Framing these theaters as a viable commercial or representational alternative to Hollywood, however, would be somewhat deceptive. The theaters themselves struggled as a result of multiple factors: the uncertain fortunes of theatrical companies, the changing tastes of audiences, a rapidly developing downtown, competition from other local entertainment venues, a global Depression, mass deportations that dramatically reduced Spanish-speaking audiences, and the undeniable dominance of Hollywood. Indeed, some theaters changed ownership and programming strategies multiple times over the course of the 1920s and 1930s, while others were simply demolished or closed. Here again, while Navarro tirelessly promoted the offerings at these theaters, he also dispensed advice to impresarios and theater owners about how best to attract local audiences and weather the downturns that were a persistent fixture of local Spanish-language entertainment in Los Angeles.[146] Regularly stressing innovation and novelty as a means of attracting audiences, he advised theater owners and producers to draw more consistently from the substantial pool of underemployed or undiscovered Spanish-language talent assembled in Los Angeles.[147] But he also continually stressed the potential of theater to uplift and educate, advising that presentations should be "dignified, elevated, and something worthy of being called cultural."[148] He even scolded theater owners for promising star appearances that never materialized, warning that such a practice would ultimately erode the trust of audiences, the reputation of talent, and the theaters' revenue.[149]

Operating in the shadows of Hollywood required reckoning with the influence and gravitational pull of Hollywood at multiple levels. Put bluntly, many of the Spanish-language theaters, particularly before the regular production of Mexican cinema in the mid-1930s, relied on exhibiting Hollywood films to survive. In other words, they could not exist "outside" of Hollywood, in terms of either cultural influence or financial survival. At the same time, many in the city's Spanish-language theatrical world, whether actors, dancers, technicians, or musicians, sought or relied on employment in Hollywood as part of their livelihood. For Navarro, sustaining these venues was paramount. If this could not be accomplished by staging live theater, then it might happen through the exhibition of cinema that spoke to the cultural sensibilities of his readership (or at least did not insult them as Mexicans).

Realistically, there was nothing Navarro's largely disenfranchised readers could do to remedy the plight of Latina/o talent, to change the minds of producers, to alter the economics of the film industry, or to resolve the financial difficulties of Spanish-language theaters in Los Angeles. Ultimately they seemed powerless to control how they were represented on screen. Rather than capitulate or reject mass culture in its totality, Navarro believed in the potential of cultural forms like theater and cinema despite the unequal social and industrial conditions that characterized their production and dissemination. Like other critics of his time, he believed in the power of culture to uplift, educate, and build community. But unlike European immigrants who eventually gained access to both Hollywood and claims to whiteness, Navarro's community was still not fully acknowledged as human, much less as part of a lucrative market. In many respects, Navarro fought to see his audience acknowledged and normalized.

Confronted with the vicissitudes of an ever-changing yet resolutely discriminatory entertainment industry but hopeful about the possibilities of media, Navarro in the 1930s briefly highlighted the efforts of Mexican American youth who formed their own film clubs.[150] He even encouraged readers to become amateur filmmakers in addition to being fans and moviegoers.[151] He argued that such a wholesome, educational activity would allow young Mexicans to build meaningful, collaborative friendships and see themselves on screen. Of a piece with his general orientation toward culture, a rhetoric of uplift was never far from the surface of even these articles, as Navarro imagined this alternative use of cinema as a counterbalance to the perceived dangers of mass media. In this respect, Navarro's enthusiasm for amateur filmmaking resonates with the calls of reformers, including Jane Addams and an early generation of Black filmmakers, to reorient the purpose and context of film production and to harness its potential in the service of social betterment.[152]

We may never know if any films were actually produced or what ultimately became of any that were. But Navarro's interest in amateur filmmaking gestures toward an unexcavated history of Latina/o media production beyond the industry. Such a notion, even if not an immediately attainable reality, was valuable as a forward-looking aspiration, anticipating the use of cinema for political activism and community in the 1960s and 1970s. Navarro's faith in the power of media-making spoke to the deep engagement by ethnic Mexican audiences with cinema in the early twentieth century. As incomplete as our view of Navarro's work might remain, his journalism and fiction offer a valuable window onto the complex migrant culturescape of early twentieth-century Los Angeles that melded mass media, performance, and print into a vibrant space for the contestation of identity and the production of belonging across borders.

FICTION

Gabriel Navarro.

LA SEÑORITA
ESTELA
(Historia de un amor.)

Talleres gráficos de
"EL HISPANO AMERICANO"
San Diego, California
1 9 2 5

Title page of Gabriel Navarro's novella, *La Señorita Estela (Historia de un amor)*, published in 1925.

La Señorita Estela (A Love Story)

La Señorita Estela (Historia de un amor), published by Sociedad Editora Mexicana in association with *El Hispano Americano*, San Diego, California, 1925

Dedication

I was about to dedicate my book to "the Women and Men I Have Befriended Abroad," when I realized I lacked the former and have not had the rare fortune of winning over the latter. So then: here is a slice of life turned into a novel, for the daily readers of Spanish-language newspapers. It is written briefly and carelessly, under the guidance of lived experience and with the hope that reading it will awaken dormant memories of youth that we all preserve in the hidden sanctuaries of our souls. My most ardent desire is that it be treated with affection, with the kindness that you have extended to my less serious works.

Gabriel Navarro

I

Becoming restless, Fidel Murillo nervously folded the program in his hands.

The hall was resplendent with light. Hundreds of picturesque Japanese lanterns adorned the bulbs along the ceiling of the spacious salon. At the end of the room, standing out like a black, lustrous monster, was a grand Steinway concert piano on a platform, awkwardly adorned with little flags and garishly colored ribbons.

Bit by bit, the salon filled with happy young women dragging their mothers, who were as severe and silent as barking seals, toward empty seats. The benches were gradually populated with that bustling humanity, which exhaled with the enormous buzz of a beehive.

None of those who had arrived knew the young journalist. He had just come from Mexico to this foreign city, and this was his first contact with the people of his country. Colonel Velasco, an old friend of his father's who had likewise fought in those bygone revolutions, had found him this morning and handed him the program that he now held in his hands: an elegant leaf of glossy paper adorned with a border in the three colors of the Mexican flag and an unfortunate portrait of Hidalgo, over whose head like a halo were placed the four numerals of a memorable year: 1810.[153]

Because tonight the "Indo-Latina League"—as they had pompously named that club composed almost exclusively of Mexican expatriates—was celebrating the anniversary of Mexico's declaration of independence. The best elements of this population's high society, the old colonel had told him, would be gathered here.

Despite having promised to come, the colonel had not arrived. Murillo was becoming impatient without being too distracted by the more or less attractive and scandalously painted faces of his little female compatriots who passed alongside him speaking English, recognizing him as a new arrival.

"Evidently," he thought, "I stick out here."

At that moment, among the crowd that had already formed a barricade between the entrance and the salon, there emerged a pair of open arms hanging from a body, irreproachably dressed in a tailcoat and topped by a youthful face with eyes and mouth wide open.

"Fidel! But, my boy . . . is it really you?"

Hands landed almost brusquely on his arms, squeezing them with enthusiasm. He seemed to recognize this wide-eyed face . . . he hesitated for a moment . . .

"Man . . . you're Calles . . ."

"Yes, my brother! What happy luck! The last thing I expected was to run into you here. So tell me: when did you arrive? How is Mexico? Come here and sit next to me."

He began remembering more clearly. It was Pepe Calles, his old friend from school: that old rascal Calles . . .

Then came a tight hug of truly warm affection. Then the two friends, chatting without the least reservation, went to sit down on one of the benches placed up against the wall perpendicular to the rows of chairs.

"Come on, man, tell me. When did you get here?"

"It's been just two days. Do you know Colonel Velasco? He found me this morning and extended his invitation . . . look, this one . . ." (He showed him the paper, already crumpled.) "And so here I am, not knowing anybody, looking like an idiot."

Murillo's loquaciousness began to awaken after being contained for so long. He even felt his initial bad mood dissipating, like a light summer cloud. He also realized that his face must be taking on a more human expression.

"Let me tell you. After leaving Mexico City when all that trouble happened—do you remember?—I began working for a small opposition paper in Guadalajara. I was there when "all hell broke loose." I automatically enlisted in the military, I, who had such an aversion to a career in the armed forces. I achieved the rank of Lieutenant Colonel and I traveled the country from top to bottom, always living the bohemian life of a revolutionary. I finally got married and it's been . . . let me see—I'm trying to remember—it will be four years in January, this coming January. Then the government fell and I returned to the world of journalism, more as a hobby than as a profession. I had the good fortune of making a few cents during the revolt and I am now happily spending them."

"Then you're not working here?"

"Yes and no. I'll tell you. I came with the intention of establishing a purchasing agency, but on a small scale. Taking advantage of my trip, 'Mundo Moderno' newspaper has named me a correspondent who will send them articles about current topics. Los Angeles is all the rage right now in Mexico because of cinema. This is the focus of my correspondent work. And you?"

Pepe Calles moved his head slightly, inclining it toward his left shoulder as he tightened his closed lips.

"I've been okay . . . I get by doing whatever I can. I've been a journalist, a musician, a singer . . . You remember that I played piano, right? Well, I've taken advantage of that training to occasionally join American orchestras, but they annoy me. You know me: I like to live freely and I hate being tied down at all . . . So you won't be surprised to learn that I've even resorted to . . . Okay, let me put it this way. You should know, in case you don't already: here it doesn't look bad to do whatever it takes to earn money. Here, as I was saying, I've resorted to being a dishwasher at the Alexandria, the best hotel in Los Angeles," his friend noted, slightly ashamed of his confession, "if you can believe it . . .

"But that didn't last long. Now I sing in the afternoons from time to time until I have enough for the following week and I stop working. That's my life."

The exchange of confidences continued. Pepe Calles ended up having the doors of Mexican society thrown open for him. Everyone praised him for his easygoing confidence and his pleasant conversation, which was always festive despite being slightly vulgar. This very night he was performing an extra number. He would be singing the Mexican song "Los ojos tapatíos."[154]

The "patriotic" program had already begun to unfold. A long-haired pianist, carrying all the weight of his Aztec features on his shoulders, banged away pathetically on the Steinway. The hall was filled up to the doors and almost everyone observed a strange silence; the notes from the piano could be heard better than is usually the case in this type of Mexican gathering. When the pianist finished, everyone applauded. No one, including Fidel, had any idea what had been played. He was so absorbed in conversation with his friend that he had only a vague awareness that he had heard music.

The program followed its course without there being anything worthy of catching the attention of Murillo, who continued chatting casually with Pepe in a low voice. Suddenly, something prompted his attention to shift . . .

A beautiful girl had just stepped onto the platform. According to the master of ceremonies, "she had graciously agreed to sing for the audience that night in honor of the 'celebration' being celebrated." A true woman. One of those women who seems predestined to change the face of the world with the magnetic power of her beauty. He turned back to his friend, inquiring about her with a movement of his head.

"That's Estela de la Garza, a pretty girl from the Mexican colonia. She's from a good family in Monterrey. You're about to hear her sing. She's not so bad."

The young man then listened with all the attention he could muster. Indeed, her voice, with a lovely soprano timbre, was not all that bad. While singing, Señorita Estela didn't look bad either. Tall and graceful, although, based on our friend's assessment of her, with something seemingly innocent in her eyes and an inexplicably childish face. As she finished, a storm of applause made her blush. Visibly moved, she thanked the audience in turn with a fresh-faced smile like that of a doll, which seemed to be one of her greatest charms.

Calles sang afterward, with a beautiful baritone voice. Following ancient custom, the program, which read at the bottom that it "would not be altered," was entirely transformed by not delivering any of the promised numbers. The piece by Señorita Estela, in Murillo's opinion, was the best—the only one worth being heard. So begin many stories that end in tragedy . . . or in farce.

After Pepe's number, everyone stood up. The evening had come to an end. With a solemn tone, the president of the League read the Mexican Declaration of Independence, interrupting himself constantly to wipe his eyes. And Murillo recalled the celebrations of this glorious anniversary in Mexican administrative offices, which, due to the scarce resources at hand, only highlighted in an unfavorable way the shabbiness of these men and their ceremonies. This gathering reminded him a lot of those commemorations . . .

For a few moments he didn't hear the solemn words of the president, absorbed as he was in memories.

The vibrant notes of Mexico's national anthem then followed, majestic and grand. And Fidel observed how everyone's eyes filled with tears, which struck him as very natural. For a moment, all these fine people forgot their intrigues, their gossip, and the sorrows of expatriate life to feel as though they were back in their own land, in the Mexico of yesteryear, which almost all of them had left against their will. The voices of over a hundred people joined in a hymn, the sacred hymn of liberty and war, which still stirs the multitudes beyond the longed-for banks of the Rio Grande:

". . . And the earth trembles from within at the resounding roar of the canon . . ."[155]

II

They had already picked up all the chairs in the salon to arrange them against the walls, and the place had been transformed by this action into a beautiful and spacious dance hall. An orchestra—which was not the one that had played the national anthem—tuned their instruments in a disorderly fashion as the light from the lamps split across the forehead of the pianist to form a sort of sparkling halo. The mothers, almost all of them together, had already taken their seats as the couples committed to the first dance.

"Will you give me the pleasure of this first dance, Leila?"

"Sure. But you know how you step on me . . ."

In the corner of the hall, Pepe Calles introduced his friend to Señorita Estela, who smiled placidly.

"I place myself at your feet, my lady . . ."

Murillo bowed in somewhat of a Parisian manner. He was delighted to strike up a friendship with this girl who had the freshness of dawn and the face of a religious statue.

"What an interesting little person," he told himself.

Naturally, as the first chords of the orchestra sounded, they had to dance together, weaving between smiling couples to the unrestrained rhythm of a fashionable foxtrot in which the banjos wept strangely in their contralto voice. The drum's tambourine squealed and its most extravagant machinery played out of time with the music. The couple had become irretrievably lost in conversation.

Estela had been in Los Angeles since the first revolution, during which her father, an honorable colonel of the ex-federal army, had been killed.[156] They gathered what money they had and, after selling their small house to a lender, had managed to arrive in this city that she seemed to think they wouldn't be leaving for a long time. Her mother was always yearning for her homeland, but Estela didn't understand why. In the United States they had tranquility, relative comfort, work . . . the news that arrived from their distant home made it apparent that misery had taken hold of the cities to such a degree that many had died of hunger . . .

"Exaggerations, miss. I've just come from there. While it is true that things aren't like they were in the thriving Mexico of the good old days, the conditions that newspapers here assure us dominate the country don't prevail there either . . . Mexico, and the capital in particular, is very lovely."

The girl shrugged her shoulders. She had become accustomed to life in Los Angeles, and she had aspirations of going east to study: to New York, to Philadelphia, perhaps to Europe. But going back to Mexico? What for?

The foxtrot ended after three repetitions in a row. Fidel hadn't even noticed, as his bad mood had completely disappeared. He then had to accompany Señorita Estela to sit next to her mother. Estela introduced the journalist to her.

"Mr. Fidel Murillo, an intelligent journalist who just arrived from Mexico . . ."

"By God, miss, you're going to make your mother mistake me for Reyes Spíndola . . . madam, you know your daughter is being too polite . . ."[157]

She didn't know what to say. The chubby woman extended her hand, inspecting him with the viscous gaze of her watery little eyes that reminded him vaguely of little Estela's beautiful, starry orbs.

"Are you from Mexico?"

"Yes, madam, I just arrived . . ."

Her mother was charmed. She made the young man describe the current situation to her, especially what was going on in Monterrey, which she had left ten years ago. The newspapers said horrendous things but she so desired to return, as much as she had the very first day . . .

"Just think: that's where my Jorge is buried . . ."

In the face of this sad memory, the watery eyes of this good woman seemed to gloss over even more and her face took on a noble expression of pain.

There was no way around it: the conversation dragged on extraordinarily at her request, as she clearly enjoyed the young man's stories.

Every now and then she interrupted him:

"You probably want to dance, and I . . ."

Fidel assured her otherwise, although his internal compass wanted to be out there, twirling around the floor with the sweet Estela, feeling her close to him with her pleasant little warmth and a perfume that provoked irreverent reflections.

When the dance ended shortly after midnight, Fidel, who had also been introduced to Estela's two dark and stocky brothers, bid the family farewell with the promise to visit them one day "when they least expect it."

As he took Estela by the hand, he realized that he was pressing it too hard. He immediately looked into her eyes for complicity, but her sweetly indifferent expression told him nothing.

Moments later, the car carrying the Garza family home receded down the shining street and Fidel stood immobile on the sidewalk, gazing at the shadow into which it had disappeared . . .

Pepe Calles, happy as always, said his goodbyes to other girls.

III

Fidel Murillo felt very good in Los Angeles. He'd managed to rent an office in the Bradbury Building and had begun to advertise his purchasing agency, which, as it was phrased in the newspaper, would send goods to Mexico and South America.

In truth, he felt the need to be alone in some kind of office, just so he wouldn't spend all his time at home like the best of the middle class, playing with his little boy and listening to the simple-minded small talk of "the missus."

The "missus" was María Luz, a pretty girl from Veracruz who had fallen stupidly in love with his captain's uniform during the adventures of the revolution and had lured him into marriage. No, it's not that Fidel hated conjugal life, but since he felt he had been born an artist, he had not accepted his role as reproducer of the species. And so, once the natural enthusiasm of the honeymoon had passed, he ended up discovering that his wife was not as beautiful as she had appeared in those early days, that she tended to have bouts of very feminine foul moods, that her legs were not at all straight . . . so many things! What was certain is that he had begun to find defects in her that he had not seen before and that, perhaps more than ever, he found himself attracted to other women, those who were not his wife, possibly out of a desire for adventure; something like a morbid curiosity . . .

Hence his isolation. For him, a clean room, a shelf of books, a table with a white blotter and two or three well-chosen pictures were sufficient for him to spend his life between the four walls of his retreat, composing verses and thinking always of his latest romantic conquest.

Internally, he justified this detachment from home with the notion that he had been enslaved at a very young age, that he had not been given enough time to travel the world, and that, naturally, the conjugal impediment only ignited his inclinations toward the carefree life of single men.

Aside from the old Colonel Velasco, he had no friend in this thriving city other than Pepe Calles; the two were almost inseparable. He had taken him home to introduce him to María Luz as "his dearest" friend from school and ate with him almost every day in American restaurants or in those "cafeterias" where customers serve themselves, the two amused by the practical nature of the ruddy and soulless faces at neighboring tables.

Summer had already expired, but beach resorts were still brimming with people from all over the country who came to enjoy the delicious California climate, a climate that to them seemed extremely good, almost marvelous. Perhaps it was because they'd never had the good fortune of being anywhere in Mexico, where the weather is always lovely.

Pepe Calles, always sarcastic, had said one day:

"Our American cousins sure do make it a 'big deal.' Think about it, man. If this is the best climate they have here, how bad are the others?"

Tourists continued coming to Los Angeles, spreading across the beaches where they spent their days lying belly up on the sand to receive the sun's caress, which didn't take long to make their skin shed like that of snakes.

One morning, Pepe Calles arrived at Fidel's office, insisting that they go walk around Venice, one of the most fashionable beach resorts in the country. It was only separated from Los Angeles by a few miles of handsomely paved road that swarmed with automobiles during the day and that by night looked like a fantastic procession of lanterns.

"I have some correspondence to take care of . . ."

"Let's go, man. You won't lose millions if you answer it tomorrow . . ."

The two friends, equipped with the best of intentions, took a car that quickly left behind the last boulevards of Los Angeles as it headed toward the beach, which seemed like something of a promised land to Murillo.

They finally arrived in Venice. In a sparsely populated plaza from whose center arose a kind of giant conch shell, a band unleashed its chords. Its conductor twisted around like an epileptic to keep time. Farther ahead, the massive shape of a roller coaster rose over the rooftops. Fidel had a peculiar aversion to its cars, since one of them back in the Ciudad de los Palacios had nearly put a final end to his earthly adventures.[158] Then, a street that undoubtedly led somewhere disappeared, overwhelmed by a gullible crowd that stopped now and then to contemplate some new game, or to listen to a barker, or to stand before the door of his attraction, pondering the sensations they might experience on entering the "cabinet of mysteries" or the "tunnel of laughter."

They walked up the street and were soon looking upon the ocean from the end of a reconstructed pier crowded with fishermen catching nothing, except maybe a fever, with the perpendicular rays of the sun beating down on their heads. Murillo contemplated the ocean, the ocean from which he had come and at the other end of which his distant home could be found, where the memory of his wilder days resided. And, buried there in a modest cemetery, were the remains of his parents in side-by-side graves, beneath the same cross.

To his right extended the yellowish beach, studded with colorful umbrellas that from a distance looked like jockey caps haphazardly strewn about. Over the steaming sand, hundreds of immodest bathers were lying out naked in the sun with that self-assured ease of women from the North who hardly care what passersby see, since none of this is prohibited by law.

The multitude of women of a respectable age, provocative little girls with hair as blonde as yellow ants, men with rubber-rimmed glasses, and children all intermingled. Every human specimen had its place in that heterogeneous crowd, whose mood struck the friends as confused, like an enormous buzzing of bees at times pierced by ringing laughter or by the sharp cry of some woman who had found the water too cold.

"What do you think?"

"It's far from what I imagined," responded Fidel. "I don't know why, but the abundance of nudity, instead of awakening a restlessness produced by the sight of feminine flesh, looks to me like a gigantic butcher's table strewn with inert drumsticks intermingled with fish that are losing their sheen. By herself, I might find one of these girls attractive. But like this, all together: I can't explain it . . ."

"Our homeland is still fresh in your memory, and there's something in your assessment—you have to admit it—that comes from the prudishness of our grandparents that still persists over there. You thought you would find an alluring spectacle and instead you discover something that, although you don't even realize it, clashes with your deepest feelings of shame. Those feelings have stuck with you since you were a little boy; they made you feel like the naked dolls on postage stamps were immoral . . ."

"No; I promise you that's not it. I think it's seeing flesh in this way, in such an abundance, that doesn't awaken any desire. And also, you know that while I'm looking at all these sunburned blondes, none of them is interested in me . . ."

A bump on the back cut him short. Before he could compose himself, he heard a gentle, feminine voice murmur in a serious tone: "Oh! Excuse me . . ."

He turned his head. It was a girl of about sixteen whose gray eyes looked at him with the expression of a supplicant. Pulling on a fishing line that had broken, the girl lost her balance, landing precisely on the young man's back as she was just about to fall.

Fidel wrapped her in a gaze. She was a delicious doll, half-dressed in a tight, one-piece bathing suit over which one could make out the small nipples of her budding breasts. Over the suit that barely covered her most concealable parts, there was a cape whose straps crossed her chest. She was barefoot and her little head was concealed beneath a white rubber cap with blue bands.

She explained the accident in two words. Pepe Calles responded with courtesy that "it was quite all right." Fidel also tried to say something with the scarce English he possessed, which went on strike at the exact moment he needed it. The girl—whom the journalist didn't find at all displeasing, with her big, dreamy black eyes and her fresh smile—smiled again and asked them to help recover the hook and line, which had stuck in a knot of the pier's wooden support just a few feet below the platform. She then thanked them politely, with another one of those looks that says more than a lengthy speech, and returned to her initial pastime.

"There you have it," continued Murillo. "That girl was attractive to me, and not only because she was more or less naked than the others. It was not her skin; it was the eyes."

"I suspect," and Pepe Calles laughed silently and sarcastically, "that what's happening is that you are seduced by all things feminine. I bet you're already thinking about a conquest . . ."

"And why not? That wouldn't be so strange."

They left the pier a little bored. Upon entering the crowd, Fidel turned his head, noticing that the blonde was following him with her eyes. Then, a smile made it clear she was flirting.

"You see? That little gringa was starting something. Now we just need to invite her for a drink and there you have the adventure you've been seeking."

The whole enterprise wasn't difficult at all. The two friends returned and after an introduction from Pepe Calles, who had an enviable coolness, they began to converse. The chat ended in a café full of bathers who wore shawls or sweaters over their shoulders so as not to break the dress code.

A Hawaiian orchestra, dressed in white and with leis around their necks, wailed a melody about the islands. Everyone ordered sandwiches and soft drinks . . .

The boys and their little companion had been seated; a waiter as big as a bear leaned over them.

The girl ordered first.

"Ham and egg sandwich and a Coca-Cola."

She ordered with that kind of confidence, as if she were either a woman of the world or extremely familiar with those who had invited her.

"She's secretly a prostitute," thought Fidel.

But he was hesitant to believe that that young girl, given her age and with that fresh face reddened by the sun, could be selling love.

But what about the audacity with which she crossed her naked legs in the presence of two men whom she had just met? She had assumed the most comfortable position that she could and rubbed her toes together to remove the fine sand that covered them, making them look like candy covered in sugar. She chatted about trivial things.

By the time lunch was over, they were good friends. Murillo's English had been tamed and his tongue seemed less clumsy, although at times he reversed some expressions that the little American went out of her way to correct. Pepe Calles, as one would imagine, was incredibly bored despite his proverbial outgoing nature.

They finally parted ways. Murillo, saying goodbye to the blonde, doffing his hat courteously in the Mexican fashion, carried with him the hope of a new conquest. And in the folds of his wallet he had written down a new address and telephone number . . .

"Now there's a lucky man," said Calles as they left the pier to stroll along the beach. "If I had spent the afternoon making eyes at that 'blondie' I wouldn't even be able to look at myself in the mirror. You, on the other hand . . ."

"But I picked her up off the street! Isn't it obvious that we're talking about a young woman who is secretly a prostitute? And those . . ."

"No, no: let me stop you there, man. She's an honest girl, I'm sure of it. I've been in this country too long for someone to tell me how things work. I'm not surprised this happened to you. Look: in our land a woman is honest by nature because she is taught to be that way. There, a woman who does what that girl did would be a lost cause, you can bet on it. There, they don't accept your first invitation just like that, nor do they greet you in the nude, nor do they adopt a cocky attitude in your presence unless they are simply trafficking in pleasure. It's different here. That girl you've seen . . . what's her name?"

"Betty."

"Okay, well, this Betty is a little girl whose parents have let her walk around Venice. They could have been out there as well, naked and lying belly up on the sand, keeping an eye on her from afar . . ."

"Impossible . . ."

"Let me explain it this way. Back home, when a woman—I'm talking about an honorable woman—when a woman, let's say, gives you a passionate kiss, one of those that you wish would never end: you can count on it being a conquest, almost certainly. When a woman walks around with you by herself late at night, there is no doubt about what you and she have been doing while absent from the view of others. Here, girls kiss you, they let themselves be kissed, they even let you pass an irreverent hand over their feminine charms. And just when you think you're dealing with an easy woman, you find yourself before a marble tower that resists your attacks and that calls you a beast as soon as she notices that a desire has awoken in you . . .

"Here you can hang out all night with one of these trivial little blondes who seem to like you and she will remain untouched. In a word, women here are fortified with a glacial soul that is perfectly defended, while our women are weaker. They get confused and allow themselves to be led by the hand down the path of love until arriving at the irreparable. Those of us who come here from there suddenly awaken in this environment of apparent licentiousness and have the impression that all women are easy . . . and we crash up against hard reality. This is the gospel truth."

"I guess so . . ."

"Don't doubt it. So I advise that you mingle with those 'girls' as little as possible. They promise disappointment, in a big way."

They continued walking along the crumbling sidewalk with their bags beneath their arms and their necks turned into accordions from the heat. On the corner a very fat man, whose red, chubby face looked like it was about to explode, struggled to wipe off the sweat beneath his Panama hat. A married couple, holding a little child by the hand, came out of a soda shop; the three were dressed in bathing suits, with their arms and legs in the open air and their feet covered in sand. They were definitely fighting. She fired off incomprehensible words while wearing an unmistakable expression of authority on her plump yet pretty face. He, without letting go of the child, did not respond. Instead, he was turning the butt of a cigar around between his discolored lips. He wore an incredibly humble expression. The child wasn't even looking at them.

When they passed close by, the young men could hear the woman suffocating the husband's first attempt at an explanation with a brusque:

"Aw, shut up!"

For Fidel, all of this was very amusing. For Pepe, this was the most natural thing in the world. He even wondered if he hadn't been witness to scenes like this all his life.

They accidentally arrived back at the little plaza where they were playing music and destroying a tune from *Madame Butterfly*. The conductor continued to jerk around like an epileptic. Suddenly, from afar, they could make out a familiar face, a fresh, dark-skinned face that smiled at them as a hand raised high to catch their attention.

"Take a look, conquistador: there's Estela . . ."

It was indeed the pretty girl from the night of the fifteenth who was waving at them from a distance. She was with some friends and her mother as an escort.[159] They were drinking soda in one of those open-air shops that are everywhere in Venice, and one of her cute little companions invited them to come over with a gesture.

Fidel felt that inexplicable sensation of attraction toward the girl from Monterrey rekindle, and he recalled that a few nights before he had held her hand tightly as a sign of understanding. He squinted and saw her from a distance; he couldn't help but murmur between his teeth with concentrated resolve:

"How beautiful you are!"

Yes, he liked her in an extraordinary way. He felt that it wasn't the vanity of the romantic conquest that attracted him, but something more profound, something spiritual that had nothing in common with the desire that the blonde from the pier had inspired in him just moments earlier.

Once they all found themselves at the soda shop counter where they were frying hot dogs on an electric stove—and after the handshakes that are as indispensable among Mexicans as they are absurd among Yankees—came the same question as always, the customary yet useless question:

"What are you all up to?"

"Nothing . . . just out for a stroll."

IV

Someone knocked discreetly on the door of the office.

"Come in!"

Fidel, awakening from a daydream, arranged himself in his seat and mechanically straightened his tie.

The disheveled silhouette of Pepe Calles appeared in the doorway.

"Come on, man! You could have come in without all the mystery. I thought it was . . ."

"Just remember, you never know if you're alone . . ."

Indeed, some time ago, Pepe walked in like he owned the place, only to discover the presence of an opulent blonde, her body spilling over the chair in which she was rocking as she carelessly crossed her legs. He suddenly understood that he shouldn't have been there. Since then, he knocked.

"It's not always the same thing."

Fidel sighed, as if thinking about something sad. They lit a cigarette that filled the room with its perfume. Soon the spirals of smoke flattened out against the pictures of performers that adorned the walls.

"Have you seen Señorita Estela?"

"I knew that you were just thinking about her. No, I haven't seen her. But I have something to tell you about that 'girl.'"

"You too?"

Murillo's voice began to waver. Some naysayers had told him something about her; it was driving him half-crazy and had him in a bad mood.

"Yes, me too. I see that you're in love with that girl and I'm your true friend . . . All the same, you know what you're doing . . ."

There was a long silence. Pepe pretended to look at the portraits on the wall. Fidel occupied himself by gazing at the smoke from his cigarette as it rose in opal spirals . . .

"I see you're in a bad mood. I'll go."

The bohemian got up and went to grab his hat.

"I don't want you to go. Okay? Look, don't take it the wrong way. You know you're one of my best friends, the dearest one of all. Yes, I'm in a bad mood. But you know exactly what's happening to me and instead of lifting my spirits . . ."

"No, old man, you're unbearable. Look: you're stupidly in love with this girl who won't give you the time of day, simply because you haven't told her you love her. And believe me, I've spent more time in this city of intrigue and rumor: this girl is not for you. I know what I'm talking about."

"So you think . . . ?"

"I'm sure of it. You already know that the walls have ears and that there is nothing secret in this world. Estela has a very bad reputation among the good families. Have you noticed how they shun her? They say terrible things about her, and you . . . well, I've already told you. You know what you're doing. If you love her like that, as a woman, why don't you do something to woo her? But if you love her with the airs of a dreamer, it will never happen . . . it's not worth it."

"And . . . tell me . . ." (Fidel stressed his words theatrically.) "What are they saying about the girl?"

"Well, nothing concrete, to be honest. But there's a lot of talk about a certain affair that she had with a tenor from the Spanish opera last year. No one could ever make him spend a cent, but he became generous toward her . . . and her mother, of course. A miracle. He took them to the beach, bought them nice things . . . well, I won't say more. People began to talk. Some said he was with the mother and others with the daughter. I mean, one day someone swore they saw the two of them coming out of a house alone . . . you don't believe me, of course. But with all those things, you understand . . ."

"Vile slander!" raged Fidel, throwing his unfinished cigarette across the room. "They're swine! Let me explain: you all, *you all*, I say, are envious of that girl who has more talent than all of those idiots destroying her reputation. You all are disgusting!"

He stood up, furious. The phone rang . . .

"Hello!"

It was María Luz, asking if he was coming home to eat.

"I'm telling you once and for all! I don't like you calling me at the office! If I don't show up, just eat alone and deal with it. The boy? Well, if he feels sick, take him to see a doctor . . ."

He hung up the phone brutally. Pepe didn't look at him and appeared occupied with reading a newspaper he had grabbed once Fidel began insulting the gossips.

But the phone had just barely returned to its cradle when it began to ring again. Fidel turned toward him, blanketing him in an angry look. He hesitated before answering, but ended up doing so, asking brusquely:

"Hello! Who is it?"

His brown face suddenly lit up. The voice of Señorita Estela reverberated on the other end of the line.

"Is this Mr. Murillo?"

"Yes, miss. Oh! What a pleasant surprise!"

"I wanted to call and congratulate you on your verses in yesterday's issue. And I regret not being there in person to shake your hand . . ."

"Thank you very much. You don't know how much . . ."

"Not at all: they were beautiful. Above all, with a bedrock of truth like a mountain. Count me among your followers."

"Oh! Miss, you embarrass me."

"No . . . just a moment . . ."

After a second her voice reverberated once again.

"Hello? Mother says hello and wants you to come for tea with us this afternoon. Will you come?"

"I'd be delighted, miss. I will be there."

"Good. I won't take up more of your time. I'll see you this afternoon."

"Goodbye!"

Now he hung up the phone with care, as if he were afraid to break it. And his face had been almost magically illuminated. Pepe looked at him coldly.

"Did you hear? It was Señorita Estela! Oh! And let them say what they want . . . they're a bunch of pigs."

Pepe shrugged his shoulders and murmured between his teeth:

"You're in love, like a dog . . ."

V

Mrs. Garza's house was located in a pretentious neighborhood in West Los Angeles, where the most well-off families of the Latin colonia in Los Angeles famously live. Although the Garzas had fallen on hard times as the result of some past reversals of fortune, they still conserved the custom of hosting their most intimate female friends from time to time for a "five o'clock tea." It was typically savored, alongside delicious little cookies, with the most scandalous gossip. As in the pages of a film magazine, everyone in town made an appearance as subjects of the cruelest accusations. Naturally, on the Saturdays that they talked about Tula and Laurita, it was because they hadn't shown up, regardless of the fact that they would make up for it nicely the following week, tearing apart the personal lives of their critics from the week before.

That afternoon, the gathering consisted of Lupe Moreno, Laurita Carrillo, and Señorita Estela. Mrs. Garza, who had suffered a terrible migraine the night before, had not appeared in the salon all afternoon. So the girls, intimate friends all around the same age, chatted nonstop, muttering tidbits about their peers to their hearts' content.

"Yes," said Laurita, absentmindedly crumbling a ladyfinger between her sharp fingers, "María Teresa thinks we'll believe that her family was 'high society' in Jalapa, since she doesn't stop repeating it . . ."

"So curious!" interjected Lupe, with those mannerisms of hers that oblige you to believe her. "Over there she would be what she is here: a washerwoman."

"What do you mean, washerwoman?"

"Yes, you didn't know? How strange! Well, in the neighborhood we all know that she works at a laundry on 32nd Street, although she would have us believe that she's visiting all day."

"Girls: but all you have to do is look at her hands," Estela gently chimed in with her sweet soprano voice as she served more tea to the insatiable

Laurita, who was holding her cup delicately. "You can see that they're a mess. Let me tell you," she continued, setting the teapot on the lacquered table, "one night, the night of the dance at the Martínez Salazar home, we were sitting down to chat before you all arrived, when I noticed that her nails weren't long and sharp like they were before. People notice everything! Then I realized that she had been working. I wanted to see how she responded and I told her:

"'Oh my god, Tere! What happened to your fingers?'

"You should have seen the look on her face! She quickly put on her gloves and told me some story about how the maid didn't show up one day and she had to take care of the house, and so on! At that moment Jorge arrived and she stood up to dance with him. It seemed imprudent of me to keep talking about it."

"There you have our 'aristocrats,'" Laurita said, stressing the last word. "All of us here say we came from the best families, but people are starting to figure it out."

"Well, what about Carmela? Those who find her so attractive at dances and gatherings would never guess that she works like a black woman in an overalls factory where I think they pay her twenty-five cents a pair . . ."

"She doesn't want you to know that, either. But the thing you try to hide the most is the first thing that comes out. There are a dozen other girls just like her who work like slaves during the day at packing companies, but at night they seem so haughty."

"Carmela was so excited about that young man who just came from Mexico. If he only knew!"

"From Mexico?" asked Estela. "Who is he?"

"I don't know him, but they say he's very handsome. I think he's a journalist . . ."

"Ah, yes! You know which one, Estela? The one who goes around all the time with Pepe Calles, that vagabond. No one knows how he makes a living."

Estela seemed to become more attentive. They were undoubtedly talking about Murillo, and she seemed interested.

"So Carmela is in love with that guy?"

"That's what they say . . ."

"But the guy is married. At least that's what Pepe told me. I don't think there's any hope for her."

"No, nor do I. But you know how she is. She has those eyes that everyone has told her are beautiful, but that almost disappear behind all that mascara. She thinks everyone is crazy for her. She has a predilection for recent arrivals. You remember Santelle . . ."

"The one who was urgently called back to Mexico?"

"That's him. I think something suddenly 'came up' for him. Here he was living the bohemian life, remember?"

"Well, in terms of that guy," said Estela, "I don't think there's hope for her. I know him, and he's a very talented young man. His name is Fidel Murillo."

"What was that?"

"Fidel Murillo . . ."

"How curious! Look, let me show you."

Lupe Moreno carefully took a small newspaper clipping, carefully cut, from out of her purse woven of silver wire.

"This morning I was reading yesterday's newspaper and I found these verses that I kind of liked, so I cut them out. And look, here's the name: it's him."

With her ringed finger she pointed at the signature written in dark black letters. Estela grabbed the clipping and began to read.

"He speaks a great truth," she said once she finished, handing it back to Lupe.

"Let's see . . ."

Laurita also looked over the verses, making a kind of grimace once she finished.

"I don't like it," she said.

"But it's speaking a great truth," reiterated Estela. "The thing is that not everyone has the bravery to say it. As you can see, it states that love, true love, the love Christ showed us, is far from existing between human beings. We all love selfishly, for the pleasure that the possession of the beloved object brings us. But none of us are capable of hopelessly sacrificing ourselves for that love. When we do make what we would egotistically call a sacrifice, it's only with the hope that, upon learning about it, our absent loved one returns. And that if they don't love us enough, that love will intensify. And we do this with the intention of feeling loved, of feeling happy; more for the satisfaction of knowing a man loves us than for the pleasure of loving properly . . ."

"Ah! That's not true," said Lupe. "I assure you that I have truly loved unselfishly, and I have sacrificed myself for a man. You remember Rubén . . ."

"I'm going to prove to you that the opposite is true. You loved Rubén, right?"

"With all my heart."

"And he loved you?"

"I think so. But on a crazy whim, you know, he got married and . . ."

"And he turned his back on you. Isn't that true?"

"Naturally, if he loved another woman, how could he love me? If he wasn't free, why would I love him?"

"There's the proof I'm talking about. At first you loved him because he was all yours. But once you saw another take him away, that he went to her instead of listening to you, you turned your back on him. That's not love."

"I don't understand."

"Let me explain myself. Now that Rubén is married, would you be capable of loving him?"

"No, because that would naturally be a mistake."

"Then, if you loved him before, it's because you believed that he was going to marry you, because you felt that he was yours alone. So you didn't love him for him, but for yourself. Now you don't love him. Who told you that love is so fleeting? Love is eternal. Of course I'm talking about love, true love, the one and only, about which Murillo says:

"'It is the sacrifice

"'Of all that exists in the name of your beloved,

"'Who smiles calmly in the face of agony.'

"Our generation, with very few exceptions, loves in a very strange way. We love for ourselves. In other words, we love ourselves in the image of others. I have to confess that I haven't loved either, just as the poet says in that clipping. I've played around at love, but it's always been about me. I've sadly realized that I love myself more than others. I put myself first."

"That's egotistical . . ."

"How else does humanity live? Ego and ego alone. Self-love—not the love of a woman—is what obliges our men to kill each other 'over her.' They say that jealousy is the best proof of love's existence. And what is jealousy? It's excessive ego: the tendency to have something for yourself and all to yourself without wanting to share with others. Why do men generally kill women who cheat on them? Why do lovers commit suicide when the ideal they've pursued slips between their fingers? Maybe you have an answer . . ."

"Come on," Laurita chimed in, "this is starting to sound more like a seminar on love than a visit . . . That's enough of these stories."

Lupe, on the other hand, was not completely convinced by what Estela was saying, nor had she taken the time to reflect on it. Instead she heard the words of a girl getting worked up about her explanations, like a distant rumbling. She was thinking about everything except what she was hearing. Laurita's intervention came as a godsend. They began making small talk again.

Later on, the doorbell rang and Estela came personally to answer the door; kisses, feminine voices, and happy laughter were heard in the hallway.

"Come in, Tere . . ."

María Teresa was now here. She was a radiant peroxide blonde whose golden hair was belied by her dark brown eyes. Estela, with her arm around her friend, entered the small salon with her. The two visitors instinctively looked at the hands of the new arrival, but her gloves were firmly in place, thwarting the inspection. The blonde smiled happily, showing everyone her teeth through the provocative opening of a large mouth that was scandalously painted.

"You see," said Laurita affectionately, addressing Lupe, "I told you she would come . . ."

"You were really thinking of me?"

"Of course! We missed you so much . . ."

Loud, exaggerated kisses were repeated and the new arrival sat down on a cushion without taking off her gloves.

Noticing this detail, a quick, knowing glance flashed across the eyes of the three young women, traveling like an electric spark. There was a long moment of silence. Then María Teresa crossed her elegant legs, refined and slender, covered in whimsical silk stockings that simulated a serpent. They ended in two slightly large feet that were crammed into small silk shoes.

"How is your mother?" she asked.

"A little bit under the weather," Señorita Estela answered. "My, what beautiful gloves you have on!"

The blonde girl smiled purposefully. Then, before the vigilant eyes of the girls, she removed the glove from her right hand.

"Take a look . . . fifteen pesos."

And she held out the glove to Estela with a pink, transparent hand, on whose ring finger shone a diamond ring.

Her nails looked like mother-of-pearl, and were elegantly cut and filed.

Lupe and Laurita shot each other a sidelong glance.
The glove passed from hand to hand.

VI

Decidedly, just as Pepe Calles had so picturesquely phrased it, Fidel had fallen in love "like a dog." Yes, like a dog. Because he was content to spend entire hours inhaling the perfume from one of Estela's handkerchiefs, which he had secretly taken from the "five o'clock tea." Like a dog because he felt that nothing was capable of dissuading him from that supreme aspiration, just as being beaten couldn't dissuade a hungry canine's designs on a piece of meat left to dry in the sun. The rumors had inundated his office. Everyone had something to say about that girl with the face of a saint who was surely the object of the most vile slander engendered by envy. Fidel only saw that she was the kind of woman he'd always dreamed about. A cultivated woman who sang and played the piano delicately; a young, beautiful woman with a worldly perspective that allowed you to understand her, like an open book . . . he recognized that he had made a mistake. María Luz, his pretty and very feminine little wife, never debated the direction of politics with him, nor did she sing or play piano. What's more, Estela composed poetry, spiritual and very feminine verses that were slightly daring for a woman. By contrast, María Luz made delicious little cookies and kept the house very clean and the little boy well groomed. But this was not enough for the heart of a poet who had dreamed of spending his life at the side of a woman who would perform Villanueva's "Vals poético" or one of Chopin's Nocturnes sotto voce as he looked for the right consonant rhyme in an erotic sonnet. A woman who was intelligent enough to understand him, to listen intently to his complex conversations about art and modernism. He had been dreaming of a woman like that, and just when he thought it was impossible, she crossed his path . . .

"Ah! But too late!"

"Too late?"

An ignoble thought swirled around his confused mind, beating its wings against the walls of his skull like a bat blinded by the light. Too late? No: it's never too late . . .

But just as he considered that unspeakable idea that he wasn't sure about dismissing, the image of his little boy smiling, holding his arms open, arose in his mind . . . Yes: he was resolved to go through with it. His only regret would be his boy. Her? Bah!

On the wall, in the middle of his collection of portraits of performers, he had hung a large picture of Señorita Estela that he contemplated in ecstasy from his seat, scrutinizing all of its details.

Every now and then he closed his eyes halfway and murmured with determination:

"How beautiful you are!"

That day, like the others, an unpleasant scene had taken place at home. Everything had been bothering him for a while now: the food, the arrangement of the rooms, the whole house itself . . . and that morning the only thing María Luz could do was explode.

"You've been unbearable for a while. Everything disgusts you even though I'm going out of my way to do things for you . . . Something's going on with you."

"Yes, something is definitely going on with me . . . I've had enough!"

He left in a rage, without consoling his beloved wife as he had before. And she, resigned and humble, was left thinking about how to bring back the affection that someone was taking from her, although she didn't know who . . .

As if sprouting from the ground, Pepe Calles appeared in the middle of Fidel's office with a sarcastic smile.

"See: now I don't knock, I sneak in!"

He had a strange expression on his face. His eyes shone in a particular way and were made larger by some suspicious bags under his eyes.

"Sit down . . ."

He obeyed. Fidel took a good look at his friend. It didn't take much work to figure out that he was drunk. Pepe, for his part, only laughed heartily, as if witnessing the most comical scene in the world.

"I'm laughing . . . I'm laughing at life. Because this life is rubbish . . . you won't believe it, I'm not making it up. Someone has already said it, but it's true."

"Hey, you're . . . well, you're soused."

"I don't deny it."

"And what about Prohibition?"

"What do I care about that? Look, now it's just a matter of spending an extra peso or so, but there's more than there was before. I should know! Let me tell you: I have a friend I met at the Alexandria working as a dishwasher like me. Now he has an automobile . . ."

"And so . . . what does this have to do with what I'm telling you?"

"Hold on. He has an automobile because he's been selling wine since Prohibition started. I think he even makes it. You can already see what a treasure he is."

He didn't know if it was being around his friend—whom he'd begun to like less because of his stories about Señorita Estela—or if it was because he thought of her constantly, seeing her before him all day as a backdrop to everything else, sometimes near and sometimes far away. Fidel felt the urge to numb himself like Pepe. He thought about looking for refuge in vice, to forget who he even was for a moment.

"Do you want to come with me?"

It was Pepe asking the question, looking at Fidel as intently as his condition would allow, as if waiting for a negative reply he was ready to reject.

"Where are we going?"

"I'll show you a secret little spot. I made some friends two weeks ago, one afternoon when I was with Colonel Velasco—your friend whom I can't stand . . ."

"Hey: who doesn't rub you the wrong way?"

In short order their departure was arranged. The two friends called a taxi. Pepe wanted to ask him something, but despite his inebriated state he didn't dare. Finally, closing his eyes, he let it out:

"You haven't seen Estela?"

Fidel answered sadly, pointing to her picture:

"You can see: I look at her every day."

Pepe made an effort to find the picture among the multitude of portrait cards adorning the wall. He finally found it and smiled in a peculiar way. Then, as he had the other morning, he again murmured:

"Yes, yes: like a dog . . ."

The car stopped in front of a bungalow almost entirely covered in vines. The little house was cute, like a toy. The blinds, completely drawn, gave it an alluring air of mystery, like a rare perfume.

"Thank you . . ."

After receiving his fare, the driver doffed his cap politely and his car headed down the street. Pepe and Fidel approached the door that was almost hidden behind the vines. Pepe pushed the white button of the doorbell, which stood out among the tender greenery of the silent little house.

They heard some distant, light footsteps inside, muffled from afar by rugs. Then the door opened without a sound and a chubby blonde appeared with a cheerful, "standard" smile plastered carefully on her face.

"Hello!"

Right there on the porch, Pepe Calles made introductions. "Madame St. Pierre . . . Mr. Murillo . . ."

A classic handshake. Then Madame St. Pierre invited them in, speaking English with an unmistakable French accent. The door closed once more, as silently as it had opened, and the footsteps of the three were muffled by the carpet that was as soft as a cushion.

They entered a little salon decorated in a simple American style. In the corner stood an immense black piano that occupied the greater part of the room. Beyond that, a column covered with a bronze pot holding shade palms. A table in the center with a large flower vase. In the corner opposite the piano, a Victrola, one of those cabinet phonographs, also black. Various chairs upholstered in a fabric with wide stripes and a garishly colored Persian rug complemented the furnishings.

Madame St. Pierre might have been thirty-five years old. She was rather short and plump, but she had a blonde head that had preserved the charm of her impetuous youth. Her eyes, blue and indefinable, were trimmed with splendid eyelashes that must have been fake since one of them, headed toward her rosy little ear, had parked itself on a small, provocative squarish mole.

Murillo had already guessed: she was an aristocratic pimp.

Madame St. Pierre broke the ice—and it didn't take much to do it—after assuring the two friends that they were in an honorable house, considering the counterfeit wines she served and the prices she charged for them. She asked what liquor they preferred.

"A whiskey for me . . ."

"Do you have any good cognac?"

You're asking if a Frenchwoman has cognac? If she were at the end of the earth, at the North Pole itself, she would do all she could to present us with a bottle full of colorful labels that displayed the renowned names that had made cognac famous.

Moments later, on the center table, the vase had been displaced by two beautiful bottles of "the real stuff" and a tray with three small glasses.

A fashionable foxtrot bellowed away on the Victrola. Pepe commented on it enthusiastically, as he had cheered up noticeably at the sight of whiskey. Madame St. Pierre attended to Fidel, who had started a conversation with the rotund madam, trying to dust off his French from the distant days of preparatory school. She had been in the United States for seven years—she came during the war—but she had already lived in England and for some time in Spain. Fidel saw the life of that woman pass through his imagination, just like a movie. A seller of love in her youth, she had understood that the profession has a more lucrative side than falling madly in love with some jealous crook who only gives her the occasional slap and ends up drinking all the francs she's earned through so many sacrifices and, above all, the greatest sacrifice. She had become convinced that the business could provide a living if properly exploited, just like any other commercial enterprise, especially given the experience she had accumulated roaming Parisian boulevards. And that's how she went from country to country until arriving in this charming city, where she had bought an elegant bungalow right on Wilshire Boulevard, the most aristocratic area of Los Angeles. He saved her the time and relative bother of lying as she told her story to Murillo. He already had it perfectly figured out.

The song had ended, and Pepe got up to put on a new one. Madame St. Pierre insinuated:

"If we weren't so all alone, at least . . ."

Fidel had no doubt left—as if there were any remaining—as to the true nature of that little house that was so curiously occupied by a single woman. He had also seen more than one elegant brass bed with bleached-white cushions as he passed in front of the bedroom doors. He murmured:

"Well . . ."

Pepe had fulfilled his strenuous mission with the phonograph and he interjected into the conversation:

"You can call some of your friends to come, Madame."

"Certainly! Only one?"

He saw Fidel gently interrogating him with his eyes.

"No," he muttered. "Two: that would be better."

There was no objection. After serving a new glass, the blonde excused herself to use the telephone to call her two intimate friends, to make the gathering more pleasant. Soon they heard her from the next room asking the operator for a number.

The delicious Hennessy began to go to Murillo's head. And strangely enough, although he was hoping that being drunk might let him forget the sight of that girl who drove him crazy, she was somehow even more present. He saw her pure smile "in mentis," her suffering gaze, the one that had inspired the verses that he had just published in "El Mundo Moderno":

"'You have the gaze of la Dolorosa

"'In your dark eyes of a celestial houri;

"'And it is your saintly image so beautiful and pure

"'That instantly recalls the pious image

"'Of Christ praying at Gethsemane.'"[160]

He recited this aloud, completely forgetting that he was not alone.

Ever attentive to the Victrola, Pepe Calles pretended not to hear him.

"It's so true . . . very true. She has the face of the Virgin of Sorrows. Doesn't that verse ring true to you, Pepe?"

"Yes, man: I've already told you so at least eighty times. But you keep up with this madness . . . Hey: why don't you speak to her more directly? Look, don't get upset, brother, just talk to her. It would be good on two counts. First, you'll see if she loves you in the same way . . . and that's 'bocato di cardinale.'[161] Second, you'll find out if everything they say about her is true."

"Impossible. Pepe, I don't feel the least bit of carnal attraction to her. You know me, right? Believe me if you want to or not, but I'm telling you . . ."

" . . . ?"

"What? That none of the women I've come across in the world have inspired such pure adoration in me as Señorita Estela has. I haven't even noticed the charms of her body. For me it's only her soul that exists. I love her, but in a spiritual way, as I have never loved anybody else . . . much less in this day and age."

He seemed to be in a dream. He unbridled his poet's soul while talking about Señorita Estela, like an enlightened man. And his speech was animated, perhaps a little bit because of the cognac, and even more so because of the memory of the woman he adored.

"Yes, it's only her soul that I love. What do I care about her physical charms? That's how I love her: soul to soul. Because of who she is, because she is the woman I've dreamed of as an eternal companion along the bitter path of life. Her, and after her, no one. You'll see, Pepe. The day will come, I can already see it, when I can't stand it anymore. Then I'll have to go and tell her and wait on my knees—just like in the novels—for her to tell me that she loves me, and to then kiss the soles of her feet. And if not, to shoot myself. Yes, don't laugh: shoot myself . . ."

"You're drunk."

"Could be. But I'm reasoning with my full faculties. Estela and my life. It seems like there is nothing in the world without her. Other women are eclipsed by her presence. What am I saying? Eclipsed just by the memory of her. Right now, as we're waiting for these girls, I don't know if I can make myself be friendly to them . . . you're laughing . . ."

"What else can I do? I'm laughing at you. Do you want me to be more blunt? I'm laughing at you. Don't be stupid, Fidel. Stop with the daydreams and let's have fun. Look, the girls are coming soon and it's not good for you to be having those schoolboy thoughts. What do you say we don't talk about Estela?"

"Whatever you want. But you're also right. Her name, the name I adore, should not be spoken on the grounds of this house of ill repute. Her name should be spoken in the solitude of night, alone, under the immensity of a sky sprinkled with drops of silver . . . 'Estela.'"

"Cheers."

They drank the last drop from the bottle. The song had finished on the phonograph and Pepe got up to change it. The diabolically happy face of Madame St. Pierre was gleaming from behind a curtain.

"Just a moment. They said they won't be long."

She was talking about the invited guests. Enthusiastically, just like a peddler who extolled the merits of a trinket that he was trying to sell at full price, the madam sang the praises of her little friends. Like sugar cubes, the two of them. One of them was French and delicate as a porcelain doll from Sèvres. A charming girl who had the romantic refinement of her people but who nonetheless was very discreet. The other, a very cute "Spanish" girl with beautiful eyes, only came in extreme cases when she had guests as kind and decent as they were. Because indeed: the girls were decent from head to toe, and discreet above all. They weren't running the risk of encountering just any girls. No, she was knowledgeable about her trade and the people she handled. In addition, she thought they would spend an extra peso here and there since the girls, being a bit expensive, were fit for a king. They were certainly worth it . . .

Now it was Madame St. Pierre who seemed to be dreaming. The drinks had made her tongue loose, and she had no qualms about sharing details that would make a libertine blush as she talked about the girls who were on their way to the house at that moment. And it was safe to say that Pepe and Fidel, who were men after all, were savoring the anticipation.

"This one's done."

Pepe was trying in vain to drain the bottles. Nothing, not even a drop. But Madame St. Pierre was no ingenue. Two seconds later the bottles were full again and the transparent, amber liquid sparkled in their glasses once more. While waiting for the prostitutes, they drank two more glasses.

Two minutes. Then they clearly heard a car stop in front of the bungalow and some delicate footsteps made the planks of the porch creak. The doorbell rang.

"Marcela is already here . . ."

Madame St. Pierre left to open the door and then returned with the new arrival, who stood in the door for a moment and greeted them graciously. The owner of the house had not exaggerated. The new visitor was a true apparition: tall, spiritual, peroxide blonde hair, full lips painted in the shape of a heart, and eyes radiant with evil. She was elegantly dressed and wore around her neck a large white fur that reflected its whiteness on her fresh and tastefully made-up face.

"Mademoiselle Marcela . . ."

"Messieurs Calles and Murillo . . ."

Marcela greeted them in correct French. She then took off her hat and fur to sit in front of Fidel, brazenly drinking half the liquor in his glass.

Pepe went to change the song. Madame St. Pierre sent a knowing signal with her mischievous eyes to her friend, who sat down unceremoniously on Fidel's knees as he smiled with satisfaction.

Suddenly the doorbell rang and the Frenchwoman went to open the door as she did the first time, while the affectionate couple lit a cigarette that they would take turns smoking.

Calles had stayed in the corner next to the phonograph. The poet and his friend, next to the table and in front of the entrance, formed their own little group, taking little drags off the same cigarette. Madame St. Pierre entered once more.

"This is Miss . . ."

She did not conclude her introduction. By her side, in the frame of the doorway, the enchanting face of the new arrival appeared, and the smile that was flowering on her lips was instantly cut short. Fidel Murillo pushed Marcela away from him and stood up in horror. Señorita Estela had just arrived.

Fidel's terrified eyes opened incredibly wide and he couldn't articulate a word. Estela remained standing for an instant and then, releasing a sigh, collapsed on the carpet, pale as death beneath the layer of rouge that covered her cheeks.

Madame St. Pierre didn't know what was happening, but she ran to bring something from her dresser to revive Estela, who was still lying inside the doorway.

Fidel indignantly stepped over her body and went out to the street. He almost even felt the urge to kick her.

Pepe stood still as a stone in his corner. For her part, Marcela, with eyes wide open, could only manage to ask with bewilderment:

"What is the matter?"

VII

Now the four walls of Murillo's office were congested with portraits of performers . . .

Through the window that opened onto pretentious Broadway, a horrible mixture of sounds arose in every hue and tone. And a cold gust of November wind agitated the pages of the calendar nailed to the front wall. Estela's portrait was still there, triumphant in the middle of a group of postcards and photos of naked performers. An innocent smile was traced across her delicate mouth, hiding so well her sewer of a soul . . .

Fidel Murillo lit his sixth cigarette and sprawled out in his rotating chair, putting his feet on the table in that horrible American custom. For Latinos who come from a country of practical methods and a very sensitive attitude toward immodesty, there was nothing easier than assimilating to bad customs without the remotest hope that the good customs they once observed would reappear out of habit. Fidel smoked distractedly before the portrait of Estela, whose smile now seemed mocking, sarcastic, like she was making fun of her own provincial naivete. She was there; also there in that transparent space full of colors was the unforgettable scene from the night before. The shameless Marcela with her puzzled look, Pepe Calles with a dumb expression on his face, the madam running to her dresser in search of smelling salts . . .

Horrible. Yes, horrible . . . Only now he was disgusted more because his love had been injured and his idol broken than he was by the fact itself . . . After all, what's the big deal? She was a woman, a passionate woman, almost a textbook case. One of those women like Messalina who would clear the brothels of men who left exhausted yet unsatisfied after an afternoon of pleasure.[162]

He felt humiliated, stepped on, deceived. He, who had put her and her saintly expressions into verse; he, who had become indignant in the face of rumors that he had always considered saturated with the nauseating slime of envy . . . He felt as if he had dreamed it; but no, he had seen it with his own two eyes. He had stepped over her body with the intention of kicking it to pieces, of spitting on it, debased, beaten, the victim of his most painful ridicule.

After all this, why had he not been able to rip the photo off the wall in front of his desk, where he had contemplated it in ecstasy, like an idiot? He felt more like crying than despising that fickle and shameless woman.

Upon arriving at his office, he had tried to tear it into a million pieces. Just like that: two, four, eight, sixteen, until almost reducing it to dust before spitting on it, trampling it as she had her innocence, her honor, her image . . . But was she the one to blame? Truthfully, Estela had never assured him that she was pure: she had never feigned any ridiculous chastity . . .

And nonetheless . . .

The seventh cigarette. Now the silver ashtray supported by a playful bronze dog was full of smoldering cigarette butts, many of them half-smoked when he abandoned them out of nervous tension.

Three discreet little knocks sounded on the door.

"Come in!"

Fidel violently removed his feet from the desk and arranged the knot of his tie with an instinctive gesture. A feminine figure walked in, her back turned to close the door.

"Estela . . ."

Yes, Estela: Señorita Estela. And he was unsurprised and unphased by her arrival, as if it were the most natural thing in the world. Nevertheless, he never believed the girl's audacity could reach these extremes.

Audacity? But why . . . ?

There was no doubt: it was her. Her majestically beautiful figure looked adorable wrapped in that peacock-blue outfit, crowned with a large, feathered hat like one worn by a musketeer of Louis XIII.

Her face bore a serene expression. She murmured:

"Good morning."

Fidel shook the gloved hand that she extended to him and had the impulse to kiss it . . . An eternal second. Estela looked at the four walls of the office and sat down carefully in a chair without crossing her legs. Her eyes still had the expression of la Dolorosa . . .

"I don't know what you must think of me, Mr. Murillo. But I felt a duty to come here in person so that you can let out your anger. I'm ready for anything; I'm listening . . ."

Fidel lost his composure. Blinded by the unexpected vision that hadn't provoked even the slightest gesture of surprise in him, he tried to respond:

"Oh! No, miss . . ."

"Please, Mr. Murillo, don't address me that way. As you know too well, that name is reserved for honorable women . . . or at least those who have not experienced the disgrace of being caught . . . as I was."

She spoke with composure, with a sad yet firm tone. Fidel ended up feeling ashamed. He believed that she was apologizing, that she had been caught off guard. Yes: he was disposed to believe everything, everything that came from her lips, even that she was as pure as a newborn.

"I understand. And save me the trouble of hearing you apologize. And above all, forgive me for having doubted you. I certainly . . ."

She raised her tiny gloved hand as if ordering him to be quiet.

"Please don't go on, Mr. Murillo; I didn't come here to make excuses. I've made a mistake, a grave mistake perhaps, that would kill my mother if she found out. But I don't want you to think I'm innocent, or a hypocrite. I went to Madame St. Pierre's house knowing what it was."

Then it was true! Señorita Estela was one of those poor women who are slaves to luxury, sacrificing everything—even the honor of their virginity, if they have it to give—just to have a little money to purchase some of the necessities demanded by their position . . . One of those victims of the shop windows who, having qualms about going out on the street in an old hat, doesn't hesitate to offer her lips to kiss the first libertine she comes across in a brothel . . . Fidel felt compassion for her. Better yet, no, not compassion exactly, but something like sympathy that could only make him more disposed to forgive her. In addition, his internal compass wanted to apologize by repeating the Arab proverb "A woman should not be harmed, even by the petal of a rose," knowing full well that he only wanted to deceive himself or to let himself be deceived. The passion that he had always felt in his chest was now reborn, like a fatal phoenix from its own ashes. Estela was there, two steps away from him, as beautiful as ever . . . No, more beautiful than ever, wrapped in her outfit of blue silk that sculpted her Venus-like shape and looking at him with the eyes of la Dolorosa that were now more like those of Manon: passionate, provocative, like one of those looks that makes an entire people change its destiny entirely . . . [163]

She realized that she had gained ground. She crossed her legs delicately and gazed fixedly at the point of her satin boot.

"Honestly, Mr. Murillo, believe me. I am extremely ashamed . . . that's right: ashamed. But I know you have a big soul, a soul that is free of our society's prejudices. I also know that I should not doubt the discretion of a gentleman. But I wanted to come here in person to receive your reproaches and to accept anything, even if you throw me out of here like a fallen woman. But only in exchange for one promise . . . can you guess what it is?"

Fidel tilted his head in silence.

"Yes," he continued after a few moments, "you don't have to worry. The secret will die here inside of my chest. Above all, I am a gentleman."

Estela's brown face lit up with happiness and her eyes sparkled. She was going to say something and even began opening her lips painted a discreet pink . . . but the words did not come out of her tempting mouth. A long sigh lifted her breasts . . .

Now they didn't speak, but their eyes wove burning gazes. He remembered the night of the Independence Day celebration, when she had squeezed his hand voluptuously . . . ; and then her effusiveness during his visits to her house when her mother wouldn't stop asking him to talk about Mexico, there, where her greatest love was laid to rest . . . And now this transfigured gaze that he didn't recognize, this gaze of a wild young woman that seemed to be daring him. And those open lips that lightly trembled . . .

Without knowing what he was doing, he got up from his seat and went toward her to extend his hand. He clumsily tried to justify his sudden actions:

"Yes . . . don't you worry. I'm a gentleman."

He had her little gloved hand pressed against his and casually put his other hand on her shoulder almost without realizing it and without her making the least effort to resist it. For a split second, he remembered the words of Pepe Calles and repeated to himself:

"Yes: like a dog . . ."

He didn't know when he had placed his lips on hers; she only trembled slightly and closed her eyes. A silent, long, deep kiss . . . and they squeezed each other's hands nervously as if they were going to break apart.

Pepe Calles was on his way up in the elevator when he ran into Estela at the entrance to Fidel's floor. Taken by surprise, the young man bathed her in a look that she valiantly resisted. Estela retained enough composure to greet him with a slight movement of her head, but he didn't respond in kind. Ah! He felt the urge to shout at the top of his lungs right there about who she was: beneath the camouflage of a decent woman was a corrupt body, available to all appetites . . . She sickened him.

Estela's triumphant look told him what had just happened. Behind him he felt the elevator descend and felt a deep and urgent wish that the mechanism's cables would break, ending once and for all that misguided life, that swamp in which his most beloved friend was becoming mired.

He rushed into the office. Fidel received him with his feet on the table and smoking his eighth cigarette. His face radiated with a glow of happiness and his eyes shone in an extraordinary way.

"Hello!"

"Hello."

Pepe answered just like that: dry, without any inflection of friendship. He let himself fall into the same chair that Estela had occupied. He could only manage a single glance at that imbecile who thought he was a god . . .

On the desk there was a tiny portrait of María Luz with the little boy in her arms; right there, close to the heel of one of Fidel's boots that was about to knock it over.

And Calles sat there, looking intently at his friend with more sadness than indignation. Then he removed the portrait of the faithful wife out of harm's way and put it in the center of the table. Murillo didn't notice this maneuver as he followed the bluish spiral of smoke through which Señorita Estela smiled at him from her place of honor, in the middle of the portraits of his favorite performers . . .

"You know what? You disgust me . . ."

The subject of this statement raised no objection. After two seconds he responded, resigned yet cynical:

"Yes, I feel the same way about myself. But there's nothing I can do."

VIII

There are few places as appropriate to set up a "love nest" in Los Angeles as the little hill on Buena Vista Street. A series of unremarkable small chalets stretches out from a little bit beyond the city jail, ending in a little cottage at the crest of the hill. The descent on the other side is vertiginous and full of rough stones. But up the hill, the street is impeccably asphalted. It's the same story with all of these paradoxical cities that are so proud of their modernity. Next to a beautiful cottage, a garbage heap so foul, with not a policeman or street sweeper in sight. The whole city is full of contrasts; it's not unusual to see, right next to one of the best theaters dedicated to opera, dreadful vacant lots where pedestrians who have the bad fortune of walking by past eleven at night are robbed with impunity. In the same way, just two hundred meters from the grandiose courthouse building and a hundred meters from the city jail, we find a row of mysterious little houses, all of them with the same old sign reading Rooms for Rent. They are nothing more than nests for supposedly married couples that only go to the house once a day without anyone, much less the landlord, giving it a second thought.

In one of these little chalets, ten feet above street level, Fidel Murillo had established what he called his "nest," a cute little apartment covered with vines on the outside and on the inside with portraits of Estela in every pose and size. He enclosed himself between those four charming walls to dream with his beloved, to live the illusion that he had found his other half, the one who understood him, one who, like his ideal woman, wistfully played the piano, singing in almost a whisper, and occasionally composed ultra-modernist and ultrasensual verses that even the least scrupulous editor in these matters would have hesitated to publish. He had found that this girl, this flower of evil, was truly a jewelry box full of whimsy. She could dream, sing, write, love like no one else . . .

Murillo frequently compared her to other women—even to his own María Luz—and he always found her to be above them. He recalled details of this one or that one, perhaps his infatuation of the day before, and they all seemed ridiculously provincial to him, or vain women full of hot air whose memory made him cringe. In the afternoons, when he was busiest at the office—his business was taking off—he always had her image present in his mind. He had taken her portrait from the front of his desk at the insistence of Pepe, who had made him see that it was disrespectful to María Luz. In more than one visit to his office, his wife had looked at it with an expression of concentrated rage, although she had never permitted herself to say anything about it. Because she suspected—with that rare and particular instinct of a deceived woman—yes, she suspected that someone was taking from her the love that she felt drifting away on the wind. Nothing had worked to stop it so far: not the effort she made to care for the house, not the constant surprises at home, not her flirtation, not any of the things that an honorable woman has at her disposal to attract her husband without ceasing to be honorable. She knew that there was someone occupying her old place in Fidel's heart, and that portrait occupying a place of honor had made her shudder. Murillo had never introduced her to Señorita Estela, but she had seen her in "Liga" gatherings where she squandered her charming voice or plucked out sweet melodies on the piano under the envious gaze of all the single men, who undressed her intimately to their liking. And just the presence of this damsel had made her suspicious—women are never deceived. There was something about her she didn't like, from which she deduced that she was stealing the love that she had worked so hard to preserve. Who else could it be?

That's why Fidel had taken down the portrait. He had certainly never understood the sad look that María Luz had given it when she arrived at the office. But Pepe, who was on top of everything, had told him one day:

"Hey, you need to take that portrait down. It's disrespectful to poor María Luz."

And he had obediently taken it down without objection, only to later hang it up on the walls of his nest, the nest that nearly disappeared at the end of a steep staircase between the complicit ivy vines that seemed to be planted for the purpose he intended for them on Buena Vista Street. In effect, from behind the vines with the window open, he could look down to one side on the entire street and see what was happening from the corner on Temple Street. In front of the house, the most complete panorama of Los Angeles stretched out before him. For him it was the most beautiful city on Earth, the place where he had—at last!—achieved what he considered to be supreme happiness.

The great clock on the courthouse was the only thing that reached the height of his love nest. It had just chimed six, and its sphere began lighting up as a defense against the shadows of the night. Fidel was at the window, looking at the entrance to Temple Street through the conspiring vines. At any moment would come that small figure with the jaunty stride, her little head almost disappearing inside a warm rabbit fur. He had waited for her there for a month, almost every day. And every time the last chime of six rang out, she quickly turned the corner, arriving moments later out of breath and flushed with fatigue.

But the clock rang six today and she had not come; every minute that passed seemed to him an hour, a day, a week. With his eyes fixed on the corner, moments passed as he waited to see her familiar silhouette emerge and throw herself into his arms right away as always: smiling, affectionate, devouring him with kisses . . .

In front of the house, night began to stretch itself out like a blanket of shadows covering the neighborhood, which was dominated by the water tank of a gas factory that emerged like a watchtower. Here and there the darkness began to be sprinkled with tiny luminous points until it transformed into a great web of lights, from which a faint, hazy glow rose to the sky. Like small meteorites, streetcars passed in the distance from one side to another, stopping their burning heads at the corners to then resume their progress, ringing their bells loudly. Far off toward the north, old Broadway was congested with the coming and going of fireflies, growing and shrinking according to distance. Two steps away in the Mexican plaza, one could hear the distant sound of the bass player of a bad charanga band giving a serenade . . . [164]

But Estela didn't come.

It began to get cold, and Fidel, instead of closing the window, wrapped himself in his coat. On the floor of the room shone scattered cigarette butts that he had not finished smoking, nervous as he was about the long wait.

The little hand of the courthouse clock changed slowly until resting at a right angle with the hour hand that pointed downward like a black finger: 6:15 . . .

A deep sigh of satisfaction.

Finally the familiar silhouette appeared on the corner. But instead of turning quickly, it stopped for an instant, only to then continue on. No, surely it wasn't her . . . But yes, now he could make her out. She had remained stationary beneath an incandescent light. It was indeed Estela, but

. . . she was not alone. In front of her familiar silhouette he could make out a masculine silhouette trailing behind that he did not recognize and didn't remember having seen before. It was the silhouette of a man advanced in age—he concluded this from the slightly clumsy movements and his obese figure—who bid farewell without ever saying goodbye. Then the masculine hand caressed the chin of the girl on whose face a smile seemed to appear. Not a bit of resistance on her part. Oh! But this was atrocious . . .

Fidel decided to come down from the apartment. He grabbed his cap from on top of a chair and launched himself down the stairs muttering curses. He would go to see him in person and teach that dirty old man what it meant to mock him . . .

He hurriedly descended the staircase, which now seemed longer than ever. But upon arriving at the door, he abruptly found himself before the smiling face of Señorita Estela.

"Where were you going, crazy?"

She scolded him sweetly, kindly, making a familiar gesture.

"What is this? It's not enough that you arrive so late, but you make a mockery of me on top of it . . ."

"Let's go upstairs. Don't be a dummy . . ."

She grabbed him by the arm, and, like a cat, she rubbed her painted face against his, which was hot as a burning ember despite the cold. They headed up to the room.

Once the incandescent light was turned on and the blinds prudently lowered, Estela took off her hat in front of the mirror adorned with postcard portraits of her.

"Hey: who was with you?"

"Let me tell you: it was that old devil, the colonel . . ."

"That was Colonel Velasco?"

"Yes, wait. That old devil was the reason that I almost didn't see you, my love. I couldn't get him off my back."

"And why did he grab you by the face?"

Estela continued to arrange her hair without pausing and went to give him a kiss.

"Don't be silly . . . you know that I see him as a father."

"Yes, a father . . ."

"Really. Look: he knew my father very well and my mother is very friendly with him. Think about how worried I was when he said, right as I arrived at the corner, that he was determined to accompany me home."

"And how did you respond?"

"Naturally I told him no, my love. I ended up telling him a lie about coming to visit some girlfriends on this street and that's how I got him off my back."

She continued putting her hair back in place. A cream-colored silk sweater balanced on a rocking chair. It was still warm as she had just taken it off. With her delicate, provocative arms raised in that way, she looked like a strange Hellenic amphora. Estela had gained a little weight, but without her figure becoming deformed. Just a little more flesh on her hips, which she needed, and even more on her arms, which had become quite full, threatening to stretch out her skin. Behind her, Fidel contemplated her hungrily.

"Today we don't have much time to be together. I have a rehearsal at the Ruiz home at seven."

Murillo jumped out of his chair.

"At seven!"

"Yes. But don't worry; I'll go at 7:15."

It seemed like such little time! For days he'd been realizing that he missed her too much. Despite all that happened during his daily life, trivial as for all of humanity, he always saw her present: her smiling image, that "look of la Dolorosa" . . . It had become just as necessary for him to see her, to throw himself into her arms, to devour her with kisses, as it was to live life itself. That's why, when he lost just fifteen minutes of seeing her, of looking into her eyes, it was too much for him.

He objected, trying to come across like a tyrant:

"No. Then don't go."

She smiled at him. Then, after giving him a kiss on the mouth and biting on his earlobe, she responded very formally:

"Yes, I will go."

"You're disobeying me?"

"No, my boy. But let's not be ridiculous. Look, if I don't go to the Ruiz home for my rehearsal (which I also hate with all my soul because I'm not seeing you), they will find out at home tomorrow and I won't be able to explain where I was during that time. And from there, suspicion after suspicion, they'll find out everything . . . you have to know that people are already talking . . ."

"They're talking . . . they're talking. And what do we care if they talk? Don't you love me? Don't I love you? What's the problem . . . ?"

"I'm with you, my boy. But . . ."

"Are you ashamed of me?"

"What a question!"

"Then what do you care if they know or don't know that we love each other?"

"Look: can we stop talking about this? I know what I'm talking about. I know these people like the back of my hand . . . and they can always build a castle out of a grain of sand. For my part, I wouldn't care. But you know that my mother, my brothers . . ."

"But I don't think it has anything to do with your mother finding out. She'd be sharp enough to understand that you're . . . well, that you can't be mistaken for a ten-year-old girl."

"What do you mean by that?"

She blurted out the question in a way that seemed perturbed, almost aggressive.

"Just that: she wouldn't believe that you don't have a boyfriend . . . I mean . . . and that . . ."

"Yes, but . . . ," and she looked at him intently, "but you're married."

Fidel felt like a bolt of lightning had struck his feet. Married! He was indeed married . . . and she knew it before they started seeing each other. She wanted it that way. But Fidel had never paid any mind to that fabric of prejudices they called social norms, according to which a man had no right to make mistakes in his life . . . Married . . . yes, unfortunately. And now she was throwing it in his face: married . . . married . . .

The sweet, simple image of María Luz crossed his mind slowly, delicately dressing their little boy, just as he had left her this morning at home, getting ready to go out shopping. And crazy as he was, he desired with all of his heart that this selfless woman and his loving son—who could not go to sleep every night without a kiss from him—would dissolve into thin air, that there would be an earthquake, a sudden epidemic, something very powerful that would give him his freedom . . .

Estela had her arms around his neck in an expression of delightful abandon and the eyes of la Dolorosa looked into his. She asked him in a soft voice:

"Did I upset you?"

"No."

"Hey, look at me." And she struggled to focus her eyes on his diverted gaze. "Look at me and answer: do you still love me?"

Their lips joined in a long, passionate, silent kiss . . .

"Do I love you? You always ask me that question and I'm always the one who wants to ask you first. You ask me for no reason, just to be flirtatious, for the pleasure of hearing me say yes . . . the day I ask you, I will be tormented by the most terrible of doubts, perhaps fearing the answer . . . Of course I love you! Ask the many hours I've gone without sleep, turning in my bed with your image grabbing hold of my mind, like a giant claw thrusting its talons into my gray matter . . . ask the entire nights when, in the darkness of my thoughts, of my indecision about the future, I see nothing but your almost faded image behind everything that passes through my mind, as if it were a film about my life . . . Ask yourself, you, you . . . Wouldn't you have to be blind not to see that yes, it's true, and that nothing or nobody could make me forget you no matter what happens, no matter what may come?"

He placed stress on these last words like a man convinced, as if he felt deeply sure of them, as if he were daring Destiny, Time, and everything to put his will to the test . . .

She responded with a sigh:

"I too, Fidel. I also love you, as I have loved no one else in my life. And no one else has ever loved me this way . . . don't think it's hard for me to love you. No. You know very well that no woman can resist a man who loves the way you do. And you, my prince . . ."

Another long, deep, endless kiss . . .

At 7:15 they parted. In the door of the love nest they gave each other a last kiss, almost being caught off guard by the owner of the house, who passed by, coughing. Then Estela went running down the stairs, headed to the Ruiz home, her soul full of the joy of loving . . .

Fidel Murillo remained at the top of the stairs, with the memory of that last caress floating in his mind. The lights of the city paraded before his indifferent, numb eyes. On the sky, blackened by the day's smog, shone a myriad of sparkling stars like a trail of silver . . .

IX

Three months of madness and abandon had been sufficient to create deep roots in two young souls, the happiness of being in love. Estela and Fidel now loved each other madly, adamantly, passionately, with a kind of ferocity.

And theirs was the love of man and woman, a jealous love of constant breakups and reconciliations, the love of illicit lovers . . .

What remained hidden in the catalog of erotic pleasures that they had not tried, thirsty like pilgrims in the desert when they discover an unexpected oasis!

Fidel realized that he loved Estela more than anything, as he had never loved anybody. He, who had written those verses that were like a prelude to his love with this woman from Monterrey, she with the look of la Dolorosa and a passionate, Moorish soul . . .

But not her. She loved him above all things in the outside world, above all her memories and even her scruples, since she was aware of his marital status. But she did not love him above her own name, above her false reputation as an honorable woman . . .

No, her mother would die the day she found out that Señorita Estela . . . the horror! Just thinking about it made something very cold and heavy run through her veins, like a drop of quicksilver. She loved Fidel passionately and in a feminine way, but not with sufficient madness to make her forget social norms. And at times the idea had taken root "in mentis," in the apt solitude of her celibate bedroom . . . and it scared her just to think about it. But in the love nest, their love nest, the passionate girl gave herself to her lover with all her soul, forgetting everything, maybe everything. And who knows? Perhaps even the very reputation she cherished like a treasure . . .

When it occurred to her that they could not go on like this, that the day would come when people found out, it scared her very much. For his part, poor Murillo had fallen hard and completely, defenseless and without a struggle, into a hell of intense erotic abandon. As in every other case like his, he was disgusted by his home life, by his wife, by his poor María Luz, who clearly understood that someone was robbing her . . . and that she had no other refuge but her tears.

Their little boy once saw her crying.

"What's wrong, Mama? Did Papa hit you?"

For this innocent boy, there was no reason to cry aside from being beaten.

She smiled painfully, wiping away her tears. Without answering, she pulled him into her arms and covered him in kisses.

But that was all. A resigned martyr, she never had a complaint or reproach for her dissolute husband, who stayed out all night and who these days arrived home two or three times a week with the first light of dawn.

That silence weighed heavily on Fidel. He would have preferred to hear her protest, scold him, shout, to vent her poorly contained rage so that he would have a personal pretext that justified his actions . . . nothing. María Luz, always submissive, always humble and complacent, never tried to penetrate or clarify the mystery of his nights. And when Murillo's arrival found her crying, she always pretended to be asleep. But she felt in the depths of her soul that she was being robbed, that she was being robbed . . .

Three months went by this way. Spring had begun to smile on California, famous for its idyllic climate. The gloomy vines of the chalets on Buena Vista Street had begun to thicken with flowers.

Over the silent waters of the lake, the moon smiled complacently . . .

There was music in Westlake. The miraculous park of a thousand amorous hideaways was flooded with the soft melody of banjos whose tenor voices trembled in the distance. On an islet nearly in the middle of the lake, an orchestra conspired to help lovers dream. And over the silent crystal waters shimmered the strangely shaped canoes, carrying couples to the most shadowy banks of the lake, where they whispered stories of love to each other.

"Do you still love me?"

The question sprang leisurely from her lips whose makeup had been removed by kisses under the moonlight. Estela rested her head on Fidel's chest, and her divine eyes, the eyes of la Dolorosa raised toward the beard of her lover, seemed to affirm the answer rather than await it.

Fidel let go of the oars. They had arrived at a lovely bend, a sort of little bay completely surrounded by overgrown grass that would be hidden from indiscreet gazes. Then he took her beloved face into his hands and gave her a kiss on the forehead. This was always his answer to the eternal question, convinced as he was that the question had been formulated by her feminine coquettishness and not by the heart of a woman tormented by doubt.

Then he spoke in a dreamy voice. His words came out slowly, smoothly, as if they were flowing from the depths of his soul.

"Love! All the ridiculous definitions of philosophers are words, only words. Have they ever felt love? Have they understood it? No, no, they have only imagined it so as to coldly analyze it and explain it according to their own standards, thinking only about the impression their definitions will create in the future. But who would dare to define it as a 'misunderstanding,' as a 'contact of skin,' or some other nonsense like that, when you feel it throbbing within you? Surely all these wise men," he scornfully emphasized, "have a profound knowledge of life, but their wisdom is incapable of understanding love, just as it's not enough for them to decipher the woman-sphinx. Love can only be defined by one who is so in love that he isn't concerned about defining it. He who has felt love is incapable of offering an opinion precisely because he no longer feels it . . . love is forgetting everything—everything—for that which you love. And the person in love feels nothing else when he has the figure of a woman engraved in his mind as if on a photographic plate in a darkroom. When he thinks he sees traces of his beloved in the face of every woman, when even the most absurd human beings share some of her features. When above every conversation, above all the confusion, floats a large, very large and pure, very pure, feminine presence. That's when you feel love, and when only a lover could define it. When you've loved and it's over, it's only then that the brain can analyze it, because your heart no longer feels it. For my part, I have a definition: love . . . is you."

"You have such beautiful thoughts . . ."

"No, it's not me who has them. They are dictated by your gaze, your breath close to my face, the warmth of your body. Without you, when I'm not by your side, I am incapable of putting two words together. But here . . ."

In the distance, on the opposite shore, one could hear the languid groaning of an Oriental foxtrot. And the eyes of Estela glazed over bit by bit, looking off into infinity, as if she were busy counting the stars sprinkled across the firmament high, so high up.

Fidel felt a light shiver shake the body of his beloved, who was resting on his chest, and his fingers unconsciously caressed the little curls that fell over Estela's forehead. The banjos continued to groan with melancholy and pain on the little island that seemed far, so far away.

"What are you thinking about?"

"Me? Nothing."

"I don't believe you. You are always thinking about something: about that leaf, about that star, about that oar. But you're always thinking. Tell me: what's on your mind?"

"I told you: I'm not thinking about anything."

And Estela forced a smile, but she was betrayed by her big eyes so full of tears they nearly overflowed. A very deep sigh lifted her breasts softly, as if her very soul were being exhaled.

"See? You can come out and say it. You're thinking . . . should I say it? You're thinking about . . ."

"Yes, it's true. That's what I'm thinking about. I'm thinking about him: that scoundrel who made a mockery of my innocence with his colorful words. You're not mistaken. You know that music has that evocative power . . ."

Fidel shrugged his shoulders the best he could.

"Don't be silly: forget about it. I know very well that you don't regard him with love and that's why I'm not jealous. Who was he? I don't know and I don't want to. Just forget about it and think about the present and me, about us. Yes, I know you're going to tell me that this is the last thing a woman forgets. But dwelling on the past is for weaker and less scornful souls than ours. The past is dead; bury it. Tomorrow our love will also be in the past . . . despite everything we'll have to bury that too . . . wait and see if I give up. But for now let's live in the present and throw caution to the wind while our love and youth lasts, since we only have one chance. Let's live in the present, Estela . . ."

Another kiss. But this one was firm, certain, less virtuous than the previous one, and more real. A kiss on the mouth, a kiss that bites, that draws blood . . .

The banjos fell quiet and the voice of the poet began to resonate serenely in the silence of the night.

"This is the great balm of love: to forget . . . to forget. To be happy, it's necessary to forget the past and to dwell very little on our future existence. After all, what do we amount to in this world? What will we be tomorrow? No one knows. And more than that: what will become of our bodies that have loved, our bodies that have imprisoned our souls, when we no longer exist? A bit of rotting flesh maybe, and then dust, nothing . . . And when the last man on earth dies in agony, everything, everything will die, all hope and even illusions of glory. That's why we have to live in the present. Loving, but loving feverishly, letting ourselves be carried away by a feeling that always guides us with invisible hands. Letting Destiny play with our lives as it wishes, laughing at the vicissitudes of our insignificance as dreamers . . . you already know what we'll become afterward . . ."

"It's true . . ."

"Yes, it's true. Of all the beings that inhabit the earth, the most unfortunate are those that occupy themselves with the past and that regard the future with terror. It has been written, as we know, what we will become once we pass through this valley of misery; the laws of Destiny are immutable. There is nothing sadder than thinking about this, nor nothing more useless. Your body, the body I have covered with my kisses, will turn into . . . nothing, nothing . . ."

"Yes, but what about my soul?"

A very deep sigh. Fidel looked up at the stars.

"Who has returned from there?"

A majestic, solemn silence weighed on them for a few moments. Then, on the distant islet the banjos began to wail a fashionable melody. Outside the lovers' refuge, a canoe passed by, silently brushing against the grass. And a carefree, happy, feminine voice sang the lyrics of the melody plucked out by the orchestra:

"You know you belong

"To somebody else

"So, why don't you leave me alone?"

A noisy laughter followed and Fidel seemed to recognize it. Then the voice suddenly interrupted its singing to cry out in terror:

"Help! Help!"

The laughter stopped and one could hear the splashing of water, as if someone had fallen into the lake. Standing in his canoe, Fidel moved the oars to the side to see what was happening. A pair of lovers, the kind that filled this pleasant park night after night, had overturned their canoe, perhaps with careless movements. Near the shore, where the water was not too deep, a man emerged from the lake carrying the sopping wet body of a little woman on his back. She was kicking about happily, trying to resume the interrupted song:

"You know you belong . . ."

In the light of the moon, Fidel recognized Pepe Calles carrying Marcela over his shoulders, the little French friend of Madame St. Pierre.

And despite his own philosophy, he couldn't help remembering the past and sighing deeply.

X

That morning, tragedy erupted in Fidel's home. He had spent all night tossing and turning in his bed, thinking about Estela, yearning to have her at his side, missing her knowing caresses, her erotic abandons, and that vampiric sucking that left him half dead, leaving him with the anguished sensation of emptiness in his brain, and with an even more voracious desire to meld together with her in one of those interminable caresses that were like the pagan consecration of their love.

When he woke up, the sun filtered through the curtains, breaking the shadows in the room. It sounded like someone was crying in the next room . . .

"Is that you, María Luz?"

The sobbing voice of his faithful wife responded. She had spent the night by the side of little Fidel, who was burning up with fever. Murillo, wrapped in his pajamas, approached his son's bed.

"What's wrong with him?" he asked coldly.

"As you can see, he has a very high fever. He's been delirious and calling out for you . . ."

Fidel smiled with a skepticism that wounded María Luz.

"You always try to use fear for him to hang on to me," he said between his teeth. "If he's sick, call the doctor and get it over with. Why all the fuss?"

"This is serious. Do you hear that little wheezing? I think he has pneumonia . . ."

"Bah! I'm fed up with you. I hope you and he both bite the dust. Yes: don't give me that stupid look. Y-o-u and h-i-m. Am I making myself clear?"

He tried to turn around quickly as if trying to flee from that place that sickened him . . .

The resigned calm of his wife had reached its limit. With a fierce pounce she rushed at her husband and grabbed him by the shoulders. She spit in his face with rage and contempt.

"Scoundrel! Scoundrel! Scoundrel! While I was the one being insulted, I wasn't worried about your despicable behavior. Now that you don't even care about your son, that you only care about that whore that you're stupidly in love with, now that you hurt my feelings as a mother I have no choice but to explode. Get out of here!"

Her tearful and unkempt figure, with its hand extended toward the door, had the look of incredible resolve.

"Didn't you hear me? You're standing there like an imbecile. Get out of this house . . . and never come back! My son is a piece of my soul and he needs only me."

And not able to handle it anymore, she threw herself crying on her son's bed where he was babbling weakly with his eyes closed, as if sighing:

"Water . . . Mama, water . . ."

Fidel Murillo left the room. He got dressed and left the house, cursing under his breath . . .

Six in the evening. In the love nest, Fidel looked like a madman. He tried to contact his house during the day but nobody answered the telephone. When his conscience tormented him, he told himself that it was nothing serious and that they would have run over to inform him if it were. In his soul all humanitarian feeling and the paternal instinct latent even in wild beasts had receded to leave space only for the uncontrollable passion for that woman who had driven him mad. He felt that he couldn't live a minute more without her.

Estela still hadn't arrived. Fidel struggled to drive a thought, which had always tormented him when she didn't arrive on time, from his feverish mind. The scene from Madame St. Pierre's house passed across his imagination; Estela, going to a brothel to prostitute her body under the caresses of another, to kiss the mouths of men who were strangers just the day before . . . It was too much for him to handle. She had sworn on her own honor—how ironic!—on the honor of her family that she hadn't given herself to another man since they fell in love, but his mind couldn't help tormenting him with doubt. If that woman had been born perverse, if he had discovered with her avenues of pleasure that he was unaware of before meeting her; if she had taught him so many unknown pleasures and unnatural acts in their intimate moments when they forgot the world existed, so many caresses of the most refined sodomy . . . ! Despite everything, he agreed that there was no other path than to run far away with her, where she could belong only to him, where he could always have her at his side, without the fear of high society that haunted this lost woman with her double existence as a prostitute and a woman of irreproachable social standing. He was ready to tell her so tonight, to leave right away, to take the first train, carrying her away as his beloved prisoner, to put the largest stretch of land possible between . . .

He heard desperate steps that made the porch creak. Then, the sound of the metal door that slammed closed, and finally the sound of his own doorknob. Someone was trying to come in . . .

A moment of anxiety . . .

The door swung open all at once and Estela burst in like a bullet, closing the wooden door behind her. Then, leaning against it with her back and her hands extended as if to defend herself, she looked at Fidel with her eyes wide open. He sat up on the bed on which he had been lying and gave her a quizzical look.

"I just had a terrible scare. My brother, my brother . . ."

She was gasping, unable to put words together from a lack of breath . . .

"My brother. You know, Abel. For a couple days he's been following me, but I didn't pay it much mind. Just now it seemed that when I was going up the stairs I saw him turn the corner, headed in this direction. I didn't have time to do anything but run and rush in here like that. If he were to show up . . ."

"Don't be silly. You know well that your brother is incapable of believing that you would come here for this . . . to see me. What's more, if someone told him, he would rip out their tongue. Calm down."

The girl moved away from the door and came to give Fidel a very long kiss. Then, with her back to him and in front of the dresser mirror, she began to carefully take off her hat. Fidel gazed at her, as crazed as ever. What a body! What hips! What arms! To him she was the best woman in the entire Universe. And to think that he hadn't found her sooner! Once Estela had removed her hat, she came to sit on the knees of her lover, who looked intently into her eyes.

"I have something very serious to tell you," he told her.

"I'm listening. Very, very, very much serious?"

The eyes of la Dolorosa had taken on another expression: that of an intimate lover, the one destined for him.

"Yes, more than I would like it to be. It's about us getting out of here."

Estela looked at him with a smile, believing that he was just joking. Then, as she noticed that his face had a more determined expression than she'd ever seen before, her smile began to freeze until it disappeared from her face. She looked deeply into his eyes, as if she were trying to read his mind.

"Are you being serious?"

"Entirely. I can't carry on here. Look, Estela, the moment I've always feared has arrived. Do you remember? The moment in which life is impossible without you, without being by your side, gazing at you, looking at myself in your eyes. Don't think that I'm trying to be poetic or that this is a schoolboy infatuation. I always thought this terrible moment would arrive, and here it is. I can't live anymore without being at your side. My home is hell; this love nest is Paradise. I'm resolved that we make a life together. I will marry you, I will do whatever you want. We'll go far away, far away to our Mexico, to South America . . . wherever you want. There, at last, our dream will be realized and we'll belong exclusively to each other and no one else, without a single cloud tarnishing the clear skies of our happiness . . ."

"But Fidel, have you thought about the scandal that could arise?"

"Scandal . . . the world . . . What does the scandal of that rotten high society matter to us, when they will just slander us in spite of the fact that they secretly envy us? The overreaction of some hypocritical old women and the fuss raised by four old men who have become moral authorities only because they can't function as men of the world anymore—what is it to us? Nothing, nothing. Our happiness is everything. We were born for each other. Look: I have some money here that can help us with the trip. We'll leave tonight for Mexicali in a car, just as we are right now. And tomorrow we'll take the train to Sonora. Once there, if you want, we can go south to the heavenly Isthmus or to Guadalajara, the most beautiful land on Earth. If you think we're still too close to the high society that you're talking about, we'll keep going south, all the way to the Cabo de Hornos, if you so desire. We'll go to Spain, where we can live as we please; to Italy, if you want, where you can perfect the art that you love so much, and we can go on to travel around the world. Don't believe for a moment that I'm rich, but I have enough for us to make the trip. Even if after that we'll lock ourselves in a shack to die of hunger, alone with our love . . . You told me it didn't matter to you if we were poor, very poor, if you had me forever. Don't you remember? Well, now I'm taking you at your word. Won't you come, my queen, my heaven, my life?"

Estela had become very serious. The look of la Dolorosa, that other expression, had returned to stretch across her divine eyes that began to shine, flooded with tears. A few seconds passed without an answer, and then she responded slowly, in a feeble voice, as if she were talking to herself:

"Yes, that has been my dream, Fidel. But you forget that I have a mother, that I have a family. My brothers would move heaven and earth to find me. My mother would die of sorrow and then . . . the scandal, my reputation and theirs . . ."

He shook his head slowly with his eyes fixed on the corner of the room, where a little porcelain dog seemed to be looking back at him.

"See? You don't love me. No. No, you don't love me and I should have understood that long ago. You don't love me, you liar, you hypocrite. Your mother! Your brothers! Your reputation! You think I'm not sacrificing anything for our love? Do you think I give a damn about social convention, about my wife, whom I have ended up hating for you and only you? My own son, who is now in agony? Once upon a time his illness would have killed me with sadness, but I only care about you today! But I love you as you should be loved: above all things, with the love that Christ extolled . . . I'm the imbecile for believing in your words, and now . . ."

He was on his feet and pacing around the room nervously, talking to himself aloud, so loudly that the neighbors must have thought that he was quarreling. Estela watched him go back and forth, and she struggled mightily with herself, trying to overcome temptation at all costs. She really did want to go far away with her lover. How could she not? It was her supreme desire! But what about her mother? And her brothers? And above all, what would people say about her? She had passed for a virtuous girl in high society, which had accepted her with open arms on that condition alone. Her love for that man, whom she had truly loved more than anyone else in the world, was about to conquer her, but social convention stopped her . . . Without realizing it, she broke into bitter sobs and covered her face with her right arm that she supported on the bed frame. Fidel kept pacing desperately.

"You know what?" he said as he stopped in his tracks in the middle of the room. "You know what? I left today with the firm intention of never going back home. Either I go away from here with you wherever you want or I kill myself right here. Yes, don't look at me with that frightened face. Right here in front of your eyes. I'll prove it!"

From the pocket of his bag that was hanging on the rocking chair, Fidel took out his revolver, pulled back the hammer, and raised it up to his head.

"Do you understand? I'm killing myself, I'm killing myself so that this agony is finished once and for all. But no . . . I'm going to kill you first . . . I'm going crazy, forgive me. You heard correctly: a shot will end my sorrow. Estela, will you go where I want you to?"

Murillo was intensely pale, and his eyes had opened extremely wide. With his right hand trembling with emotion, he had pointed the barrel of the gun at his chest, ready to pull the trigger. And over his eyes passed something so strange, so ferocious, so unknown, that Estela ran to embrace him.

"Fidel, for God's sake!"

She covered his face with passionate kisses, bathing him in tears. Estela was trembling from head to toe. Her resistance had been overcome. A new question came hoarsely from the lips of the desperate man:

"Will you go, Estela?"

She nodded her head intensely in the affirmative without separating her face from that of her lover. Then, between sobs, her soothing voice whispered near Murillo's neck:

"Yes . . ."

Estela finished drying up her tears with an overflowing powder puff and put on her gloves. Murillo had called a taxi stand to order a car for the corner of Buena Vista, just a few steps from his love nest. That very night they would make the trip to the border in the taxi. They would be greeted the next day by the sun in Mexico, their Mexico, the future paradise of their happiness. And after a long kiss, they said their last goodbyes to the little love nest, in which all the memories of their madness and joys continued to float, finally crystallizing into reality after all this time. Before pushing the button to turn off the light, Fidel regarded, one by one, the four walls of their love nest and sighed. She, preoccupied by the seriousness of the step they were about to take, didn't speak a word and kept trying to put her gloves on; she couldn't manage to get her fingers to fit inside. Fidel's voice finally rang out, sweetly, with an unknown accent.

"Now can I call you my little wife?"

"Always, my prince."

Yet another kiss, already on the porch and hidden by the flowering vines. Then, they began to go silently down the stairs.

On the corner, sitting by itself, they could make out the silhouette of the car that would carry them to the border. Fidel saw it and released a deep sigh. She seemed to meditate deeply inside of her being . . .

"There it is. Let's go, my queen."

"I'm afraid . . . I don't know why. Look: I'm trembling."

She showed him her arm on whose fine skin had risen smooth little bumps like those produced by the cold.

"Bah! Don't you worry, silly girl."

They finally arrived at the taxi. The driver respectfully doffed his cap, opening the car door so that Señorita Estela could get in . . .

At that very moment, a horrific cursing thundered through the relative silence of the young night. On that same corner, as if by accident, Estela's brother Abel de la Garza had just appeared, muttering obscenities ...

"Stop right there! Where are you going?"

Estela saw that all was lost. Her reputation as an honorable woman was forever destroyed. High society would repudiate her like a prostitute. Her mother would go crazy with the pain ....

The voice of her ego spoke on her behalf.

"Help me, Brother, help me! I'm being kidnapped!"

Suddenly, two flashes of light shone out in the shadows of the street. Abel had opened fire on Señorita Estela's seducer, who collapsed heavily, raising his hands to his chest just as a stream of blood emerged from his mouth. Then Abel jumped into the car beside Estela, who was unable to move. Holding her in his arms as though he was afraid they would steal her away, he nervously exclaimed:

"Yes, my dear. I knew it: that scoundrel . . ."

Then, addressing the driver, who barely had his wits about him:

"Hurry, West 27th . . ."

Moments later, a circle of curious bystanders who had heard the shot gathered around the body of Fidel, who had fallen halfway into the gutter and from whose mouth blood continued to flow.

"Hurry, call an ambulance . . ."

XI

Covered in bandages and surrounded by soft pillows, Fidel slowly recovered from his physical wounds. The shots fired by Abel de la Garza had entered his right lung and broken a rib, which had to be completely amputated to save the young man's life. It had been a month since the confrontation, and fortunately the police were aware only of Fidel's version of events. When he was well enough to talk, he declared that he had been assaulted during a robbery. And since in those days in Los Angeles you could be assaulted at six in the evening, just as you could have been in the mountains of the Yaqui, that's what he claimed in his statement.[165] Afterward, the patient asked to be taken to California Hospital, in whose rooms, in the care of a nurse and under the almost maternal vigilance of María Luz, he was slowly but surely returning to life.

By a true miracle, his son had also completely healed and accompanied his selfless wife, who had forgiven him for everything. That night, seeing that Fidel hadn't returned, a vague foreboding made her suspect that something serious had happened and she called the police stations. They told her that a "Mexican" had indeed been found dying on the corner of Buena Vista at around seven at night. And right then, leaving her son in the care of Lupe, an old housemaid she had brought with her from her homeland, she went to the emergency hospital, where she found the body of her unfaithful husband pierced by two bullets. No reconciliation was necessary, and Fidel didn't ask forgiveness from María Luz. Since he saw her at his side in the sterilized hospital room, insisting that he take a spoonful of the potion that the doctor had prescribed for his fever, he understood everything. Nothing but the version of the story about the assault had reached her ears, although Mexican society knew the story forward and backward: Señorita Estela de la Garza was on the verge of being kidnapped by Fidel Murillo, and Abel, her brother, had saved her from the clutches of that letch with two well-placed shots. For that feat they had lavished the warmest congratulations upon him.

One afternoon, as a result of this incident, Pepe Calles ran into Colonel Velasco, who told him very indignantly:

"Did you hear the news? Your scoundrel of a friend has tried to rape Estelita de la Garza and . . ." He came closer as he continued, "he's now in agony as a result of the two wounds Abel gave him, as Abel also escaped certain death. I'm telling you," and now he raised his voice, "these days you never know when you're being deceived . . ."

"Indeed," responded Pepe, who was thinking the same thing, but about a different person, "you never know . . ."

The old colonel assured him that Fidel, if he didn't die from his wounds, was already dead socially. The "Indo-Latina League," which in a moment of enthusiasm had vested him with the title of "Honorary President," had met to address his case. In a solemn session they had agreed to remove him from this position "for engaging in undignified conduct," replacing him with the young de la Garza, who had saved his virtuous little sister from the clutches of such a monster. Estela had been visited by all of her friends, who had reiterated their regard for her and assured her that despite the dark intentions of that brute Murillo, her reputation as an honorable and virtuous woman had not suffered in the least, and—as if that weren't enough!—congratulated her on her presence of mind in a moment of danger.

Colonel Velasco finally departed with a comment at the level of his intelligence:

"How outrageous! How outrageous!"

Pepe Calles watched him leave, strutting off on his callused feet, with a look of contempt:

"Imbecile!"

Then he returned to the hospital, where the patient was already showing signs of life. There he found María Luz, whom he greeted affectionately, offering his condolences about the incident and recommending that she not believe anything ridiculous she might hear about Fidel. The Mexican colonia was boiling over with gossip, and Murillo had plenty of enemies. She shrugged her shoulders and affectionately embraced her husband's head as he looked at her tenderly.

One afternoon during his convalescence, the doctor advised Fidel that as soon as he was up and around, he should leave the city for a change of climate. The wound in his lung had left him very delicate, and it would be necessary to prevent tuberculosis. María Luz became very happy.

"We'll go to Mexico," she said, jumping with joy.

"That's a great idea," advised the doctor. "I've been to Jalisco, Mexico, and it has delightful weather. I think it would be good for you all to go live in Guadalajara."

And so the trip was arranged for the happy day of his complete recovery. Pepe Calles, who had already reconciled with Fidel, was put in charge of liquidating outstanding accounts, closing the office, and selling the furniture to the highest bidder. Finally, one day—on the first of August, to be exact—Calles accompanied the Murillos to take the train at the Southern Pacific station. They walked hand in hand with their little boy, who had already grown up a good deal.

The friends embraced affectionately.

"Don't forget to write me."

"Don't you worry, as soon as I arrive . . ."

Fidel suddenly paused. Among the crowd on the platform, he discovered the gaze of la Dolorosa persistently fixed on him. He felt his heart skip a beat and he managed to avert his eyes. Moments later, from the window of the Pullman car, he once again recognized her among the indifferent faces that filled the station: the enchanting eyes that had been the great love of his life. Estela was there, dressed in black, lost among a multitude of little American girls chewing gum and telling dull jokes. Her eyes shone through her veil, full of tears.

The train's last whistle sounded, and Pepe gave his friend one last hug from the platform. A few moments later the conductor's coarse, raspy voice was heard:

"All aboard!"

The convoy slowly began to move. From the window, Fidel looked out at the city of dreams, where he had been so happy for four months, where he had been on the verge of abandoning his life . . . The figure of Estela was still burned into the retina of his mind, but the image was so blurry and faded that he feared losing it definitively.

The little boy was very happy and waved a handkerchief from his window. María Luz cleaned the sweets off his little face, and Pepe Calles waved goodbye with his hat. Estela's eyes continued to shine somewhere. Fidel felt that he still loved her. Despite himself, he looked for the face of la Dolorosa among the crowd so that it could bathe him in its divine light through its tears . . .

XII

In the cheerful city of the Granadian towers and the blue lake, Fidel and María Luz had begun to savor the delights of a second honeymoon.

With the arrival of spring, and thanks to the marvelous climate of the Sultana of the West, the last shadows of danger had disappeared like a light summer stratus cloud dissolving in the turquoise sky.[166] True conjugal peace had returned to the broken home, ashamed of its exile during those dark days in the city of cinema beyond the blue line of the Rio Grande. Of that terrible adventure there remained only the dissolving memory of a nightmare that became blurrier every day. True love had returned to bestow its smile on the peaceful home in the Colonia Moderna, the kind of love that can't be replaced by the passionate flames of two unbridled souls. Every night Fidel and his eternal companion, with the little boy between them asking questions timid and curious, spent hours looking toward the future and the sky . . . Two blue things that Fidel had not occupied himself with before but that were now taking shape in his restful mind, now that his son's little blond head was reaching his in its implacable march toward its golden youth . . .

Fidel arrived at the front entrance of his house, which was covered in flowering vines, reminding him of two memorable porches in Los Angeles. He came with joy ringing in his soul after realizing the dream that had kept him up for many nights: establishing an arts magazine in Guadalajara that, in his estimation, would be at the forefront of publications in the region.

As his feet made the first steps of the short staircase creak, a child's voice reached his ear:

"Papa! Here comes Papa!"

Fidelito, very tidy and well groomed, came out to greet him at the door. His father grabbed him from the doorway and raised him up to his height, covering his golden curls with kisses. The little boy kicked his feet around, overcome with joy.

"Come here, Fidelito; you're going to get Papa dirty . . ."

María Luz's heavenly smile appeared in the doorway. Behind her could be seen the interior of a little house that looked like a love nest, purer and more noble than the one on Buena Vista Street, and one in which everything seemed to be part of a mutual happiness.

Once in the lovely little living room, his wife handed Fidel a package.

" . . . ?"

"I don't know. It came from Los Angeles. They look like newspapers."

His pure-hearted wife had spoken about Los Angeles with sadness. She had passed the darkest stage of her life there, feeling every day that she was being helplessly robbed of her only treasure, her only love . . .

It was all she could do to choke back a sigh.

Indeed, they were newspapers: two issues of a new magazine in Spanish sent by his good friend Pepe Calles, from the looks of it. He remained abroad, carrying on with his bohemian youth, his childish heart open to everything that seemed good.

Fidel felt a sort of strange sensation as he opened the package that carried the scent of that land of his fleeting happiness, where he had felt the greatest love of his life. He cut open the wrapper with a little shell-handled knife.

The magazine was beautiful. It was a true revelation of Mexican progress in a foreign land. In the first issue he opened, he saw something that made his heart skip a beat. Under the title "An Aristocratic Marriage" appeared the portrait of a bride and groom who had just been united forever. The bride was Señorita Estela. The groom, Colonel Velasco.

Below there was a brief summary in very fine print, justifying the inclusion of the engraving:

> The 20th of this month, in the aristocratic church of San Pablo of this city, the ever-virtuous Señorita Estela de la Garza and the honorable Colonel Don Mariano Velasco, both very distinguished members of our most exclusive Mexican society, entered into the unbreakable contract of matrimony. We adorn our pages with this portrait of the happy couple, wishing them an eternal honeymoon.

Fidel looked at the portrait for a moment. Estela was there with her look of la Dolorosa, her lips contracted in a triumphant smile that seemed to contrast with the expression in her eyes. She was clothed in the white dress of a virgin, and her head was crowned with orange blossoms. The old colonel looked like he was stuffed into his jacket, and his freshly shaven face revealed the deepest satisfaction.

Murillo felt that the wounds on his heart had not yet healed, although the others had left behind only a small bluish mark . . . and María Luz must have seen something pass across her husband's eyes. Casually and warmly she went to stand next to him to get a look at the couple.

Did a spark of truth and a woman's intuition cross her mind? Did she realize that this was the woman who had stolen her happiness, who had been on the verge of causing the greatest tragedy of her life?

She looked serenely at Fidel, giving him a kiss on the mouth, and said sweetly:

"Sir, if you please, your breakfast is ready . . ."

He answered her with another kiss and left the magazine on a table in the living room without even leafing through it. Then, on his way to the dining room, he started talking enthusiastically about the dreams he had fulfilled, about the founding of his magazine . . .

On the table covered in flowers, his steaming hot chocolate was waiting to be savored. María Luz gently ordered the maid:

"Leave me alone here, Lupe, and see that the boy doesn't get into any trouble."

During breakfast, between bites, dreams kept spinning around Murillo's mind and he spoke to Luz warmly about his new enterprise. She listened very attentively, her eyes fixed on him as if he were her only faith.

The shrill voice of the maid shouted from the living room:

"Miss! Just look at what the baby did. He tore up some papers."

The child's footsteps were heard running toward the dining room. He ran to his mother, out of breath, looking both cheerful and scared, trying to hide between the folds of her skirt.

"What did you do, Fidelito?"

"Nothing, Mama. Me, nothing . . . lookie . . . ."

With his adorable little hand, he showed her a small paper boat made precisely out of the magazine page featuring the portrait of the newlyweds. Luz looked at her husband intently and he began to laugh, taking the folded paper from her child's hands to examine it up close. Then he looked up, his eyes meeting those of his wife.

Fidelito looked back and forth at them, as if waiting for a verdict.

"You see, miss? Do you see?"

Lupe came in from the living room, pointing at the little boat.

"He ripped up the master's papers. You see, miss?"

María Luz lifted up her child and, looking at him intently, gave him a kiss. A flash of gratitude passed over her eyes.

The paper was now crumpled into a little ball; Fidel threw it away and continued enjoying his hot chocolate.

The happiness of the hearth floated through this peaceful environment, the bourgeois happiness of ordinary folk. But in the end, it's the only happiness left in this very short journey full of disillusionment that we call life.

FIN

Coronado, Playas del Pacífico
1925

BARBARA LA MARR
A STORY OF PLEASURE AND PAIN

Barbara La Marr: Una historia de placer y dolor, published by
Casa Editorial Lozano, San Antonio, Texas, 1926

PREFACE

This book goes to print absolutely devoid of literary pretensions. Its pages
lack those theatrical scenes that, unrealistic in order to draw attention,
fill the pages of ordinary novels. Like life, its ending is simple. It develops
normally, without providential interventions that come just at the right
moment to save the heroes in danger, at the same time lifting a weight
from our soul that we had felt while reading the story, delving into the false
lives of its characters, experiencing their moments of anguish or happiness.
The tale between the front and back covers here is simple, simple like life
itself. The tragedy is narrated without the splashy effects that give a story
unusual points of interest but that also destroy whatever life there is in it,
transforming it into one of many pleasant fables that have sold in book
markets from the foggy times of typographic history to our present days
that are so hectic and full of a lust for life.

Instead, this story is truth in its essence, and even its most trivial incidents have been lived by the same characters who parade through the novel.
It is the story of an unfortunate woman, mortally wounded by the fatal
hand of destiny precisely when the dawn of fame, companion of triumph,
was starting to be glimpsed.

In real life, Barbara La Marr was rarely the seductive and malevolent
vamp that the studio publicists, with commercial aims, always painted her
as in order to create a buzz for their films. Neither was she the victim of
her wild living, nor a moth that burned its wings in the flames of pleasure.

She was a beautiful woman, extraordinarily beautiful and extraordinarily unfortunate. Blessed with a talent exceptional for her sex, she lived from disappointment to disappointment for thirty years, always in search of a supreme ideal that she never managed to find: true love. Brought up from infancy amid the treasure of books, she realized too early that the supreme power that universally rules life is selfishness; disguised as piety, as love, as charity or as benevolence, but selfishness in the end. The visionary spirit of the Latin race that nestled in her dreaming soul, however, refused to resign itself to this cruel truth. She struggled to find the ultimate proof in her life without ever attaining it, and she took the bitterness of her defeat to the grave.

To the reader who hopes to find in the pages of this true story the theatrical shocks of the ordinary novel: close this book. The tragedy of Truth doesn't have dramatic scenery or artificial complications: it is stark, rough, lacking interest at times for those who haven't lived through its moments, moments that are only intense for those souls that suffer them. But if you loved this unfortunate woman, if from time to time you asked yourself what truth there was in the web of legend that was woven around her pagan goddess figure by the malevolent spider of publicity, if you want to face the unvarnished truth and later meditate on the influence of Destiny on each life, turn the page and read:

CHAPTER I

THE KALEIDOSCOPE OF LIFE

As she tugged the silver chain with a gloved hand, a pearly light extended over the room, accentuating the curves of the furniture, setting off sparkles from her jewels, exaggerating the orange tone of the silk bedspread. Barbara took off her ermine cape and gave the usual order to her black maid, who waited respectfully at the door, same as every night:

"You can go to bed."

The girl's step faded little by little, cushioned by the Persian rugs that covered the room next door. The young woman looked at herself in the mirror, sighed, and took off her high heels to then begin moving her toes, which had been crammed together by the narrowness of her shoes. A silk dress slipped over her statuesque curves, giving way to the caresses of a flannel robe. Barbara took her hair down in front of the mirror and entered the bathroom silently. From the platinum clock encrusted with diamonds that was on the little nightstand, three chimes rang, one after another . . .

That night she had been at a party given by the restless Mabel Normand, who was just beginning her slide down the slippery slope of decadence; one of those parties called orgiastic, which had contributed so much to forming Hollywood's reputation and which nevertheless were nothing but gatherings of merry people who wanted to relax, to find healthy outlets after arduous labor in the film studios. At two thirty, despite the revelry that continued at its peak, Barbara gave signs of wanting to leave, signaling a headache she didn't have. After unsuccessful entreaties, the revelers opted to let her do as she wished, knowing that one way or another she would get her way: this always happened. Her character was firm in its resolutions, invariable, incorruptible. Someone had said that the star's way of being had only one remedy: Love.

She had moved her head sadly, responding in her favorite language:
"*L'amour? Connais pas . . .*"

When the water had caressed her soft flesh for some time, she got into bed, carelessly grabbing a book of poems that was on the nightstand. She opened it randomly and read:

> You, the ingrate I adore
> might see when the black veil
> of near death covers my eyes,
> virgins, listen to my ultimate plea:
> take him my goodbyes and tell him
> that his name was my last utterance . . .[167]

She smiled sadly, and an expression of disgust, like a whitish veil, spread over her countenance. Then, half closing her eyes, those eyes that were like two splendid agate almonds, she murmured:

"How beautiful it must be to be loved like that . . . !"

The cloudy scenes of her life began to parade on the imaginary screen of her mind. She remembered as a little girl learning a language that wasn't the one she had heard in the first days of her life, spent, she didn't know where, but someplace strangely associated with a rippling sea, with threatening green waves capped by pure white foam. Then her new life in the care of some good, middle-class people in that small town of Yakima; her school days; her first sensation of love . . .

Since she was a little girl, the blood of her unknown acrobatic ancestors had been putting pressure on her brain, pushing her toward a theatrical career. It was at seven years old that she finally made her debut in an insignificant small part with the Allen Company, which had passed through Yakima by chance. The memory of the applause that she received still rang in her soul. Then came weeks, months, years of study, and then the first vexed incident of her life made her vaguely doubt the parental bona fides of those good people who, until then, had treated her like a daughter. One night, leaving a dance, an unknown force, perhaps a mysterious atavism hidden in the interior of her being, had drawn her to follow a young rake who ultimately tried to take advantage of her innocence on the outskirts of town. When she went home, with the light of dawn already very clear, everyone refused to believe that she was as pure as the night before. Her adoptive father, Mr. Watson, had imprudently made a veiled allusion to her origins, an allusion that shed slight clarity on her past. She linked the bitter words of Mr. Watson to her first memories of life, with that vision of waves crowned with foam, with the contrast between her black hair and the red hair of the Watsons . . . and doubted. That night she cried for a long time until she made a firm resolution at the break of day. She fled her paternal home, wandering without a goal, until a masculine figure put himself in her path, making her an invitation that sounded like new music to her ears.

The man who so providentially came to her aid was Jack Lytell, a rancher of a certain social standing who was seduced by the freshness of her fifteen years. A quick trip to Mexico followed, a trip that ended in the growing town of Mexicali in front of a civil judge. That was Barbara La Marr's first husband . . . !

How she remembered her curiosity about this new life, married life without love, without any other desire than the instinct to take refuge in some arms that would give her shelter, and a table at which she could satisfy her most urgent needs! What did she know then about love, about marriage, about home! Yes, she had an enormous, insatiable hunger for fame. She saw herself triumphing on stage, loved by everyone, lavished with attention, carried to the heavens by the incense burned at her feet. Her first conjugal adventure lasted a short time. Jack died one night after just a few months of marriage, and she found herself abandoned, not knowing where to go. Her unbreakable pride, which had made its existence apparent since she was a little girl, stopped her from knocking on the Watsons' door, as they had wounded her dignity. She saw a vision of herself in mourning, vacillating about which road she should follow. She was only sixteen.

The Carvilles, a family from the South, opened their doors to her, and there she passed her adolescence between the cuddles of Virginia—the little girl of the house—and the innocent jokes of Bob, her brother, who later would also become her husband. She saw herself, later, drawn by her thirst for fame, forming part of a theatrical circuit, dancing with [Bob] Carville, united with him in matrimony because of the need to comply with a legal requirement that would have prevented her from working in the theater at such a young age. She loved this man . . . Yes, but she loved him like a big brother, like a comrade, like a close friend. Love never knocked on her door, not even during the sweet nights of her honeymoon, almost all of them spoiled by fatigue from the theatrical show. The figure of Bob, whom she continued to love like a brother, soon disappeared from her mind to make room for that of Bernard Deely; he was introduced to her by her own husband and would later give her his name and his hand. For a moment she thought that Deely would make her love him passionately, with all the passion of her eighteen years, but she soon became convinced that her soul was not made for love. She looked upon men with a certain respect, with the fondness that little schoolgirls in coed schools feel for their classmates. Perhaps she may have once felt a carnal trembling upon thinking of one of them or of chastely uniting her mouth with that of her husband, but her heart remained unmovable. Then, Phil Ainsworth . . .

Barbara tried to count to 200, her favorite remedy when sleep would not descend sweetly over her body, making her forget love. Impossible. Throughout the mechanical count the human figures who had passed through her life intertwined diabolically in strange contortions, some of them making macabre faces or looking at her with eyes out of their sockets. The face of Phil Ainsworth, dressed in the infamous striped prison uniform, filled the screen of her mind in a menacing "close up" that made her tremble reluctantly. At first she saw him full of feigned charm, trying to conquer her heart with the cloying sweetness of a European-style performance. Phil had only been her fourth husband, and that marriage had been another of those juvenile whims. She had met him in one of those loud cafés in the Mexican barrio of Los Angeles, in the era before Prohibition, when she was the neighborhood favorite with her seductive dances. He had murmured words of love in her ear, and she thought it opportune to try again, guarding the secret of Bernard's existence very carefully (she had been separated from him for some time already). It was then that she changed her name, Reatha Watson, to the more sonorous Barbara La Marr, in the hope that Deely would never find her again, that he would think she was dead, en route to an unknown world . . . What did she know! Marriage made her sick, but nevertheless she fell into this new trap, hoping to finally find the true love for which she had long been searching. Nothing. A month of disenchantment, and then Phil had been arrested by the police, accused of stealing an automobile, and incarcerated in Leavenworth prison. She was alone again, owner of an unenviable reputation, desperate, uncertain.

The clock slowly let out four chimes. The clear, frosted light of dawn began to filter through the room's curtains. Barbara La Marr sighed again and turned off the light on her nightstand. At her feet wiggled the tiny figure of "Pom-Pom," her favorite dog, her only companion during her desperate nights of voluntary solitude, letting out a sigh that was almost human.

"Are you cold, my love?"

And her divine body, poorly covered by the sheets, straightened up on the bed and extended a rosy arm toward the animal. Over her extended hand, as if it were one of those tiny silk cushions scattered on the living room divans, Barbara brought her precious one toward her face, kissed its little white head, and eventually settled the pet on her chest as if it were a newborn baby. The lips that had known so many kisses shifted briefly into a new, bitter smile to let the words pass, practically imperceptible in the shadows of her bedroom scented with incense and flower petals:

"And to think that you are my only love. What man would have your loving resignation, your selflessness, your faithfulness?"

And, wrapping herself in the covers, she prepared to enter the enchanted kingdom of dreams.

CHAPTER II

JACK DAUGHERTY

In Metro's studios that were then on Cahuenga [Boulevard], the sets on which the emotional scenes of *Black Orchids* would be performed were built under the knowing direction of Rex Ingram.[168] Among the previously established cast figured truly prestigious actors and those with wonderful artistic promise. Among the former, the stately figure of Lewis Stone stood out. Among the latter, the supreme beauty of Barbara La Marr and the bold virility of Ramon Novarro, the first Mexican to reach the enviable heights of American cinema. At nine in the morning the lot on which the bulk of the giant castle stood could be compared to a beehive; a group of extras swirled around the assistant director, the "cameramen" arranged the machines that would later transmit the scenes performed on the sets to nitrate film, and Rex Ingram, a bit impatient, chewed his pipe, passing his megaphone from one hand to the other with the air of a general meditating on his movements before a decisive battle. Next to him, dressed in a uniform and with all his gallant bearing, was Ramon Novarro, his arms crossed over his chest, observing the coming and going of the extras. Rex turned toward him:

"Has Barbara arrived?"

In a gesture characteristic of him both on screen and off, the Mexican shrugged his shoulders before answering. His well-pitched voice formulated a response:

"They just told me that she is getting dressed."

Now it was Ingram who shrugged his shoulders, going back to his silence. Ramon continued:

"Don't you think that Barbara is going to be a magnificent success in this film? Her scenes with me have been done with such care on her part. She is a hypersensitive woman who is never satisfied with her work. I believe she is a true artist who will make it very soon. Maybe sooner than we think."

"I hope so," answered Rex. "I'm only afraid that she won't know how to take advantage of her successes. She is a woman . . . how would I put it . . . very strange, unruly perhaps . . . Beauty, like success, also has its decline. You don't know yet how the public is, Ramon . . ."

"Oh no. You're wrong, Mr. Ingram. Barbara La Marr is misunderstood. I have never seen a more sincere, generous, aware woman in my life. All this about her money problems is nothing but the fruit of her generosity. She doesn't know how to watch anyone suffer. She wants everyone to succeed with her, to live well. In the future, after she becomes a great actress, she will know to retire when it becomes necessary, if not with riches, then with the satisfaction of a duty fulfilled. At least if I am not mistaken, that is . . ."

Before Ingram could answer, a murmur erupted from the entire company. The group closest to them opened to make way for a beautiful woman, dressed in black with a hat of the same color. In the depths of her made-up face, her huge eyes shone like two large opals, exerting an inexplicable and magnetic attraction. Her lips, painted so that they resembled a blood-red carnation, separated lightly. Essaying a smile, she greeted the director:

"Am I a little bit late? I almost couldn't sleep last night. How are you, Mr. Ingram? What does our handsome Mexican friend have to say?"

Ramon smiled before her lavish attention and extended his open hand to Barbara. From the black gloves emerged the tip of her hand, aristocratic and feline.

"Buenos días," she said in an enchanting, broken Spanish.

Ingram's voice carried over the crowd, resounding against the false walls of the "sets":

"Ready . . . !"

The continuity clerk sat on his canvas bench and opened the yellow pages of the thick script. The head cinematographer turned the visor of his hat around and a relative silence fell over the set, fully bathed by the sun. A few moments later Ingram's voice could be heard again, with an imperative:

"Camera . . . !"

And the crackle of the cameras, which in the silence produced a sound like that of a distant motor, dominated the crowd. One of the most sensational scenes of *Black Orchids*, Ingram's masterwork, was soon filmed. Barbara, who put all her soul into her part, was transfigured by artistic emotion. She had ceased to be Barbara La Marr, transforming instead into "Zareda" of the script, her divine eyes widening with an expression of lust that she had never known in real life. In contrast to many screen talents, Barbara was always a different woman in front of the camera; she folded up her real personality, her ordinary self, into the depths of her soul to make another radiate, the one that the public knew and that made them think about this seductive woman, enchanting with the fascination of a snake, rapturous like a mermaid, thirsty for caresses like a sophisticated woman.

At the lunch hour Lewis Stone introduced her to a petite, faded blonde with an insignificant appearance, tangled hair, and tortoiseshell glasses. She was a reporter from one of the American film magazines and had come to ask for an interview. As in similar cases, she began by asking common questions about details that were best left private. With her characteristic sweetness that had a tendency to prevail, Barbara stopped her:

"I don't think," she said, "that the public has the least interest in my private life. Actresses need to give the public our art, our effort to interpret the characters that we are entrusted to play, and nothing more. You know that an actress is a woman like all women: with her little passions more or less disguised by the education that she has received; with her weaknesses and her small vanities. The day that the public knows all the private acts of their favorite actresses, they will cease to burn the incense of their admiration at our feet."

"And why? It doesn't have to be so terrible . . ."

"You haven't understood me, my dear. Haven't you heard it said that there is no man greater than how he appears in the eyes of his valet? It's the same thing. The human acts, the life functions that make us equal to those who admire us on screen, give them the right to see us as equals in a certain sense. This destroys the charm . . ."

Then, before the reporter could argue, she continued:

"We will talk if you like about my aspirations, my cinematic goals, or my artistic past. In a few words, I will tell you that I would like to perfect myself to the extent humanly possible; that my career proper began with that 'Milady' that Douglas Fairbanks gave me in *The Three Musketeers*, that Mr. Ingram, to whom I am deeply indebted, chose me for the mermaid in *The Prisoner of Zenda* after various attempts on my part, and finally that I hope that *Black Orchids* is a complete triumph . . . to the extent that this triumph might interest everyone."[169]

Her last words had been underlined by a meaningful smile. The reporter persisted on the topic of love. She talked about how the public said this or that about her mysterious and reserved character, confident that she was a woman whose heart was invulnerable.

"No such thing. What has happened is that I haven't yet found anyone in the world deserving of being loved . . ."

Barbara realized her indiscretion a little too late. One could see expressed on her face, underneath her makeup, the irresistible desire to take back this risky assessment. On the contrary, the blue eyes of the little blonde with the tortoiseshell glasses shone jealously behind the lenses. Undoubtedly those words had been more interesting to her than the entire interview. In American magazines, and in those all over the world one might add, the central interest of articles about film artists resides in intimate details. The public adores and applauds the celebrity at a distance when they see their image on the silver screen, but they are anxious to know how she is on a personal level, in the course of everyday life. Barbara thought it advisable to explain:

"But I beg you not to print that idea. It was an opinion between the two of us."

There had been in her beautiful eyes such an expression of supplication that anyone who wasn't a reporter, a Yankee reporter, would have vacillated before denying her. The girl with the uncombed hair promised:

"Oh, don't worry! I won't . . . if it's up to me."

A handshake, a look at the clock whose hands were at a sharp angle, marking one on the dot. Then Barbara La Marr went on set again to continue filming her scenes, the majority of them in the arms of Ramon Novarro, to whom she gave "make believe" kisses more than twenty times.

At five in the afternoon, with work over, the star was taking off her costume in her dressing room when they announced a visitor.

"Mr. Jack Daugherty . . ."

The maid waited a moment for the answer from her mistress, who was facing away from her in front of the mirror with a marble comb between her teeth. Without moving, she murmured:

"Tell him to come in. I'm ready."

The figure of a young man of twenty-six years appeared in the doorway of the dressing room, through which it seemed that he wasn't going to fit. He had blond hair and very light eyes. His smile was the kind that makes any of us swear that we are in front of a man as honorable as Quixote. He was about six feet tall and beneath his impeccable tuxedo one could make out the musculature of a Roman gladiator. Without daring to sit down, he said:

"How are you?"

Barbara turned around to face him and reached out with both her hands. Her unbraided brown hair fell over her chiseled shoulders, and her face had the other expression, the one that the public never saw. With her face illuminated by a reflection of happiness, she responded:

"Sit down for a moment. I'm about to finish."

"Am I on time as I promised?"

"Absolutely, I was waiting for you."

The actress deliberately lied, one of those innocent lies that all women engage in once in a while. She had forgotten that the night before at Mabel's house, Jack Daugherty, who had just been introduced to her, had promised to come for her at the studio in his car to drive her home. And there he was now, the enormous Irishman with his innocent face, with his huge eyes radiating frankness, fulfilling the pledge made under the mist of that happy night.

With the help of her maid, Barbara finished dressing quickly and left the studio on Daugherty's arm. While she got into the actor's car, after he ordered the driver to take him to his house, two girls from the group of extras that were in the doorway looked at them expressively:

"Five down," said one of them.

The other smiled maliciously, repeatedly tilting her head, halfway closing her small blue eyes with the expression of someone who had understood the entirety of a situation with a single phrase.

Chapter III

A Night in Montmartre

For those unfamiliar with the deceitful environment of Hollywood, the Café Montmartre holds the prestige of a mysterious, exotic, almost otherworldly attraction. From six in the evening, the hour that actors begin to leave the studios near Metro, Paramount, and, in a word, all the studios spread along Sunset Boulevard, its tables begin filling with elegant loafers anxious to find out how the most famous screen idols really are in the flesh and blood. An Italian orchestra that could play a modern "Charleston" as easily as an undulating island melody interpreted in the Yankee style weaves a net of harmonies over the heads that move anxiously in front of the little white tables loaded with glasses and steaming plates of food. From time to time, a head with jet-black hair parted down the middle in a style they would call "lacquered" strikes an exotic note amid that garden of gold plating; now and then a carefree laugh can be heard to signal the telling of an off-color joke, and the spirals of smoke that float toward the sky, only to crash into the stucco of the ceiling, form like some extraordinary vegetation that arises from libertines with golden heads and precious jewels, irrigated with the prodigious water of subtle and intentional gossip. Barbara La Marr came to find refuge at this café with her new friend, that Irishman with the face of a sweet boy, an inoffensive smile, and big diaphanous eyes that put a ray of frankness in all of his expressions. As the star passed between the tables, the voice of Nita Naldi, who was there accompanied by some journalists, rose up to greet her:

"Hello, Barbara . . . !"

An infinite number of heads turned toward the recent arrivals as soon as the noisy and provocative laugh of Naldi erupted, as she had deliberately tried to draw attention to her friend's arrival. It was then that all the newspapers began to occupy themselves with the nascent prestige of Barbara La Marr. Illustrated magazines in the United States fought for the honor of publishing her portrait on their covers, and the most impertinent of the curious journalists began diving into the intimate life of the artist, discovering details that even she could not explain how they could have known. This homage to curiosity over, Barbara and Jack went and sat at a small table far away, alone, face-to-face.

"Are you feeling okay?"

"Never better . . ."

"I believe," he responded, managing to underline his words with a marked intention, "that I have never seen you more beautiful."

She looked at him for a moment, her huge eyes filled with an expression of censure.

"Don't be like that; at least give me the pleasure of thinking that you are different from all the others."

"It's that I can't be any other way, Bobby. Will you let me call you that?"

Before Barbara's silent assent, Jack continued:

"I said that I can't be any other way; I like you extraordinarily and I'm ready, when the time comes, to demonstrate my devotion in any way you want."

A waiter, bowing in genuflection and making whimsical curves in the air with the "menu," approached the couple. Later, with a napkin over his arm, he took out his notepad and was poised to take notes with his head inclined slightly to the right and without losing sight of Daugherty.

They ordered something. A hot chocolate with pastries for her, and for him just a glass of milk with a rich, American-style cake. The conversation, interrupted by the waiter, picked up again as soon as he turned away. Barbara enveloped Daugherty in one of those looks that throughout her life had had enough power to make men throw themselves at her feet. He continued:

"I know what you're going to say, Barbara. This isn't the right place to talk about these things, but I assure you . . ."

The tiny white hand rose as if to stop the conversation.

"Look: How about if we don't talk about this now? You've understood well enough that this is neither the time nor the place. We'll talk about it later . . . maybe tomorrow, maybe in a month. For now, let's be friends: give me the pleasure of considering you my friend."

He tilted his head. In the back of the Café the orchestra roared out a popular foxtrot. Nita Naldi's voice continued rising above all of the sound in an intonation that would have made anybody think she was calling for help. Jack and Barbara, with the food on the table, began to devour it silently.

All the advice that circulated about his beloved came to the young man's mind like a rushing whirlwind. People had told him about her scandalous adventures; the reprimand of a Los Angeles judge who had sent her home after a night in jail with the recommendation that she not come back to the city, because she was "too beautiful" for it. Then the reputation that the studio publicists had concocted, the rumors, the fame she had of being a siren, the legend about the hardness of her heart, which had remained unmoved by the tears of so many men she had vanquished and abandoned . . .

And despite everything, he felt that he loved her ardently, with the passion that the sons of Ireland, with dispositions so similar to those of Latinos, approach everything.

For her part, while she brought the silver spoon to her mouth, red like a bleeding wound, she let her imagination roam free and combined her memories with her aspirations. She recognized that she had never loved anyone and that this big guy, candid, a little simple, interested her extraordinarily. Would this meeting be her happiness? Would her much-desired moment of love finally come into her life?

Then they got up to dance. And while they twirled around to the sensual melody of a foxtrot that had a great deal of tango in it, their minds kept trying to resolve identical problems, just from two different points of view. They spent several hours like this.

It was after ten at night when Jack's car stopped in front of the aristocratic home of Barbara La Marr. She turned to her companion and, showing all her teeth in an innocently diabolic smile, extended her gloved hand to him.

"Until tomorrow," she said.

His only response was to take her hand and lift it to his lips without Barbara making the slightest attempt at resistance. Then, perhaps emboldened by that attitude, he took her head between his two enormous pale hands and placed a chaste kiss on her pink mouth. She looked at him sadly:

"Jack? Why did you do that?"

He responded without lifting his head, as if he were embarrassed by his outburst: "Because I love you, Bobby; because I love you . . ."

Even though she had spent most of the previous night awake, it took Barbara a long time to fall asleep that night. When she was finally able to enter the enchanted dominion of the inexplicable, the figure of Jack occupied almost all the space in her mind. For the first time in her life, she felt the unmistakable shivering that precedes the arrival of love. And, also for the first time in her life, she felt full of hope, with a goal in her life to which she could dedicate all her efforts and all her suffering . . .

CHAPTER IV

IN THE PAGES OF HER DIARY

> . . . Men . . . Bah! It makes me sick to think of them. The admiration of men, the so-called love of men!
>
> I have been married many times and from that I may have learned everything I know in life. The love of men is the least satisfactory, the most disappointing in the universe. The girl who only has one boyfriend, who grows up and finally marries him, is lucky. In her ignorance she keeps her faith in men and that is already something. The woman of the world at whose feet men prostrate themselves like lambs can't call herself lucky.
>
> If by chance we find love—true love—between a man and a woman, it's because heaven has sent it. But I've been forbidden this happiness; this is why I have adopted this child . . .

At the precise moment that Barbara's delicate hand traced these lines, a weak cry could be heard in the alcove next door. The actress suspended her work and, lifting her head, called out:

"Cristina!"

"Everything is fine, ma'am," a voice responded from behind the door. "His pacifier fell."

She smiled for an instant, picked up the gold pen and put it to her lips as if she were trying to organize her ideas, and then continued writing in the immaculate pages of that diary:

> That is why I have adopted this child. I know men too well, the world and its temptations, and this will make me raise Marvin as he should be, to make him the man that I dreamt of for myself and that I could never find. I still remember when I saw him in an orphanage in Texas. I was walking

through rooms full of infants when this little man smiled at me. His smile was a child's smile, like any other, but it tugged at my heart.

"Oh, please," he seemed to say, "I want to belong to someone; they've never rocked me; no one has kissed my little fingers in my entire life. No one loves me and I so need a mother . . . "

With tears in my eyes, I picked him up from the crib and since then he's been mine. Mine! Little by little I familiarized myself with this idea to the extent that I began to believe it seriously. I will never tell him that I am not his mother. I think I would even kill the person who revealed [the truth].

How many women envy my life . . . it seems romantic to them, interesting, full of divine emotions. Success, admiration, riches; servants who are almost slaves; men who think they are in love with me. Silks, jewels, automobiles . . .

But all of this is ashes. Unless we have someone to love, someone to triumph for, someone that loves us, all is ashes. Love can't be bought with beauty, nor with fame, nor with money. The only thing that can buy love is . . . love itself.

Barbara went over what she had written with her tiny handwriting in the leaves of that intimate notebook. "Someday," she thought, "I would like to change my way of thinking about love and about men: when I meet someone who makes me forget what I have suffered."

And her big eyes filled with tears as she put her little diary away in a tiny drawer of her "secretary" and returned to her bed.

Fame had crowned the temples of Barbara La Marr with the laurels of success. After the release of *Black Orchids* with Ramon Novarro came *Thy Name Is Woman*, with the same Mexican whom she had grown to love.[170] That film, without a doubt the most human that the unfortunate artist performed in during her short life, launched her to the heights of fame. Now her name shone brightly in incandescent letters over the sinful avenue of Broadway; her servants had multiplied and there was an inconceivable difference between the dilapidated room on Main Street where she began her turbulent career and the palatial residence in Beverly Hills that she now occupied with little Marvin. Those who knew Barbara as a seminude dancer, contorting on the stage, barely applauded by the old men who went to the theaters more to enjoy the display of female flesh than the art of the Yankee dances being performed, admitted her notable evolution. Now rich, she followed the path toward definitive success, which is the supreme consecration, her real personality hidden beneath the decorative name, her persona increasingly well known in the far corners of the civilized world. But the Barbara La Marr whom everyone saw in her films, lustful and fiery, her eyes shining with cruelty and her lips contorted by desire, only existed in front of the implacable lens of the cameras. In her real life, she was always much more beautiful than in the Cinema, with charms of a distinct kind. Her mouth, bigger and more sensual than the screen revealed, had an expression of goodness. The expression of her eyes was also different. Sometimes they had something of the innocent curiosity that surprises us in the eyes of a little girl who attends a marvelous spectacle for the first time, but they were always covered by a veil of sadness that surely reflected the disappointment in her soul, this thirst for true love, the kind that makes us believe in the existence of God.

The love affair with Jack Daugherty that began that night at Montmartre had been extremely truncated. The next day the young actor wrote her a note asking her forgiveness for his impulsive act and left for New York. When he returned, she had become famous and had picked up little Marvin, on whom she now pinned all her hopes, from an orphanage in Texas. Sometimes Barbara thought with fondness about that man whom, she said to herself, she could have loved seriously one day if he had persisted in the struggle to conquer her heart. But then she smiled at the idea that could only be a dream, a desire for adventure, a momentary attraction provoked by the rumors that had already spread far and wide about her eventful life, more deserving of sadness than shame. Jack had not been a new man but another man. And when this idea came to mind, her mouth opened in a sad chuckle, like those heard sometimes from clowns, from acrobats; one can't decide at any given moment whether it is laughter or a cry of pain.

Once in a while they had seen each other in this or that Hollywood party or on the studio lots. He had looked at her with that peace, with the serenity of his big blue eyes, and he had managed to greet her with a:

"Hello, Bobby . . . !" in passing. She, prideful like all women, had barely answered. And that's how those souls carried on, perhaps loving each other privately but with a love so faint, so weak, that it wasn't enough to quiet the shouts of their own vanity.

Barbara had been remembering all of this that night, and, with her eyes refusing to close, as when we met her at the beginning of this story, she sat down to write in her personal diary, satisfied by being able to say how she felt to someone who would never betray her.

CHAPTER V

WHEN LOVE IS REBORN

That night Jack Daugherty had resolved to drown his illusions of love forever in a whirlwind of mirth. Since the night after the one when he had gone with Barbara to her little palace in Beverly Hills, he had convinced himself that any memory of him had left her soul forever. Then he had read that interview published by *Movie* in which the reporter put offensive statements about men in Barbara's mouth. That had convinced him to agree that in the end it wasn't worthwhile to spend nights tossing and turning in bed, with her image stuck in his head like a cursed claw, just for such a frivolous woman. The reporter, despite her promises, not only had published the star's words in her magazine but also had intentionally twisted the interview, painting Barbara as an arrogant, haughty woman who scorned men instinctively and at the same time as an insatiable pleasure seeker. Such was the image that the public wanted of its favorite star, and she had to be portrayed that way. Naturally the little blonde had not come back to the studio where Barbara worked and always took the precaution, before entering the others, of asking whether they had seen her around. The story had reached her ears that in one of her frequent fits, Miss La Marr had sworn to gouge the reporter's eyes out. Barbara would never be capable of doing such a thing, but it is a fact that she and the reporter never saw each other again. On the other hand, the work of slander that studio writers had crafted about her, perhaps with the best intentions of creating publicity, had cooled the primitive emotion in Jack's soul a bit.

That night he had found refuge in a Chinese restaurant in Los Angeles, accompanied by Betty Hill, a pretty brown-haired girl who had changed her French name in order to enter the back door of the studios with hopes of winning the prize of fame. At the Wi-Peng-Fu you could just as easily find veritable luminaries of the screen as well as high-class women with double lives as prostitutes and housewives, or prominent functionaries who passed their nights there incognito, and not precisely for the motives that the famous Harun-Al-Rashid had for doing so.[171] Betty had brought him with the hope of securing his promise to help her scale the heights of fame. Jack began to feel attracted to the French girl, but in spite of everything, the dark-haired figure of Barbara La Marr floated above her—immense, bigger than ever, magnified in comparison.

A band of Chinese street musicians extracted from their instruments what the proprietor of the café claimed to be music. To the profane ear, perhaps unaccustomed to Oriental refinement, it was nothing but a succession of monotonous squeaks without rhythm or cadence, whose only virtue was putting one's nerves on edge. While the café had been filling with people of all appearances, the couple occupied one of the discreet reserved tables.

When the orchestra quieted, Jack and his companion noticed that there were two half-drunk men talking very loudly at the next table.

"Let's get out of here," murmured Jack. "All of this noise is making me nervous."

Betty grabbed him by the chin and, looking into his big blue eyes, moved her head without responding for a moment. Then, with a smile that showed all her teeth behind her carefully made-up lips, she whispered:

"Not yet . . . later."

And a lightning flash of desire passed across her dark eyes.

The neighbors continued talking loudly. Their words could be halfway heard, as they were intermingled with the laughter of some women farther away who were having fun with two old libertines. Even farther away, you could hear Spanish being spoken. Some young journalists, correspondents from Mexican magazines, had also taken refuge in the "Wi-Peng-Fu" with two dancers from the Princess Theater.[172]

Precisely at the moment that the orchestra—or whatever it was—returned to perpetrate another one of those inexcusable numbers, it seemed to Jack that he heard his own name at the next table, where the voices that first bothered him could be heard. The interference of the Chinese flute kept him from hearing what they were saying.

During the song he was nervous and barely tasted the delicious "chow mein" that the waiter, dressed in traditional Chinese garb, bowing in genuflections and beaming with rabbit-like smiles, placed on the table in front of him. Finally, as all calamities must come to an end, the orchestra stopped again. Jack then fixed his attention on what his neighbors were saying. With a little forced concentration he realized that he had not been wrong. But now the issue was more serious: they were talking about Barbara La Marr.

"I've known her since then . . . and I knew Converse," said a baritone voice that, based on the tone that reached all the way to Jack's table, must have belonged to the man facing him. "Barbara danced in a café on Main Street and there . . ."

A mocking laugh, coming from the table where the other girls were holding court, completely blocked out this interesting development. Jack became all ears. He answered Betty's gesture of surprise by putting a finger perpendicularly against his lips, with such a look of resolve that she considered it dangerous to insist. Shrugging her shoulders, she began to eat her "chow mein" with gusto as if she were all alone.

The voice could be heard again:

" . . . agreed, but you don't know what you're talking about; she herself told me that she had to come to California to rest . . . because of the life she was living, she had to begin writing for the studios after abandoning Deely, who was already the third. There she met Douglas Fairbanks, who, as you know, puts up little resistance to love, and he gave her the part that you remember in *The Three Musketeers*, which is how she began her career. Now, of course, she doesn't know me . . . or pretends not to know me."

A voice that could be heard less clearly, a circumstance that presumably meant it came from a person with his back turned toward Jack's table, continued:

"Bah! . . . . don't believe it. A woman who has led a life like that can't change her way of being. God knows who her lover is right now. I've heard a lot about this . . . What's the name of that actor, the big guy from Universal?"

"Daugherty?"

"That guy; Daugherty. But you've seen: it was a dream . . ."

Jack was in such a state that he could barely keep himself in his seat. A trace of self-control stopped him from jumping up to go see the faces of these slanderers.

The conversation continued:

"And how much do you make of this?"

This produced a brief silence. It seemed as if the other man was trying to remember before giving a definitive answer. At last he spoke, waveringly:

"Well . . . I don't remember well, but then, like now, she was everyone's woman."

A huge hand driven by a ton of force landed on the mouth that had just said these words. Jack Daugherty, to the stupefaction of Betty, had leaped from his table to the other like a tiger and punched the cad in the mouth. The man fell next to the table, holding his jaw. In front of him, with his fists up, legs still open on guard, was Jack. The big blue eyes, almost innocent, had been lit by a fire he hadn't known until then. Half oaths flowed through his gritted teeth.

"What do you want?"

It was the man who'd been knocked down, formulating the question with a timidness justified by Jack's threatening fists.

"I'm here to break both your faces. I'm Jack Daugherty."

The recently knocked down man, who had begun to open his eyes in preparation for standing up, closed them again. Maybe in his heart of hearts he considered it prudent to follow the advice of Pobre Valbuena.[173] The other guy went intensely pale and froze like a rock in his seat.

The incident had created a terrible scandal. One of the good-time girls with the old men faked a fainting spell; Betty, who generally knew what to do in these types of situations and in places of ill repute, took advantage of the confusion to leave the café. A Chinese man sounded the alarm and the two Mexican journalists stood on stools in order to see better.

"It's Barbara La Marr's boyfriend," said one of them.

"It seems like they were bragging about her. That made him furious."

"I'm a friend of Barbara's. She'd like to know about this . . ."

A "policeman" the size of an elephant entered the premises, revolver in hand. Upon his arrival, everyone began to throw bottles under the tables, producing a noise like the shattering of a cantina window. Jack pulled down the cuffs of his blazer and managed to calm himself.

"What happened?" asked the policeman with authority.

"I smashed this scoundrel's face," responded Daugherty, "because I caught him talking about a woman I love."

"Is the wound serious?"

The injured man got up to prove that besides a broken molar and the swelling that he was beginning to feel on his cheek, everything was "all right." The officer smiled kindly, holstered his revolver, gave Jack a pat on the back and said:

"You have to control yourself, Jack."

"Do I know you?"

"My wife is crazy for the cinema and sometimes drags me with her. Just last night we saw your Jack triumphant.[174] What bravery, friend. What shrewdness. And then when you carried the heroine to safety through the flames. Wow! . . . I wanted to meet you in person."

And he extended his hand, open in a cordial greeting. Jack gave him his. The Chinese orchestra started its infernal melody again. As he left the café, the injured man used his sleeve to brush off his hat, which had fallen from its perch at the moment blows were thrown. His interlocutor had already disappeared.

At the reporters' table, the younger of them insisted:

"Tomorrow I am going to tell Barbara by phone. She's going to like it a lot . . ."

Jack Daugherty was just finishing dressing the next morning after exiting the bathroom, when his valet entered the bedroom, upset:

"Mr. Daugherty . . ."

The young man turned his head without lifting his hands off his head, which he was giving a reasonable unction of aromatic pomade.

"What's going on?"

"Miss La Marr is here . . ."

Jack opened his arms like a man who had just been shot; his eyes got so big that to the valet they looked like porcelain plates decorated with blue. Then, taking the boy by the shoulders, he looked him firmly in the eyes, almost yelling in his face, with a drowned voice:

"Do you mean to say . . . Barbara La Marr?"

The valet nodded his head yes a few times, while at the same time his face had the expression of confusion that comes over us when we don't know whether the news we've delivered is good or bad, but we can tell that we've caused a sensation. A little bit calmer now, he focused on the actor's hands still on his shoulders, dirtying the sleeves of his shirt with pomade, and discreetly tried to tell him so. The news had made such an impression on Jack that he didn't know whether to run and throw himself at the feet of the recent arrival or hide so she wouldn't see him. He wiped his hands on a towel, fixed the knot of his tie in the mirror, and went out to the foyer with determination.

Barbara was there, indeed; more beautiful, more rapturous than ever. A silk and gold dress clung to her pagan goddess flesh, outlining her prodigious curves. Her head was topped by a little hat of fur inclined cutely over her left eyebrow. Upon seeing Jack, she stood up.

He moved forward, extending his hand to her with a remorseful expression. Barbara without a glance took him in her arms:

"Jack, oh Jack! Why did you do that?"

He felt that his voice was knotted in his throat as he tried to inquire about her behavior. He likewise clasped her mechanically in his vigorous arms, putting his hand over her darling head covered in fur. In the end he could only say:

"Barbara, Barbara . . ."

And before either of them could explain how, their lips had already united in a long, deep, intense kiss, as if with it they wanted to communicate their own souls.

"I heard about it this morning, Jack," she murmured, looking into his eyes and finally halfway untangling herself from their embrace. "You see how happy I am. I finally know that you really love me. Finally, finally, I know what love is."

He didn't know what to say. He gave up on trying to say anything loving, convinced that he would seem ridiculous. He just murmured now and then:

"Barbara, Barbara . . ."

And their lips came together again and again.

When the burst of affection had passed, she sat down again on the Persian divan over which a floor lamp still spilled its uncertain light, accentuating her divine profile.

"How did you know . . . that?" he asked.

"They told me this morning by phone. I knew that you were with that odious Frenchwoman." Barbara's divine mouth twisted into a contemptuous grimace. "And I had phoned your house. You couldn't hide from it. Oh Jack, you are magnificent . . . magnificent . . . !"

The heart of the naïf burst. At first in a rush, then repeating, with the vehemence of those sincerely in love, he told her all he had suffered since that one night; he told her about the effort he made to forget her, of his desire to be swayed by the slander that had ripped apart her name, saturating it with the vitriol of an abominable reputation. But all the articles he had read were written by deceitful chroniclers, an echo of the popular voice that was wrong as ever: the day he heard it, he couldn't resist a moment more . . . and that was all.

He started his story from the beginning, and he repeated it ingenuously, with new flourishes, with new literary cloaking, but always with the same spirit: that great love that held his being in an eternal flame, love that until then he had only seen in the novels of Elinor Glyn.[175] She invariably responded, full of admiration:

"Oh Jack, you are magnificent . . . magnificent . . . !"
And new kisses tied together the bond broken that night when the pride of a woman overcame the vehement call of her very own heart. When the lovers separated, the afternoon already upon them, she carried in her soul a unique pleasure, the kind that makes existence tolerable: she had felt the arrival of love.

CHAPTER VI

"DON'T BE TOO SURE"

Rome, August 1923
My friend, I never realized how comfortable I would feel in Rome, since my health has returned . . . . just like my Jack. In passing I want to ask your forgiveness for not having written to you earlier, but the truth is—and you know this too—that during a honeymoon one is a little thankless, even with your best friends. What would you think if I told you that during these delicious nights I've even forgotten Marvin himself, my beloved child whom I love so much?

But there is a plausible and good reason for this. You know, my dear friend—because I have opened my heart to you numerous times in Hollywood, where nobody understands you, where everyone lives this artificial and egotistical life—that I have never known true love. Just like that: never, never. I never imagined that one day I would come to feel the desire to throw myself at the feet of a man if he asked me to in exchange for one kiss from him. Now, I assure you that if Jack! my Jack! asked me to, I would do it without hesitating.

Nor did I ever imagine that there would be a man so handsome, so good, so adorable as him. We have known each other for some time: you know (you're the only one) the circumstances of our reconciliation after that horrible night in the Chinese café. From then until our marriage, which was arranged with such haste as you must remember, we were convinced every day that we had been born for each other; that ours was a true love, the kind that can't be faked, the kind that builds its bridge between souls and not between bodies. I am so lucky!

Jack is very sweet to me, but he likes to be the "head of the family." What he says is done; his word is law. I love this and wouldn't allow the contrary. I like a man like that: dominant, arrogant inside his masculine castle, but with all the sweetness of his heart dedicated completely to me, which I very much need. You know what I have suffered in my life . . .

You will tell me that you can't be sure about my assertion; how can I know if this time true love has knocked on my door? Didn't I think the same in my previous marriages? Right? But to this I have a reasonable response. That wasn't the same; It never could be. Now that I reflect,

I think that the previous cases could have well been affection but not love. You know how easy it is to confuse sympathy with love and you already have proof of that in your own life. My first marriage was a case of hallucination: the rest of them affection, all of them. If I were to tell you that my first husband was fifty when I was just sixteen . . . !

Forgive me if I can't stop talking about Jack. You know that when one is in love, as I am now . . . and always will be, one feels the desire to share, to have everyone participate in their own happiness. My Jack isn't like the other men, I assure you. All of them want to have a woman at their side who is wife, mother, waitress, in agreement with their beliefs and point of view, seductive siren, and housewife at the same time: sensational and substantial. Where is the woman who contains all these qualities? Not Jack; he wants me to be his baby, his doll, his little girl . . . that I be myself, in a word. Aren't you jealous of me from over there?

As you know, we've been here shooting scenes for *The Eternal City*, and I'm the only woman in the cast.[176] During the day we film with Lionel Barrymore, with Bert Lytell, Montagu Love, or Richard Bennett. At night, Jack and I go to Roman cafes, so loud, but sincerely joyful . . . If I had to speak frankly, the cabarets of Los Angeles and New York might be more sumptuous, more magnificent in their luxury, but in these cafes people live their own lives, so happy, so delighted to have been born! Jack and I frequently mingle among these people when we don't have some invitation from nobles. You know that I am half Italian . . . you are up to date on the story and know that I am not the Watsons' daughter . . . let's speak of something else. I was telling you that as I have Italian blood, I've identified with these people and we understand each other very well. Sometimes, most of the time, they invite me to parties that I almost always refuse to attend so I can be alone with him. I was sick for a few days and he almost died of regret. It's a dream to have someone take care of you in such a way.

You'll see how delightful those Roman nights are! Sometimes by the light of the moon, we walk along the banks of the Tiber, dominated by the historic mass of the Castle of Saint Angelo, telling each other silly things like two students. I, who have always deeply desired to visit this city, mother of the world, to find pleasure in the silent contemplation of its monuments to the past, haven't had any time to dedicate to looking exclusively at them. Jack, Jack . . . Jack is all that fills my existence for now.

I am going to triumph soon; I feel it, I see it coming as a natural consequence of my mood. Before, life was an eternal struggle for me, at the end of which I was going to find that I had achieved what I wanted . . . for what? Who was going to enjoy my triumphs, to be proud of them and of me? Now I have two souls for whom to live and triumph: Marvin and Jack. One is my beloved son, who is part of my own being. The other is the only man for me in life. What more could I want?

After all, the only conclusion is this: happiness, true and authentic. Not the struggle to reach false pedestals, but rather the struggle that comes from the depths of our being and that can't be created by external success. I already know that you are going to tell me that no one obtains it, but this is precisely what makes it desirable for all eternity. The cows grazing in a field . . . that's conformity. But happiness, nebulous, fragmented, today in a good book, tomorrow in the eyes of a friend, later in the security of feeling loved . . .

Live the twenty-six years I have already lived, experience what I have experienced, and you'll agree with me. For now, Jack and Marvin. After them, and you, dear, nothing, nothing . . .

Yours,

Barbara

In front of the mirror of her dressing table, to which she turned with her face covered in cream, Virginia carefully folded the letter she had just received and guarded it in her bosom.[177] The vision of Barbara happy, finally achieving her deepest longing in the Eternal City, passed through her mind. Then a sigh elevated her breasts for a long time and her lips opened to murmur like a prayer:

"Poor Barbara! After everything, she deserved all the happiness that might come her way, if there really is complete bliss in the world . . ."

Outside, like a terrible omen, like a response to Virginia's thoughts, the opening notes of a popular song could be heard from the neighboring house:

"DON'T BE TOO SURE . . ."

Furrowing her brow, she went to close the window of her bedroom, but the music kept filtering in through the panes with a mocking and cruel insistence:

"DON'T BE TOO SURE . . ."

CHAPTER VII

EN ROUTE TO AMERICAN SHORES

The Daughertys' honeymoon trip lasted two long months. The scenes of *The Eternal City* done, the tempestuous Barbara and her husband boarded the *Aquitania* to return to America; she, anxious to continue climbing the ladder of fame in the studios of the enchanted Hollywood; he, desiring with all his heart that the voyage would never end. Meanwhile, the star's name had become known around the world; the enchantment of her smile reached the gaze of the universe's cinemagoing publics who admired her at a distance, lavishing her with applause that she would never hear but that translated into magnificent ticket sales for the exhibitors, who began to ask for more and more films by Barbara La Marr.

Thy Name Is Woman, in which her persona had been so wisely foretold by Fred Niblo, spread throughout Latin America like a clarion call of triumph. Her name was linked with that of Ramon Novarro, the cinematic Apollo of the future. Her salary rose considerably and the whole world threw itself at her feet in a gigantic caravan, opening its arms, offering her their hearts, scattering before her path the roses that would not have had time to fade when the Hour of Glory arrived.

Now her name shone brightly in luminous letters over the wide and tempting thoroughfare of Broadway. Everywhere they talked about her celebrity loves, her domestic extravagances, her Oriental luxury. Her most notable virtue, generosity, was always interpreted badly. Barbara La Marr lived for others, succeeded for others, and if in her life she never denied herself the pleasures money could buy, neither did she forget those who suffered in orphanages, on the streets, in the poor neighborhoods to which she extended her caring hand and magnanimity with the sweetness of a handkerchief that dries a tear.

Barbara returned to America under these circumstances. Her arrival in New York was celebrated by all the newspapers, and rounds of admiration were fired off in her honor from the shiny pages of the magazines. The dock of the *Aquitania* was full of photographers and reporters anxiously jockeying to be the first to greet her. The old beauty hunters, the millionaires of that den of wolves that is Wall Street, auctioned off the honor of being the first to kiss her white hand, silky and perfumed. Only they didn't say a word about Daugherty. They pretended that the star wasn't married. They ignored that she had someone who already legally enjoyed her caresses, and Jack's name was barely murmured by any of those who search the cinema news to be able to brag about knowing everything that happens—and sometimes what doesn't happen—in the deceitful world of the screen.

During their brief stay in New York, Daugherty began to suffer the grief of being married to a world celebrity. He clearly felt his smallness, and his heart filled with bitterness before the attention lavished upon his wife. And he divined in the gazes of the lovestruck the immense desire for an earthquake, an epidemic, a cyclone, something that would come and leave

Barbara free to accept the love of those who were ready to make a carpet for her out of their hearts.

One night, the evening just before their departure for Hollywood, she had to notice the sadness of her companion and interrogate him about its cause before he would find the courage to speak up.

"You don't have time for anything, Barbara! How much would I give for you to stop being what you are and truly become my beloved darling, the woman of my house, the light of my home . . ."

She became nervous, and for the first time in her married life she spoke to him in a sharp tone:

"Don't disappoint me, Jack," she said. "I have tried to believe that you were different, without the egoism of the rest, without their lack of faith. You men will never ever be able to forgive a woman the sin of being famous and admired: to be something more than an ordinary housewife who mends socks and prepares the table to await her husband's arrival."

He was silent, a bitter silence that had made him spill tears of desperation when he was alone at night.

Their arrival in Hollywood was a new test. Everyone in that deceitful city fought over the honor of meeting the woman who had returned famous and who previously, in the sad days of her anonymity, had never drawn their attention. There was even someone who, inviting her to a dinner in her honor, insinuated that it would be advisable to leave her husband at home. Then, on to work with even more zeal for the conquest of cinematic fame. Entire days of fatigue, at the end of which she retired to her luxurious residence in Beverly Hills, only to cry for no apparent reason, victim of a desperate, nervous irritation. Fame has always been conquered at the cost of personal tranquility, of sacrifice by the famous person and for the benefit of those whom they love the most. That's how the first months passed after their return.

One day, terrible news made the house of cards of marital peace sway in the home of the two actors. Bernard Deely, abandoned in harder times, discovered the whereabouts of his wife and showed up in Hollywood. The Los Angeles newspapers, attuned to everything that might signify a new scandal in the disreputable city of cinema, published the news of his arrival illustrated with his portrait on their front pages. In short order there was talk of a looming legal mess. A lawyer came to the star's house offering to quiet the scandal in exchange for a large sum of money, but with the threat of making the scandal even louder in the event of a negative answer.

The mess, which tore up Barbara's delicate health, continued and caused a temporary separation between the recently married couple as a measure of the most fundamental precaution. Deely, meanwhile, worked to be received by his wife, without achieving that desire one single time.

It was then that the voice of slander extended across the world with a sweeping force. They talked about her tempestuous past, her supposed orgies in bad parts of town with people of the lowest class. They associated her character of the cinematic vamp with her real life, and her reputation was left in tatters forever. The star, at the apogee of her glory, felt profoundly unlucky for the first time. While the case continued in the courts, the hand of destiny struck Bernard, who died suddenly and mysteriously during a trip back East, as soon as his lawyers tried to blackmail the star. Barbara, for her part, had fallen into a deep despair.

An offer by film producers to go to New York came to take her out of that suffocating atmosphere. But Jack didn't want to go with her, and after a terrible scene in which she threw his lack of sacrifice in his face, his absolute indifference to the woman whom he had adored more than any other in his life, Barbara La Marr departed for the East Coast, cutting off, painfully, what everyone had believed was an unending love story.

That night, at her palace on Lexington Drive, Pola Negri gave one of her rowdy parties, whose reviews always occupied so much space in the global press. The main salon on the lower floor shone like an ember made of gold over which rained a waterfall of precious stones. As their crystals sparkled, the chandeliers were pierced by the light. A group of the Polish countess's favorites had gathered at the house, among them some luminaries of the screen, two or three Los Angeles journalists, and a millionaire who had been admitted almost as a special favor, anxious to mix the useless prestige of his riches with the most famous talents of Cinelandia. There was Charlie Chaplin, the genius of cinema, his head now sprinkled with the silver of his years, without his eternal clown suit, his forehead knit in a meditative pose; Antonio Moreno, the Spanish actor who after a long, painful ordeal had come to be a millionaire in the film colony, with his fortunate marriage to the most exquisite woman known to Hollywood, Daisy Danzinger; Mabel Normand, eternal victim of newspaper scandals and in reality less perverse than they tried to make her seem; Ramon Novarro, the nascent favorite of Hollywood, ambassador from Mexico to the American art [cinema]; Ruth Roland, the heroic "White Eagle," rolling in her millions since, less of a dreamer than her companions, she abandoned her film career to dedicate herself to the complicated operations of real estate; Patsy Ruth Miller; Luis G. Pinal and Fidel Murillo, young representatives of Mexican magazines in Hollywood; and Jack Daugherty, always sad, eternally closed in his incurable melancholy, with the image of his absent siren stuck in his brain like an implacable and torturing claw.

Murillo had been talking with Barbara's husband after the sumptuous dinner, while a little orchestra from the studios played melodies by that sad Pole, Frederic Chopin, who imprinted his struggle with tuberculosis on his musical compositions. The violin moaned the strains of a nocturne in D, and over this melody that unwound in the manner of a strange drunkenness, Jack's voice embroidered intimate confessions in front of the Mexican journalist, who listened to him religiously in a corner of the living room, over which a vertical lamp let its rain of tenuous, opaline light fall on the silk cushion of a divan.

"I swear to you, my friend," Daugherty said in a low voice, "I wanted to make her happy and achieve my eternal bliss by giving her my name and my hand. But the most terrible thing that can happen to a man is to be married to a movie star. And to think that if she had not become famous, we would have been so happy with our life . . .

"The husband of a star is always a 'nobody,' and you know that no man who values himself wants to play such a role. When I became something in her life, I was . . . the background against which her prestigious and envied figure moved, the opaque screen on which the Chinese shadow of her tempting image was reflected. Nothing more . . ."

"You always exaggerate, Jack," responded Murillo, with a smile that he attempted to make comforting.

"Exaggerate? Bah! I could tell you about a hundred incidents in our married life that showed me the light. Look," he arranged himself in his seat, "when we were in New York, coming back from our honeymoon, Barbara was greeted with frenetic enthusiasm. That was something that filled my heart: I was so proud of her that I barely noticed that no one even realized that I existed. She was the only one who from time to time, grateful, turned her beautiful eyes toward me. God bless her for that!

"One night we went to a party at the residence of a certain family, one of the most aristocratic families in the Marvelous City. I have to confess that never in my life had I seen luxury that was more Oriental, more outrageous, more over the top. Barbara was introduced to everyone, and the men kissed her hands and gave her passionate compliments. However, no one worried about introducing me, and everyone looked me up and down as if they admired the impertinence of my being there, smiling like a dummy, when no one paid attention to me. Soon the woman of the house noticed me and, as if she had remembered something important, called the attention of those present to introduce me. 'I've forgotten,' she said, 'to introduce you to Mr.' . . . (she vacillated for a moment) 'to Mr. . . . '

"I was on edge. Finally, the good woman, giving up on remembering my name, introduced me as 'Mr. Barbara La Marr.'"

Murillo really would have liked to have laughed at this, but the deadly spark in Jack's eyes held him back. Jack continued:

"That woman never knew how close to death she had been at that exact moment . . ."

They lit cigarettes that Jack took out of his gold cigarette case. When he opened the case, Fidel could see on its lid, in enamel, a magnificent portrait of Barbara. When the spirals of smoke had begun their journey toward the ceiling of the room, the conversation continued.

"All of this, and more I could tell you, will impress on you how bitter my life at her side was. In the end, only the love that I knew she felt for me deep down made me resist protesting for so long. But in the affections of a star, cinema comes first. The husband is in a supporting role, a consolation, if that; her career is her life, her love, her only ambition. The suggestion of the roles that she interprets in the studios, and the continuous emotional tension, turn her into a different woman than she might have been otherwise. Soon my own individuality was erased from her life, and I couldn't resist anymore. Because of that I felt that there wasn't room for both of us.

"A man can't be a satisfactory lover or husband when he suffers such frequent humiliations. A woman like her needs a strong man, dominant, rough . . . and I, who loved her so much, could never be that. Her personal success, I have to be honest with you, never shocked her, but it completely changed her way of living. Barbara is completely careless about money. The huge salaries she earns only mean more luxury, more extravagance, more of the good things in life for her. So she began to spend in proportion to what she was earning without thinking about the future. My salary, which is large, was a pittance compared to hers. That, my friend, humiliates a man who respects himself."

"Egoism, dear Jack."

"And what else is life itself but egoism? To release oneself from it you need to achieve supreme perfection, a perfection that is prohibited to humans. Now I think that there may be someone who could be happy as the husband of a star. But this guy would need to completely abdicate his personal pride and have not an iota of jealousy in his entire body. He needs to think about the fact that she is famous, that all the men will throw themselves at her feet, and that he is nothing but a hindering and bothersome figure for all of them. He can console himself with the thought of having a famous woman, and with the blind security that in the end she prefers him to the others. But if this man is like me, like you, like all of those who have grown up with the general concept that a man has of woman and marriage, the same thing that happened to me will happen to him. And I feel bad about it, as she should feel bad about it, because at the beginning at least, we loved each other very much. But now . . . it can't be . . ."

A sharp silence passed between the two friends; the smoke of their cigarettes continued rising in bluish spirals over their heads, writhing in the gold flecks of the lamp, crashing into the rich stucco of the walls, later dissipating in the air as an illusion dissipates, as a wish dissipates. Jack finished by repeating, as if it were an echo:

"It can't be."

At the opposite end of the room, the strange accent of Pola Negri stood out among the fabric of murmurs formed by the conversations being woven, embroidering capricious arabesques over a canvas of general happiness. Patsy Ruth Miller, a flatterer, made jingle bells with her silver laugh, without giving credence to something that Luis Pinal assured her of with the most seriousness in the world. The serene voice of Ramon Novarro made an effort to explain something about the Mexico of the Aztecs to the mature beauty of Ruth Roland.

On a small lacquered table, a portrait of Barbara La Marr, indifferent, with her eyes in supreme ecstasy, obsessed Jack, who despite his silence continued repeating to himself, like a comfort, like an excuse, like a supreme renunciation:

"It's a shame . . . it can't be."

Chapter VIII

"The Moth"

Meanwhile, word on the street began to attribute new love affairs to Barbara. She filmed the burning scenes of "The Moth," a film that gave her that nickname and that conflated, in the eyes of the public, the part she played in front of the cameras with her own life.[178] The sobriquet quickly became popular, especially among Hollywood types; even on the date of her mourned disappearance, a newspaper omitted her proper name to use "the Moth." The power of publicity was made clear in this case, as in many others in which a woman is the victim of attacks against which she can't defend herself because it would hurt her interests. The principal masculine role was played by Ben Lyon, a new actor, born in the heat of competition between Latin lovers and Anglo-Saxons. They attributed a novel eroticism to both artists when in reality it only existed in the popular imagination. The truth of the matter was that Barbara, at the apogee of her fame, began to live life intensely, hurrying to take huge gulps from the cup of pleasure. No aristocratic corner of the Phenomenal City was hidden from her. She went everywhere accompanied by Ben, and the bills she paid always reached outrageous totals. She wanted to shock herself, to live life fully in an effort to forget the unforgettable. Like all women in her situation, Barbara drowned herself in pleasure without managing to erase the obsession with her beloved from her mind. She always woke up the day after one of those sprees, which were never as out of control as was reported, with the memory of that sincere man who held all the charm of a first love for her. With the release of *The White Moth*, her popularity reached its height, and the advantageous contracts, with offers fit to appear in the story "One Hundred and One Nights," rained over her "secretaire." In front of the camera, she feverishly brought to life *Sandra*, *The White Monkey*, and other films of lesser prestige, many times without worrying about her artistic future, which she considered secure.[179] Unfortunately, after *The Eternal City* and *Thy Name Is Woman*, Barbara La Marr's prestige lived exclusively in the memory of those two cinematic triumphs. But riches and adulation continued to surround her name, and she continued to live almost entirely at night, wrapped in a whirlwind of life, with a thirst for oblivion that she could never quench.

One night, when she and several friends were out being stunned by the clamorous orchestra at Rectors, the first advances of the Relentless One were presented to her. She had tired of dancing and of laughing. The bill, which she wanted to pay alone, grew by the instant in the register of that aristocratic restaurant. It was already morning, close to the hour she usually retired to her quarters, where the word on the street had her bathing in milk and perfumes, living in the complacent half-light of a salon in the Baghdad of Harun-Al-Rashid. She felt indisposed and insinuated that they should hurry up and leave. Ben Lyon, who was at her side, solicitous and caring, asked her a little anxiously:

"What is going on with you? You are very pale and have circles under your eyes that I have never ever seen on you . . ."

She smiled sadly, trying to brush it off. But a few seconds later a terrible cough erupted, a funereal omen that loomed over her life and strangled her voice just as she was going to explain that it was nothing but a trivial bout of dizziness. Her fine silk handkerchief that she had raised to her mouth was spattered with bloody flowers. Lyon was alarmed:

"Quickly, the car. Barbara is not well."

And the cheer was cut off by their hasty departure. Now in the luxurious apartments, the servants were awakened by a voice of alarm:

"A doctor; quick, a doctor!"

Her maids undressed her and put her to bed. In the anteroom Ben Lyon, Anna Luther, Frank Mayo, and a young millionaire named Worth milled around restlessly. Dr. Brent finally arrived, greeting them briefly and passing toward the room that was lit softly by the tenuous light of its opaline lamps. He found the sick woman with anxiety on her face, making him try in vain to offer an optimistic smile.

An eternal minute. The doctor examined the patient in silence, his stoic face not revealing the slightest impression. When he had finished, she questioned him with a look, and he moved his head lightly, putting away his tools in a little leather case.

"There is no need to be alarmed," he said at last, "but you'll need to make sure you get a lot of rest. Do you have something to do in California?"

"No. Why, doctor?"

"It would be best to live in a less harsh climate than that of New York. I fear that . . ."

In Barbara's mind, like a sudden dazzling light, appeared the memory of something that had happened years earlier. During her marriage to Deely, and her marriage to Robert Carville before that, she had had to seclude herself in hospitals, prisoner of a "nervous condition" whose exact diagnosis no one wanted to reveal. Then the early deaths of her [birth] parents. This unlucky event had always had a veil over it. Suspicious whispers had emerged the one time that the issue had been talked about in the Watsons' house . . .

"I understand, doctor," she said, her beautiful eyes full of tears.

The doctor didn't say a word. A few minutes later, after having prescribed a creosote-based syrup, he left the room.

In the antechamber Barbara's friends beseeched him with supplicating and inquisitive looks.

"A change of climate is necessary . . . and above all else, there needs to be more calm in her life," he said. "That might still extend her life a bit."

And bowing deeply, he departed the room, leaving the four friends upset, looking at each other with wide eyes. No one spoke, but the same terrible idea moved through their minds.

Inside, in the alcove that had received her body so many nights after those interminable parties, which she had filled with her dreams that in the end disappeared like a fragile summer cloud, Barbara La Marr continued coughing desperately, with the silk handkerchief over her lips, lips that hours before so many would have given half their lives to kiss.

In her imagination a vague figure took shape and finally emerged. It was a virile young man, strong and healthy, topped by a blond head whose face shone with a sweet smile of optimism and life. And for the first time in her impetuous life, the sick one associated the figure of Jack Daugherty with those of the good old couple, almost forgotten, who gave her their name and took care of her during her childhood, and whom she had abandoned in a moment of madness in that town of Yakima, lost in the spacious plains of Washington State . . .

CHAPTER IX

SETTING SUN

How different was the Barbara La Marr who returned to Hollywood after a long absence, during which the echo of her extravagances in New York reverberated through the gossip mill in the city of Cinema, shredding what little was left of her poor reputation! This time the "White Moth" returned almost in silence, devoid of all of the train of Oriental luxury that had almost always preceded her arrival in American cities. A half dozen of her friends went to greet her at the Santa Fe station in Los Angeles and a caring hand brought her a huge bouquet of flowers. Profound traces of the illness that undermined her had already begun to appear in her face; her smile was no longer that of a woman of the world, irresistible, the smile of a tigress or a vampire. Her huge, light eyes no longer looked as if they were full of lustful thoughts; her lips had an expression of goodness that few had seen. Installed in a house belonging to Mabel Normand, since hers had been sold during her stay in New York, with the hope of never, ever returning to the enchanted city, Barbara began to organize her accounts, to put in order all her affairs for the first time in her life. She regulated her expenses that had been so careless and showered caresses upon little Marvin, now a cutie who extended his chubby little arms to her, smiling with a tiny tooth barely sprouting from the bright pink of his gums. The night of her arrival she picked him up late and was writing until twelve thirty in the morning.

The next day she sent out a long letter to the Watsons, her adoptive parents, forgotten during her period of fame and pleasure. The old couple received the letter at their house in Fullerton, where they now had a photography studio, and cried when they read it. The prodigal daughter was calling them to her side, asking their forgiveness for her thoughtless outbursts, prostrating her prideful soul of a woman of the world at their feet, anxious to kiss them since it would be "maybe the last time."

This observation, underlined in the letter, alarmed Mrs. Watson. Her husband explained to her that, in effect, the girl had been weak in her infancy, and that later she would have this or that relapse, but that he didn't think her condition was dangerous.

"You know her, Rose," he said between puffs on his pipe on the porch of the house in Fullerton. "She's always been pessimistic and prone to exaggeration. Tomorrow we'll leave for Hollywood."

The woman dried a furtive tear that had been teetering on her eyelashes and agreed with a movement of her head. After all, they had pardoned her before. And how could she not, if she was the soul of her soul, if she had given her life to her during those first years after they came and deposited her at their door, with a note that her father, the count, had died days before in Paris? That night they made preparations for the short journey, and the next day both presented themselves at Barbara's house, creating a tender scene of familial love.

Upon seeing the woman arrive, Barbara took her in her arms, sobbing with emotion. For a few minutes they stayed like that in a strong hug, unable to talk because of the knots that the tears had formed in their throats. Mr. Watson, standing silent, contemplated the scene with his noble face illuminated by the smile that was habitual for him. Finally, Mrs. Watson was the first to speak, but only to say two or three words:

"Daughter . . . my daughter . . . my little girl . . ."

Then came one of those long conversations that always follow a family reconciliation. Mr. Watson found Barbara "very well" and smiled at her fears:

"Bah! Doctors always exaggerate. A bit of rest will do you good and above else no worries, no strain. The idea is ridiculous, my dear daughter . . ."

The good man, with his index finger raised in front of Barbara's eyes, threatened her lovingly, as when she was a little girl and had committed some naughtiness in the neighborhood. Oh, the endless indulgence of parents, who have seen us day after day in our march toward maturity, toward their graying heads! Mrs. Watson took a look at her in turn with an appraising gesture and said:

"Okay, then . . . I will take care of this and turn it into a home. You have some very careless maids, my daughter."

Barbara felt completely happy. In the depths of her soul, she calculated that she would have given all her adventures in the deceitful world, all her luxury, all her moments of pleasure and vanity for another moment like this one. Even the cough, which hadn't abandoned her except at intervals since her arrival in the city of the studios, seemed to have left her in peace. That night, from the bottom of her heart, she gave thanks to the all-powerful in whose hands she put herself, resigned, supplicant, and devout. She had to live for those two old people, for her little Marvin, who had already begun to walk with an unsteady step on the sunlit porches, under the watchful care of his nanny.

Shortly after their arrival, Barbara began to film the principal female role in *The Girl from Montmartre* for United Artists, playing against the energetic, virile majesty of Lewis Stone.[180] As weak as she felt, she thought it prudent to accept the contract offered, as much to not create suspicion about the illness that afflicted her as to replenish her estate, which was a bit deteriorated by her life of financial disorder and eternal generosity in New York.

One day, when the cameras were already ready to start filming the first scenes of the production, Barbara was talking with Stone when something happened that let everyone know about the misfortune that loomed over the poor woman. Lewis Stone had opined something about her characterization, and she tried to respond:

"I don't see it that way; my character, according to the script, should . . ."

A horrible coughing attack cut off her words. The veins of her neck swelled alarmingly, as if they were going to burst; her eyes filled with tears that melted the Rimmel adorning her eyelashes, and her skin turned livid underneath her makeup. Everyone looked at her, terrified.

One of her maids who was on the "set" ran to her aid with a silk handkerchief. Moments later everyone saw how blood stained the delicate fabric. The director sent for the studio doctor. Poor Barbara, lying on a divan, managed to smile and convince her coworkers that it was nothing. But in front of everyone the horrible truth of the relentless phantasm of the white plague, whose clear symptoms definitively betray its appearance, had already revealed itself.[181]

Dr. Wilson, who answered the call, of course recommended two or three days of rest if the contract couldn't be broken. That night in the house in Beverly Hills, he had an interesting conversation with Mr. Watson.

"This girl needs to take care of herself," he said. "If you want to extend her life, you need to take her to live in the hills as soon as possible. There's Altadena, where the air is pure . . ."

"But her contract?"

"It will have to be broken . . . or whatever you like. The fact is that Miss La Marr needs absolute rest and a strict regimen."

Barbara, despite everything, refused to break her contract. She assured them that she would have the strength necessary to work during production and that she only needed them to provide her with a nurse at hand, to film with more peace. Four days later she returned to the studio, thin and weak; her colleagues received her with a compassionate silence. Stone, a great friend of hers, was the only one who dared to encourage her:

"Bah! Don't worry. Once the film is done, with a little bit of rest . . ."

The director, scared of what might happen, filmed scenes in which Barbara would appear in advance. That way they avoided work for her and saved the company any resulting loss in the case of an unfortunate event. In this way Barbara continued working with the help of a nurse who periodically gave her spoonfuls of medicine. The young woman only filmed four hours a day.

One afternoon, after having done one of the last scenes, she fainted on set and that fateful little thread of blood that alarmed all who loved her came out of her mouth again. Dr. Wilson, now severe, prohibited her from working a moment more and, with all the energy of a general in charge, ordered that the artist be transported to Altadena. Meanwhile, Mr. Watson had obtained a house on Boston Avenue, small but surrounded by all the conditions necessary for his daughter to recover her health.

Crying, she said goodbye to her coworkers the next day. When her automobile—the only thing that was left after the bankruptcy—left with her inside, her angled hand thrust out of the window waving the silk handkerchief, there were tears in some eyes. The woman who had had the world at her feet from the proud pedestal of her fame was leaving, perhaps never to return.

CHAPTER X

A NIGHT OF ANGUISH

That terrible night. A night of ruthless delirium, during which the specters of a past more unhappy than guilty paraded in front of the White Moth's eyes in the fertile shadows of her chamber of agony. Three months had passed—three long months—since her move to Altadena, and the outside world seemed to have already forgotten about the woman it had loved madly, the woman who had motivated the making of a carpet with men's hearts, the admiration of the poor and the rich, the yoking of the souls of men to her triumphal carriage. Next to the white bed, a nightstand loaded with little flasks of medicine reminded the poor woman of the danger of an end that was near. Would there be a miracle in the spring of 1926 once the sky was clouded with dark swallows, touching the rosebushes of the orchards with their magic wands to make them erupt in flowers that emitted new fragrances, new illusions, new life? Dr. Wilson had assured them that if Barbara lived to the first spring day on her bed, her heart still beating, life would return lost vigor to her lean flesh, lost brilliance to those beautiful eyes, and the freshness of better days to her parched lips.

Only the compass-like tick-tock of the platinum clock on the nightstand made one believe in the presence of life in that solitude. The entire room was submerged in a shadow of uncertainty and agony, like her heart, like her brain, prisoner of the most horrible hallucinations. In the outer chamber slept the faithful maid, and even farther away, lying in an armchair, Mr. Watson waited his turn to stand guard near the head of the sick woman's bed. Meanwhile, the room filled with visions of the past; the memories of hours of pleasure and of pain ran swiftly by, ceding space to intangible masculine figures that melted into one another as they either laughed or threatened her. There was the figure of Phil Ainsworth again, like a curse, with his striped suit, smiling diabolically; the threatening specter of Bernard Deely, the man who had preceded her in his march toward the unknown, who already knew the secret of the eternal mist, where he perhaps waited to take his wife in his arms again . . .

Then a strong figure erased the fugitive shadows to take possession of her chamber of agony. She half closed her eyes in order to recognize him and was at the point of letting out a shout: It was Jack, Jack Daugherty . . .

But the figure didn't speak or change its position. She observed clearly that it was her own illusion, a product of her feverish delirium, and nevertheless everything suggested that it was him, him . . . Why didn't he clasp her to his chest? She had already forgiven his abandonment, she had sworn that the day he showed up at her side she would take him in her arms as always, with that love that had been, after all, the only real love in her life. In the background of this nebulous vision, she saw the verses that she had written for him in the paroxysm of her love, pulsating in letters of fire:

> . . . I would turn to sink like a slave at his feet,
> to wait the surrender of myself, complete . . .[182]

But the vision, like the other vain shadows, evaporated slowly to give way to a more dismal scene. A man dressed in denim dug in the dirt, dug without rest. At his side was a big pink box, abandoned on the ground on which the grass began to sprout. She was curious to know what it contained, the box that she of course began to recognize because she had seen it before, in her dreams, in the course of her real life . . . She went to open it, cautiously, before the man who was digging, drenched in sweat, would have time to turn his face . . .

Horror! In the bottom of that pink coffin was the figure of a woman whose face was her own face, whose half-closed eyes were hers, whose marble white hands interlaced over her gaunt chest were her own . . .

Finally, the man took the box, and then it wasn't another woman who looked like her, but she herself whom he lowered into the recently dug grave. The man began to shovel soil over the top, and the clumps of dirt made a deafening noise. She wanted to scream but she couldn't, until the sound stopped. Then the man whistled a popular tune and left the grave and her alone, very alone, in that frightening mansion of death. She made a last, huge effort and let out a piercing scream, so horrible that she came to. She was in her bed and at her side the solicitous and loving Mr. Watson asked her, anguished:

"Little girl, little girl . . . what's wrong, my daughter?"

Outside, Hollywood played on in the eternal rush of time, crazy with pleasure and love, like a courtesan in ancient Babylon. In the shadows of the alcove, two souls watched with the same dream, the same hope, eyes toward God. And the spring, that elusive wizard who quiets the mortal gales of winter with its arrival, took a long, long time to arrive . . .

CHAPTER XI

LIKE A VOTIVE LAMP

Thus was extinguished the life that knew all of the joys and pains of pleasure in the world. The unlucky Barbara was consumed slowly, clinging to the last hopes that materialized, only to find her tensed hands clutching at the last outcroppings of the abyss. One day she asked to see her son, kiss him, and hold him in her arms, and Mr. Watson, with his eyes full of tears, wouldn't let this desire be fulfilled. He didn't want the innocent boy to be a victim of the illness that was taking his adoptive mother, who dreamed of a promising future for him. She also had the intention of asking for Jack, but the request always stayed in her head, before her brain gave her tongue the order to formulate it. Meanwhile the winter receded with a cruel slowness.

The twenty-ninth of January, a Thursday, Barbara woke up notably better. The anguish that sat like a huge rock weighing on her gaunt chest had vanished, and she felt the desire to get up and run through the fields, breathing deep breaths of life's perfume. Her maid, overjoyed, went to see Mr. Watson, who slept in the outer chamber.

"Sir," she said, her face illuminated with happiness, "Miss feels really good and wants to get up. Oh, Mr. Watson, thanks be to God, she's been saved . . . !"

The old man felt a shudder run through his body from his feet to his venerable head.

He knew too well that lives, like lights, like the fire of the sun, acquire an extraordinary brilliance, a miraculous intensity, moments before going out forever. Hiding his feelings, he went to see his daughter. She waited for him in her bed, happiness spread out over her countenance, her checks brushed with a light pink, her eyes shining and her lips moist.

"Papa," she said, "God has heard us: I am well . . . well!"

"Thank God," Mr. Watson answered. "Rest now, don't overdo it."

"But I want to go out for a walk . . ."

He looked at her, surprised. Was it possible that their prayers had been heard in the dominion of he who can do all things? He himself, despite what he knew about life, despite his pessimism just a few moments ago, began to doubt. After Barbara's supplications, he sent the chauffeur, diligent and full of joy, to arrange the car, and it was ready within a few moments. Wrapping her completely in her silk clothes, he helped her get in the car, accompanying her and beginning a drive down the boulevard. The news was transmitted to all her friends, and in the studios, where the martyr had left bits of her life, it was the topic of the moment. Everyone considered her recovered. The era of miracles, then, had not disappeared from the universe forever.

From her car, which drove slowly along the boulevards, she took in deep breaths of morning air. Her voice, opaque because of the long illness, soon acquired an extraordinary brilliance, and she began to speak, seized by the greatest happiness:

"Blessed be God," she said. "Now I can take care of my Marvin all of his life. I will raise him to be a man . . . but a man like the man I dreamed of for myself for so long. Then, once I am reestablished, we will go on a voyage to Europe to see those enchanted and marvelous lands once more. We will go to Rome . . . Rome! Such beautiful memories . . . !"

She paused to take a breath, and continued:

"Can you believe, Papa, that I have never felt better? Look, my chest now rises without any effort; I don't feel pain, I don't feel anguish, I don't feel that weakness that was killing me anymore. Now that everything is over, was it true, Papa, that I was very sick? Look: there is the Wrights' house, and then the Murrays'. I see from here the proud residence of Elliott Dexter, crowned with ivy. What exquisite taste that man has! I'll have one like that when we return to Hollywood, Papa, and when Marvin is already going to school. How beautiful life is! But . . .

"Why don't you answer me; why are you crying?"

Mr. Watson made an effort to stop his tears that already peeked out traitorously from his eyes, having overflowed his heart. He then tried to answer but felt a knot in his throat and managed to smile instead, since his face was inexpressive.

She kept speaking crazily, building dreams about the future, creating castles in the air that she herself would destroy in order to build new ones and then more new ones, erected on their ruins. The afternoon began to fade when they returned to the little house in Altadena. They found that the maid had received some telephone calls asking about the newly well woman, and she, very proudly, had answered that "the mistress is now well, that she had been saved, that the illness was now nothing but a silly suggestion, inventions of the doctors to make money." Barbara returned to her alcove, and under the threat of severe punishments they made her lie down. Mr. Watson left for a moment to change his suit in order to put himself again by the side of the poor sick woman's bed.

When he returned, Barbara was terribly pallid. The pink that her cheeks had shown during the day had given way to a horrible earthen color; her lips were dry and her eyes were half closed. The old man shouted, terrified:

"Daughter, my daughter . . . my baby . . . !"

She opened her already glassy eyes, which had that macabre shine that the pupils of consumptives get in their moments of agony. Her lips parted for an instant and three words escaped that mouth that had been the ambition of so many men:

"Jack . . . my son . . . !"

Then, mouth and eyes closed forever. Her coma lasted until the next day, and at four thirty in the afternoon, to the astonishment of her loved ones who didn't believe the end was so near, she took her last breath. Her face sharpened slowly, taking on tones of old marble; her beautiful body got cold little by little, and her soul flew to the unknown regions where the souls of the good go, those who have suffered and loved what she suffered and loved in her life . . .

Five days later a large funeral procession, accompanying that pink coffin that she had dreamed of, passed by Washington Avenue en route to the Hollywood Cemetery, which would be the last stop for her sinful and desired body. At one of the intersections there was a closed car from which a man dressed in black peered out through the windows. When he saw the coffin go by his eyes filled with tears and he cleared his throat in which a repressed sob had formed a knot. His lips opened halfway and he murmured slowly.

"My poor little girl . . . my queen!"

And hiding his face in his hands, he truly broke into tears, with that bitter sob of men whose eyes flood when there is no longer any space in their hearts for so much pain. Some passersby who had seen him through the car windows looked at each other. One of them asked a question that the other answered in a low voice:

"It's Jack Daugherty, the only love of Barbara La Marr . . ."

FIN

Hollywood, 1926

FAME

BY TEODORO TORRES JR.

I don't remember where I read what has always seemed to me the best definition of fame. The writer said that fame is the sun of the dead. In each particular case, we've been able to prove the truth of this admirable synthesis. We can observe it now that the film star Barbara La Marr, whose departure was noted this morning by the newspapers, has just died. The final, painful news of her life has, in a burning flame of admiration and enthusiasm, revived the curiosity of the public that goes to see her in films; that went to see her—until recently—to admire her carnal and tempting beauty, the arousing curves of her body, her voluptuous movements that raised swarms of Spanish flies in unquenchable passion; films that opened young women's eyes, widened in the shadows of the theater upon discovering in the artist, who knew how to perform roles of sinners so marvelously, traces of a love story that the splendid woman had lived in real life; they had gone to see her that night in the cinema with a new feeling, with a slightly morbid curiosity, similar to that which pushes us to the mortuary chamber of a beautiful woman to examine her last gesture and record in our retina the final manifestation of her beauty.

Cinema impresarios had been promoting the name of Barbara La Marr—the romantic invalid of Altadena, the woman who would die for having lived so intensely—in their advertisements for an opening that would take place this Sunday; one that had already caused a stir among the girls who each Sunday inspected the newspapers, not so much to find out how the doomed woman's health was but to see whether, by chance, some indiscreet chronicler had given them a new detail of the erotic tragedy that surrounded her. It was like inspecting "from top to bottom" the bed of the bride, according to the classic and beautiful verse of Cristóbal de Castro.[183] Perhaps the film being announced—the first one they had exhibited since the artist's illness—would give them the key to the story. Maybe her fiery eyes would reveal a new episode in the dramatic life of the new Margarita.[184]

And when all the fashionable young people, the girls who lived for nothing else but to make themselves beautiful and then go to see their "flapper" figures reproduced on screen . . . as they were getting ready to go to their colonia's respective cinema, then came the news that Barbara La Marr had died. Simple curiosity turned into a yearning, aching desire; the theaters filled—they are full at these times—with a sort of funerary committee that had gone to see "the dead one." No one felt very comfortable this time, despite the company of the boyfriend and the friendly environment of the cinemas that invite one to recreation. Because in the middle of the explosions of love, in the middle of the passionate chapters in which the always dashing figure of Barbara La Marr was revealed, a cold breeze blew, chilling the enthusiasm and making her flame crackle—like that of the pillar candles that surround the dead—toward that corner of California where at that precise moment the body of the star, rigid and pallid, exhibited for the last time the remains of a beauty that the illness had smashed to pieces.

Strange spectacle that we witnessed just a few moments ago, one in which, through a miracle of science, we could see the woman who had just died appear as real and present as if she were living flesh, one that rendered the image on the screen that looked at us passionately and emitted a strong sensation of life, of health and youth, that made the news of the night before seem like a lie, an exaggeration of the newspapers!

The girls didn't let loose the singing stream of their voices in laughter. Instead, they whispered fearfully. After perking up a bit at an impressive scene or to comment aloud on some episode, they returned to their meaningful muteness, to their silenced comments that sounded like prayer and supplication.

But there was no triumph bigger in the life of the beautiful artist than that of the night of her death. The cinema owners did a colossal business: people were standing in the walkways of the orchestra seats, obstructing

movement, and in the entrances of the cinema a great multitude waited
their turn to go to see, full of life, the woman who had just died.

The actress must have dreamed of such a triumph many times. She
would have given, we are sure, some of her success as a woman in love for
this moment of supreme glorification in which all eyes turned toward the
victor and all figures were made opaque before the one that implacably
monopolized attention.

And now, as always, the moment of her supreme triumph had also been
the moment of her supreme failure, since it's a failure and a very painful
one to die in full youth and beauty; upon lifting herself to the zenith, the
sun of glory had come to kiss only the suffering face of a woman who was
the incarnation of life, and who was in the end defeated by death.

"Everything comes to us late!" said our Duque Job, intuiting our early
end.[185] Barbara La Marr must have said the same upon learning of her
growing popularity in the bitter days of her illness. During her existence,
as long as it might have been, she would never have obtained a success like
the one that she just had; on the contrary, it's very possible or almost certain
that through the passing of the years her name would have been forgotten
and her figure obscured, like those of so many stars who burn out after a
sorrowful and long languishing. But as she has died, the painful moment of
her disappearance has also been the moment of her consecration.

And luckily the public was not as stingy in paying homage to her as
with others. Don José Echegaray lashed out at the public in one of his
acclaimed dramas, referring to the delayed admiration that enveloped the
author of *Don Quixote* in resplendent glory:

> . . . the subtleties of ingenuity
> would be of no interest
> until three centuries after
> the dead man said them.[186]

In the case of Barbara La Marr, if the homage hadn't taken place "in
the heat of the moment," it would never have taken place. Not all works of
art are destined to last as long as the book of chivalry.[187] The "star" would
be forgotten in the end . . . and it's already a great deal that the sun of her
glory shone, at least while the earth received her beautiful remains . . .

Mexico, January 31, 1926.

THE CITY OF NO RETURN

La ciudad de irás y no volverás: Novela de la vida en Hollywood,
published serially in *La Prensa* (San Antonio, Texas) from
December 19, 1926, to April 21, 1927, and left incomplete

[December 19, 1926]

Mary Pickford's face lit up with that Good Fairy smile that Laura had admired in the films shown in the theaters of her home city. Douglas Fairbanks inclined courteously, offering her his bent arm in a very "Don Q" attitude, and both entered the salon, illuminated like an antechamber of the sun.[188]

Pola Negri and Charlie Chaplin, lazily seated on a sofa, chattered discreetly. Over the gray hair of the magician of laughter, the rays of the "kliegs" broke into a thousand sparks that filled the room with a clarity the day would have envied.

They were in that grand studio that had strange pointed windows through which one could see the immense blue sea, populated with mermaids that from time to time poked out their heads, crowned with flames, only to dive back into the water, making the moon smile over their silvery scales that at times gave off blue sparkles, as if they were illuminated by a violent flame of alcohol.

"Would you like anything else, miss?"

A Nubian slave bowed in front of Laura Cañedo until he touched the silken carpets with the bands of his brown hair. His back glimmered with that shine that only fish have when they are released from the hook; it was divided by a discrete groove that barely signaled his dorsal spine, then cut off brusquely at the waist before the imperious mural of a black leather belt with incrustations of diamonds and topazes. Next to the curved, servile body, on a tray covered with garnets, stood a bottle of Rhine wine; at its side, like an obedient son, shone a cup of pure gold in whose depths, like a drop of blue nectar, was a giant turquoise cut in the form of a tear. That sign of disillusionment had fallen from a pair of light blue eyes, which carried within them much of the sky and the sea and deep water, like the material from which the incomparable eyes of Mae Murray were made.

"No, nothing else for now . . ."

Laura heard her voice almost without recognizing it. She knew she had spoken, because she felt her tongue vibrate between her teeth and heard the intention of a sentence in the interior of her brain, but the voice she heard wasn't hers. It couldn't be hers. It had strange and unknown inflections; it seemed like a coo that passed through a radiographic amplifier without losing the roundness of its tone, but vibrating powerfully like the sound of a bell that rang out overhead.

The slave drew back and disappeared upon reaching some shifting, iridescent curtains, not as if he were hiding behind them, but rather as if he had disappeared softly at the magic spell of a Hindu enchantment. It was then that Laura looked in front of her. Bowing in the gallant greeting of a knight from the times of Louis XIII were three masculine figures dressed in different costumes. Involuntarily, as if someone inside of her being was guiding her movements, Laura made a sign with her hand to the three men, who straightened up smoothly, almost lazily, and advanced without lifting their feet as if moved by one of those escalators that one finds in the modern dime store in the United States. One of them dressed in the suit of a Spanish naval officer with big gold braid on the sleeves, his face adorned by two heavy sideburns that reminded her vaguely of an antique illustration she had seen, a portrait of Méndez Núñez giving orders to his men under the imposing roar of the ship's cannons.[189] The other appeared dressed in a suit from the cover of a French novel: tight velvet breeches and a small capelet that hung from his shoulders. On his feet, two diamond buckles stood out against blue patent leather shoes.

The third straightened up majestically beneath the virile trappings of a Roman prince; around his dreamy head was a white belt over which peeked out the curly mass of his hair.

She recognized them all immediately—and how could she not if she had seen them so frequently on the silver screen—Antonio Moreno, John Gilbert, and Ramon Novarro.[190] They stopped suddenly, two steps away from Laura, and the sailor broke the silence majestically with the tinkle of his silvery voice:

"Miss, you come from lands in which they speak the language they taught me in the happiest days of my life. My motherland, Old Spain, greets you in the name of all her sons, who sought to cushion your path with their bleeding hearts. Greetings!"

The gentleman who resembled the old engraving fixed his two eyes upon her, penetrating and full of passion. Opening his ardent lips, he let the following words escape from them:

"Daughter of the most beautiful land of América. The fire of your eyes has ignited the flames of my heart like a spark; your slave is here, to steal you away, astride the finest white horse, and to defend you with the shining leaf of his sword. Give the command, and your wish will be granted as if you have picked up a prodigious amulet. Your divine lips, nest of kisses and smiles, have the power to give me life or death. Command me, my beauty . . . !"

And the other said simply:

"I greet you, sister. You come from the land that heard my first cries and was brightened with my first smiles. Tell her when you return that I fight for her with all of my soul, that her memory gives me new energy daily to conquer fame, whose reflections will illuminate her flag and lift up her name. Welcome, beautiful Mexicana . . ."

Thus spoke the three idols of the screen. Later, before Laura could explain how, without even trying to explain it, they vanished in plain sight, little by little, like a cinematic image that ended with an artistic "fade out" . . .

All of this seemed marvelous to her. She had arrived just the day before—she remembered it very well—and they were already paying queenly tribute to her. Without knowing how it happened, she was dressed in silver and purple. Her hand held a scepter that she didn't remember having brought, its ends set with diamonds that emitted sparks that almost seemed to release a sound, reflecting powerful lights hidden who knows where. She felt sure she was in a cinema studio but couldn't remember precisely how she got there. She only had a vague notion of having boarded an airplane that had gone up so high that there was a moment that the clouds surrendered submissively at her feet. She had then found herself on this throne, like one who had awakened from an enchanting dream and now contemplated all her favorite stars moving with restraint, as if to the compass of a gallant minuet whose music you couldn't hear. Through the pointed windows she continued seeing the sea, immense and mysterious, splashing at times in brilliant points like a trail of stars, when over its eternal swaying appeared hundreds of mermaids . . .

All of a sudden, a horrible bell rang through the regal room. The lights of the "kliegs" transformed into shadow, and the sea blurred as if a gigantic hand had passed over a fresco that had been painted by mysterious artists. She perceived running, murmurs, jumps in the shadows. The giant bell kept ringing . . .

Laura Cañedo opened her eyes, frightened. The alarm clock that she had put on the decrepit table of a cheap hotel room rang rapidly. Through the window, imperfectly covered with worn-out shades, filtered the calming sun.

[December 26, 1926]

She tried to move but couldn't. Then, closing her eyes, she'd tried to restart the marvelous dream, but the infernal racket of the trolleys that went by on the street beneath her window didn't allow her wish to be fulfilled. She felt tired, exhausted, as if she had come on foot from far away and her legs couldn't hold her up for an instant more.

Faceup on her bed, halfway wrapped in the not very clean sheets, she began to mechanically count the corners of the ceiling, forcing herself to find human forms in the huge stains that indiscreet leaks had left in the stucco. That one had the shape of an old man with a long beard and without eyes. No: better yet, a goat-man, if the stain had been a bit longer in order to form the twisted horns of the cabalistic beast. Scenes from the day before passed cloudily across her captivated imagination: her arrival in the big city whose noise contrasted so rudely with the mystic quiet of her Guadalajara, the charmingly provincial city she'd come from. Later she relived her encounter on the railway platform with a Mexican from whom she asked directions to a cheap hotel: then, the unscrupulous driver raced, passing street after street with her, twisting to the right, then to the left, and later retracing his path via a parallel street. That coming and going had given her the clear impression that he was cheating her vilely, taking her around and around the city, with the goal of having the taximeter mercilessly tabulate a fare that was less than reassuring. The detail reminded her of a story her aunt Valeria would tell her from her travels, in which the wife of a blind friend would lead him around a yard all night to make him think that he had walked a long distance, until they finally took refuge back at their own home in the early hours of the next morning. And how aunt

Valeria liked telling her this tale, which was one of her favorite stories. What would aunt Valeria be doing? Surely Laura's sudden disappearance, briefly explained in a note she left on the dining room table the last night she spent in Guadalajara, had made her aunt very sad. But by now she would have calmed down upon receiving her first letter in which Laura would talk about the imaginary triumphs that would not tarry in bringing the real ones. Later the scenes passed through her mind like a newsreel: the furtive trip to Manzanillo and then the departure from the port toward Mazatlán, aboard an American boat whose captain had been on the verge of derailing her life. After this, a long interlude of irritation opened in her mind in order to jump to the scene of "crossing the line" in Nogales. She remembered the migration officials, a bit crude, asking in broken Spanish about things that surely would have mattered little to them personally but that, following orders, they would need to verify with all the detail of a confessor. Where had she come from, who was she, how much money did she have in her purse, what brought her to the United States . . .

And why did the unfriendly officer with the short mustache, incipient baldness, and glasses with gold hinges smile that way when she said she was going to Hollywood to try her luck in cinema? Did her notable resemblance to Pola Negri go unnoticed? No, that was impossible. That surprising resemblance had been validated by the young women of Guadalajara. They nicknamed her "Madame Dubarry" in remembrance of that eminently tragic Pole who appeared on screen in the role of the unhappy French courtesan.

The thoughts filled her head rapidly, almost without logic, like a fistful of steel springs that would soon vanquish any resistance, each jumping in a different direction with the violence of vertigo. What would they say in Guadalajara about her flight? What new sensations would she encounter in this environment, only known to her for the most part through deceptive magazines that reached even the enchanting city of the west?[191] Would all that they said really come true? What was Rubén doing right now? Surely he'd already gotten up and gone to the office thinking of the pretty fugitive, whom he had dreamed of making his wife. But wouldn't it have been an embarrassment to marry a common bureaucrat when she had this future in the mysterious world of cinema ahead of her? But the future wasn't well defined after all. She didn't know anyone, and the little English she understood, after long months of study and solitary practice, didn't give her much confidence. Bah! You don't have to be a pessimist. How had so many others, unknown like her the day before their glorification, reached the peak? She was willing to fight energetically until she was noticed; success would have no other choice but to smile on her. She already saw herself famous, her image scattered all over the world on rolls of film; her aunt Valeria, smiling through her tears, would show her friends in the cinema:

"That one. That's my girl . . . !"

Putting aside with distaste all the probabilities that could work against her, she now jumped to thinking about what name she would pick once she was in the struggle for celebrity. Hers seemed too pedestrian, too commonplace, to make any impression. She would take a romantic name like Ramon Novarro, like Pola Negri, like Rudolph Valentino. Besides, English doesn't have the letter "ñ" in its alphabet, and the last name Cañedo would be unpronounceable, just as happened with Ramón Samaniego's last name, which became Samanyagos, Samenigos, and God knows how many other absurdities.

Decidedly she would be called . . . What would her name be? Yes: Lyda Mac . . .

No, that name doesn't sound glamorous. Then, Gloria Stella. But . . . Gloria seemed like a servile imitation of the name of the Marquise de La Falaise.[192] She needed something original, new, something that had the phonetic features to make it memorable to the multitudes. Alicia . . . no; there was already an Alice Terry, an Alice Lake, an Alice Joyce . . .

She forced herself to combine letters in the most bizarre manner in her mind. A name would come to her, and she would reject it out of hand to substitute another. What she needed was a pretty [*linda*] combination . . .

Finally!

She spelled the name slowly, letter by letter. But Linda what? She suddenly remembered her mother's name: Valentina Celis.[193] She could twist the last name and adapt it to the Italian pronunciation: Chel-ee, which it surely derived from. Let's see . . .

She spelled the name slowly: L-I-N-D-A C-E-L-L-I. With the prolonged double "l" it had an elegant, chic tone of novelty. She didn't have to go around in circles anymore. Her name would be: Linda Celli.

Not wanting to think about it anymore, lest a new name that might make her reconsider her decision come to mind, Laura jumped out of the bed, which seemed to groan in a cry of pain; the sheets fell from her body, leaving her virginal nudity uncovered, nudity that she was not in a hurry to cover up again. Wasn't putting aside all absurd modesty the first condition for a woman who was fighting for glory? The American girls who looked for opportunities appeared in choruses seminude. Why not her? Since she was little, she had observed that her skin was whiter than one would expect in a criolla.[194] Later, when she was fifteen, she noticed with happiness that her curves had taken on artistic proportions, soft curves that only she had admired in the big mirror of her dressing table. She approached the cloudy mirror of her room, but it offered her a wavy image, horrible like those cursed mirrors in cheap hotel rooms. When she succeeded, she would have magnificent Venetian mirrors, framed in gold . . .

Linda Celli, Linda Celli . . .

While she brushed her short brown hair, she went over her favorite name in silence, stopping each time on the double "l" of her new last name. On the irresistible screen of her mind, letters of fire appeared like the prophetic inscription at the supper of Belshazzar: Linda Celli, the only rival of Pola Negri.[195]

And quickly finishing her hair, she left that room in which she had abandoned the remnants of her old life to give birth to a new one, still unknown and full of romance and adventure.

[January 2, 1927]

The story to date:

Laura Cañedo, a beautiful girl from Guadalajara, has abandoned her homeland in search of fortune in Hollywood's studios. Her friends all assured her that she bore a striking resemblance to the beautiful Pola Negri, and this assurance prompted her to leave Guadalajara in secret to make the voyage. In the first chapter of this story we found her dreaming of success in a cheap hotel on Main Street. That morning she decided to change her given name to a more resonant one; after careful meditation she chose Linda Celli. She left the hotel to make her way to Hollywood in search of Paramount Studios.

Hollywood is the land of beautiful women. Few places in the world could pride themselves on giving the visitor such an impression of youth, enchantment, and happiness that feminine beauties give its boulevards. Blonde heads that are little jewels of gold inset with big dreamy turquoise eyes that emit who knows what ancient spell; androgynous little bodies that move with lascivious twists as they walk, as if they were sliding over the waxed floor of a ballroom; mouths that are like a bleeding wound in the rosy snow of their faces.

From time to time a brunette with ebony hair parted down the middle passes by, provoking in us an involuntary sigh, as if we have suddenly found ourselves in front of one of those vamps created by cinema, whom American films always characterize as the evildoer, a villainess who has a mysterious charm and the obsessive gaze of a cobra for the men who suffer the torment of the Marquise de Freneuse . . . [196]

Laura Cañedo hoped to run into her favorite stars on the street. It seemed to her that turning any ordinary corner she would come face-to-face with Pola Negri's smile or the big agate eyes of Gloria Swanson. Sometimes, walking slowly along Hollywood Boulevard, she thought she recognized a familiar figure in some little blonde who passed alongside her, swaying her hips with the air of one who knows she is admired by the men that walk by. She followed her with her eyes and ended up abandoning her, later telling herself with a little bit of doubt still in her body:

"Bah, she's no one . . ."

When she left the hotel, the day was already well underway. She figured out as best she could which trolley to take to get to Hollywood, and by chance, guided solely by the enthusiasm of her faith in her success, she had headed to the city of her dreams. She found it, there in the depths of her being, less interesting than the mirages presented in stories published in Mexican magazines had led her to believe. She carried in her handbag a little notebook full of the addresses of studios, patiently noted one by one, and she decided to visit Paramount Studios, then still located on Vine Street. Frankly, Hollywood looked like any other town, its streets full of inflated masculine types puffed up by cinematic self-importance. Absorbed in her observation of all these figures that seemed strangely familiar to her, she suddenly found herself on a corner with a blue sign that read in white painted letters: N. VINE STREET.

She felt her heart give a leap. She was finally going to find herself at the gates of those laboratories of fame, where seamstresses were converted into marquises and European adventurers into global idols. She turned nervously to her left.

She didn't walk very far before she discovered, along a block perforated by endless gates without any adornment, a large sign that she recognized from having seen it an infinite number of times on the screen, at the beginning of her favorite films: "Paramount Pictures." Without knowing how, she was already in front of the building where the eternally famous

Marquise de La Falaise and the latest of her "Latin" idols, Ricardo Cortez, had emerged.[197]

Laura felt the distress of a dream realized. Many times, in the warm intimacy of her virginal alcove, she had thought with a delightful curiosity about what she would do when she was in front of the first studio she would visit. But in that moment her heart didn't feel anything extraordinary. Faced with the crystallization of her hopes, brusquely, without any type of struggle, she remembered the philosophical words of the great mystic of Nayarit:

"Okay . . . so what?"[198]

They were only a few seconds of contemplation. She rehearsed a phrase in English in her mind that would open the door of any studio, as a golden key could open the iron gate of a fantastic fairy castle. She thought about it for a few minutes . . . how would she say it? Whom would she ask for permission to penetrate the walled enclosure of that celebrity factory that seemed to offer itself, without resistance, as if ready to receive a visit from anyone, just like churches, libraries, and museums?

She finally found the sentence that would serve as her "open sesame." Practicing it mentally one more time, she approached what seemed like the main gate.

She entered a small office that had the appearance of a prison reception area. A short gate cut off her path, and up against the walls were greasy benches on which folks were packed tightly together and dressed outlandishly as if in a desperate struggle to attract attention. She asked a young man in uniform who passed by with a basket of papers:

"Is this the entrance to the studios?"

This person looked at her for a moment before answering. Then, indifferently, with a completely American naturalness, he exited the door to the street and pointed with his index finger to the left:

"The third door."

And he went back in, without making much of anything of the grateful look that illuminated the eyes of the aspirant, at the same time that her lips moved slightly to pronounce the ritual expression:

"Thank you . . ."

Transported to the threshold of the door he had indicated, Laura suddenly found herself nearly face-to-face with a girl with short, almost masculine hair, who chewed a piece of gum while she read an adventure magazine. In between the two women was a wooden gate with a turnstile that barely reached her waist. In front of this female guard was a little table with various papers and a hand-held telephone. She asked:

"Is this the entrance to the studios?"

The girl laboriously lifted her gaze from the pages of her magazine. With a sharp expression, without stopping her chewing, she answered with another question:

"Who would you like to see?"

Laura had not counted on this new question. As if by the work of a strange spell, the convincing phrase she had practiced in her head faded away. She had counted on an affirmative answer, for which she had prepared an explanation. With the quickness of her criolla intelligence she understood that only if she were going to see a specific person would the doors of the studio open to her. After a few seconds of hesitation she said, with a very natural expression:

"Miss Pola Negri."

"Do you have an appointment with her?"

It was too much. If the first question [was issued] with what seemed an outrageous attitude, the second, also unexpected, was at the point of disconcerting her.

She swallowed and:

"Well, you see," she said finally, "I don't have an appointment with her per se but . . . I'd like to see her about something important."

The telephone girl understood what it was about. So many dreamers called at this gate every day, asking for impossible meetings, that she recognized the situation at first glance. She looked at Laura with a vague expression, as if through fine onion skin, and murmured through her teeth:

"Miss Negri doesn't work today."

And lowering her eyes, she went back to burying her pert nostrils in the cheap romance of her magazine.

"Do you know when I'll be able to see her?"

This time she didn't even lift her eyes. Turning a page in her notebook and chewing her gum more hurriedly, she managed to move her head in a negative gesture.

Laura felt all the weight of her failure over her little brunette head. When she turned around to go out again onto the street, she had the impression that someone had laughed silently behind her back. She didn't hear anything, but she felt the painful twinge of a secret joke. And this humiliated her more than an insult; it discouraged her more than a palpable obstacle, before which at least she had recourse to an intimate explanation—to herself—based on the difference of strength.

[January 9, 1927]

The story to date:

Abandoning the land of her birth, Guadalajara, Laura Cañedo arrived in Hollywood in search of a film career. After a strange dream during the first night of her stay in Los Angeles, she woke up to go to the studio, heading to "Paramount" as a first step. At the gates of that studio she encountered her first difficulty. She left the studio with a heavy heart and for the moment without a fixed destination.

It wasn't until then that she noticed that up against the walls of her new location were wooden benches similar to those she had seen in the previous one. Alone on one of them was a man who looked at her, smiling with one of those stupid smiles we put on in front of strangers who seem friendly, or simply to convey that we have good manners. But the weight of her shame was such that she shifted her gaze and went out without thinking about anything except her failure; that failure that instead of giving her new determination, as was the case for strong souls, had caused a strange discouragement to extend over her being. She experienced the sensation of something very cold that ran through her veins like a drop of mercury . . .

"Miss, miss . . . miss!"

She turned away toward the street, fearful of meeting one of those professional flirts that she knew abounded on the streets of the enchanted city. She saw in front of her a young face, which she quickly identified as the face that had smiled at her at the precise moment of her shame.

"How can I help you . . ."

"Are you Mexican?"

"Yes, sir. Why?"

"Oh, nothing. It gave me so much pleasure to see someone from my country, and since it seemed to me that you are new around here . . ." Laura also felt that calming sensation one experiences when someone speaks to us in our own language, so many miles from our native land. The soft accent of her interlocutor contrasted with the new, slightly disagreeable inflections that she had noted in all of the people who had asked her what she was doing this morning, words coming from faces that were inert, inexpressive, cold . . .

A quick glance was sufficient to tell her that she wasn't talking to a hunter of innocent beauties. The man in front of her was a youth of about twenty, with a fresh and optimistic face that would have looked good on the shoulders of a boy of fourteen. His extraordinarily beautiful and optimistic eyes had an expression of naivete, a little bit out of place in a young man of that age. He didn't wear a hat, and the rays of the midday sun broke over his hair, combed down à la Valentino, giving off sparks like a lacquered helmet. His suit consisted of a blue jacket paired with wide, pearl-gray pants.

"I caught up with you to tell you that they tricked you."

"What?"

"Yes; I saw the countess enter the studio a little while ago."

"The countess?"

"Yes. Pola Negri. You know she is the Countess of Dąmbski . . . or at least she was.[199] Anyway, Miss Negri is working today."

This wasn't news to Laura. Her natural instinct had told her the same thing the moment the telephone operator at Paramount had turned her back on her, but this confirmation made the taste of her failure even more bitter. The young man continued looking at her with his face illuminated by that somewhat childish smile.

"Is it true that you are new to Hollywood?"

"I arrived in Los Angeles last night and today I've come to . . ."

"You've come to look for a job in the movies, no? Your bearing, your manner, everything about you tells me that this is your objective. What's more . . . ," and he paused, looking at her with almost comical attention, "did you know that you look a lot like Pola Negri?"

"Really?"

"Yes, yes. Now that I see you a bit better, you have the same heron eyes; the same expressive mouth, almost the same height . . . Do you have any references?"

The girl shook her head no and her lips spread out in a sad, discouraged smile. She opened them to say almost with fear, with a sweet provincial brevity:

"No . . ."

He clicked his tongue between his teeth two times, with the expression of someone who laments a misfortune.

"I think we are in the same boat," he said. "I came from El Paso with every intention of making my way. Why not just say it? We Latinos are dream chasers.[200] Most of the time we run after hope until we find a grave in our path. And even in that grave, who knows, one might still feel a weak hope. Our cases, from what I see, are the same."

Laura would have liked to prolong the conversation, which she found consoling, but the provincial courtesy of our country girls held her back a bit; accustomed to always seeing a man as the macho lying in wait for an erotic opportunity, and not as a buddy or pal. It seemed incorrect to prolong her chat with this stranger who hadn't even waited to introduce himself before diving into the conversation. He must have read in her big blue eyes the thought passing through her head, because he took a wallet out of his chest pocket and from it a card that he held out to her with a beautiful gesture of courtesy.

"Pardon my forgetfulness. This is my name . . ."

Laura took the card in her long fingers with pink fingernails. In gold italics she read a name and an address:

Raymundo Nava
Hollywood, California

"Thank you very much."

"And yours, miss?"

She vacillated for only a second. Her birth name almost vibrated in her head, but she remembered her resolution that morning.

"Linda Celli," she said with a firmness that surprised her.

"Linda Celli? It sounds like an Italian name . . ."

"It's mine, sir."

"Ah . . ."

The conversation had ended with this exclamation. Now both of them stood on the sidewalk face-to-face, blocking the path of passersby. Raymundo was the first to break the silence.

"Miss Linda," he said with jovial courtesy, "would you permit me to accompany you to the corner? It doesn't look good for me to keep you lingering on the sidewalk."

Laura assented with a smile of goodwill. Her new name, pronounced for the first time by a stranger, produced the effect of a celestial harmony in her ears. It sounded very pretty, infinitely more pretty than her own, and, what's more, she was sure it had made a good impression. He ceded the sidewalk to her and both began to walk toward the boulevard again.

"Yes," she repeated, "Linda," as if wanting to renew the interrupted chat. "I arrived last night, and I am determined to get into the studios. You know more about this than I do. What's your advice?"

"I repeat, we are the grand chasers of hope, but the business doesn't stop being difficult. I've been here for over three months and haven't obtained a thing but hope. Tonight they've promised to introduce me to Ramon Novarro."

She opened her beautiful eyes as wide as she could. She knew Novarro very well through his films but didn't know he was in Hollywood. Deep inside she felt a very human envy toward her fortunate friend in this adventure.

"To Ramon Novarro?"

"Yes, miss. His secretary and I have become friends. But if you knew what suffering, what bitterness, in the face of the smallest opportunity! It's because of this I paused when I saw the woebegone expression on your face. When that horrible blonde girl refused to let you see Miss Negri, I felt strangely drawn to you. I hope I can be of service to you . . ."

She felt as if a door had suddenly opened to the future, filling with light before her eyes. She rapidly calculated that this providential friendship could serve her well in her career, in the career that would later make her famous, just as she'd dreamed. She went so far as to think that Raymundo was nothing less than a heavenly angel that her lucky star had put there to meet her at the beginning of the road . . .

[January 16, 1927]

The story to date:

Abandoning her native land of Guadalajara, Laura Cañedo arrived in Hollywood in search of a career in films. After a strange dream during the first night of her stay in Los Angeles, she woke up to go to the studios, heading to Paramount as a first step. At the gates of that studio she encountered her first difficulty, signaling her failure. She left with a bitter heart and without a fixed destination for the moment.

One of those fast friendships that are born without knowing how, and which are so frequent in our impulsive Latino lives, took root rapidly in her soul, in the same way that you've sometimes seen in educational films, where a tiny plant blooms in an instant until it becomes an enchanting rosebush. Her companion seemed handsome and well intentioned. She resolved to prolong the conversation herself.

"You say that three months ago . . ."

"Yes, three months ago I went around to all the studios in hopes of an opportunity. During this time I've worked as an extra, but no director has noticed me so far. God knows well how hard I've worked but the competition here is fierce. What's more, I've learned that finding your bearings in this profession is a matter of time, patience, and perseverance. Are you going to take your train?"

"I don't know what to do. I will tell you the truth. I didn't come in search of Pola Negri, but rather in search of an opportunity to get into the studios. Crazy—I know—with the remote hope of finding someone to give me a start, some director . . . What do I know! I came ready to see one of the heads of the company and talk to him frankly about my aspirations. So many have succeeded that way! But now that I've met you . . ."

And a blushing smile somewhere between innocent and daring underlined those last words.

To many of my readers this attitude will seem unnatural; they will think that a young Mexican woman brought up in our environment so full of prejudices and conventional modesties would not have been able to enter into conversation so suddenly with the first man she met. But it's because they have not been in a country in which one word of Spanish sounds glorious, because it brings a cherished memory; they have not resolved to embark on a career at any cost, spurred on by a desire for fame that is practically sinful. In the environment in which our story takes place, Laura Cañedo's attitude is perfectly logical and natural.

"I'd love to be helpful to you," he said. "I'd enjoy seeing a compatriot climb the ladder of success, even if only to demonstrate to our people the value of perseverance and faith. Count me among your friends."

"Thank you . . . I hope the same. Eh?"

Raymundo smiled in that way his new acquaintance was beginning to like. It almost seemed that his eyes, beautifully masculine, had watered with the emotion of hope.

"Among my friends, you say? I don't count you among them," and he intentionally emphasized the word *them*, "because I still don't have any; but I will count you as my first . . . and hopefully the only one. If it's not an indiscretion to ask, where are you from?

"Me? From Guadalajara . . ."

"From Guadalajara. My mother was from there. You must know the Camarena family."

"Yes, by name . . ."

Laura began to fear she had risked too much. She was tempted to regret having given her new name to that frank and friendly fellow without disclosing the mystification that he could discover at any given moment. The Cañedos are very well known throughout her native state. With a tranquility that she tried to conserve in her interior, without letting any shadow whatsoever appear on her smiling face, she continued asking questions.

"Have you been there?"

"No, but everything about that blessed land reminds me of my mother, whom I lost about a year ago in El Paso. Allow me to say that you interest me more than ever."[201]

The distance that separated the old Paramount Studios from Hollywood Boulevard was very short. The new friends had arrived at the point where they would surely need to separate. At that precise moment, the train headed to Los Angeles was stopping on the corner with a squeal of the brakes and the gasping puffs of its vapor exhaust. Raymundo, understanding that she needed to take it, murmured:

"So . . ."

"It was a pleasure to meet you, and I hope it won't be the last time . . ."

She offered him her hand, much to her regret. He took it softly, asking her more with his eyes than with his voice:

"Will I see you again soon?"

"Hopefully. I think so. We'll see each other now and then around here unless something happens . . . Goodbye."

But at that precise moment of this goodbye, the trolley began to move again, having closed its automatic doors. When Laura stepped down from the sidewalk onto the road she saw it pulling away and said, with a displeasure that only thinly disguised the happiness in the interior of her being:

"You see that? The train left me . . ."

Raymundo drew on all his gifts as a budding actor to fake deep shame.

"I'm so sorry! I recognize that I am an impertinent charlatan. Now, and only due to this stupidity, you are going to have to wait longer."

She looked at him fixedly, inwardly sympathizing with the confused expression on his face. In order not to mortify him, but in reality with a hidden happiness, with this intuition that is a natural gift of all women without distinction of age or race, she replied:

"It was providence . . ."

"Well said. It was providence . . ."

And with a wide smile, they said something that they would not have been able to explain to each other in a conversation of two hours.

[January 23, 1927]

The story to date:

Abandoning her native Guadalajara, Laura Cañedo arrived in Hollywood in search of a career in cinema. Her extraordinary resemblance to Pola Negri, noted by everyone, made her renounce the comforts of home to embark on this voyage. After a dream she had on her first night in Los Angeles, she woke up to go to the studios in search of an opportunity to ignite her career. She changed her given name to Linda Celli, which seemed more sonorous and cinematic to her. At the gates of the studios she encountered her first difficulty, signaling her failure, and she left with a bitter heart, without a fixed destination for the moment. But right there she met Raymundo Nava, a lively young striver for cinematic glory, and they began a conversation, mutually attracted to each other by a secret affinity. Now, follow the novel:

The trolley incident offered the new friends the opportunity to dare to externalize a desire born of the moment and mutual liking. It had just struck noon, and from everywhere working girls with serpentine walks and young men with a cinematic air rushed to the doors of the cafés: it was "lunch" time. Hollywood in those moments is nothing more or less than all American towns that are subject to the discipline of work. Work stops automatically at the whistle of a turbine or the ringing bell of a wall clock. Everyone hurls themselves out of their offices, their workshops, their studios just as they might if someone shouted "fire." Moments later, lined up in front of a counter that could be a more or less elegant eating spot, they devour their hot food in a rush so as to return to their work half an hour later. From the construction workers—invariably Mexican—who work building sets to the film magnates, everyone recognizes this hectic hour as the time to eat. No matter if appetite is lacking; American life is standard, disciplined, and uniform. Just as in a big barracks the lunch hour is just that and nothing more: the "lunch hour."

Raymundo Nava accompanied Linda—it's time now that we, as she has put it into our heads, call her that too—toward one of the best cafés on the boulevard. Mentally, while both walked on the sidewalk that divided the almost vertical shadow of the buildings, he went over the balance of his small fortune. Twenty, fifty . . . yes, it would cover lunch for both of them, and there would even be, if his calculations weren't wrong, a twenty-five-cent coin to allow him to leave a rarely appreciated tip on the table.

Face-to-face at a small reserved table, Linda and Raymundo each sipped a cup of soup with evident delight, both taking care to make no sound with each spoonful they brought to their mouth. It is so difficult to achieve this elegant silence! Whoever doesn't think so can try it and would have to take great care not to produce, at the moment the hot liquid passes from the spoon to the mouth, this modest and peculiar little sound that has lent itself to so many epigraphs in humorous magazines in the United States.

But they took these precautions mechanically, out of force of habit. Neither one nor the other was actually thinking about the "lunch." Linda, forgetting for the moment her recent defeat, began to feel delighted by the encounter with this likable young man who had won her sympathies almost at first sight. How would their encounter end? Underneath her friend's cover of irreproachable manners, would there exist the satyr, the hunter of beauties that she had seen described so many times in novels? She had begun with innocent and ridiculous stories of Carlota M. Braeme to advance little by little toward the limits of Vargas Vila.[202] The latter captivated her with that strange attraction that morbid things have. At the beginning she didn't know whether to admire or reject with alarm his crude, almost savage, realism. But after her aunt's prohibition, one night when she found her stealthily reading *Flor de Fango*, she ended up deciding to devour all the works she could by the same author. In our rebellious temperament, subconsciously refusing to accept a prohibition with meekness, this fact is not one bit strange.

For his part, Raymundo was only thinking a little bit about his new little friend. Like all worshippers of the goddess of dreams, his entire mind was fixed on the studios, imagining ways to open the gates of those stubbornly walled enclosures to realize a hope that had put down deep roots in his dreaming soul.

When the coffee in thick porcelain cups steamed over the intimate table and the hour of confessions sounded, he pointed out one of the waitresses who passed by his side to Linda, greeting the girl with a slight nod.

"Do you see that girl? That one with the straightened 'boyish' hair, the one that is picking up the dirty plates on the table in the corner . . ."

Linda nodded. She was a woman who could have more naturally worn the silks of a queen than the somber white apron of a waitress. She had deep blue eyes, a blue that produced a remote and involuntarily glacial impression.

But the lines of her face were symmetrical, and the totality of her features could be called beautiful without indulging in hyperbole.

"She's one of the many defeated," continued Raymundo. "I met her three months ago when she, like me, wandered from one studio to another, pushed by hope lit by her craving for fame. A friend of mine introduced me to her. Her name is Betty . . . Betty Clark, if I'm not mistaken.

"Her success seemed very sure when I met her. She spoke of directors and stars with familiarity, calling one and another by their first names alone. Anyone would have said that two months later her name would be shining brightly in incandescent lights over majestic theaters on Broadway. But no one can be sure of anything in this incessant struggle. After fruitless ventures that left the bitterness of disillusion drop by drop in her soul, she lost hope and gave up on immediate glory. She struggled desperately to find a job as a waitress, as a factory worker in Los Angeles, anything that would rescue her finances that I figure must have been in bad shape. Just a week ago she was able to find a spot here, and it seems like her life has normalized. The last time I saw her in the street I confess it gave me a profound feeling of shame. She had on twisted heels, a worn hat, and a dress that despite being scrupulously clean betrayed its age. She told me she had lost several pounds. She was no longer the haughty conqueror sure of the effect that her beauty—I don't deny you she's pretty—would produce in any of the directors the instant they saw her. Now she had a melancholy smile full of kindness. Even the hard expression of her eyes had softened. Now do you see how difficult it is to put yourself on the path of success in this city of disenchantments and the disenchanted?"

"She must be a decent girl," Linda ventured to say, while she discreetly stirred the coffee in her cup in which she dissolved two cubes of sugar, "otherwise . . ."

"I have reasons to think so. And there is one of the thorniest points to deal with in this chat. If you only knew . . ."

"Come on," she said with an encouraging smile, "say it. Between us, comrades, soldiers under the same flag, there's nothing you can't say, especially now that you've taken me in your confidence. What is it that 'if I only knew?'"

She looked deeply into his eyes. Raymundo hesitated an instant. Then, lowering his head as if he were entertained by playing with the German silver teaspoon, he continued:

"It's that, Miss Linda, this place, Hollywood, is full of small tragedies that very few know about. In the field of cinema, disgracefully—and I don't say it to discourage you—with rare exceptions, women who cast aside the social norms of our land are the only ones who succeed. I have not seen even two women, among those who have reached the top, who haven't first endured a painful renunciation of their virtue. Knowing that the most beautiful women in the world come to Hollywood, many times armed only with a divine dream, shielded by their hope and relying only on the blessing of their beauty, a true school of sharks have established themselves here, ready to take advantage of these circumstances. Why say more? You understand . . ."

[January 30, 1927]

The story to date:

Abandoning her native land of Guadalajara, Laura Cañedo arrived in Hollywood in search of a career in films. After a strange dream during the first night of her stay in Los Angeles, she woke up to go to the studios, heading to Paramount as a first step. At the gates of that studio she encountered her first difficulty, which to her signaled failure. She left with a bitter heart and without a fixed destination for the moment.

After a sip of coffee and a drag on his cigarette, Raymundo continued, as if emboldened by the silence of his friend.

"I've told you before that these women only had their beauty and not the talent they might have had. This detail will save you. You have always seemed like an intelligent woman to me . . . No, don't blush. I'm speaking to you from the heart. I don't think a woman of your education faces as many difficulties, but the contest continues to be hazardous.

"Hollywood is an inferno of temptations. Confronted with the spectacle of the fast life, lavish and always gay for more fortunate women, the recent arrival can scarcely avoid suffering the mortal blow of envy. She begins by cloaking herself in her virtue, naturally, but then she realizes how easy it is to wear jewels, a silk dress. It changes, in a strange way, her manner of thinking. On the one hand, the temptation of luxury, a wounded self-esteem, the arrogant looks from those who were once her companions in the struggle—they are everywhere, and she encounters them at every turn. On the other hand, the ever-growing difficulty of getting into the studios and attracting attention, the funds that run out, the disenchantment that begins to take over her soul . . . The woman who does not have extraordinary strength of character is lost. This is the moment that the men I spoke of earlier take advantage of, and they always have the sound judgment to appear when resistance is almost gone. Afterward . . . who knows to what extremes a moment of recklessness might lead?"

Linda sighed deeply. Her friend's last words rang in her ears, like the notes of an organ that linger over the moldings of a church nave once the pipes have finished sounding. "Who knows to what extremes a moment of recklessness might lead?" But she felt strangely fortified by this new friendship, with that affection—why not think it?—that began to grow in her soul. Suddenly, with one of those decisions so frequent among women, decisions that they make almost mechanically without thinking about them for an instant, she seized one of Raymundo's hands with hers and looked him directly in the eyes with an imploring expression:

"You won't leave me . . . right?"

He was surprised by this attitude. That look that beseeched, the fixedness of those almost tear-filled eyes, huge like two big agates, seemed so extraordinary to him that he resisted believing it was true. Recovering his composure, he put his free hand over those of his friend and, making an effort, he let escape these words, almost under his breath:

"No, together we'll risk the same fate. Do you authorize me to defend you if the moment comes?"

Now, Linda didn't respond with her lips, which nonetheless opened halfway into a smile, slight but full of happiness. She nodded her head repeatedly and the jubilant look in her eyes appeared to underline the response. Before that day, it had always seemed that what others called love at first sight was only a silly excuse, a way of explaining the fascination that is so frequently confused with love. Now she felt close to this young man as if by invisible bonds, as if she had known him her entire life. She saw him in front of her with his eyes very wide as if he weren't resigned to believing he was awake. It almost seemed to her that he, contrary to everything she had seen in other cases, had blushed. Raymundo managed to murmur, as if in a state of surprise and hope:

"Linda, Linda . . ."

They slowly unlaced their hands to put them back in their original positions. He rearranged the lapel of his jacket with one of those involuntary movements we use at times when we have nothing to say or when we don't know what else to do. He seemed to recover his serenity and continued:

"Yes, Linda. If you will allow me, I will look out for your safety and endeavor with my own example to provide encouragement for your own success. Until today, I have been alone in my struggle: now we are two people pursuing the same end, not independently, not with an individual hope, but rather two uniting as one. If I succeed, you will also succeed. If we both fail . . . we'll resign ourselves to our fate and . . . only God knows."

He took a breath. Now he felt imprisoned by an overwhelming loquacity. He wanted to say many things that roiled in his head, but he controlled the words before they got to his mouth. Finally, almost in a whisper and as if talking to himself, he continued:

"Do you believe in Destiny? After what has happened today, I'm inclined to believe in it. Just yesterday at this time, nobody could have told me that we would be like this, with a new hope in my heart, with a new dream I'll fight for until the end. This morning I had nothing to do in Hollywood, and to kill time I went to Paramount Studios without any perceivable prospects since I hadn't ever tried again after my first disappointment crossing its threshold. I remember that I felt a strange inclination to go there even though, at least apparently, there was nothing there of interest to me. Several times I mechanically followed Vine Street, and many other times I tried to retrace my steps to find something more productive to do. In the end I told myself, 'Let's see what's attracting me to this place. Tonight, I'll write in my diary about this strange impression I felt, maybe for the first time in my life.' And . . . but tell me with frankness, don't you think we had to meet today?"

"Yes, if I had to speak to you from the heart," responded Linda in the sweetest tone she could muster within the chromatic range of her soothing voice. "I confess that I didn't predict this right now. But after meeting you, it seems to me that I've seen you somewhere else, that your face is familiar. What do I know! In Mexico, I've heard about those whom you so graphically call sharks, and I feared meeting one of them. But from the first glance I felt that I'd be safe with you. If I didn't believe it would be going too far, I would say with complete frankness that I like you very much, but . . . within our upbringing such words are forbidden to a woman."

They looked at each other for a few moments in silence, as if they wanted to say so many things to each other, without daring to do so. Raymundo remembered the trolley incident and the "if God wills" that had given him so much hope. Almost without knowing it, mechanically, he repeated the same little phrase:

"If it's God's will . . ."

A waitress, notebook in hand and shimmying like a leech, came up to the two friends. Focusing a flirtatious gaze on Raymundo, she asked:

"Would you like anything else?"

"No, thank you. Nothing for me . . ."

The girl wrote some numbers in her notebook, tore off the page and gave it to Raymundo with a smile that anyone would have thought promising. Linda felt a little bit uneasy. Who would have thought, with their friendship barely started, tenuous, that she would be jealous? When the waitress withdrew, she followed her with a disdainful stare. Raymundo saw her, divining what passed through his friend's mind with that masculine instinct that exists in such cases. As if she had asked for some sort of explanation, he said in a tone that revealed a timid apology:

"No, I don't know her . . . I've never seen her before."

And they both laughed at the incident while getting up from the table to go out to the boulevard.

[February 6, 1927]

Laura Cañedo arrived in Hollywood in search of an opportunity to start a career in cinema. She abandoned her native land, Guadalajara, to flee to the United States, encouraged by the resemblance to Pola Negri that everyone saw in her and by her very feminine desire for romantic adventures. After a strange dream in the cheap hotel room where she spent her first night, she woke up and went to visit Paramount Studios, where she suffered her first disenchantment. Leaving there inconsolable, she providentially encountered Raymundo Nava, a young Mexican struggling to make it in cinema, just as she was; the two took a mutual liking to each other. After having lunch, they sealed a friendship and resolved to struggle together to conquer fame. Now, follow the novel:

Not all the cinema studios are in Hollywood. Twelve miles away arises Universal City, which is a true emporium of cinematic activity, and no less than six miles away is Culver City, which prides itself on the MGM and Cecil B. DeMille Studios. Even farther still in Burbank, First National has erected the walls of a new city, which would take more work to enter than if it were a fortified stronghold in wartime. It is in huge studios where they make films called "spectaculars," for which they almost always need extras of every type imaginable. You might say that their outskirts have become inhabited by a strange new population from which characteristic traces of nationality have been erased. Malformed dwarves alongside giants who reach seven feet in height, old men with white beards together with unkempt individuals with protruding eyes that one might think just escaped from that Court of Miracles that Victor Hugo speaks of in Notre Dame.[203] Haughty Hindus with the classic turban, Chinese that have adopted Western customs and who speak English bursting with "l"s; patriarchal-looking Russians, Mexicans always ready to risk their lives in adventure films for a miserable pittance. All of these people make their living from cinematic productions . . . Well, at least they try to make their living from them. Directors try to set their scenes with authentic types to the extent possible, and the houses in charge of contracting extras receive orders to hire this or that number of "old salts," of Orientals, of ambiguous types that could pass for Spaniards, South-Americans, or primitive inhabitants of the South Sea Islands. At the time our novel takes place, there hadn't been a demand for Mexicans except in the cheap studios, whose extras, poorly paid and treated even worse, held on to work obtained months before, appearing in all the films and grasping any opportunity that came their way.

Linda had taken up residence in a boardinghouse on Gower Street that Raymundo had recommended to her. There Raymundo had gallantly ceded her his room and moved to another place. From the morning of their first meeting, which she saw as providential, the two friends began seeing each other almost every day, sharing their impressions, giving each other mutual encouragement. The promised meeting with Ramon Novarro never took place due to his sudden departure for Europe, and Raymundo had felt one of his best opportunities to start his career slip away.

She had visited almost all the studios in a week in search of a placement. Soon she realized that in real life the difficulties that compassionate journalists speak of to discourage the hopefuls that go to Hollywood in search of fame are dinner-table chats stripped of all pain, of all the tragedy that the pilgrimages from studio to studio hold for the eternally persevering. In a week she had worn out her best pair of shoes and taken out another pair from her trunk, which was taking the same path as the first. They were all useless trips; sometimes words of hope from those in charge of casting, at other times ruthless insults from those who pursued the same goal and saw in the new aspirant a possible threat. But above all Linda realized something that she had never dreamed of when she saw the future through rose-colored glasses: around the studios there were women so beautiful it was almost supernatural. The proud creole beauty who had boasted about her slight resemblance to Pola Negri, those facial characteristics that she had always considered winning in the moment they were mentioned, seemed ridiculous next to the beauty of all the aspirants, as unfortunate as her, as ambitious and full of dreams as the rest of the young women who struggle to find the door to fame.

That night Linda had gone to bed very late, beginning to worry about the state of her finances. She saw clearly that if a golden opportunity didn't present itself, she could only live for a month and only by producing economic miracles. She washed her underclothes herself, holding on to religiously pay the miserable pension that she had arranged for her room and three meals in the boardinghouse that were more illusory than real. She dreamed for the first time since she'd been in the United States of her dear aunt Valeria and her friends in tranquil Guadalajara. She dreamed that she had become famous, dripping with diamonds, wrapped in furs, and at the station a group of gentlemen she had never seen before were there to greet her, all of them wearing silk hats; a band played a favorite tune . . . What song was it? As much as she tried to remember it the next morning, she could never reconstruct its triumphant beats. She went to hug her aunt, whom she had seen on the platform with tears in her eyes, when she woke up . . .

Someone knocked on the door. Through the window, curtains filtered the rays of the pure California sun, which seemed to shine with more happiness in those skies than in those that cover other, less fortunate regions.

They told her through the half-open door that Raymundo was on the phone. She jumped out of bed, wrapped in a dressing gown. She put on some embroidered Chinese slippers and went out into the hallway where the phone was. When she got close to it, Raymundo's voice could be heard on the other end:

"Is that you, Linda?"

"Yes, go ahead . . ."

"If you can, get ready quickly and let's meet at eight in front of MGM Studios. You know, in Culver City. Remember that building we visited on Friday? I am going to work, and I've arranged for them to contract you too in the cast of extras, possibly for three days. Anyway, I'll tell you all about it, if you can come, that is . . ."

Linda felt her heart palpitating with a threatening violence. She was finally going to see the inside of a studio, to test her abilities as an actress. She felt her blood rise. Maybe a director would notice her . . . and . . .

She hung up the receiver with a hurried "Thank you. I'll be there in a bit" and began to get dressed. She was nervous. It seemed to her that her face wasn't made up well; she brushed a bit of powder over her cheeks more than twenty times, and she wiped her eyes to redo them no less than ten times. She chose the best dress in her collection, and later, after six or seven consultations in the slightly dishonest mirror in her room, she left the house without accepting the breakfast that the good "landlady" offered her.

At last! She felt buoyed by more enthusiasm than she had on that first morning when she traveled from Los Angeles to Hollywood. Now she wasn't just trying her luck: Raymundo had perhaps taken charge of finding her a true opportunity to act in front of the cameras, and he had modestly hidden the magnitude of the occasion to give her a surprise. It probably wouldn't be like that, but "who knows?" During the voyage she gave a "dime" instead of a penny to the bus driver and stepped on various ladies who were on board. She was surprised now and then before the curious looks of some little boys who rode in front of her and then noticed that she was laughing without knowing at what, almost speaking out loud as if she were rehearsing something she had to say later.

She found Raymundo in front of the big entrance full of columns at MGM Studios. Her first question, after nervously shaking his hand was:

"Am I okay?"

"You are always okay, Linda. Did you already eat breakfast?"

"Why?"

"There's time for you to eat if you want to. The others won't arrive for another twenty minutes . . ."

(To be continued . . .)

[February 20, 1927]

The story to date:

Laura Cañedo arrived in Hollywood in search of an opportunity to start a career in cinema. She abandoned her native land, Guadalajara, to flee to the United States, encouraged by the resemblance to Pola Negri that everyone saw in her and by her very feminine desire for romantic adventures. After a strange dream in the cheap hotel room where she spent her first night, she woke up and went to visit Paramount Studios, where she suffered her first disenchantment. Leaving there inconsolable, she providentially encountered Raymundo Nava, a young Mexican struggling to make it in cinema, just as she was; the two took a mutual liking to each other. After having lunch, they sealed a friendship and resolved to struggle together to conquer fame. One day, at last, Raymundo called her at her boardinghouse to invite her to take part as an extra in a film with him. She accepted, and they met each other at the gates of MGM Studies. Now the story continues . . .

In front of one of those small counters in American cafés that demonstrate so clearly the hectic lives of these people, Linda ate breakfast hurriedly. Raymundo, tranquilly smoking a cigarette at her side, contemplated her with pleasure. Never had she been more deserving of the name she chose that uncertain morning in her Los Angeles hotel room. Linda, yes, in both name and appearance; the agate, almost Slavic, almonds of her eyes, with almost straight eyebrows that pointed a little upward like Cleopatra's, moving as if a head full of contrary thoughts boiled behind them. She ate without worrying about how she looked, and in all her sublime animality she was even more beautiful than under the affectation of social norms. Raymundo looked at her from the side, anxiously surveying everything that the little hat with short feathers and discreet furs of her coat left uncovered. The tip of a little ear that you might call pink peeked out beneath the curly mass of her recently cut hair. Then, a bit lower, the allure of a tempting alabaster neck was lost in the fur of her coat. She was, decidedly, more beautiful than ever . . . or so it seemed to Raymundo. Unconsciously, incapable of controlling his enthusiasm, he whispered:

"How beautiful you are . . ."

But Linda, lost in her thoughts before the unknown that could decide her fate, didn't hear the "compliment." She thought . . . What did she know about what she thought? In an instant of uncertainty about the future she constructed a vision of success and later the voluptuous caress of a dreamed-of popularity. Rapidly, images of Raymundo, her aunt, the absent boyfriend already half forgotten, and descriptions of the studios that she had seen in magazines from Los Angeles and New York City mingled in her head. She drank her coffee without sugar, and it wasn't until the last mouthful that she discovered why it tasted bad from the beginning, vaguely, as if she were still under the influence of last night's dream. Raymundo kept watching her, being careful not to give free rein to his impulses or he would have kissed her right there. Finishing, she wiped her divine little mouth with a paper napkin and, turning toward her friend, said simply:

"I'm ready."

Without another word they walked toward the studio entrance where a group of extras waited for them, while a strange-looking individual, rather poorly dressed and with hair almost down to his shoulders, called them from a list. When he saw them arrive, he turned to Raymundo to ask:

"That's your friend?"

Raymundo replied with an introduction to which the other paid no attention. Eventually the group made its way to a small gate to the left of the main one, and they all entered the studios in silence. Meanwhile, the man with the long hair kept count in front of the gate, the same way one would count a herd of cattle entering or exiting a corral.

Once inside the premises, the women were separated from the men and Linda said goodbye to Raymundo with an affectionate look. They put her in a room in which there were lots of wrinkled dresses and various used hats piled up on the small, dirty counter. She was to put these on for the scene that they had to perform that would be in a film whose name none of her companions—all American—could tell her. To Linda all of this seemed very curious. She got dressed with everyone else and then she looked at herself in the mirror.

She was transformed into a prostitute of the slums, one of those women who abound in second-rate nightclubs in some parts of Europe. They gave her some paper flowers so that she could put them in her hair, and they went out again toward the "stage" that had been built in the middle of a patio with green lawns, with the grass cut two inches from the ground. Next to the shack with a glass roof were some others, seemingly silent on the outside, but within which stirred multitudes shooting single scenes from different films.

It was there on the "sets" that she and Raymundo met again. The scenery represented a criminal underworld café in Paris, according to the absurd directors of American films. A counter full of utilitarian bottles, various dirty wood tables with rough and mismatched wooden chairs next to them. She barely recognized her friend. Raymundo had transformed into a figure that could have come out of those illustrations that adorn the covers of Ponson du Terrail novels.[204] He wore the huge cap of an Apache, locks of hair peeking out from underneath it and next to his ears, falling halfway down his face. A black scarf covered his neck and its corners fell over a checked shirt. His eyebrows had been amplified to join over his nose with a touch of makeup, and over his always clean-shaven lips he had placed a small crooked mustache that barely underlined the base of his nose. If it weren't for his friendly smile, she would have had to work to identify him. He asked her:

"What do you think?"

She smiled dumbly, answering with a light shrug of her shoulders.

"Look at how they've done me up . . ."

"Okay. You never dreamed of seeing yourself ever dressed like this. But that's not even half of it. I've played, as an extra, the part of a diver, Indian, Black, and God knows how many other parts. They've thrown me twenty times from horses in scenes from cowboy movies: I even remember having played the part of a Chinese . . . and, well, my type is not the best for that role. Don't give up; the day will come when you can dress as a countess or something more dignified than this. At least you got a job, you can be sure."

She shrugged her shoulders again.

"What else can you do?" she said.

They handed out cigarettes, as they had to be constantly smoking and the place was supposed to be full of smoke. The electricians arranged the lights, swearing now and then in a low voice, and an individual wearing golf pants, in shirtsleeves with a visor over his eyes, gave orders to others who listened with servile attention.

"That's the director," said Raymundo.

To Linda the preparations seemed interminable. Two hours passed like this, without the scene being formalized. Later, when it seemed that everything was ready, the director turned to the multitude to explain what each person needed to do. Luckily for our friend, Raymundo arranged for them to place her at his side so he could dance with her at the right moment. It was just as well like that. They rehearsed a few times without the cameras on. For this or that reason, the director scratched his head and at times seemed ready to say something offensive when one of the extras hadn't followed his orders to the letter. This struck Linda as a type of crudeness that she didn't expect to find in a man of his appearance, which suggested a certain education. Another hour passed like that.

The nervous tension was discouraging. When were these people going to begin shooting? Linda didn't know that in every studio and in all cases, there are times when you work all day to shoot just one of those scenes that passes on the screen without interruption, one after the other, within a few minutes. She had a very different idea of how they made films, but as she didn't see any of her companions showing signs of impatience, rather only an Olympian indifference, she didn't dare protest to her friend.

At last they filmed the scene. In total, two parts of a foxtrot danced by some couples, a bottle that flew through the air, and everyone running, looking for refuge somewhere. At the end of this the assistants to the director said to the crowds:

"All right, that's all for today."

It was exactly time for lunch, which this time was eaten by the two friends in the studio's own cafeteria, which was outfitted with all the little necessities of life. Inside the MGM Studios was a barbershop, a shoeshine stand, a restaurant, and so on. Linda and Raymundo sat in front of the counter dressed as they were.

"But that's it?" she said.

He answered with a nod of his head.

"And what's worse," he added, "is that we won't act in that film again. I've told you that sometimes you have to wait a month to find another opportunity. But don't be discouraged. Didn't we agree that we would struggle together, come what may, until we conquer fame or death ends all our hopes . . . ?"

She grasped Raymundo's manly hands in hers.

"You are so good," was all she said in response.

[February 27, 1927]

After abandoning those rags to put their street clothes on again, the two friends left the studio. An elegantly dressed individual approached Raymundo, smiling at him with an expression that would have made anyone feel honored. He was a man about forty years old, on the thin side, and with an, oh, I don't know, aristocratic air that produced the impression of a vulgar feminization. He wore a blazer, and under the bell of his impeccably cut pants peeked the gray notes of a spat like a bridge between the fabric and the dazzling patent leather of his shoes. Leaning forward with a servile Parisian gesture, he extended his hand to the young Mexican:

"My dear friend! What are you doing now?"

Raymundo vaguely remembered that this person had been introduced to him as someone with a lot of influence in the publicity office of one of the studios. At that time he was running an office that he had established in Los Angeles, apparently to furnish new actors, new faces as he said, to film directors. His name was . . . What was his name? An entire list of names spun in the young man's head with the hallucination of a carousel before he could shake the hand that was offered to him and say waveringly:

"Oh, how are you Mr. . . . Mr. . . ."

"Sharkey. Frank Sharkey. Have you forgotten me so quickly?"

Raymundo told him what he'd just finished doing and this or that other triviality. Meanwhile, Linda observed the recent arrival with a woman's penetrating look. Suddenly Raymundo said:

"How absentminded I am. I forgot to introduce you. Mr. Sharkey . . . Miss Linda Celli."

The gentleman leaned over in a gesture of courtesy that revealed his incipient baldness (in the manner of a tonsure) that adorned his head [*illegible*] with great care. Linda extended her hand with a sociable smile, that is to say, in the friendliest way she could:

"It's a pleasure to meet you . . ."

"The young lady works in the cinema?" he asked Raymundo with a gesture of feigned surprise. "Gloria Swanson and Pola Negri better be careful. How are they treating you in the studios, miss?"

Linda blushed underneath the layer of rouge that discreetly covered her cheeks.

"Not so much, surely, Mr. Sharkey. I am a mere striver. Nothing more than that . . ."

"Well . . ." and he stood looking at her fixedly, half closing his small blue eyes, "did you know that you have a beautiful future ahead of you? If I had met you a week ago, when they requested a new starlet for the Hollywood Studios, we would have both made a fortune. Exactly your type was what they required. Yes, exactly those eyes, those facial contours, that profile, that height. But where have you been, Nava, my friend, that you haven't come to see me with your little friend? This is something neither she nor I will ever excuse . . ."

Raymundo apologized as best he could. Frankly, he didn't initially remember this person who from the start had produced a bad impression. But now he thought, even if I had remembered, it would not have been good to bring Linda to his office. In his eyes, even though he had no reason to affirm this suspicion, Mr. Sharkey was one of those "sharks" that he had told Linda about in their first conversation. Sharkey went on, rubbing his hands together and looking at the young Mexican woman from head to toe, more with the air of someone reviewing a head of cattle than that of someone trying to find the artistic side of a woman.

"Miss Celli," he said at last, "it's never late when you get off to a good start. You and I need to be in continuous contact. Here is my card, so that

you can come to see me when you want and I'm sure that we'll make . . .
I mean you'll make a lot of money, if you follow my advice. Have you
heard of Ethel Romer? Of Viola Lee? And the gorgeous Mary Sullivan?
Well, all of those ladies would give anything to have your qualities. Their
success is completely due to what I have done for them, if that wouldn't
be an immodesty on my part. Now they are actresses of renown and are
on the path to being true stars. And a year ago . . . Bah! A year ago, they
were nothing but poor strivers who had lost all hope and were at the point
of taking desperate measures, as you will have heard said about those who
cannot succeed as quickly as they'd like, as they'd dreamed. But you, oh
you, you are very different . . ."

He held out an elegant card to her on which she read in raised letters
in brilliant blue ink:

Mr. Frank Sharkey
Ambition Building. Hollywood Boulevard.

During all this time Raymundo had not said a word. Linda promised
to go see that angel savior who had appeared so unexpectedly in her path,
two days later. Still saying goodbye, Mr. Sharkey bowed with a servile
gesture and advised her:

"Don't forget to come. I'll be waiting for you; your future is going to
depend on this visit. Don't forget."

And turning around, he entered the studio gates while Linda and
Raymundo went down to the sidewalk.

They walked together to the bus that waited nearby and on which
many of the extras who took part in the morning's scene had taken seats.
At last Linda broke the silence to ask Raymundo, looking him in the eye
forthrightly, almost lovingly:

"What do you think I should do?"

He shrugged his shoulders. Later he responded with a little bit
of hesitation:

"Well . . . I don't know. The truth is that when it comes to success one
shouldn't pass up a single opportunity, but . . . in the end . . ."

"Do you think it could be dangerous?"

"No, for you, no. But it seems to me you should be very careful. I
don't know why, but that Mr. Sharkey doesn't inspire a lot of confidence,
you might say."

She moved her head sweetly.

"Apprehensions, Raymundo. There is something inside of me that tells me that I'm on an unmistakable path."

And both remained silent, meditating on different topics, but all of them related to the visit arranged for two days hence. When they separated, she carried in her body the presentiment that her future was made. He could not contain a sigh as he said goodbye to her.

[March 6, 1927]

The story to date:

Laura Cañedo came to Hollywood in search of an opportunity in the cinema, abandoning Guadalajara, her homeland. After a strange dream during her first night in Los Angeles, she got up to go to Paramount Studios, where she suffered her first disappointment. Leaving disconsolate, she providentially encountered a young Mexican man, a striver like her, Raymundo Nava. They liked each other. After having lunch, they sealed their friendship and resolved to struggle together to conquer fame. One day, at last, Raymundo called her at the house where she was living to invite her to take part in a film being made at MGM Studios. When they left the studios, she disheartened by work as an extra and he regretting having brought her there, they ran into an American, Mr. Sharkey. Astonished by the young lady's beauty, he invited her to his office to "carve out her future." She hesitated a bit, but the ambition to be famous is great and . . .

But continue with the novel:

The days pass rapidly for those who are enveloped within their personal idea of happiness. But for someone who is waiting, with that anxiety of youth, for the opportunity to succeed in life, for the first spark that may ignite a bonfire of fame, two days are two eternities. Linda Celli spent the next forty-eight hours gripped by a terrible agitation. Would she go see Mr. Sharkey, on whose goodwill an enviable future could depend, or would she pay heed to Raymundo's warnings? After all, nothing had proven to her that Sharkey wasn't an honorable man. She dared to think that it was jealousy, Raymundo's stupid and irrational jealousy, that had made him think that behind the American's friendly manner was hidden the typical "shark" he had spoken of the day of their providential meeting. What's more, wasn't she sufficiently intelligent, sufficiently grown up to protect herself against any male trickery? Mr. Sharkey had done nothing but offer her disinterested help . . . or rather, he offered to make a business deal with her in which they both could make a small fortune. She remembered an infinity of cases she knew of in which the dumb jealousy of a man and a woman's affection for him had been the reason a career had been cut off forever. She herself, hadn't she abandoned her home, her Guadalajara, dearer now than ever, her aunt, her boyfriend, to run in pursuit of fame? Bah!

She leaped from her bed, where she had surrendered to the previous reflections. It was exactly fifteen minutes before the hour of the appointment with Sharkey and she was still in her slippers with no makeup on her face. She wrapped her exuberant form—she had gained a little bit of weight in the past few days—in a simple silk robe. She went into the bathroom and came out five minutes later. Once she had dressed and carefully made up her face, with that flirtation so natural to women, she grabbed Sharkey's card and went out to the street in search of the Ambition Building.

Now [she was within] the four walls, crowded with portraits of cinema artists, that made up Frank Sharkey's main office. Wedged inside the cushioned easy chair as if she were encased, Linda waited nervously for her providential protector to appear. Upon entering they had told her that he was not in the office at the moment but had relayed orders to welcome her and ask her to wait a few minutes. Linda passed her gaze vaguely over the portraits on the walls. There were some that seemed a bit daring: artists without tights, others in attitudes that seemed more like classical "poses" for a pagan frieze; here and there a loving dedication to Frank. Later, over the desk chair, an artistic enlargement of a portrait of a pretty woman. Over the glass top of the work desk was also a small portrait of a young girl. Everywhere women, women, nothing but women . . .

Unfamiliar with these women, whom she supposed were artists, Linda convinced herself that they had been discovered on the street, as she had, by the prodigious scout who had later lifted them to fame. She imagined her own portrait, pictured in one of the works whose interpretation she had been entrusted with, later added to the others on the same wall, now as a star, a testament to her discoverer's ability as a publicist.

She heard footsteps outside the office and with an instinctive movement, Linda took a tiny speck of powder and passed it discreetly over her nose. Looking at herself quickly in the little mirror of her "vanity case," she returned her legs, which had been crossed, to their normal position and waited, feeling her heart give tremendous leaps, threatening to jump out of her chest. The door squeaked like a groan and Mr. Sharkey entered the office, rubbing his hands together while over his faun-like face was drawn a smile that tried to appear friendly.

"What a pleasant surprise! Have I kept you waiting long?"

Linda said no with her best smile. Mr. Sharkey came to shake her hand and brought it discreetly to his lips before she could do something to impede this extemporaneous gesture of courtesy. He noted that the greeting seemed a bit familiar and, settling into a chair, explained:

"I beg your pardon if you didn't expect that kiss of your hand. It's a continental custom, learned in Europe . . . I suppose I haven't hurt you by it."

Linda felt embarrassed by her first thoughts. She thanked God she hadn't let herself draw back her hand from the caress of those slightly withered lips; what a rube Mr. Sharkey would have thought she was if she had done so. He leaned against the back of his armchair a bit and, resting his elbows on the arms of the chair, put his palms together in an almost religious gesture. Then slowly he spoke:

"I don't know if you came with your mind made up about what we talked about, Miss Celli, but before we get into that subject, I will tell you that I am sure that your future depends on this conversation. Many beautiful women have come to this office, first a bit timid and later more hopeful, in search of the celebrity you have ambitions toward now. Some have sat in the same chair that you occupy, and now . . ."

He pointed with a long, aristocratic finger at the diverse portraits that adorned the walls.

"Now," he continued, "all of them are grateful for the little that I could do. With you, however, the case is different . . ."

Linda straightened up in her chair, a bit alarmed.

"Do you think that I can't . . ." she began to say.

He interrupted her with a sweet smile, halfway closing his eyes and moving his head rhythmically from right to left.

"You haven't understood me," he said in a soft voice. "With you it's different because you have more than half the road traveled. They were beautiful and full of aspirations. You are simply enchanting."

Linda calmed down a bit. Sharkey continued, watching her with those small, penetrating, reptilian eyes without abandoning his ecclesiastic position. When he saw the effect that his words produced, he continued, slowly softening his voice until it seemed like a murmur:

"You will accomplish a lot in the cinema. But you mustn't forget that the beginning is difficult and that the road is full of sacrifices that are necessary, but not for that less painful. Many women have retreated from them, perhaps because of a silly instance of impetuousness, and have lamented the consequences later. When they exit through this door, I never let them enter again . . ."

The telephone rang stridently. Mr. Sharkey interrupted to lift the receiver:

"Hello!"

. . .

"Oh, Cecil, how are you?"

. . .

"Unfortunately, I can't. I have an appointment with the governor of California, who has begged me to dine with him. Maybe another day . . ."

. . .

"I swear, I can't, Cecil. Oh, yes. Right now I have a young Mexican woman here, ideal for the starring role you've been looking for these past few days. She will have a great future . . ."

. . .

"Don't worry about it. I appreciate your confidence. You know that the people I recommend show up. How much can this young lady earn?"

. . .

"That doesn't seem like very much. She is a woman of great talent—simply a star in the making. Could you go as high as $2,500 a week?"

[March 13, 1927]

The story to date:

Laura Cañedo came to Hollywood, abandoning her native land of Guadalajara, in search of an opportunity to make her way in the field of cinema. After a strange dream the first night of her stay in Los Angeles, she got up, resolved to present herself at the studios, first having changed her name to Linda Celli. At Paramount Studios, after her first disappointment, she met Raymundo Nava, a striver like her, and they immediately liked each other, resolving to struggle together to open a path to Fame. One day, after having achieved her first opportunity to work as an extra at MGM, she met an American publicist, Mr. Sharkey, who was struck by her beauty and made an appointment with her at his office to give her an opportunity to ensure her future. Raymundo warned her about this individual, whom he distrusted, but she overcame her repugnance and went to see Sharkey two days later. She was speaking to him when Sharkey received a telephone call from a famous director to whom he proposed his new discovery. When everything seemed to have been arranged satisfactorily . . . But continue with the story:

There was a long silence during which Mr. Sharkey seemed to listen very intently, inclining his head frequently as a sign of approval. Linda waited with an indescribable anxiety. Nothing less than her future success, the opportunity of her life, was in play at that precise moment. Finally, Sharkey spoke.

"Sounds good," he said. "I don't think I have any objection. Two thousand two hundred dollars weekly, to start, and then progressive increases . . . When can we come to see you, my friend?"

. . .

"Aha, yes. Bye . . ."

He hung up the receiver with a care that made it seem like he was afraid of breaking it. Then, letting out a sigh of satisfaction, he looked squarely at the girl to tell her with that honeyed smile of a few minutes ago:

"You are as fortunate as you are beautiful. My friend, the great director Cecil Brown, has agreed to contract you for $2,200 dollars a week. What do you think of my goodwill toward you?"

Linda did not know how to respond, overwhelmed by emotion. She didn't have time to focus on the name Cecil Brown, which was unknown to her and probably the entire world. The idea of success overwhelmed her; she felt herself drowning amid glory. Finally, feeling that she was blushing to the tips of her fingernails, she could only say:

"Oh, thank you, thank you . . ."

Sharkey got up slowly from his seat and moved closer to her, slowly, as if he were afraid of making noise and awakening her from her dream of happiness. Before Linda realized it, he was already at her side, grabbing her chin with one hand and throwing his right arm around her neck.

"Your future is assured, my dear," he said with that same soft and intoxicating expression, "but now we have to talk a little about my conditions. You said you were ready for anything, isn't that right?"[205]

Too late, the girl began to understand what had been behind that apparent favor. Violently, without her being able to stop him, Sharkey kissed her on the mouth, filling her with the nauseating stench of burned tobacco. She made a supreme effort and stood up, trembling with indignation.

"Mr. Sharkey," she said in a tremulous voice, "what does this mean?"

He maintained the glittering gaze of his agate eyes that seemed to get bigger with surprise and anger. Retreating three steps, he fixed the lapels of his jacket and answered:

"Remember that your future is in my hands. All those women that you see there have succeeded because of me, and you can count yourself among them if you want. Those who have been silly, as it seems you want to be now, have left through these doors never to return again. On the other hand, I am a discreet man and no one else besides us will know about our intimacy. What do you say to that?"

"I say that you are a scoundrel. The women of my race prefer poverty to dishonor. You are completely mistaken, Mr. Sharkey, and I warn you that if you persist in this attitude, I will call out or throw myself out of this window. Goodbye."

She turned around to try to exit the room, but he grabbed her with a strong arm, so strong that he hurt her. When she turned her face, all appearances of the false goodness had disappeared. Sharkey looked at her with those flashing eyes, and even the tone of his voice had become forceful. In a distressed voice he said quickly:

"I warn you that if you leave here, you will never come back, ever. In turn, if you reflect on this tacit proposition, you will have everything: happiness, money, fame, prestige. I have a chalet in Beverly Hills at your disposal for our improvised 'honeymoon.' When after a month you've tired of me, you can begin to work, and we will never remember this. I am a man of my word and I keep my promises until the end. For the last time, what do you say to this?"

Linda couldn't find words to express her anger. With a rapid movement she unloaded a slap on the libertine's cheek and got free of his clutches, leaving a shred of her silk blouse in Sharkey's fingers. He recovered a bit, and before Linda could get to the door he began to talk in the same sweet tone that he had used before that insolent proposition:

"You are truly interesting. I've told you that no woman who has rejected me has come back to see me ever, but as I think your Latin temperament is impulsive, I will give you another chance. When you have thought about your future, when you have meditated serenely about what you risk by rejecting such a small thing as what I am asking of you—to lose a whole career full of riches—you can come to see me. I will always be ready to receive you. I'll see you soon, Linda . . ."

She had reached the door already, but she could hear all of the satyr's words. With a violent bang the door closed, and she rushed through the gallery that contained the elevator. Within five minutes she was again on the boulevard.

Upon arriving at her room Linda found a carefully folded paper underneath the door. She opened it nervously and read with frightened eyes an "ultimatum" from her "landlady," giving her a deadline of that week to pay her rent, which she had failed to pay for the last two weeks. She put the paper on the table and, opening her handbag, took out her checkbook, leafing through the receipts to make sure of the amount that was left.

She was at the point of screaming, as women do in novels when they've suffered a tragic surprise. Of the amount she had deposited in a Hollywood bank when she arrived in the enchanted city, there were only five and a half dollars in her favor. The single room alone cost twenty . . .

From that moment her martyrdom began. She undressed mechanically, and then, latching the bolt on the door of her room, she threw herself on the bed, unable to contain her tears so much so that contrary thoughts roiled in her head, torturing her mercilessly. Why had she made that gesture of modesty in such dangerous moments? Was she sure that she wouldn't regret her attitude later? The idea that she was alone there, without a friend besides Raymundo, who was as poor as she was; that she didn't have a roof to shelter under; that in the end she might not have another road to pursue other than that degrading but productive option, made ice run through her veins. The evening found her still crying, half thrown across her bed, tired as if she had walked all day, thirsty, her spirit exhausted from disillusion. When a little bit after seven they knocked on her door to ask if she would come down to dinner, she responded in a hoarse voice, straightening up over the brilliant white bedspread but without getting near to the closed door:

"Not tonight. I don't feel well . . ."

She heard the slow fading away of her landlady's steps, without an insistent entreaty, without the least effort to investigate what happened in her heart. She felt even more alone, even more full of that bitter pain that had been making tears flow from her divine eyes all afternoon as if the spring of her sobs had no bottom . . .

Her night was one of insomnia and horror. Close to twelve, she got up slowly, taking off her clothes to put on her silk pajamas, one of the vestiges of her previous wealth. In between the sheets, she kept thinking, thinking . . .

Why did she leave her land and with it all the comforts of her home, modest, but always vigilant about her tiniest necessities? How true was all that she had read about the city of disenchantments and its small, intimate tragedies: of the bitter cries that the fanfare of the triumphant never allowed to be heard outside of that place that was mysterious to some, full of bitterness for others, and loved by all!

She had finally fallen asleep when the light of day filtered through the curtains. She dreamed of Guadalajara again but without remembering, any more than she would a nightmare, the dark hours she had passed far from there. Her aunt Valeria had come to wake her to announce that the chocolate was ready, waiting for her on the brilliant white table. She found a bunch of roses that her distant boyfriend had sent very early with a messenger. Yes, it seemed that she had dreamed everything, that Mr. Sharkey had been nothing but a horrifying nightmare. Life smiled on her again and she forced herself to breathe, to fill her lungs with the fresh and life-giving air of spring.

[March 20, 1927]

It was already very late when Linda left the bed, entering the bathroom to refresh her bronze flesh. She got dressed quickly and went out of the house without knowing where she was going. She needed air, distraction, something that would make her forget the tragedy that she felt beginning, that she saw coming irreversibly, scared to think about the immediate future. She found herself on Hollywood Boulevard, just as on that golden spring morning when for the first time her eyes were gifted with the magic spectacle of the enchanted and smiling city. Only this time she felt crushed, insignificant, as if the months that had barely passed had already left the snow of years over her lovely little head.

How different her spirit had been that day! Then she had moved along the sidewalk crowded with idlers, with hope buzzing in her body, with the curiosity of someone on the threshold of an enviable future, with the emotion of one who sees herself one step from the golden door that looks so easy to pass through. Now she carried in her soul the skeleton of an illusion; she dragged the broken-down baggage of her hopes, heavy and enormous, a great bundle that someone had tied to her tempting body. She passed by the "Montmartre," that aristocratic restaurant that she had read so much about in magazines from Spain, and in which she always glimpsed a continuous party of happiness, a conglomeration of joyous people who didn't remember yesterday nor even think, like her, with horror about tomorrow. There was a group of people on the sidewalk who seemed to be waiting for a European monarch to pass by, an exotic figure even within the diverse cosmopolitanism of Hollywood. She had to stop too.

She saw a woman of medium stature, wrapped in a spring coat with ermine trim, leave through the glass door. Under the short feathers of her little white hat, wings of brown hair that barely covered the bulb of one little ear also peeked out; it might have been a rosy pink, as all the charm of life beat within it. Behind her, a man dressed in light colors, with a large pipe between his lips, emerged through the doorway. At the edge of the sidewalk, a brand-new Rolls-Royce waited, at whose door a lackey made servile genuflections. Somebody at her side said very quietly, as if they did not want anyone else but her to hear:

"It's Gloria Swanson . . ."

And she recognized the smiling face of the man as that of the Marquis de La Falaise de La Coudraye, whom she had seen before in the New York magazines. Gloria, with a firm, quick step, went first to the door of the auto, barely turning her head in a rapid movement, making her heavenly smile shine before those who admired her in silence. She was radiant with beauty and happiness. Her big pearly eyes, just covered by the short brim of her hat, revealed all the joy of living.

The car finally left, silently, like an exhalation, and the group dispersed, leaving a clear path for the young dreamer. In her head a cascade of contradictory thoughts was unleashed, and she felt her blood pulsing in her temples. Envy, the most explicable of the human emotions, made her tremble with anger, an impotent anger, that she at first didn't know how to explain. Why had that woman, just a few years ago a poor pharmacy employee in Chicago, become the idol of the masses? Why did she herself—young, beautiful, and intelligent—pass by anonymously on the sidewalk without anyone stopping in her presence, when just a few seconds ago admiration had woven a web of commentary around the figure of another woman? She compared her misery, her grief, with the proud prosperity of the star, and without knowing why, she felt decisive about everything in that moment. What was a moment of dishonor, the sacrifice of a social concept that seemed very insignificant in that environment, compared with the entirety of a happy life, of world admiration and satisfied desires?

She felt poor, a failure, spiritually dead to the world, but conserving the precious jewel of her virtue . . . and she extended her lips in an involuntary smile that was more like a painful grimace. Virtue! Who values virtue when its possessor is at the point of dying of hunger?

She continued wandering almost by chance, without a fixed idea, without a premeditated destination. She passed stores whose display windows offered constant temptations; restaurants out of which wafted appetizing aromas; and flower carts that were packed with bunches of roses, marvelously beautiful but deprived of scent. This made her think that in California, the flowers and fruits are like the women themselves: they look tempting, with a prodigious robustness, but lack spirit, flavor, perfume. Soon she felt thirsty, as the rays of the sun beat straight down on her head; she had walked far, she didn't know how far. At the corner of the boulevard she saw a sign for a drugstore, and she headed toward it resolutely.

They served her an orange soda on the fake marble counter. At her side was a throng of little blonde girls with colorless heads, cinema dudes with large sideburns, shabby businessmen who devoured "lunch" with an air of resignation. American drugstores will just as soon fill a medical prescription for active poison as they will serve you an order of tasty Texas tamales, a poor imitation of the Mexican product. When she had quenched her thirst and tried to pay her check at the cash register's metal window, her fingers found a wrinkled card inside her handbag. Linda paid and went out to the street, taking out the little card and letting her womanly curiosity guide her. Reading it, her heart gave a leap. It was Mr. Sharkey's, and over it she had written a telephone number whose digits appeared to vibrate, to shudder over the immaculate parchment before the girl's eyes.

What strange mandate of Destiny put that reminder in her hands at the precise moment when she began to struggle against her concept of honor? When she touched it with her fingers inside her handbag, she didn't remember what it could be; later, guided by curiosity, she wanted to see it, and now the numbers grew in front of her eyes, pulsating like the biblical inscription at the festival of Balthasar:[206]

Hollywood 3770

She gave it no more thought. She walked resolutely to the drugstore's phone booth and asked Central to connect her.

[March 27, 1927]

While she heard the short squeaks that announced a connection being made, Linda's heart palpitated with such force that it seemed to want to jump out of her chest. The bell sounded three, six, eight times . . .

At last she heard the peculiar sound that the receiver produces when it's lifted from the cradle. A high-pitched voice said:

"Hello . . ."

"Hello, could I speak to Mr. Sharkey?"

A moment of silence reigned during which it seemed that the person who was on the opposite end undertook a brief investigation. Then the shrill voice could be heard again.

"Mr. Sharkey's not here right now. Who's calling?"

"Tell him," responded Linda quickly, feeling that she was drowning with emotion and fury, "that Miss Celli called him; Linda Celli."

"Oh! Miss Celli? One moment; don't hang up."

A different voice sounded on the other apparatus after a three- or four-second pause. The soft, convincing, and warm (if you could call it such) accent of this new voice made Linda tremble in the deepest part of her being. She recognized Sharkey as her interlocutor.

"Is that you? How can I help you?"

Linda had thought all of this would be a lot easier. Listening to the voice of the satyr, insinuating, friendly, she wavered before answering. She didn't want to offend him, because she was ready to do anything; nor did she want to show him her weakness, remaining proud in the midst of her desperation. She took advantage of the chance to clear her thoughts and respond:

"Mr. Sharkey, I need to talk to you."

"I'm at your service, Linda. Remember what I told you when you left my office. I'm deeply interested in you and I forgive that moment of impetuosity. Come when you want and tell me what you need. I'm at the point of telling you I love you . . . but that isn't prudent at my age. Will you come to see me, Linda?"

"Tell me when . . ."

"No, but not so coldly as that, Linda. Whenever you wish, I will be waiting for you. Will you come today?"

It seemed in good taste to vacillate a moment before answering this last question. She would have liked to have gone right away, because she had the feeling that if she thought about it a bit, her romantic notion of honor would overwhelm her desire. Nevertheless, like someone who thinks before deciding, she answered:

"No, but I'll be at your office early tomorrow morning. At eleven. How does that sound?"

"Delighted. I will be waiting for you, my dear, with true pleasure."

Then pausing at each letter, managing to underline the word with all the intention he was capable of, he said:

"I will be alone. A-L-O-N-E."

They said goodbye. Linda hung up the phone carefully and went out to the street in search of fresh air. She felt her temples throbbing quickly to the beat of the thoughts that tangled up in her head, turning into a formless mass, without deciding to go in any particular direction. Now, walking down the boulevard again, she let herself dream about her fantasy, seeing herself as famous, respected, envied, rich. She managed to rid her mind of the troublesome idea of the price she would have to pay for that rosy future, to feel herself leaving that zone and emerging into the light, with her own wings, forgetting the past as the multicolored butterfly forgets that it has been a repugnant caterpillar. Who reproaches the past of women who triumph? Who draws back the discreet veils that cover a wound, when the one who bears it has had her faults pardoned with the indisputable power of glory? Names of famous women, from Teodora, the actress who occupied the Roman throne, to Sarah Bernhardt passing for the picturesque Nell Gwyn, circled in her feverish imagination.[207] It was done . . . she was on the verge of becoming famous. That was all she cared about.

[April 3, 1927]

"In every way, you are the type that we want. If things go well, you'll be contracted for some time. Come and see me tomorrow at ten in this same office for the final details."

And with the dryness of the Saxons, a bit brusque, the director Shelley got up, giving the young man the signal to leave.

Raymundo's first thought upon leaving the office was to talk to Linda. First he called from one of those phones that they install in American drugstores, inside a booth that contains the greatest number of discomforts that could occur to a brain devising tortures. The line was busy. He waited for a bit and picked up another handset, obtaining the wrong number from Central. Later, since he was getting close to the house, he realized that the phone line continued to be occupied by some unrepentant conversationalist. At that moment only two streets separated the boardinghouse where he lodged from the one where his friend stayed. He was determined to walk this distance to tell her the good news. He had so many happy plans in his imagination! So much so that in traversing the distance that still separated him from the house, he went along daydreaming, formulating in his mind the speech that he was going to blurt out to the young woman.

"Linda," he would tell her, "I've caught a glimpse of success, in all its splendor. Tomorrow I sign a contract that will surely be advantageous. Well, even though it won't carry with it a sum of millions, it will give me the opportunity to appear for the first time in important roles. And who knows what later? Well, Linda, since you still haven't achieved this for yourself you will tell me that . . . No, I want to say what you will say to yourself: 'Great, and why should I care about this? I want to triumph myself. I want it to be me who shines in the sky of the screen' . . . But then I will tell you, not in my mind as you have said it: 'Yes, Linda, but my triumph signifies your own. In the first place . . . we will get married.'" (Here—thought Raymundo—she would pause for a moment.) The first moment of surprise past, he would tell her in a passionate voice, coming near her, kissing her hand (the right or the left?), well, whichever one was closer. He would tell her, kissing her hand:

"Don't speak, Linda, let me finish. In the first place, I address you as 'tú' because I love you, which you know very well even though I've never told you. I know that you do not want to marry me, because what you want is to have a career, but I'm getting precisely to that. We'll marry tomorrow, next week, within two weeks, whenever you've thought about it, because I know that my proposal is a bit sudden. We'll marry and you will continue working in cinema but now promoted by me, recommended, introduced by a gallant young man, not as his wife, but keeping your name that you love so much. I will be a companion for you in the struggle, as I have been up to now, a help, a source of respect . . . and at the same time an obedient, ideal husband . . ."

Raymundo stopped at the mouth of the street to let a car pass that was just about to hit him. Then, the danger having passed, he continued with his meditation on the opposite sidewalk.

"Maybe it would be better not to say anything to her about marriage. I'll simply tell her about my new contract, and it will encourage her to hope, promising to do everything I can for her; I'm sure she will succeed. This young woman only needs an opportunity, however small it may be, to prevail. As soon as she attracts attention, her future will be secure. Later, bit by bit, I will speak to her of my affection. We'll dine together today, and coming home in very American style, without preamble, I will propose marriage. That might be better . . ."

He had already arrived at the door of the boardinghouse. He didn't know how he went up the steps, and he barely greeted a very pretty little neighbor whom he had been courting for a few weeks before his new friend arrived in Hollywood. At last, before the closed door, he stopped for a moment to catch his breath and then, fixing his hair, hat in hand, he knocked. No one answered. He called again, a bit louder, and then letting a few moments pass, even louder still. Nothing. Linda had just left to meet Mr. Sharkey. It was then that Raymundo noticed an explanatory note, well folded, stuck in between the door and the frame. He read it:

[April 4, 1927]

"I'll be back tomorrow. Don't wait for me tonight, Raymundo. I have a lot to tell you if you look for me in the morning—Linda."

That was it. Not even a plausible explanation, nor a detail that indicated where his friend had gone. Raymundo scratched his head as everyone does unconsciously in moments of indecision. Giving the closed door one last look of sadness, he went down to the street.

Once on the sidewalk, he remembered that he was hungry. Emotion had not allowed him to feel this necessity before, and now it awoke in him with the force of a reaction. With his head full of dreams forming a lovely web that was punctured now and then by thoughts of Linda, and full of worry about where she was in those moments, he entered a café on the boulevard and ordered dinner.

The next morning Raymundo woke up early to get ready to meet his new savior. All night long he had tossed and turned in bed, without being able to sleep except at intervals during which he dreamed about strange things. He saw himself famous, prestigious, coming back to a home where Linda waited to hear news of his latest triumphs. Then he dreamed that his name in glowing lights stood out over the luminous way of Broadway, crowning the portico of an aristocratic theater. Who at the point of deciding their future hasn't felt this sweet sensation? At midnight, considering that if he stayed up all night he was going to look awful the next day, he resolved to sleep. He counted to two hundred, then he started again, and later still, lost count. He mechanically went over the numbers again and again, following a familiar method for falling asleep, but in the middle of counting he would be surprised by the memory of his beloved, of that novia to whom he had never said a single word about his affection. His thoughts were related to his career, confused images of the director Shelley, of Linda, and the slightly blurry figure of Mr. Sharkey . . .

When this person appeared in the movie of his memory, Raymundo felt his heart do a somersault and all the first part of his dream disappeared. Without knowing why, he linked the memory of the satyr with that of

Linda Celli, and he trembled from his worry for her and for his dream of happiness. Would the girl have paid attention to the slick words of the professional libertine and fallen into his clutches? Because to him there was no doubt about Sharkey's true intentions, his name only a symbol of evil and treachery. He remembered that he had advised the young woman not to go see him and that she had smiled at his fears and . . .

This thought was what tormented him the most for the rest of the night. Finally, at dawn, he managed to stay asleep, with that heavy slumber that produces alertness; but upon waking he still felt tired and nervous, as men feel after a night of dissipation in which there has been abundant liquor and the happiness [*illegible*] of vices.

In a few minutes he had completed his "toilette." He took a poor bath and cut his face twice while shaving. He smiled at his bewilderment when he realized that in place of shaving cream, he had covered his face with the "Stacomb" cream that he used for his hair and that he had, without thinking, put a little bit of shaving cream on his toothbrush. Finally, he went out on the street, not without having put on his best suit and having made sure in front of the mirror that his appearance was above reproach.

On the sidewalk he bought the morning newspaper. He had the habit of reading all the daily headlines, and his eyes met with one that made him linger on the body of the article. It said:

A POLICE RAID . . .
An elegant residence in Laurel Canyon, about which there were vehement suspicions for days of it being a center of vice and prostitution, was suddenly visited last night by the Hollywood police. Since agents arrived when nobody was expecting it, they were able to capture several known screen personalities that were engaged in a veritable bacchanal. The police recovered various gallons of moonshine, two cases of gin, and some bottles of imported gin.

[April 5, 1927]

According to the details of the "raid," the partygoers had been surprised in an outright bacchanal and not a single one of them had time to escape. When the police arrived, someone had sounded the alarm and several women had thrown themselves toward the windows, breaking the glass, but with such bad luck that detectives stopped them before they dared jump into the garden. One of them got out to the sidewalk, where she fainted. The police picked her up there. It seemed that this unhappy soul, fearful that her name would be wrapped up in the major scandal that would break, tried to gamble everything and threw herself through the glass of one of the windows, injuring her face and her hands. Her strength had failed her upon hitting the sidewalk and there they had picked her up. In her clothes they had found some morphine pills. The woman was completely intoxicated. Later, at the end of the article, came the name of this victim: her name was Linda Celli.

Raymundo was on the verge of screaming, horrified. Surely there had been an error. It wasn't possible that Linda, yes Linda! and the cursed delinquent were the same person. He went to the phone to call the young lady's house, but the line was busy. Meanwhile, the hour of his appointment with Mr. Shelley grew closer . . .

He hesitated a few moments. Should he go to the boardinghouse to prove with his own eyes that it had been a mistake, or hold off on that investigation until later, suffering meanwhile the pain of uncertainty, which was even worse than the pain of disappointment? After all, a name didn't mean anything. He kept reading to see if he could find something else that would allow him to rest easy. Lower down in the article it gave certain specific details. The detained person had been taken to the emergency hospital where she had received her first treatment. There they had discovered that she was a young Mexican woman hoping to make it on screen. Somewhere else, in the list of those arrested, appeared the name Frank Sharkey, "known trickster," whom the authorities in New York had tried to extradite some time ago. His real name, according to the newspaper, was John Sullivan.

With these grim details, there was no doubt in Raymundo Nava's mind. But how had Linda kept this relationship secret, and how had she fallen into Sharkey's net after the warning he had given her? Consumed by anguish, he walked toward the building where Shelley's office was.

Signing the contract took minutes. Raymundo left there, under circumstances that would have made anyone else happy, with a copy of it in his pocket. The door of fame had opened before his eyes, and riches seemed to await him just a few steps away. His long-held dreams were at the point of being realized. He had achieved success, or at least had begun to climb with firm steps the rungs of the ladder that leads to success. But . . .

Anyone who's been in these situations knows that when a tragedy darkens the soul, the trumpets of fame cannot, with their metallic noise, lift the spirit. Raymundo's secret dream since that day at Paramount Studios had been that both he and she would triumph. He could offer her his hand and his name, the start of a fortune. And now his beloved had fallen, maybe forever, in her career, had stained a name that was respectable, and in the process had destroyed, without meaning to, a heart that was full of affection for her!

At the police station they told him that Linda was in the hospital, where she probably would remain for more than a month. Her face had been severely injured by the glass of the broken window, and they thought it likely that she would have a permanent scar. Asking here and there, he was able to find out that the sentence imposed on the young woman, in the event her culpability was proven, would be no less than six months in jail.

[April 6, 1927]

What weeks of anguish for those two hearts that had been united by a single will and for whom fate charted such distinct courses! While Linda slowly recovered in the General Hospital, Raymundo had to leave Hollywood to shoot scenes for his first film, in Baja California. In a hospital bed, Linda received a passionate letter every day, full of condolences, saturated with the perfume of true love. She had been reading these letters with indescribable shame, without daring to answer them. She didn't feel worthy of that affection, having fallen in one jump to where her Destiny had thrown her. But this afternoon she had resolved to answer, at first with a trembling hand and then more assuredly. She wrote for almost an hour. In the end she put her name at the foot of those sheaves filled with tiny script, lines squished together, and vacillated a moment between mailing them or ripping them up and throwing them in the wastebasket. She had written this:

> Dear Raymundo:
> Your letters fill me with shame, and that's why I have not been able to answer them all this time. Nevertheless, as you anguish about my fate in your last letter, since I notice that you fear for my life, I consider it fair to tell you that, unfortunately, I remain alive. Following your instructions, I'll speak to you informally for the first time in this letter, as you address me in yours, because it also seems to me that we are closer to each other that way. I, like you, embraced those dreams when I began to be your friend: I also dreamed of an eternal union, of when we would have triumphed, and God knows how fortunate I would have been having you next to me forever. Now, as you well know, it is too late.
> As you've been insisting that I explain how I came to fall into that web of infamy that has killed all of my hopes in one fell swoop, all of my dreams for the future, I think it's right to put you at ease by telling you that it wasn't all my fault. That afternoon I had been to see Mr. Sharkey to

ask for his protection because, like you and like all strivers after the ideal, I did not possess the resources to reach the goal that would make us all happy. Sharkey invited me to that party without telling me anything about it. When we arrived, when everything betrayed an impending bacchanal, I wanted to leave but he would not let me. No, I don't believe that I am a child. I know that I could have screamed, resisted going in or, once inside, I could have left by any means possible. But you don't understand this ambition for Fame. I closed the windows of my repugnance towards that party, which exceeded all the horrors that I had imagined, and decided to drink the cup of my trial to the last drop. Almost upon arriving, Sharkey had introduced me to someone he said was the director Cecil Brown, and who, according to what I've read in the papers afterward, I've learned was nothing but an assistant film director, as perverse as Sharkey and, like him, using a name that wasn't his.

They made me drink some cups of liquor and soon I entered into the liveliness of the moment. Why lie to you? I also needed to forget, to numb myself, and the occasion was propitious. You know that when we do something bad in isolation, our attitude seems monstrous to us, or simply reproachable, according to our larger or smaller sense of honor. But when everyone around us does the same thing, when we don't have the opportunity for comparison, it seems as if we aren't doing something entirely wrong. If everyone else does it with freedom, with that *sans façon,* why not try it ourselves?[208]

I don't know what happened later. There was a moment in which panic made itself felt in the gathering. A voice murmured in my ear: "Save yourself; the police," and instinct did the rest. Then suddenly I recovered my lucidity to realize the disgrace that has fallen over me and over my future . . . and, sincerely I thought of you, Raymundo. I tried to flee without knowing what I was doing, and the rest you already know. The morphine pills that they've said to have found on my body are a mystery. I don't know who put them there, nor did I see them. It could be that it was a mistake, since I remember that I had a little box of aspirin with me.

[April 7, 1927]

Now my dreams have been left broken and my hopes cheated. If it wasn't for the comfort that you give me with your letters, if it wasn't because I know that there is someone who still remembers me and pities me, this life would already have been over in some way. But I feel ashamed, unworthy not only of your affection but also your compassion. You were right when you told me that afternoon that aspirants to Glory in cinema were butterflies who flutter around a chimeric light in whose splendors they end up burning their wings. What would I give to have never come to this city, that more than once I have heard called "the city of no return." How much better would it have been for me and my dear ones to have stayed in my little house in Guadalajara, surrounded by legitimate affection, unknown by the public, but tranquil in my spiritual state!

I don't know what justice will do with me. I don't even know how I will get out of this loathsome place and what I will do after I have crossed its threshold. What is more, I'm afraid I will have a perennial scar that will make life even more bitter for me. I am a woman and this vanity is perfectly explicable. Who will give me even a look, if I am left deformed, marked forever with this infamous mark, with no one knowing whether it resulted from an accident or (I would die of shame) a street fight? All my hopes for the future, all my illusions, all my dreams have gone up in smoke. Yes, I feel myself going crazy just thinking about it! Right now, I would be capable of any madness whatsoever. I'd like to scream, run away, cry until I'm spent, destroy everything near me. What do I know! You who possess this magnificent soul, this soul that anyone would think was divine, are in a position to understand me.

I'm going to end this letter with something that I'm not sure was what you expected, in your noble and gentlemanly spirit. I don't know where to start . . . Well, here it goes. Of course, I beg you, in the name of this love that you say you have felt for me, that you don't write to me again nor try to find out what has happened to me. When I get out of this place, I will take back my own name, which you don't know, or maybe take another: Linda Celli was a pseudonym, a name chosen in moments in which the prospect of a brilliant future dazzled me. As far as what I was then, the spirit that animated me has ceased to exist; Linda Celli will also cease to exist. I will find work, earn enough money to go back to Guadalajara, and there hide my defeat, forever trying to reconquer the affections that I was at the point of losing forever in that blessed country. That is why I beg you not to look for me, that you don't try to find out my whereabouts. Hearing your voice would make me die of shame and to see you face-to-face . . . You have carved out your future. You have a door to success in your sight and have the right to enjoy it without someone by your side weighing you down. Forget me . . .

For the last time,
Linda

She hesitated greatly before sending this epistle in the mail. She was on the verge of ripping it to pieces. Four times and many more she stopped, murmuring:

"It's worth more in pieces . . ."

She was horrified to think about her situation, about the tragedy that had darkened her life. To her it had been something like a horrible nightmare, a macabre obsession. She never believed that it would be so easy to have destroyed so many hopes at once, so many obsessions, so many legitimate aspirations. She thought about death and she desired it with all her soul, but she didn't dare cut the chain that still tied her spirit to her body, not because of her religious beliefs, which she had almost lost, but due to an explicable instinct toward self-preservation. Suicides, generally, are on the brink of madness, and she was more lucid than ever after that blow that at first glance would have seemed incredible. Live, live . . . for what? She tried to console herself as a Christian with the idea that her dear ones would still love her, her beloved aunt Valeria, her provincial boyfriend, her Raymundo . . . and when she thought of him she felt her heart give a leap and then it would compress as if a hand had squeezed it mercilessly . . .

[April 8, 1927]

The hand of Justice was merciful to Linda. After a trial that provoked a bit of a sensation and during which they obtained testimony that was very prejudicial for certain fictitious characters from the world of cinema, the young woman left, sentenced to sixty days in prison. When she left prison and found herself in front of the court, with Temple Street extending to the right and left, transformed into a human anthill, she felt a new disillusionment, a new despair. Where would she go?

Her eight weeks of imprisonment, first in the General Hospital and later in the new Los Angeles jail, had almost completely transformed her physical appearance. Her face was even paler than usual; her eyes lacked that tempting shine of new agate that they had had before; her face was lightly scored by a scar. Fortunately for her, the doctors had worked conscientiously on her case, and the edges of the wound had closed completely, leaving only a long, light scar which they themselves said would disappear after a few months. But the naive young woman was now thin, unwell in body and soul, defeated. She felt insignificant, a human rag in the middle of that sea of people who didn't even stop to look at her, attentive to the pursuit of the all-powerful dollar that bought subsistence as well as honor and social standing. She paused a few moments in the door to the jail, and then she walked resolutely to the left as if she had made a decision.

Linda understood then the obstacle that her useless virtue had constituted for her. Any lost woman, like those who abound in the barrios of the big cities or in the cream of their deceitful society, would have had more probabilities of success in her struggle for life. She, untouched, conserving in her soul the teachings of her parents, demure and still virtuous after everything, she was there undecided, without any door open in front of her, lacking even the basic necessity of bread. She thought about picking up her things from the boardinghouse in Hollywood, in which she had spent those months of dreams, but she was overcome by the fear of a scandal. What's more, the "landlady" would surely not want to hand over anything until she had paid the weekly rent that was past due. There was no need to think about that for the moment.

She got to the corner with the post office and turned toward Main Street to the north, where she had sometimes seen little repulsive theaters, veritable shacks where they advertised shows in Spanish. How did the idea occur to her to try her fortune in one of those salons, on whose stages aficionados full of pretensions and lacking in talent paraded in turn, stars in their twilight, performers who began the race with determination worthy of better venues? I don't know what to tell you. Possibly the animalistic voice of self-preservation directed her that way, considering that mediocre hope a true gate of salvation. To think that she had fallen so far, that she had descended so rapidly, to the point of pinning all of her aspirations at the moment on performing on those disgusting stages!

But did she have theatrical experience? She hadn't acted on a stage, except on one occasion in which she had played in the [Teatro] Principal in Guadalajara during a charity festival. Nevertheless, the only studying she had done in anticipation of her cinematic career was what she had observed on screen, which seemed sufficient to her. She stopped in front of one of those entryways covered with multicolored posters and huge ads painted by hand, which promised the public an afternoon of "crazy laughter," with a fantastically titled comedy, probably the creation of some street poet. A broken-down automatic piano spit out a song from "The Tempest." In the doorway a fat, poorly dressed, unshaven character extolled the delights of the show at the top of his lungs, ending by inviting the passersby to buy their tickets at the box office in order to "not miss that opportunity of a lifetime." Little by little, individuals with a hangdog look began entering, good bourgeois men accompanied by their families who still bore the mark of their race on their uncombed heads. She approached the man who shouted, sweaty, brandishing in one hand a sheaf of programs poorly printed and even more poorly written.

[April 9, 1927]

People continued entering and disappearing into the obscure mouth of the "foyer," as if they had been devoured little by little by an apocalyptic monster. Linda hesitated an instant before deciding to speak. At last she said in a small voice, semidrowned by emotion:

"Sir . . ."

The barker continued exaggerating the qualities of the histrionic scenes that at those very moments were being performed on the repulsive stage inside. He called out at the top of his lungs with more or less successful jokes to the chicks who passed by on the arms of tall, dark-skinned men with the air of a creole pimp. Linda, convinced that he had not heard her, repeated:

"Sir . . ."

The man turned his gaze and tried to rehearse the friendliest of his smiles. Seeing the young woman approach him, he stretched out one of the programs and with a honeyed voice invited her to come in.

"Come in, miss. Come in. The great company of . . ."

"Excuse me. I would like to see the owner."

The man contained his cheap oratory to pay attention. She explained that she would like to talk with the manager of the theater, with whoever saw to the artists on stage—she had the courtesy to refer to them that way, without irony—about a very personal matter.

"He's around here," said the man. "I'll send someone to look . . ."

A little bit later Linda was in front of an individual as poorly dressed as the first one. The only visible difference was an enormous gold chain that crossed his stomach over his jacket and various rings adorned with false stones on the fingers of his right hand. He introduced himself as the owner of the theater and asked how he could help her.

"It's a little bit long to explain, sir," she said. "I'd prefer it if we went into your office . . ."

He begged her pardon. Where they were going to go, he assured her, wasn't an office but a tiny room in which he took care of all of the accounting business; as he almost never had opportunities to speak to such distinguished people—he managed to underline the phrase—the place wasn't all that great; matters related to the artists were almost always dealt with right there in the portico, or inside in the seats, while an adventure film played on screen.

He guided Linda down a hallway that smelled strongly of floral disinfectant, and at last they found themselves in a little room full of multicolored programs, wallpapered with portraits of performers cut out of newspapers and magazines. Inviting her to sit in an armchair of a very respectable age, the man remained standing.

"Tell me, miss . . ."

"I've come to see if you would like a new attraction for your theater. I think that, if I'm lucky, there will be a spot for me. You'll see . . ."

"You're the attraction?"

"Well . . . I think so: at least, I had thought that . . . you see, I am going to be entirely frank with you. I was . . ."

The impresario raised his hand as if to keep his interlocutor from talking. In his little sunken eyes a spark of lechery shone and he tried to smile in as friendly a way as he could.

"You don't need to say anything more. You suit me, precisely in these days in which the competition is getting stiff. How much do you want to make a week?"

"The truth is I don't know; I think I would be okay with . . ."

"We can pay you," he straightened the lapel of his jacket, as if to give himself the air of extraordinary importance, "better than any of the other theaters. We can give you . . . you see . . . Would five dollars a day work? Of course, we are going to advertise you as coming from the capital of Mexico, where you have had great success . . ."

[April 10, 1927]

She wanted to speak, but the impresario, knowledgeable about his business like few others, impeded her from opening her lips with a gesture that he tried to make gentle, putting his not very clean hand in front of Linda's face.

"I know what you are going to say to me, miss. Speaking plainly, I imagine that you haven't worked much in Mexico, much less in the big theaters, but the public here doesn't understand these things. If you knew how many artists we have presented this way on posters in the neighborhood![209] What do you say: accepted?"

The young woman hesitated a moment, half intoxicated by the bad smells that seeped out of someplace nearby mixed with the pungent perfume of cheap disinfectant. He continued talking, as if he were interpreting her silence as an interested hesitation:

"I understand; I understand. We might be able to offer you up to six dollars a day . . . which is subject to increase, of course. Well, we can pay six dollars to see this little face, so pretty, every day . . ."

She felt as if the blood were rising to her head: it seemed to her that her face was burning or that her eyes shone with either piety or indignation. In that man's look she had just read the true desire that lay behind his words

... and she was nauseous. She tried to resist, but the vision of her disgrace, still so recent, advised her against it. With a resolute air she answered before her interlocutor expected.

"When can I start work?"

"When? Whenever you want, beautiful. We would take a week to advertise you, if you agree . . ."

"It can't be sooner?"

"Yes: but it would be prejudicial to you. I don't want to offend you with what I am going to say, but I've taken a liking to you. What do you want? Even though I am not of the age to say such things, ours has been a case of Destiny perhaps. I am going to be frank with you. Do you have anyone here in Los Angeles?"

"I don't understand . . ."

"Well, I'll explain to you. Your husband, your friend, someone . . . you understand me?"

Yes, she understood. She hesitated an instant before replying but ended up thinking that she was faithfully obeying the imperious mandate of her Destiny; of this cruel Destiny that had made her dream of fairy tales, only to finally awaken her to abruptly face reality. She didn't know why, but she felt pushed to play with fire.

"No, I don't have anyone here, sir . . . What is your name?"

"José Rosales, miss; but call me Pepe if you like."

"Well, Mr. Rosales, I don't have anyone, and the truth is that I am looking for work because I don't have the resources necessary to sustain myself. I think that for a woman, sir, and in front of someone unknown to her, this is too much. But when would you like me to come back to see you?"

She got up politely to say goodbye. He followed her example and said to her, still very sweetly:

"Whenever you want. Please don't think it too daring if I invite you to dine with me tonight after the show. I swear you have nothing to fear . . ."

He said that with his mouth, but his lugubrious eyes betrayed his words. He was a clever impresario whose office must have welcomed an infinity of butterflies, their wings burned by the light of ambition, looking to the theater as a refuge for their half-withered beauty. On that occasion he had found a conquest by the most ignoble means that could exist: giving bread to a hungry woman. She continued operating like an automaton, without knowing why she said what she said, nor why she thought what she thought.

[April 11, 1927]

She accepted the offer, with that insensibility that had overcome her, promising to meet the impresario in front of the post office. That is to say, like a vulgar woman who had staked her pride on her virtue; like a prostitute, like someone who wasn't Linda Celli. Why did she feel so transformed? Her head ached when she tried to think about it, and she preferred to let Destiny weave its tangled web quickly. She felt hungry, but it seemed shameful to ask for an advance from that man who still didn't know if she was capable of entertaining the public from the stage. She said goodbye, making a date with Rosales for eleven o'clock that night.

The next day Linda woke up in a room that, if not luxurious, was at least furnished with a certain decency. Upon opening her eyes, she was momentarily surprised to see the ceiling stucco instead of the cold cement of her cell. She took a look around: a lightly used dressing table, an upholstered divan, an armchair, and her clothes in disarray over a varnished chair. She felt a bitter taste in her mouth and upon asking herself why, she moaned involuntarily . . .

Then, scenes of the night before, at first blurry but then with more precise outlines, passed through her imagination. She remembered having been in a neighborhood Mexican café, where she danced and drank without a care; she remembered vaguely that the walls were decorated with big deformed figures that brought to mind memories of Diego Rivera's art. Then that bottle that seemed immense; the fury with which she took the glass, slugging down the contents and asking for more, to the surprise of the impresario . . . What else? What else?

Ah, yes! She had been very drunk, and he had kissed her first on the hand and then on the mouth. She had been talking like a dummy about her adventurous past that was responsible for this second mistake, more abject and irreparable. Later she shuddered at the memory of the savage guffaw that he emitted when she confessed her virtue. He hadn't believed her . . . and who would believe her now, after two months in jail, after having been such easy prey? She felt the desire to break the bottle on his half-bald head, but in her drunkenness she thought that he was completely right after all. Was it feasible that a woman like that would have conserved her body untouched by any man, her virtue immaculate? No one, not even she would have believed it. She didn't even have the attraction of the virginity that our parents value so much as a marriage dowry.

Later there was a lacuna in her memories. She confusedly recalled that things had begun to spin around her and that later she felt her body jump around in a taxi, the tick-tock of whose meter followed her, strangely tormenting her ears. Another hole in her memories. Now that bitter taste in her mouth, that implacable thirst, that exhaustion in all the muscles of her body.

The sun started to filter its golden rays in between the curtains, like that other memorable morning in which the tick-tock of her watch woke her from the most beautiful dream of her life. Now she also awoke to disillusionment. During the hours when she had been in the enchanted domain that imitated death, she didn't even notice those figures made of fabric, animated puppets wearing purple and gold suits. She didn't remember anything but the face of Silenus, of her seducer, his caresses a bit mushy, his repugnant laugh, those foul-smelling kisses . . . how horrible![210] And to think that she had descended to such degeneration without affection, without any interest other than assuring herself a job to earn her daily bread, for the apathy of not struggling anymore! But her internal voice said that she was tired of struggling; she tried to explain the cause of all this, and she went back to falling to the conclusion that it was her destiny, nothing more than Destiny . . .

[April 12, 1927]

The telephone, which was in a ridiculous little black box pegged to the wall of the room, rang. Who could it be? At first she didn't want to pay attention to the call, but it was so insistent, the constant ringing made her so nervous, that she arose laboriously to answer. She had to make a great effort, because her legs did not want to hold her up and her head burned like a live coal. It was Rosales calling her:

"Hello! Have you gotten up yet, baby?"[211]

That familiar address seemed insolent to her. She was going to protest, but she suddenly remembered the full extent of her disgrace, and swallowing a sob, she limited herself to answering;

"No; I feel really bad . . ."

"I will come by soon . . . Listen, the truth is I didn't believe you . . . but let's talk about something else. Do you want me to bring breakfast to your room, or would you like to meet to have breakfast together?"

"I don't care. I think I'd rather not see you for some time, sir."

"See you, sir? Who are you talking to?"

"To you."

"What?!? Now you speak to me with 'usted,' dear? Don't be silly. Speak to me with 'tú,' as I do with you; like last night . . . Look, right now I'm already out on the street, I will call my house and tell them not to wait for me to eat. I'll be there in an instant. No; no objections; now more than ever you need my presence. I'll see you in a few moments."

And she heard the characteristic sound of the receiver returned to its cradle on the other end of the line. She felt disgust, disgust for herself, disgust for the world, disgust toward everything. For a moment she felt the entire burden of her disgrace on her dreamy little head, over the entire castle of her virginal illusions. The satyr . . . but did she have the right to call him that? What had that man done that any other man wouldn't have done when in possession of an intoxicated woman who had lost not only the exact knowledge of her surroundings but modesty itself, suggestive and anxious for happiness to drown the sorrows that weighed on her like a paving stone on her heart? He, seen properly and in accordance with the concept of opportunity that Latinos hold, did not bear the greatest blame. It was she, she was the only one responsible for her situation. Without knowing why, Linda started to laugh, to laugh nervously, with loud guffaws that reverberated gloomily against the four walls of her room. An attack of hysteria, a moment of craziness, that later broke open all the floodgates of sobbing that drowns us and ends up making us shed useless tears; that hardly brings us anything worthwhile beyond making us rest. In the beginning she laughed with tears; later she cried with laughter, and even later still she began to sob with her face buried in the pillows, almost without knowing why.

Rosales found her still in this position, half wrapped in a pink robe, thrown facedown over the sinner's bed, shuddering in convulsions that would have split the soul of anyone. He went to pull her up, to take her in his arms in a show of consolation. There's no reason to die over it; it was not a big deal! She had had the fortune of falling into the hands of a man who could shape her future. It's true that he was married, but after all he was getting tired of his wife, who was old and bothersome. They could live together for a while, while she found a good prospect to marry, and he himself would be the godfather, if she preferred, because . . .

Linda interrupted him with a withering glance, in which the light of her light-colored eyes escaped through the tears, like the sun filtering through the crystalline web of the rain.

"You are a swine; cruel. I don't want to see you again in my entire life."

[April 13, 1927]

Rosales was silent for a moment, and then in the sweetest voice he could manage, changing his attitude, he became romantic. He explained that he did not think he had done so much damage to her, and that if he had known her true status as a virgin, maybe it wouldn't have gone as far as it did. But he was conscious of the obligation he had contracted, and he was willing to do everything: they needed to think about it carefully, talk about it until they reached a determination. He confessed to her that he had never been involved in a situation like this; all of his conquests until then had been superficial moments of fleeting love with girls who came to the theater in search of an arrangement, more as a cover for their other activities. After all, he told her, that had been a question of inevitability, a decree by Destiny. How did she know that the wrong he had done her wouldn't lead to good for both of them? For a space of fifteen, twenty, up to thirty minutes, he was talking this way, without looking at Linda, who was lying in the bed in which she continued sobbing about her shame and her downfall. The sound of his voice was so smooth, so even, that she began to feel lulled, much to her dismay. She didn't hear what he said, but the rumor of distant words, that constant murmur of that thread of voice that did nothing more than give excuses that excused nothing, apologies that were not even taken into account by his companion. He had come to do what was necessary. When he finished his speech, Linda stayed silent with the desire to beg him to continue, but he looked her firmly in the eyes:

"My dear little girl: will you forgive me?"

And there was such meekness, such humility in the question, that she hesitated in answering with one of those outbursts that her pride dictated. He repeated the question in a softer tone, more loving, more flattering.

"Let's not talk about that, please. You did what anyone else in your place would have done. Let's forget about it and leave me in peace."

"No. I want us to go eat something: you must be very weak. Or do you want them to bring us something here?"

Linda shrugged her shoulders. He got up slowly without taking his eyes off her and went to pick up the phone receiver. Still, before talking, he consulted her with a tender look of his tear-filled eyes. In spite of her indifference, he asked resolutely that they bring something to eat to room number 446.

Once he had placed the order, he returned to her side, as if he had not left his previous position. An enormous silence spread over them both, interrupted only by the noise of the trolleys that passed below in the congested street, where people were already marching off to tackle the struggle for life. At last, he broke the silence.

"Baby, tell me now that you forgive me. But tell me looking in my eyes, here, like me. Come on, smile; show me your little teeth like last night, in the cabaret; make me happy with an indulgent word, but speak to me from your heart. Do you forgive me?"

She looked at him for a long time, without parting her lips. Rosales asked again, with the insistence of a little boy, which didn't fit his somewhat repulsive resemblance to a corrupt satyr:

"Do you forgive me?"

And then Linda managed to move her head in the affirmative, with an expression that she endeavored to make disdainful, bitter. He got even closer:

"No; but I want you to tell me with your mouth, with your pretty mouth. Tell me: yes."

Like an echo, she repeated in a low voice, looking at a corner of the room:

"Yes . . ."

"Tell me: yes, Pepe. I forgive you. Let's see . . ."

She didn't know why she answered, repeating the words of her seducer, one by one. He felt transfigured; the feeling spread like a cloak of light over his face, already somewhat worn by the years and by vice. He came even closer to her and, taking her in his arms, planted a big kiss on her mouth, which Linda had neither the force, nor the determination, nor even the intention to resist.

[April 14, 1927]

Linda's debut as a "cupletista" in the revolting theater on Main Street was an event of only passing interest.[212] Intelligent women, as a general rule, are not suited to the theater; they lack that common touch that the masses like so much. They don't know how to please them with pornographic and vulgar jokes. Her performance was a flash in the pan. Rosales, who at first really feared that he had fallen in love with the girl, convinced himself after a few days that it had been a passing ray of light in his life that barely left a fleeting reflection on his soul. Soon he transformed from lover to impresario, and from indulger to strict guardian of his interests. One night, after the show, he called her aside to tell her:

"Sweetheart: I don't know where to begin, but the truth is that . . ."

She looked him in the eyes, with a spark of irony in her agate-hued pupils, putting her arms akimbo, a pose she had learned from those infamous, fashionable *cuples*, who are the most tremendous homage to human vulgarity; he was trying to get out of the agreement.

"I know. You are going to tell me that I'm not suited for the theater; that the public wants something livelier, something with more spirit, as you say. Don't think that I'm going to offer an excuse, nor am I going to promise to improve. I'm the first to recognize that I'm not suited for this and I have no illusions about a career. Fine career one can start in a nasty shack like your theater and with an audience that would just as soon show up to watch a circus act as they would to hear a comic speak nonsense for half an hour! Don't worry, dear: I'm going to get out of your way . . ."

"No, Linda. I don't want to say that . . . ; but really . . . no; it's impossible to explain things to you. You have this genius . . ."

"Bah. Don't be stupid. I'm not a little girl and there is not a lot to discuss. Today is . . . what day is today? Tuesday, I think. Great, if it works for you, I'll be here until Saturday. You pay me and wish me good luck. Is that what you want? You see how easy it would have been to say it."

In a few weeks an abrupt change had come over Linda Celli, inexplicable to those who are not accustomed to the caprices of Destiny. She was no longer the dreamy, visionary chaser of the ideal. Her contact with that man had made her feel the entire bitter impression of disgust that well-born women feel in such cases, when they fall into the swamp of perdition. It even reached a point where she felt it was someone else who moved underneath the tempting covering of her flesh, another spirit that animated her mind. She only held on to the memory of what she had been, and even this only came momentarily to her mind. When she was alone in her room and felt her past closing in on her, either she went out on the street in search of a friend to distract her or she jumped up and down like a crazy person, rehearsing some indecent "cuple" to erase any possibility of thought from her mind. It hurt her to think about anything that wasn't the present. For her the past was dead and the future something problematic, wrapped in the mist of uncertainty. What a leap from the pedestal of her ambitions, from the very door of Triumph to the dunghill in which she now moved! Had the disillusion that poisoned the spirit been those sixty days in jail? The contact with that mob that surrounded her? It was only when for some reason a memory of Raymundo came to her mind that she felt as if a drop of mercury, heavy and cold, ran through all her veins. It was then that she called the "old guy"—that's what she'd begun to call Rosales—to shower him with faked caresses that at times had a bit of sincerity, because they made her forget her torment. In her short time performing on the stage of that fetid theater, she had managed to save some money—enough to try her fortune somewhere else—and she wasn't worried about the immediate future. She ended up feeling happy in the mud she wallowed in, without aspirations that might torment her, without memories that would make her a martyr to her feelings.

[April 17, 1927]

The separation was agreed upon almost as easily as her hiring at the shack had been. Linda worked carelessly during this last week; Rosales had resolved not to talk to her, nor accompany her to dinner as before, nor even look at her. On her last night, he had an assistant of the little theater give her a paper on which he had made a careful accounting of all that had been spent on her over the past seven days, including flowers that were supposed to have come spontaneously from the audience, the construction of a frame with her portrait, and one or another small thing. With the paper was a small envelope in which Rosales had put two ten-dollar bills and some coins as her payout. Not a word of farewell, nor a single simple expression of regret. At the entrance, the debut of another young artist "who had triumphed in Mexico" was being announced, a Mexico that not even her grandparents had known, and who occupied the head and the heart of the impresario, the place that Linda Celli had left vacant.

One of her stage companions, another mud flower who had also come to the theater through the door of perdition, was the only one with words of consolation for her.

"Don't worry, dear: you're young and beautiful, and you'll be fine wherever you end up. I and others wish we had your future. Where are you thinking of working?"

"I don't know; I'll try my luck in some of the other theaters and if I don't find anything, I'll leave Los Angeles. After everything, I'm sick of this city . . ."

Her friend hesitated an instant as if she wanted to make her a proposition that seemed too daring to her. At last, while they took off their face paint in front of a shabby mirror in the dressing room, with two fingers full of "cold cream" and without looking at her interlocutor, she insinuated:

"Well . . . I want to give you a tip, but I don't know if you'll like it. The deal isn't bad, but I don't know your scruples."

"What is it? It could be that . . ."

"I'll tell you all at once. I have an American friend who manages a cantina in Tijuana, on the other side of the border. Have you ever been to Tijuana?"

"No. I've heard people talk about it . . ."

"Well. It's not as bad as people who don't like Mexico make it out to be. Listen, there are cabarets and cantinas and the girls make good money as 'entertainers.' You know: they sing, they dance, they have a drink with the tourists, but they don't compromise themselves, ever. I repeat that the job is not very sought after because these stuck-up girls are too scrupulous, even those that might be worse than a demon in private.[213] They're hypocrites. You could, if you don't have anything else at the moment, try your luck. You don't know anyone there, I suppose—I guarantee that you won't make less than one hundred dollars a week, with tips and everything."

Linda paid more attention to what her friend was saying.

"Let's see; let's see. Explain it to me slowly."

"You'll see: you have to go in at noon, with the exception of Sundays, when you have to go to work very early. You have to sing some of your songs, and if you know some in English, all the better. You have to dance a tango or two, which the Americans like so much. Naturally, you will make friends with them, and you'll let them invite you to drinks at the bar or at the reserved tables, and for each one of those drinks they'll give you a commission; they paid me ten cents or twenty-five, depending on what it was."

"But wouldn't I get drunk like that? No?"

The friend smiled with compassion.

"Don't be silly. The bartenders know the drill, and in the place of cognac—which will be what you always order, because it is the most expensive—they will give you tea, the same color as the liquor but inoffensive, as you can understand. You will use your tricks if you like, so that the clients will drink and you will make your tips. There's nothing compromising in that. I know various good girls, left by their husbands or with children and a mother to maintain, who have never taken a misstep, despite their work."

[April 18, 1927]

"What's more," continued the girl as she passed a powder puff over her face, "I repeat that the work pays, if you know how to manage it. Your salary won't be lower than one hundred dollars a week, and if you are smart, you won't spend anything on food or lodging. In two weeks you'll have your one hundred and fifty or two hundred dollars and you can leave there and come back to Los Angeles, or wherever you like—that is, if you don't find a good prospect. There have been cases in which a girl left there well married."

Amid the indignation that started to invade her soul, Linda felt her heart give a leap. In two weeks she would have enough to go back to Guadalajara, where her loved ones still waited for her, surely, and where they would receive her with open arms. There was still a way to restart her life, and this painful interval in it would be nothing more than a sad nightmare that disappears when the sun rises on a happy day. Why not make the sacrifice? Despite the quickness with which she had fallen, Linda still retained a bit of control, and the idea of returning to her homeland gave her the courage to no longer confine herself to the dark corners of perdition. What's more, in Tijuana—a town she had barely even heard of—she didn't know anyone, and it was so far from her Guadalajara, her beloved land, that no one would imagine what her true means of living had been! Without thinking about it more, she almost interrupted her providential adviser.

"Listen, girl: when can you introduce me to your friend? I think I'd like to hear something about the deal."

"Whatever day you like. Just yesterday I saw him in his apartment. He's in Los Angeles on a business trip and wanted to take me with him to work. But I have my mom here, who does not even want to hear that I am going to Tijuana; like a lot of other good people she has the idea that it's all prostitution and vice there. You know how mothers are. If you want, let's make a date for tomorrow for the three of us to meet somewhere after the show. Here's his phone number—look, Beacon 4923."

The appointment for the following night was set for eleven at the theater itself. Linda would come once the show was over. The friend would be there and the three would go to the "Paris" to dance a bit, eat dinner, and seal the deal. When the two friends said goodbye, Linda carried in her soul a new hope of redemption. Leaving the entrance, she barely saw Rosales, who was standing there, waiting for a farewell smile. At his side was the new "tiple," a dark-skinned girl painted like a clown, who looked her predecessor up and down with an insolent and stupid air. Linda contained a gesture of indignation when she heard the girl say clearly as she passed:

"This is the famous 'Linda'? Boy, not even if she were the queen of Spain . . ."

She swallowed the insult and with a firm step exited the "foyer" where some boys were energetically nailing up portraits of the debutante everywhere, whistling the music of one of those abominable "cuples" that she had been condemned to learn by memory to please the "respectable public" here.

On the way back to her room, she didn't pay any attention to the catcalls that the night owls of Main Street, some of the worst she had seen in her life, directed at her in the little plaza. Close to the post office, a little something seemed funny to her, bringing her to the point of losing her habitual seriousness, cracking up laughing. A poorly dressed guy, with a dirty bandage over his right eye, an unkempt beard, and some pieces of surgical tape over various purulent sores on what you could still see of his face, said as she passed:

"Ay mamacita! How pretty you look. Who are you looking for so intently? Well, I'm right here, aren't I . . . ?"

In her heart she felt an intense bitterness, a depression that she tried to drown with the retort that didn't come out of her mouth. Had she reached such an extreme degeneration that this deformed entity, a living painting that resembled one of the disinherited from the court of miracles, thought he had the right to catcall her with any hope? She didn't know whether to get mad, laugh with joy, or cry.

[April 20, 1927]

A wind of fortune had blown over the head of Raymundo Nava. He had finished acting in the first film he made in Baja California, casting him as the young lead with the most prestigious actresses of the screen, and the film was a resounding success. The New York magazines, creators of reputations and frequent destroyers of popular idols, had smiled upon his work, and the harshest critics had deigned to direct encouraging words to him. Naturally, this brought a spate of interest from producers who saw in the up-and-coming Mexican a new gold mine to exploit while the boom times lasted. Now we find him filming his first role as a professional actor, in front of the serene beauty of Norma Talmadge, caressed bit by bit by the adulation of some, envied by others, desired by many women in Hollywood.

Since the rapid rise of Rudolph Valentino, who brought along with him the almost sudden fame of Ramon Novarro, no one could remember a triumph that had awakened so much interest. Raymundo's image multiplied across the continents in the pages of magazines, and his erotic figure as a Latin lover traveled from screen to screen to the edges of the Universe, provoking applause that he had never heard and the daydreams of romantic girls whom he had never seen in his life. Triumph in all its overwhelming grandeur, with all the intoxication of its prestige, had come upon him. He no longer lived as he had in a cheap boardinghouse room; now he had built his own mansion in Beverly Hills and brought there the rest of his family, half-forgotten in his native land. Six months was sufficient to carve out that reputation that already began to bear the abundant fruits of popularity. Those who had never fully paid attention to his arrogant figure of a creole boy, during his long peregrination from studio to studio in search of a place, now praised his profile as that of a Greek god, declaring him predestined for success from his birth. They found his figure attractive, his eyes full of a rapturous fire, his lips tempting. In the United States it's women who dedicate themselves to the disdained labor of interviewing stars, and they always had a word of admiration for him.

But Raymundo Nava seemed obsessed with one idea: meeting Linda Celli again. That girl had been almost his first love, the untouched virgin, for him his ideal love, to whom he had never spoken a single affectionate phrase for fear of losing her all at once. At first, when he received her last letter when he was in Baja California, he had a crazy impulse. He wanted to leave everything to run to her side, abandoning his career, future, riches, fame in exchange for seeing her one more time. But a night of bitter reflection sufficed to keep him away from that adventure that would have wrecked all of his artistic aspirations, the end of the career he had struggled so much to conquer. After all—he thought—she couldn't hide herself at the bottom of the earth. There would be time to succeed and to have her participate in that success for which she had, perhaps unconsciously, given him the required encouragement. Hadn't they sworn to struggle together that happy bohemian afternoon in the little café on Hollywood Boulevard? Hadn't they promised to fight fate tooth and nail, to succeed for each other, to make their dreams crystallize, so they would no longer be faced with mundane and threatening economic problems?

When he returned to Hollywood, he tried in vain to look for her in the places where he could ask about her. Her "landlady" told him with a

gesture of feigned piety that she was still in jail, where she had not gone
to visit her to avoid gossip. Raymundo ran to the infamous building on
Temple Street, where he obtained a vague answer to his queries. Linda had
left there some time ago and they didn't know where she had gone. She
had probably crossed the border to enter her native country, which she
never should have left. Everywhere he found uncertainty, doubt, crueler
than disenchantment . . .

[April 21, 1927]

Later his own prestige demanded that he keep more careful watch over his
name. He made one film and another, and another, and the work in the
studios had him completely absorbed, sighing now and again on remembering the eyes of that woman who seemed never to have left his life. At
times he imagined her back home, surrounded by her loved ones like a
maternal caress, having forgotten the tragic past, the nightmare that the
intent to conquer "The City of No Return" had been for both of them,
in that environment where illusions wither and where only those chosen
by Fortune reach the summit of true success. The pilgrimage to that height
is undertaken year after year by a hundred people, maybe more. At times,
among that parade that becomes less numerous over time, one or two
glimpse the light of glory before falling, exhausted, by the wayside, their
strength spent and their spirit lost. At other times no one even reaches the
midpoint of the journey and the caravan breaks up, corrupted by vice or
simply whipped by the winds of disillusion. From time to time there is
a figure who reaches the peak and can resist the glare of the sun, closing
their eyes to every vanity. These are the consecrated. But for every one of
them, how many have fallen along the path, how many have strayed from
the path in time to follow other routes more practically productive, how
many have seen over their dreaming heads the snow of a premature aging
that descends to wither all previous illusions!

Then he waited some days for a letter that never came and later tried
to forget the unforgettable. Like all those who live off the public, he had
become superstitious and acquired a blind faith in Destiny. Something inside
him told him that their lives would reunite in the end, and he hoped for
this with as much faith as he had pursued victory in previous years. He
gladdened at the thought that one day, perhaps not very distant, he would
have her in his arms, calling her his, making her part of a name already
famous, ensuring a pleasant future forever at his side. He would picture

Linda seated on his knee, before the warmth of the fire in a fireplace, remembering amid laughter their past adventures during times of poverty, shared so beautifully as they had been. But then he would wake up from his dream trying to forget, looking for relief for his sadness that even the arrival of his own mother, who had come to illuminate his new house like a celestial blessing, had not brought.

During the few months of his formal career, Raymundo had met various famous women and many fortunate actresses. The same ones who had seemed otherworldly to him in magazines now seemed crudely common, uninteresting, far from that ideal of beauty that the camera had given their images. He compared them mentally to Linda—his Linda!—and he found them so inferior that he could not contain a smile of commiseration. He had, in sum, all the symptoms that characterized the incurably lovestruck, dazzled by a fixed ideal, maybe because he had not touched reality with his own hands; maybe because the painted wings of his dream butterfly, apt symbol of illusion, had not faded between his fingers.

At almost the same time that the scenes from the film that he made with Norma Talmadge were finished, the racing season started in Tijuana. Tijuana is one hundred and thirty miles from Los Angeles and, as an oasis for Americans who wither in the desert of Prohibition, makes all its profits from tourists who travel across the border. One afternoon, a group of friends, all of them tourists from the world of cinema, agreed that upon finishing the most important scenes they would take advantage of a short break to visit the Mexican city, at whose hippodrome they made plans with the most fashionable personalities from the [European] continent. Raymundo had not set foot in his home country for a long time, and the opportunity to feel himself again in his land, or some part of it, seemed good to him. He was now in possession of a famous name, something he had lacked when he left one memorable afternoon, promising not to come back until he had grabbed the golden curls of that elusive goddess, Fortune.

[Translators' note: Although Navarro ended this installment with "Continues tomorrow," it appears that no subsequent installment was published.]

SELECTED FILM AND CULTURAL CRITICISM, 1921–1939

La OPORTUNIDAD de FRACASAR en el CINE

Por GABRIEL NAVARRO
Redactor Cinematográfico de los Periódicos LOZANO

Los Trucos de los Estudios para Nulificar a los Aspirantes que Prometen, pero que 'no caen bien'

EL EMPLEO de los artistas de habla española en los Estudios del Cinema, no es una cuestión de patria, ni de pronunciación, ni de acento; es simplemente una cuestión de calidad. Aquellos que reúnan requisitos elementales algunos, no son ni pueden ser rechazados; a los estudios les conviene contratar a esos elementos ¿y qué menos que podría ser su actitud al rechazarlos?

Las palabras anteriores, lector amigo, no son de la cosecha del autor de este artículo. Fueron pronunciadas en cierta ocasión que va siendo ya memorable, en presencia de un grupo de artistas hispanoamericanos, por uno de los más prominentes funcionarios de los talleres cinematográficos de Hollywood.

Considerando semejantes declaraciones serenamente, vale la pena corroborarse de si es o no verdad tanta belleza.—Y antes de seguir adelante, aseguramos que no discutimos el trazismo de discutir el que se tenga ejercito por ésta o aquella razón a las no peninsulares, al formularse los cálculos de campañas que filman en español.

Solamente nos parece oportuno presentar hechos, sin bordar en torno de ellos comentarios intencionados; los artistas que fracasan ante las cámaras, son, de diferentes nacionalidades y no creemos—por el momento, cuando menos—que la campaña sorda vaya enderezada hacia los que nacieron en esta parte del Atlántico, por más que muchos de los vencidos "de allá" sean directa o indirectamente responsables de que el público, ávido de sensaciones, prohíje con tanto calor versiones contrarias a esos mismos elementos.

ESTRELLAS FUGACES EN EL FIRMAMENTO DEL CINE

De la misma manera que a un artista se le da la oportunidad para triunfar, lo mismo ¿cómo a otros se les da la más franca, amplia y decidida oportunidad de fracasar ante la cámara y el micrófono. ¿Intencionadamente? Eso no lo discutimos; el hecho existe, y basta.

¡Cuántos aspirantes a la gloria del Cinema han visto derrumbarse todo su castillo de ilusiones, tras la primera prueba, de la que depende casi siempre su entrada a los estudios, o su proscripción total de los mismos! Con las desencantados de Hollywood, solamente en el terreno de la película española, podría formarse una división, lo suficientemente fuerte para luchar, si acaso, aún quienquiera de nuestras turbulentas repúblicas todohispanas. Y película dos que gran batalla trás una larga lucha en cierta ocasión, a las primeras de cambio en los elementos más afortunados; pero de los que caen—y caen a diario—no saben sino sus amigos, sus familiares y el acaso alguno de esos consejeros pesimistas dispuestos siempre a decirnos después de un contratiempo: ¿no lo había dicho yo?

—No te lo había dicho yo? No son pocas las veces que hemos visto un nombre con grandes caracteres en programas y carteles, como pertenecerán al o la "estrella" de una producción. Nos medio familiarizamos con su fotografía y luego, cuando la película se ha exhibido se reconoce si se los bulldos tirados la tierra. Ni el público, ni los productores, ni nadie vuelve a acordarse de ellos. ¡Cuál es la explicación más aproximada en tales casos?

En la mayor parte de ellos es que al artista o aspirante, se le ha dado la más amplia oportunidad de fracasar, con toda intención; pero siempre con el mismo resultado. Y aún no notaremos resulta ridículo, su maquillaje de una mediocridad que sublevaría al no fuese conmovedora; sea las víctimas del "miedo" de las que se hay antes en Hollywood.

EL CASO DE LOS CONSAGRADOS

Porque es indiscutible que el Cine, ahora que ha hecho uso de la palabra, es una cuestión primeramente de tipos. Veamos vivió anónimamente mientras fue mudo ¿cuero?, triunfando de manera episistante cuando se le convirtió en galán ardiente y dominador—que conocemos en sus interpretaciones silenciosas; a nadie hubiese interesado mucho ni poco Lon Chaney en una parte de galán conquistador, ni Lilian Gish en una de "vampiresa" resistente de maldad. Gloria Swanson iniciando los tres "Peter Pan" hubiera muerto antiestimulante el mismo día del estreno de la película, y Lupe Vélez, presentada por primera vez en una parte de ingenua o de gran dama, estuviera ahora mismo bailando danzarín en el "lirio" o en cualquier otro teatro de segunda categoría, destinada por completo de la carrera cinematográfica. Nadie puede negar con éxito—he sido gusto de partida de su carrera "cholo" plenamente triunfal no fue la "Güera" encarnación del bandido generoso que nos pinta el argumento. Por simple y sencillamente Lupe Vélez en persona, llevada a la pantalla con sus mismos maneritos, con su misma inquieta personalidad en ese momento, simpatía, por lo atrevido y cautivadora por su unindencia a triunfar; todos los convencionalismos sociales. Ese ha sido el secreto de su éxito ideal. Una vez, fue en ella la atención de los productores, vino lo que podríamos llamar la preparación.

Pero hablemos ahora de los pequeños "trucos" de que se vale la industria para descartar de pleno, y de una sola plumada, la efectividad de un valor artístico. Uno de ellos, muy conocido, es el "test" llevado a la debida preparación.

Un actor dotado de ciertas cualidades...

La oportunidad de fracasar en el cine le fue aplicada sabiamente a Cora Montez. Este es sólo uno de los numerosos ejemplos que podrían ser citados. Cora, que tiene facultades reconocidas y "fotografía bien", como puede apreciarse en este grabado, fracasó en la pantalla, del mismo modo que se le había dado la oportunidad contraria; la de triunfar. Cora, bien maquillada, bien dirigida y tomada desde el ángulo fotográfico que mejor favorece a su cara, aparece aquí atrayente. En cambio cuando quiso dársele "la oportunidad de fracasar", fue mal maquillada y tomada desde su peor ángulo fotográfico, como el lector podrá apreciar en el grabado que aparece en la siguiente página.

con un pasado artístico recomendable, llega a Hollywood en busca de una parte que sea para él la puerta por donde penetrar al recinto vedado de los estudios del Cine parlante. Después de gestiones laboriosas, en las que se ha echado mano de todos los recursos imaginables—la oportunidad es real siempre cuestión de influencias—se le llama al estudio, manifestándole que se le va a sujetar a una prueba, y él se dirige a la cita con el corazón palpitando a razón de ciento veinte latidos por minuto.

Ya en el escenario, se viste al actor de cualquier manera, se le maquilla a toda prisa, defectuosamente, la mayor parte de las veces, y se le da un pliego marón, del cual tiene que aprender de memoria una parte. Una hora más tarde, y sin preparación alguna, se le pone frente a la cámara; se le elige, así nada, una porción del "diálogo" que se le ha dado a aprender. En la mayor parte de los casos, se justamenta la parte que menos seguro está el candidato, y su nerviosidad aumenta hasta el delirio.

—Quien haya estado por primera vez ante la cámara y ante el micrófono, sabe la impresión que se siente en esas circunstancias. Frente al actor hay un grupo azarín—director, ayudantes,—supervisor, etc.—cuyos ojos se clavan sobre su figura con una ansiedad que tiene mucho de prejuicio. Y así, el ojo impasible de la cámara adquiere para él los proporciones de Fu-Man-Chú. Se hace un silencio general, que viene agravando más la situación, y luego se le invita a "vivir una parte de la tarea" en la entrada teatral. Funciona la cámara y dos minutos más tarde so corta la actuación. Ni un comentario alentador, ni una sola frase que lo haga concebir esperanzas. El resultado es que cuando la revelada la cinta de celuloide se exhibe ante un grupo de severísimos críticos, el actor o actriz que en el teatro ha conquistado grandes manifestaciones de aprobación del público, está hecho un mamarracho. Se ve sobre la pantalla su figura, que temblaba como la de un aspirado; su voz es gutural, horrible, sus ademanes inciertos, y en su mirada se adivina la angustia, el esfuerzo por recordar las "líneas" que se lo han hecho decir de memoria. El aspirante casi nunca ve esta prueba, y el silencio del productor o director en torno del resultado le dice claramente cuán deplorable ha sido su fracaso.

OTRA FORMA DE FRACASAR

En algunas ocasiones, la prueba se hace con dos elementos entre los cuales se desarrolla un corto diálogo: el aspirante, y el actor o actriz ya probado y aceptado, y quien, en consecuencia, tiene segura su parte respectiva. Se hace un pequeño ensayo. Antes de comenzar la cortísima escena, y el director, levantando la voz, anuncia llamando su nombre—toda-s las frases consagradas en el léxico de los "gangs" de Chicago, que, es una voz no es la que debe emplearse, que la entonación está baja, que éste o aquel movimiento es forzado. La figura del interlocutor queda, dentro del radio de la cámara y solamente so oye, al ver la prueba, su voz. En muchos casos, dicho interlocutor perfectamente preparado, lee lo que dice, mientras que el desdichado que está a prueba tiene que hacer de memoria. Y cuando ambas figuras son fotografiadas—da dan cuenta—el resultado es todavía peor, por tanto que la una se ve bien claro su aplomo y dominio de la escena, en la del aspirante se nota una nerviosidad que lo pone en condiciones muy desfavorables con respecto al otro actor. Tal es una de los términos de la oportunidad de fracasar.

Naturalmente, cuando el aspirante o un agente solicita una parte en una producción siguiente; el productor o su representante le dice con su sueño de lástima que extremece:

—¿Quién? ¡Ese! ¡Vamos, hombre; si no sirve para nada! Se la dió la oportunidad y ya se embarró.

Y venga usted a decir ahora que es cuestión de calidad!

Hay otras maneras de provocar el fracaso de un aspirante, cuando la prueba ha resultado medianamente satisfactoria. Se le extiende su contrato por una película, y en lo que la parte para no sobresalir. Unos días antes de la primera escena. Pero la parte en él se le administra en tal grado la personalidad propia del actor o es un tipo juvenil, lleno de la naturaleza del de vivir, se le "reparte" un papel de villano, en que un bigote que trastorna, se apodea Zapata, y durante la impresión de la escena el director está constantemente procesando-por su atuendo. Como de la película esté su aprobado, el público se convence de que el nuevo actor es una mera tranquilidad de farolillo. Para él, las puertas de los estudios están cerradas definitivamente, a menos—

La Magazín de la Opinión, February 8, 1931, page 5, with "The Opportunity to Fail in Cinema" by Gabriel Navarro.

IN THE REALM OF MEXICAN MUSICAL ART

"Por los fueros del arte musical mexicano," published in
El Heraldo de México, May 20, 1921, page 7

Some days ago the management of a well-known Los Angeles theater announced the performance of a band as one of its coming "attractions." According to reports in the English-language papers, the band was known in Mexico as the Mexican National Band.

They began by promoting the famous Police Band of Mexico, a group whose name has traveled triumphantly around the globe. But then they later announced, with a certain degree of ambiguity, that it was simply the "Mexican Government Band." Nonetheless, shortly after the first of this month, a paragraph in this city's *Examiner* gave news that the band in question had remained intact through multiple revolutions and had accordingly earned the title of the "National Band of Mexico." It was said to be composed of 125 master musicians and had been compared to the most famous of brass bands led by Sousa and Mercator.[214] These details correspond precisely to the band led by maestro Preza, who has belonged and still belongs to the mounted police corps of Mexico.[215] Together with the first announcement, this led every Mexican in Los Angeles—who was not privy to the secret of these claims—to believe that they referred to the famous Mexican musical group. Likewise, this newspaper, initially guided by reports from the American press and theater programs, spread the good news to our readers. The Police Band would be coming, the pride of Mexican Art, the paragon of military bands . . .[216]

Unfortunately, this did not happen. This week, the theater in question has been presenting a small group of relatively mediocre musicians in its auditorium, in front of a foreign audience, as the "National Band of Mexico."

Hardly any commentary is necessary. The American public believes it is hearing the famous group it has heard so much about and that is indisputably the best of our nation, despite the showmanship of another band that recently came to the United States. As far as bands are concerned, this public is forming a rather sad impression of the state of our musical arts.

And what's more, the same theater, which has a magnificent symphonic orchestra, advertised a serious program of "All Spanish-Mexican" music in which nothing truly Spanish was included except "La Paloma" and from which Mexican music was excluded altogether. We have to conclude that, in the eyes of our cultivated neighbors in the United States, our country is deemed worthless in terms of music and musicians.

We cannot allow this. If we have national music and musicians in Mexico, why not protest the fact that something is being presented as ours when in reality it is not? And why not make the necessary clarifications about the band, even if only in defense of our national art, which remains unknown to those who have not visited our country?

The band that is actually giving concerts in the aforementioned theater, although it may be a Mexican band, hardly even measures up to second-class bands in our country. I am not attacking the band or its members—who are our compatriots and have the right to make a living from their work—but instead the impresarios who sacrifice a nation's conception of art in the interest of sensationalism and profit.

Because people will undoubtedly believe that the band in question is the most famous in Mexico, the best the country has to offer, something akin to the artistic pride of the nation . . . And what easier way is there to form an impression of the state of music in Mexico, by deduction, than by hearing what has been proclaimed as the best?

That's one side of the issue. Now let's talk about the "all Spanish-Mexican program" presented on the fifteenth by the symphonic orchestra of the same theater. In the first place, said program featured "La Paloma" and "La Golondrina," two popular songs performed in their most primitive form. Being Spanish and Mexican, they are undoubtedly better known in this country than in our own. And that was it. The selection from Bizet's *Carmen* was very Spanish, of course, but it is not Spanish in origin. The Spanish rhapsody that was performed is not by a Spanish composer, nor does it have anything to do with the Mexican music touted on the program. The numbers by Rubenstein are undoubtedly majestic, but they are not Spanish, much less Mexican. The rest of the program, including an Argentine tango, is even less Hispano-Mexican, which is apparent just from reading the song's title.

This is no small matter. Reading the procession of foreign names among the composers, it's natural that the public would notice the absence of Mexican names. And, thinking logically, given the band in question, its considerable musical reputation, and its obligation to be serious and truthful with the public, one could only reach the conclusion that in Mexico there are no musicians capable of composing even a bad song, nor a truly national music. (And I reiterate that "La Paloma" and "La Golondrina" are less popular in Mexico than in this country.)

This is false. In Mexico we have Julián Carrillo, Arnulfo Miramontes, and Manuel M. Ponce, among those who are alive. Among the glorious dead are figures like Felipe Villanueva, Melesio Morales, Ricardo Castro . . . And all of them have written Mexican music in a more or less independent style. The symphonies of Carrillo and the rhapsodies of Ponce are a testimony to this. It is true that the operas of Morales, just like those of Gino Corsini, the Poet King of Campa, and others by Castro reveal the influence of studies in Europe, mostly in Germany. But it is also very true that "Nicolás Bravo" (whose overture is based on a Mexican military march), "Anahuac" (even including the failure it provoked), and the rhapsodies of Manuel M. Ponce are Mexican through and through. And there are a hundred others like these that would undoubtedly have been seen as imperfect from the perspective of harsh criticism. But they are without a doubt superior to "La Paloma" and the other song, which are furthermore not of Mexican "parentage," as I have already mentioned.[217]

Let us now move to music of a lesser character. Villanueva is the founding father of an entire school of short pieces, the majority of them waltzes. This distinction was then seized by Berger, who became famous for his Parisian waltzes, inspired by the "Poético" composed by the old master from Zacatecas. Like him, Abundio Martínez was an original composer of melodies, the creator of a style, a bit ignorant and vicious perhaps, but with an inspiration that would surely be envied by composers who graduated from European schools. And the Mexican marches of Velino M. Preza? Is this maestro not the creator of short pieces in a new style, with impeccable melodies and harmonic structures that are so whimsical? I know of no foreign style that can compare. What's more, they are all completely Mexican.[218]

The danzas of Calderón and Pomar, the waltzes of Chucho Martínez (standard-bearer of the Villanueva school), and the incorrect pieces, full of mistakes and with a motley tone, by composers from the border region like Rodolfo Campodónico, Garza, etc., also have an exclusively national flavor. This is Mexican music.[219]

With respect to "Folk Lore," we have "Mañanitas," a short piece that is perfectly Beethovian and with a melody all our own. Our popular songs (most of them from anonymous authors), the sones of the Bajío region, our jarabe tapatío, the zandungas, the danzones from Veracruz and the Yucatán (with a bit of Cuban influence because of proximity), the risqué songs from Jalisco, the "Pazcola" of the Yaquis, and so many other things that come to mind are also a testament to the fact that we have national music. Eliminating Mexican songs from a program called Mexican is therefore an unforgivable mistake by a symphony orchestra directed by a famed European musician and composed of musicians from every nation, which week after week finds success with the most complicated scores of Tchaikovsky and even Richard Strauss.

I wouldn't have decided to write this little article if it weren't for the desire to defend our national art. After a Mexican concert that was no such thing, they serve us a Mexican band that might align with the claims of publicity in terms of nationality. But in terms of art, it is a hundred miles in the exact opposite direction. Is this fair?

Let them say that one of those renowned Mexican bands (using whatever claims or terminology they want) is going to delight attendees with select musical pieces. Let them say that they will play a program of semi-Spanish music, etc. But they should not operate with the kind of carelessness that leaves us so offended.

Mexico has music and musicians.

Let justice be done!

THE CRYSTAL BALL

El cristal encantado, column published in *La Prensa*, December 14,
1924, page 16, under the byline El Mago de Hollywood

A. Rojas. León, Gto. [Guanajuato]

To be an artist of the cinema, my dear friend, it is necessary . . . simply
to be one. You say that you are sixteen years old and are almost certain of
your talent for the silent art. If that's so, come to Los Angeles, but come on
your own account and understanding the risks. It's necessary to bring money,
enough money for the bad times, or an immense amount of patience. I
personally don't advise it, but you know what you are doing. Your idea of
coming and doing whatever is offered to you seems judicious and reasonable. But do you know English? Without this requirement, you won't enter
a studio, not even with thousands of dollars. Reflect on it well and decide.
Don't forget to write often.

Manrita. Kansas City, MO.

And why in English? You had nothing to do, so you asked, eh? I have
a lot to do and so I'll answer you briefly. You are correct in your thinking
about Ramon Novarro. I don't have time to give you all the details that
you ask for, but I'll tell you that I win the bet. When you don't have "a
thing in the world to do," as your letter says, write to me. That's what I'm
here for. Yes, I am Mexican and very proud of it, little one.

C. M. R. San Antonio

Unfortunately, I can't answer your letter personally, even though you
sent me stamps to do so, because the matter that you've broached with
me is of a character entirely related to this column. Since she arrived in
Los Angeles, Pola Negri has had her secretary and her personal maids,
and I don't think what you suggest would be possible. What's more, she
doesn't speak Spanish. I talked with her about your letter, and she said she

appreciates your expressions of sympathy and she returns them. Her address, for the portrait, is 1506 Lexington Drive, Beverly Hills. Write to her in French or Spanish.

A. Flores. New Orleans, LA.

Ben Lyon is American, miss, and speaks English. He is twenty-three years old, and his address is 5341 Melrose Avenue. If you want a portrait of him, I can send it to you by return mail. See how quickly your questions are answered. Write frequently.

María de la Luz Reyes

"María de la Luz Reyes," published in *El Heraldo de México*,
January 11, 1925, page 8, under the byline Crispín[220]

It was the hour of monotonous rehearsal. Seated next to the music instructor, her childlike hands leafed through a movie magazine. I had no intention of interrogating her; but her wandering, restless eyes that anxiously scanned the illustration "captions" compelled me to ask her a few questions. And her lips—two red, robust wings across which fiery kisses seem to wander, those burning kisses she uses to show gratitude to an applauding audience—opened slightly to move with the voluptuousness of rosebuds.[221]

Convinced that María de la Luz Reyes, with the eyes of her soul fixed on the heavens, has been struggling alone to reach her life's dream, which is wrapped in lilting, sonorous notes, I proffered an indiscreet question:

"Would you like to be a movie star?"

A smile of contempt nearly formed on her lips, an Olympian, unthinkable, and unacceptable contempt:

"A movie star? No. I have another dream. I am pursuing success along a different path. I am an artist, but in a more sublime sense. Music attracts me, envelops me, subjugates me . . ."

And María de la Luz—I said to myself—attracts music, subjugates and almost dominates it. I then recall the impression that our community's maestros had of her. At this moment Luz is the youngest Mexican singer, the most beautiful, the one with the most talent and a voice that is the clearest, the most diaphanous, and the purest.

"Mary Philbin has such bewitching eyes!" she exclaimed, looking at the effigy of said artist appearing in the publication she was enjoying.

"Do you go to the movies often?"

"Yes, whenever my studies permit. I go because, above all, I do find that some productions are truly works of art. But . . . if you could see how angry I get at some of those monstrosities?"

María de la Luz is not on stage, but she makes a convincing gesture of anger. She then laughs with crystalline clarity, like a little girl.

"Which recent films did you like the most?"

"Let's see . . ."

The celebrated singer remains quiet. I imagine that she has not heard my question. As I was interested in her opinion, I prepared to express my curiosity again when she surprised me:

"I was about to say *Forbidden Paradise*. It's a bit of a fantasy film that nonetheless seduces you through the tangible reality of its scenes. That is, the overall story seems a little far-fetched, perhaps because of the ideas we have about all those tales of princesses, elves, and fairies. But the details? There is no doubt that Mr. Lubitsch is a genius. So much so that he could be compared to Chaplin himself. By the way, *A Woman of Paris* left me with very fond memories.[222] It's a film in which life pulsates with all of its characteristic cruelty and hope."

"Your favorite 'star'"?

"There are three or four. Pola Negri drives me crazy with her temperament; Gloria Swanson dazzles me with her elegance; Mary Pickford seduces me with her naivete . . ."

"And what about the ugly old men?"

"I assume that you aren't referring to Novarro or Valentino. Sticking to your question, I will respond by saying that I find so much interpretive spirit in Wallace Beery, Milton Sills, and Lewis Stone."

"And what do you think of Valentino?"

"He's a mediocre actor. His indisputably artistic temperament makes him one of the most convincing young leading men on screen. Novarro has an elevated conception of art, an art that is refined, aristocratic, and incomprehensible for a large part of the general public."

"And Norma Shearer?"

"She is a very attractive young woman who, as far as I can see, has managed to join the ranks of the biggest stars."

"What would your opinion of Ricardo Cortez be?"

"My opinion is almost as bland as his very personality. From my perspective, Ricardo Cortez has no grace, nor that Saxon 'pep,' nor 'esprit.' As you already know: he began his cinematic career in the same way and with the same advantages as Rudolph Valentino, that is, by hypnotizing directors with his 'tangos.'"

"And Barbara La Marr?"

"A woman who provokes a sea of interest; she only needs to break free of the one personality that she has cultivated in front of the camera."

And so we waited for María de la Luz's turn by talking and commenting on cinematic topics. A few minutes later you could hear the flow of her firm and luminous voice that drives us mad with those sharps that are always precise and always harmonious . . .

The company at the Teatro Hidalgo is proud to have her within its fold . . .

Cinematic Indiscretions— Why Mexican Girls Shouldn't Come to Hollywood

The Dangers of the Enchanted City; How Rudolph Valentino, Novarro, and Barbara La Marr Have Gotten to Where They Are; Disinterested Advice

"Indiscreciones cinematográficas—Porque no deben venir las muchachas mexicanas a Hollywood," published in *La Prensa*, May 24, 1925, page 12

Dear Enriqueta:

I see from your last letter that you are thinking about coming to Hollywood. And, as I consider it a matter of a certain gravity, I am going to undertake a slight digression in my weekly epistles to take up this issue with you. Within the next week I will probably continue talking about the secrets that the studios hold for the uninitiated in terms of making films that the owner of your favorite theater will present to you, skillfully accompanied by organ music, title cards in Spanish, etc.

The step you are thinking of taking, dear Enriqueta, is the most serious of all seriousness. Just because you're familiar with the trivia I tell you about Hollywood doesn't mean that you can move to this enchanted and marvelous city without more deliberation. In the end, its shelters, its hotels, its streets are crammed with girls who dared make the journey, just as you want to, and who in the end have resigned themselves to working the most dreadful jobs in order not to starve, if they haven't already succumbed to the yapping of the human wolves who howl on every corner here. All these girls are pretty like you; they have aspirations like yours; and they have heard, as you say in your letter about yourself, the neighbors of their town telling them:

"But by God . . . What are you doing here? With your looks and intelligence, you should be a movie star . . . !"

And they listened to the call of the sirens, with the painful result that I've already told you about. They should never have come. In their towns they might have married some insipid but honorable local boy who would earn enough to support them. Their houses would have already received the blessing of some adorable, mischievous children. At the least they would have remained honorable women or wouldn't have suffered so many setbacks and disappointments.

I am going to explain to you why I can't advise you to come: You have told me that your little friends assure you that you have an attractive figure; that you have seen yourself act in front of a mirror and that (without any pretensions) you haven't done so badly. Yes, I understand the words in your letter very well. You also assure me that you have enough will to withstand the reversals of fortune of the early days and you would come with endless spirit. All of this might be true, and even I, someone who knows you, am aware of other fine virtues you possess, which would help you reach the peak—if that were possible. But disabuse yourself of these notions, Enriqueta. In the film studios there isn't a single opportunity (and now less than ever). Artists whom I have seen playing principal roles are playing secondary roles with other famous "stars" in their latest films. Many of the studios have shut their gates and others have consolidated their resources to work as one firm. What's more, almost all the old studio "extras" are now working at jobs that are less attractive, although as honest as those that used to consume their energy. There is, then, much higher supply than demand.

Then there is a second issue to address, but I confess that I don't know where to start. You are more or less beautiful, have certain artistic faculties, an immense love for the sublime, etc. But you don't know how to swim. You don't, so far as I know, know how to ride a horse. You are ignorant of how your photographs come out and whether you would be a good "subject" or not. You still don't know English very well, nor do you have the resources to be able to support yourself respectably for very long without working. What's more, your beauty is one of your worst enemies. In Hollywood there are an infinite number of individuals who call themselves agents of this or that company who will reassure you that they are friends with this director, that they have a "direct line" to the studios. Neither of these things is true. They are individuals who hunt for money or feminine innocence to exploit. You would need your mother, or some other respectable person from your family, to come with you . . . and that would mean more money.

You will tell me that Ramon Novarro, Rudolph Valentino, [Antonio] Moreno, Barbara La Marr, and others have succeeded in the same way, so you can too, since you have the persistence that they had. Don't believe it. Before Ramon Novarro definitively entered the studio, he had already been a dancer in American theaters with Marion Morgan's troupe, and he had acquired a name within the artistic circles of Hollywood and Los Angeles with his danceable creations, some of which he authored; Rudolph Valentino came to his success in the same way.[223] He was a dancer for a long time and had close relationships with directors, stars, etc. Barbara La Marr is a talented writer and had already been exercising her profession in the studios. Opportunity only came to her when she was well known. Antonio Moreno worked in the spoken theater, and when he began his cinematic career he did not have the tremendous competition that exists today. I could enumerate many artists and many "stars" like this, but out of respect for the ladies who are the primary readers of this section, I wouldn't be able to tell you the lengths to which they went to get the smallest opportunity. Your intelligence is sufficiently broad to understand me.

Given all these general conditions and the way that Hollywood is packed right now with people who want to work in cinema, I don't advise you to come. And God willing you will never think of it again. There are so many dangers here for girls like you.

—Until next time, G.

ENRIQUETA'S VOYAGE TO THE OLD WORLD

GERMAN FILMS IN CUBA; ANTONIO MORENO, MADRID'S IDOL; POLA NEGRI, SPANISH?; IN PARIS THEY DO JUSTICE TO OUR RAMON NOVARRO; ANNOUNCING THE UPCOMING EXHIBITION OF *BEN-HUR*

"El viaje de Enriqueta al viejo mundo," published in
La Prensa, December 6, 1925, page 17

Dear Enriqueta,

For the pleasure of *La Prensa*'s female readers, today I am starting to publish your notes about your voyage, which might be of interest to them given that they are fans of the cinema. It might be a little strange to find your notes corrected a bit, but I haven't distorted their meaning; if anything, I've barely changed this or that word that seemed too repetitive to me. You say:

"We left New Orleans at the end of September. My parents had promised to take me to see interesting places on the old [European] continent, and that made me a bit more content to leave my girlfriends in America. But during the crossing I was deprived of going to the Cinema, as is my custom every night. What would I see in European theaters? What novelties would the cinemas of Spain, France, and other places hold for me? I passed almost the entire crossing reading the book you sent me about Hollywood's stars. How many surprises it held for me! How many artists' lives it revealed to me in a most unexpected and enchanting way! Pola Negri, Rudolph Valentino, and Antonio Moreno above all prompted me to meditate an entire night on the unexpected twists that destiny has in store for us with the turn of any calendar page. A few days later, the ship arrived in Havana.

I was determined to see the city and, above all, to visit its cinemas that, to tell the truth, I didn't find as comfortable as those in the United States.

"I'm going to tell you something very odd. In Havana, in contrast to everything one might expect, American films are not the most popular. German film dominates in such a way that when there is a screening, a giant sign at the entrance to that cinema doesn't announce the name of the film but simply says 'GERMAN FILM TODAY.'

"Berlin's U.F.A. has more control over the cinemagoing public in Cuba than any American company.[224] While in some theaters I saw in big letters over the entrance: 'Rudolph Valentino' in this or that film, in the rest the name of the star, film, and director were in small letters dominated by a luminous sign announcing the origin of the film, even German comedies! What a difference between American film, consistent and always cloyingly sweet thanks to the censors' action, and that genre of films that are vigorous, magnificently presented, in a word, superb! How I would have liked to have visited Berlin's studios. It's a huge shame that my parents didn't have this great city on our trip's itinerary. Mae Murray, Rudolph Valentino, and Norma Talmadge receive the greatest share of Cuban affection. It was so strange to me to see not a single film by our Ramon Novarro. On one corner I saw the remains of a little poster that announced, 'At the Margin of Civilization': from the images I realized that it was for that film he made with Alice Terry under the name *Where the Pavement Ends.*[225] The posters declared that the film had been made in Cuba, something that surprised me, since I had always believed that the scenes, supposedly set in the South Islands, had been filmed on the coast of Florida. But I saw nothing else about our beloved Mexican actor. What do you think of that?

"Two weeks later we were in Madrid. What a beautiful city with its picturesque characters still present in certain neighborhoods, with something of its past splendor still lingering in its people and things. I noticed that despite everything, films made in Spain don't dominate their own market. It is materially controlled by French and American films. In one Madrid cinema, where they also had a variety show, what do you think I saw? Nothing less than *Forbidden Paradise*, shown under the title 'The Queen's Cadets.'[226] A girlfriend that I made quickly in Madrid maintains that Pola Negri is Spanish, even though I proved that she is Polish by showing her the book that you sent. In the face of my proof, she smiled and told me:

"'Yes, yes . . . now they want to appropriate her.'

"Of course, I didn't insist, leaving her to her illusions. As if that weren't enough, audience favorite and idol Antonio Moreno is in Madrid. They inform me that he was just in the city to visit his elderly mother and that he left for Niza, where he was going to shoot, or was shooting, a Blasco Ibáñez film.

"Another favorite in Spain is Raquel Meller, although she only appears in French films. As I've told you before, Spanish film is almost worthless. Better than ours [Mexico's], it's true, but never at the level of American film, which I say with all honesty.

"In Paris, I found that American film also has a wide presence in the French market. One night I saw Gloria Swanson pass by on the Champs-Élysées boulevard accompanied by her husband and two other women who also looked American. What a life these stars live! Surrounded by luxury, comforts, and servile admiration. When I was in Paris, it was rumored that the Marquis de La Falaise wasn't a marquis but a poor common devil, and the newspaper gave the matter some importance. But later came the news of the war in Syria and of the bombardment of Damascus, among other cities, and the rumors that had grown around the Marquis and Marquise de La Falaise de La Coudraye quieted down.

"In my next letter, I propose sending you details about our voyage to the Holy Land, which we undertake despite the alarming rumors of war that are circulating everywhere. You will see what I see in Port Said and in Jerusalem, the holy city. I forgot to tell you that in Paris they are already announcing the film *Ben-Hur* with Ramon Novarro, whom I was pleased to see announced as 'the marvelous Mexican actor.'[227] On my return to the United States I discovered that they still haven't finished the film, but it's already contracted in Paris. What do you think of the diligence of the publicists and exhibitors?"

I assure you, dear Enriqueta, that our readers are going to really enjoy your second letter. Don't forget to send it to me promptly, so it can be published here. For now, as always, yours . . .

WHY DO YOU GO TO THE MOVIES?
A MASCULINE OPINION

"TO SEE WOMEN!"; DIAMONDS IN THE ROUGH;
THE ETERNAL ILLUSION

"Por qué va ud. al cine? Una opinión masculina," published
in *La Opinión*, August 5, 1928, page 14

I am unaware of what my colleague Rosa María is writing about this same
topic in her column that will appear opposite this one on the cinema page
of *La Opinión*. The subject is the same, but the points of view will probably
differ; since the first human being stepped onto this planet, men and women
have never agreed. So it will certainly be interesting to hear each opinion,
especially if they are printed side by side on the same page to be analyzed
by the readers themselves.

WHY DO YOU GO TO THE MOVIES?—is the topic proposed by
the editor. The response of this author is as follows, although perhaps hastily
articulated given the demands of modern journalism. But it is nonetheless
sincere, eminently sincere:

"First of all, I go to the movies out of necessity because I write about
them weekly and I must remain immersed in the sensations of cinema so
that I can convey this to readers. Next, because I consider it a complement
to our lives; a thoughtful and well-made film can be a source of education.
Although I know that virtue will triumph in the end and that the hand
of Destiny will impose a punishment on the villain that mankind is prohibited from imposing, I am still amazed by the cinematic process, which
becomes more innovative and complicated by the day, and to greater effect.
Yet nonetheless . . .

"I do not believe that cinema can serve as a school of good customs for the time being, as it is under the severe control of censorship. Life is how it is, not as we would probably like it to be. Movies are for the most part made in accordance with the sensibilities of the public that attends their exhibition, a sensibility previously observed by exhibitors and producers; cinema is not tasked with creating the tastes of audiences, but rather with projecting audience preferences. People go to the movies expecting to find what they desire: a gruesome or romantic fiction, a daring adventure, or the intense emotion of a suspenseful moment. But there are sometimes diamonds shining through the shadows of this haystack, small details that are transforming the Industry into a true art: tragic gestures, captured by the camera, that pass fleetingly across the screen, leaving us with the desire to savor them more fully. So I go to the movies to catch these details, not to blindly accept the fables presented for the benefit of the audience in the gallery. In addition—and I'll tell you a secret—I go to the movies . . . to see beautiful women. I secretly suspect that the enchanting faces projected on the silver screen are not as spiritually beautiful in real life, that the stars once off the screen are not any more beautiful or elegant than the women we encounter in the course of our daily lives. But we all enjoy an attractive lie. What would our lives be without the sweet deceit of unreal things? The truth can be a good thing, but it is not always sweet. Illusions rule our existence, because after all, what are our lives but a perpetual illusion? Someone has said that the blue sky suspended over our heads is neither blue nor a sky. But all the collected philosophies of the world could not for a moment keep us from chasing golden butterflies that may in the end be only mirages, like the green oasis and the miraculous springs that the wanderer believes he sees through the undulating sands of the desert.

"That's why I go to the movies: because I tirelessly pursue illusion. A lovely interlude that makes us forget the bitterness of existence is always desirable. Movies are entertainment for children. But who doesn't enjoy feeling like a child now and then, taking a reprieve from the perpetual duty that forces us into a web of self-involvement and interests that have become the life of grown men!"

WHY DO YOU GO TO THE MOVIES? A FEMININE OPINION

CENSORSHIP; ROMANTIC FILMS; UNNECESSARY TRAGEDIES

"Por qué va ud. al cine? Una opinión femenina," published in *La Opinión*, August 5, 1928, page 14, under the byline Rosa María[228]

WHY DO YOU GO TO THE MOVIES?—they ask me, requesting a feminine opinion like mine to be published on the cinema page of *La Opinión*. They tell me that someone else is writing about this, and that this person is a man, which will make this little inquiry more interesting. I don't know what my colleague on this page will say. But without fear or prejudice, without even knowing how he thinks, I will now tell you why I go to the Movies:

"I attend film exhibitions because I think the art of shadows is the art of the future and because it is a truly feminine art. Ask any woman, young or old, intelligent or stupid, married or single, whether she likes Cinema, and she will always say yes because it is indeed our favorite form of entertainment. The films with the most irresistible appeal to us are the erotic films—*Love* and *Red Hair* are movies of this sort.[229] Anything that could be considered too racy has been wisely cut by the censors, who are charged with protecting the morality of a generation. We presumably go to the movies to see edifying examples, not to take pleasure in lurid displays. So this supervision by censorship allows us to take our children to the movies without worrying about them asking questions we cannot answer once the film is over.

"I don't mind telling you that I love simple and innocent films in which the heroine is always played by a type like Janet Gaynor or Lillian Gish. And I think it is right to show these films so that we can avoid the traps set by men in this day and age, in which sexual liberation has degenerated into licentiousness. But no woman would deny admiring John Gilbert, Ramon Novarro, and Ronald Colman more than any of the famous actresses appearing on screen. These actors have an unmistakable masculine stamp, an irresistible attraction for a woman, more because of their acting, properly speaking, than for any other reason. Any woman, in the deepest part of her soul, has a restless inclination toward "sheik" movies in which the strength of a man overcomes all willpower and destroys every obstacle. That's why Valentino has been my favorite hero, and none of today's screen actors have yet to occupy the place that the unfortunate Italian actor held in my heart, as much for his truly virile appearance as for the feats that directors had him perform in the roles he played.

"In addition, Cinema has the power to make us forget about life's little annoyances and to transport us to an enchanting world of imagination, where we feel more like actresses than spectators. I like movies that make me cry, but also the ones that make me laugh. I can't tolerate those sordid productions in which evil triumphs, like those directed by Von Stroheim. Some say they are a faithful reflection of life, but my opinion is that we already have enough tragedies in our world without going to witness new ones on the perpendicular screen, as my film critic friend calls it.

"In sum, I like Cinema because it always makes us aspire, to cherish the hope of someday elevating ourselves to a level superior to the one we now occupy. And it presents us with the latest fashions, as if it were a society to which we don't belong but would wish to join. I like romantic movies because I am a woman and there is not one of us who does not feel the call of romance within her heart, but I prefer the films about high society that always have a love story. This is my sincere opinion to be run without any corrections, because embellishment would make it lose much of its principal value: spontaneity."

MEXICAN EXTRAS WITHOUT WORK

OUR EXTRAS SURVIVE SOLELY ON NEARLY UNREALIZABLE DREAMS; THE AGONY OF "EXTRAS"; PERNICIOUS EXAMPLES; WHEN WILL THE CARAVAN OF BREATHLESS AND STARRY-EYED DREAMERS STOP ARRIVING AT HOLLYWOOD'S DOOR?

"Extras mexicanos sin trabajo," published in *La Opinión*, September 2, 1928, page 12

The fact that some of today's prestigious film actors have ascended to the throne of popularity from the obscure ranks of common extras, from that anonymous "mob" milling around the lead actors in big-budget films, has had a harmful effect on the spirit of our starry-eyed youth. Many have been spurred on by the publicity given to cases like that of Ramon Novarro, who struggled for seven years among the ranks of extras, as well as Valentino, who came nearly out of nowhere, and Don Alvarado, who has slowly climbed the ladder of success. But for others, for the great majority aspiring to cinematic glory, the effect has been disastrous. Following initial disappointments comes a defeat that makes them feel small, anonymous, insignificant. They then remind themselves of old clichés repeated by philosophers like Juan González:

"He made it. Why can't I?"[230]

So they continue the painful struggle until they fall defeated by the wayside or decide to follow another path in life. I know many extras who played juvenile parts amid all the "hubbub" in the earliest films with crowd scenes; now that they are graying and downtrodden by disappointment, they keep playing the same parts now and then, but they are invariably overlooked when it comes time to cast juvenile roles. They continue their careers through force of habit because they no longer know to what new pursuits they should dedicate their weary existences, since they have wasted their best years chasing after a brass ring that they never captured. The Mexican colonia is full of these disillusioned individuals whose lives depend on the vicissitudes of Hollywood.

A DIFFICULT CAREER

There are numerous Mexican extras; they belong to a great variety of social classes. Among them I know a "well-to-do" young gentleman, son of a family whose name appeared on Mexico's most distinguished social registry at the turn of the century; a revolutionary convinced that his efforts were futile; an immigrant politician; and a man of the people, semieducated between the schools of his homeland and those in California. There are former theater actors who arrived in Los Angeles on a difficult tour and abandoned the glow of the footlights to try their luck in the stormy seas of the studios; "respectable" young women whose ignorant friends in a distant province back home assured them that they were destined for Hollywood; retired bureaucrats and merchants, leaders of failed coups, and, finally, deformed individuals who figured out how to capitalize on their physical misfortunes. All of these diverse miracles in the making swirl around the studio doors, each of their minds nurturing the dream of making it big someday, each one believing they have a better chance than the rest; all of them are capable of the greatest sacrifices imaginable in exchange for a career opportunity.

But finding work within the walled confines of the Cinema studios, those factories of fame, is very unpredictable. One week they hire two people, then 300 Mexicans for a film with "Spanish" ambience, and then a mandatory break could last months. The sixty to one hundred dollars earned during those seven difficult days doesn't stretch far enough to cover necessities during that prolonged recess. What can Spanish-speaking extras do during that time?

AND THE CARAVAN CONTINUES

Their occupations are diverse . . . when they have them. Some, the most fortunate class, are musicians who play in Hollywood cabarets. Others try to work in the intimate little Mexican theaters on Main Street; still others perform domestic work in hotel kitchens, always waiting for the call from an agency or individual who is charged with recruiting "talent" of a particular type to provide ambience to some production or other.

Because in addition to "Central Casting," where hundreds of individuals from our community are registered and receive calls only when they are absolutely needed, there are two or three individuals who secretly look for "extras" to work on Cinema productions. I know two of them personally, although I will not mention their names for reasons you can easily imagine. They have at their homes lists of addresses, telephone numbers, costumes from different periods for dressing extras, and that's how they make a living. They also work in films, although more frequently than their clients. There are currently more than a thousand Mexicans trying to make a living from Cinema; they lead a difficult existence with their heads full of daydreams and their pockets completely empty. They are entirely segregated from the Mexican community but have been unable to penetrate the privileged world of film actors. Their situation is difficult, but they endure their suffering with a heroic resignation of which no one had previously believed them capable.

And in the meantime, from all parts of Mexico—the border, the interior, the capital—hundreds of daydreamers keep arriving, cherishing the fantasy of making it big someday; infinite numbers of young people who while watching a Ramon Novarro film have said, with the full certainty of their convictions:

"If he made it, why can't I?"

And then they dissolve into the multitudes that aspire and dream until some unprecedented turn of events convinces them of their failure. At that point they start their lives over, dispersing into the cafés, into the factories, into the packing plants, their souls bitter, regretting their improvidence. The women almost invariably sacrifice everything to receive nothing in return, convinced only belatedly of their folly. The men use up their energy on unproductive perseverance, only to end up back where they started. And this is only if they don't find themselves in jail as the result of going on a binge in Hollywood's "Latin Bohemia," as has recently happened to a group of respectable young people who had let their hair and sideburns grow under the delusion that their resemblance to certain juvenile screen stars would open the closed doors of the film studios. And many of these young people, who end up in the press daily, are the children of talented individuals, members of aristocratic families that ruined them by trying to educate them in the United States without suspecting that their future would be so different than the one they had planned for them . . . !

A "CINDERELLA" FROM THE PEARL OF HUMAYA

MONA RICO'S MIRACLE; HOW TWO BEAUTIFUL HANDS
CAN DECIDE A WOMAN'S FUTURE; A THOUSAND
METERS ABOVE SEA LEVEL; THE RIVALRY BETWEEN
CAMILLA HORN AND ENRIQUETA VALENZUELA

"Una 'Cenicienta' de la Perla del Humaya," published
in *La Opinión*, December 9, 1928, page 14

For many of our film stars, fame has been the fruit of sustained labor and preparation, the prize for a prolonged Via Crucis during which renunciations have been followed by personal sacrifice, cruel disappointments, and the harshest of tests.[231] For Enriqueta Valenzuela it only took eight days, as the winds of fortune blew her way. This beautiful and thoroughly prepared woman won the sympathy of an astute director along with a flattering contract, and the doors opened wide, allowing her to see the first steps of the golden staircase that leads to success. Such has been the case for the new Mexican screen artist whom audiences know by the pseudonym Mona Rico, transforming both her given name and her surname, one made illustrious by honored poets, intelligent politicians, and successful businessmen.

FROM MEXICO TO CULIACÁN

Mona Rico was born in Mexico when the country first began to be rocked by the initial successes of Madero's revolution, which continues to keep our people in a constant state of unrest. Born into a family living along the border, she had barely turned two when she was brought to Culiacán, the shining pearl of the Humaya River, where her beautiful eyes first began to take in the landscapes, buildings, people, and things that surrounded her.

That's why you might say that Mona Rico is from Sinaloa. Our homeland is always that little part of the world where we grew up, whose folklore we learned from memory during our first years, whose people and things have left indelible first impressions on our malleable brains.

But the provincial ambience of the Sinaloan capital was not enough for Enriqueta. From her earliest years she had a thirst for the lights, that strange hunger for new things, for marvelous sights that are off limits to those living a small-town life, where relationships are reduced to a small social world, confined to a single population. What would be more natural than for her to desire a life in Hollywood, the land of beautiful women, that "enchanted city" that was born as if by rubbing Aladdin's miraculous lamp? Three years ago the family moved to Los Angeles to see firsthand what had only appeared before their eyes in colorful stories or rotogravure prints. Such was the start of Mona Rico's life as an artist.

THE SUPREME AMBITION: CINEMA!

Gradually becoming familiar with English, but without losing the strict social customs of our people, she began to catch the fever of our century and wanted to see the film studios in person. Her mother, a woman with an old-fashioned upbringing, now found herself in a social environment that has regressed even more in this era under the advancing influence of "Jazz." She therefore objected to her daughter's ambition to become a screen actor. So much has been said about life inside the Studios, and justifiably so! There are so many dangers lying in wait for young, beautiful women as they make their way along the road to fame! But Enriqueta had caught a fever for stardom, and nothing could convince her to abstain from a visit to the Cinema studios. Her sincere promises to avoid any twists and turns along the straight-and-narrow path rekindled confidence in Mrs. Valenzuela's soul. She gradually relented, infected by her daughter's hope. After all, who knows what Destiny had in store for her daughter? For her part, Enriqueta had a strange determination, a supreme confidence in herself and her future. And so the days passed . . .

One afternoon Enriqueta arrived home beaming with joy. Someone with influence at United Artists Studios had promised the young woman an opportunity; it was only an opportunity, however, to be an extra among the anonymous multitudes. But in the end it was a door leading to what could be the realization of a dream she had long cherished. The following morning, the woman who would later be Mona Rico showed up at the Studios to take part in a film with Norma Talmadge and Gilbert Roland: *The Woman Disputed*.[232]

The Charm of White Hands

Nothing noteworthy happened during those first few days. Indistinguishable scenes, working day and night, long waits as directors and electricians got everything arranged; sometimes there were ten hours of preparation for a scene whose filming lasted a total of five minutes. Before long, someone noticed Enriqueta's hands—white hands, like lilies plucked straight from an old painting. That's how the idea arose to have her hands "double" for those of Norma Talmadge, and they made the necessary preparations to film the scene. It was only one scene, but the actor's future and the crystallization of a feminine hope depended on it.

Once Enriqueta was ready to put her hands in front of the camera, an incident occurred that nearly derailed her path to stardom forever. Someone objected to the scene, and the young Mexican was abruptly removed from it. That's how they do things in Hollywood, where a castle of dreams can be demolished in a heartbeat. It was a moment of intense pain, but Enriqueta's determination kept her steady. She begged and used all of her feminine wiles to convince Lubitsch, the famous director of Pola Negri, to give her a screen test. Then followed an agonizing wait that lasted hours, a night of insomnia for the aspiring actress, and finally a clarion call of joy. It turned out to be so satisfactory and Lubitsch was so enthusiastic that before anyone knew it, Enriqueta Valenzuela had changed her name to Mona Rico, her new name signed at the bottom of a contract that secured her services with United Artists for five years. This contract swept away the last little clouds of uncertainty, and Mona Rico returned home overflowing with happiness to tell her mother the great news.

With Barrymore and Camilla Horn

The first film in which she took part was *Eternal Love*, with John Barrymore in the starring role and Camilla Horn as the heroine.[233] The new actress received the role of a "heavy," and everyone set off for the mountains of Canada, where the culminating scenes of the photodrama would be filmed. Once there she was presented with another test: Mona Rico had to shoot a scene a thousand meters above sea level with an abyss at her feet, in danger of losing her life at the very moment when fortune had finally smiled upon her. But she performed her role enthusiastically and with all her determination, knowing that if she died during this test her name would forever remain unknown. John Barrymore began to take an interest in his new companion and that's when there emerged a rupture in his relationship with Camilla Horn, who refused to even acknowledge our Mexican actress. But now her career had been decided. A new film with Ronald Colman, also with United Artists, will have her in the role of the heroine, sharing her fame with the favorite actor of Balzac's female fans.[234] So here we have one of the rarest of Hollywood miracles: a young, beautiful woman emulating Caesar when he came to see and conquer. But as we have said on previous occasions: for each woman who triumphs, there are so many who fall and never recover!

If she remains as she is now, modest and hardworking, untouched by the natural vanity that usually comes along with fame, Mona Rico will soon see her name in lights on the high temples of Cinema along Broadway. And with this we will have a new Mexican actress who is proud of her origins, bringing prestige to a land that until now has been misunderstood as an epicenter of revolutions, as a conglomeration of creoles, apathetic and tumultuous all at once, placing their confidence in a "mañana" that will never come. But if things continue on as they have, our poor country, which is worthy of good fortune in every respect, will soon reclaim its rightful place in the interpretive arts through the combined forces of Ramon Novarro, Dolores Del Rio, Lupe Velez, and this new star who is beginning to cast luminous rays over the spangled firmament of Hollywood.

THE INFANCY OF A GIANT

In Old Arizona COMES ALONG TO CONVINCE
EVEN THE MOST SKEPTICAL THAT FILM WILL KILL
THEATER; SOLEDAD JIMÉNEZ AND DOROTHY BURGESS;
"MAGAZINE" MEXICANS AND REAL MEXICANS; GUS
EDWARDS INNOVATES; AN OPPORTUNITY FOR ARMIDA
VENDRELL; LOOKING AHEAD TO THE FUTURE

"La infancia del gigante," published in *La Opinión*, January 6, 1929, page 14

Max Reinhardt must have a compelling reason to assure us that theater
will endure despite the fact that Sound Cinema has invaded the realm of
modern entertainment. This man has spent his life among sets, produced
the worldwide hit *Sumurun*, and presented *The Miracle*, which was, in terms
of staging, almost miraculous.[235] He can opine with impunity because his
word has all the weight of experience, because he is steeped in wisdom
acquired not from books but from the fertile terrain of Life. Nonetheless,
with films like *In Old Arizona*, the latest production from William Fox,
the ordinary mind feels assailed by very justifiable doubts regarding such
a prediction.[236] Less than a year ago I joined Herr Reinhardt in his belief
and expressed it publicly in an article printed in various Spanish-language
newspapers; I now have well-founded reasons to believe that theater faces
the threat of dying out. What's worse, that threat is close to materializing.
This film—the first to be shot outdoors with synchronized sound, isolating
the useful noises, combining skillful tricks, and doing away with rumors
that this would produce muddy sound—has played a big part in convincing
me. Sound Cinema is still in its infancy, but it has already given us such
surprises and has so many more marvels in store for us in the near future!

A REFLECTION OF LIFE

In Old Arizona could be considered a reflection of life itself. A pale reflection naturally, but a reflection all the same. It has vibrating words and pulsating action. During some scenes we even forget that we are sitting in front of a rectangular screen, creating the illusion that we are witnessing one of the most intense moments of the past; it seems that with the least bit of effort we could pull Conejito or any of the other characters off the screen to steer the conversation in a different direction than that imposed by the author. And the illusion is nearly complete if we add to this the lengthy scenes that are synchronized in our own language with very Castilian flourishes and words emanating from the mouths of people we know personally. Compared to other big pictures this year (*The Singing Fool*), this film based on the novel by O. Henry is more cinematic than theatrical.[237] The former makes us cry, combines music with human emotions, and presents us with a moving fable, but without letting us forget for a moment that we are sitting in front of a stage; the latter produces the sensation of real life. *The Singing Fool* resorts to word and song to produce emotion; with *In Old Arizona* the action speaks for itself, and words are only an effective complement.

THE WORK OF OUR PEOPLE

It would not be fair to talk about this film, especially in light of Reinhardt's predictions, if we did not highlight the work of our people who appear in it. Soledad Jiménez, who since *The Red Dance* has shown herself to be a magnificent character actor unrivaled by any other living actress of this sort, shares the honor of synchronization with Edmund Lowe and Warner Baxter.[238] Elena de la Llata also brings a Castilian touch to the screen, but all the opportunities are given to Soledad, a veteran of all things cinematic, who has lived long enough to see the realization of perhaps her greatest dream in life. This will undoubtedly mark the start of a brilliant career that will place the Spanish actress among the top ranks of her profession alongside Louise Dresser and Vera Gordon, although in a slightly different genre. It won't be long before even naysayers see this prediction fulfilled, as it is based on the luminous logic of a very promising precedent.

REGARDING DOROTHY

Dorothy Burgess, recruited from a local theater to play the part of Toña María, is frankly a disappointment to those of us familiar with our people.

The young actress plays the most important feminine role and is curiously the most affected and artificial figure in the synchronized story. American critics have heaped a cornucopia of praise on her work and she is probably convinced that her creation was masterful. But they, like her, only know Mexican women through the gruesome stories in pulp magazines and have never been in contact with one in real life. Toña María's every step exactly matches the template made fashionable by an American fantasy: she writhes constantly and speaks theatrically, while her poses and expressions recall her long career on stage. She is a Mexican woman like the abominable girl in *The Dove*, a Mexican woman in a Yankee film, a type that came into vogue with Belasco's *Girl of the Golden West*.[239] This may satisfy the expectations of a Saxon audience in keeping with its standardized mentality, but it rings entirely false to the Hispano American public. Among the actors, Edmund Lowe is the most natural, although Warner Baxter's El Conejito turns out to be the most likable character. That is, at least in the opinion of this dispassionate critic.

THE INNOVATION OF GUS EDWARDS

In order for a film of this sort to give a complete impression of reality, even within the conventions we might expect from a reproduction, all that's missing is for its scenes to be shot in natural color. But this detail of talking Cinema has also been tested out by other productions. Gus Edwards is currently shooting a short film starring Armida Vendrell in which action is joined to speech, while objects, people, and backgrounds have their natural color, or at least those most closely resembling the colors Nature uses to paint all things perceptible to sight. And as a happy coincidence, this film, which will be even closer to perfection once it is exhibited, has a title we are sure to love. It is called *Mexican*.[240]

Will Gus Edwards give us a *Mexican* in the style of Dorothy Burgess? There is no reason to believe it, since he has a perpetual source of inspiration in Armida, our favorite little girl whom we know from her days of struggle on the stages of Main Street. This young woman has a decisive influence over the man who discovered her, who is now a great friend. And from what we have seen since she abandoned the colorful bohemia of the Mexican barrio to follow a higher road, she still preserves a very clear perception of our character types that have been around since the days of La Colorada. What's more, she always portrayed these characters faithfully on the Spanish-language stages of Los Angeles. All this seems to mean guaranteed success . . .

THE GIANT IN INFANCY

One should not offer a definitive opinion about theater before understanding the potential of its challengers. Theater has given us all the evidence we could hope for during its centuries of existence; it has reached the limits of its expression and has no further resources to exploit. Spinning stages like those in *Ben-Hur*; others with moving scenery like Wagner's *Parsifal*; impressive constructions like those in *The Miracle*: they are scenarios, symphonic marvels, an impression of life from inside the three classical walls, but nothing more. Talking pictures boast the spoken word, sounds, color, and a limitless range of scenery planted by Nature within the world we inhabit. It is in its infancy, but we already hear the first cries of tomorrow's giant. Mankind has entered into an era in which the mysteries of Creation have ceased to be so. Each generation is born and grows up in a time of constant innovation. All of these possibilities make us doubt the results of this struggle on a daily basis. But sound Cinema has been convincing us bit by bit, with the persuasive power of reality. Now who could guarantee that by the end of the century theater won't be just a vague memory of the past, like old-fashioned pantomime or the symbolic dances of the tribes that populated América before the arrival of Columbus?

THE SCREEN—OPPORTUNITIES THAT SPANISH-SPEAKING CINEMA OFFERS TO OUR ACTORS

OBSTACLES TO OVERCOME

"La pantalla—Las oportunidades que la cinema hispano-parlante ofrece a los elementos artísticos de la raza," published in *La Opinión*, January 30, 1930, page 6

Within a few days the Mexican public will see a talking picture made entirely in Spanish for the first time ever. The first serious attempt in this regard has been made under the banner of Sono Art. Our readers will surely know that we are referring to *Sombras de gloria*, presented last week in one of this city's theaters. As these lines are being written, José Bohr is headed to our nation's capital with a copy of the film, where they are preparing a well-deserved reception for both. As we understand it, the film will be exhibited in the most aristocratic of Paramount's theaters and we are certain that its very announcement has caused an uproar in that legendary city of the Virreyes.[241]

But it is not *Sombras de gloria* that we will be discussing in this article, although it has received acclaim from the public and Spanish-language newspapers. No matter how you look at it, the film represents the realization of a great effort; what's more, it is the first step toward what will undoubtedly be the salvation of our language in all of Latin America. We are not going to praise here the great Argentine actor José Bohr or Francisco Marán, who in our opinion shares the honor this picture deserves. We will instead try to comment, if only briefly, on the significance of this first attempt for the Spanish-speaking public.

With the initial production of Spanish-speaking pictures, a golden door has begun to open for the future of Spanish-speaking acting talent currently gathered in this enchanted city, this golden ember around whose glow so many gullible moths from our homelands have burned their wings, and before which the enchanted castles that our young dreamers build in their minds have been toppled like a house of cards. They have been taken in by the prestige of this great laboratory of activity that someone once called "The City of No Return."[242] Writers, musicians, those working in the interpretive arts—the majority of them Mexican—cast hopeful gazes upon the beguiling agglomeration of studios. And their hopes have a solid reasoning: they have come to work in this art form, now that the first brick of the Spanish-speaking building has been laid. Because of their proximity to the studios, because of their knowledge of that environment, because of their own talent, and even because of the commercial logic of supply and demand, they hold the key to the future in their hands.

But now a question arises that in our opinion does not merit the heated controversy that threatens to surround it: the use of the pure Castilian language, with its marked accent, in the synchronization of films destined for the Latin American market. The question does not have the importance that some would like to give it, since all of our people speak what we could call "Spanish" and not the Castilian language proper—we are still referring to the accent here—which doesn't even extend throughout all of Spain, but only to certain regions where the influence of the capital has not yet penetrated. Generally speaking, those in Madrid speak the mother tongue with only a slight accent; in addition, the films that will be made are destined primarily to supply this continent [the Americas], not the old Iberian Peninsula, where the American accent would also not strike them as all that strange.

The opinion of the person writing these lines is clear and leaves no room for doubt. It is a personal opinion for which I take responsibility, and there is nothing odd about it differing from other views that may be expressed, even in this very newspaper. In my opinion, films should be produced using the Spanish spoken in América, with the natural exception of those stories that take place in Spanish provinces. It wouldn't occur to anybody to present American movie characters living in New York and speaking in the "funny" accent that Prime Minister [James Ramsay] MacDonald brought with him on his recent visit to the [American] continent.[243]

Imagine a film whose plot unfolds during the Mexican Revolution. And then a general, who may have been a bandit before he discovered the principles for which he would risk his own life, along with those of the men under his command. It would be odd to have them accenting the "c" and "z"; the language of the characters taking part in the plot would necessarily have to be in keeping with their social position, with their surrounding environment, with the education they have received, and, above all, even if for the sake of truth, with the way their compatriots speak in their everyday lives.

As we have said before, our opinion allows for an exception: those films in which authentically Spanish stories are spoken in authentic Castilian, as much as this may present a technical difficulty, which we will speak about in the following paragraphs.

Experience has demonstrated beyond a doubt that the pronunciation of the "c" and "z" in front of the microphone, even from the mouths of legitimate Spaniards, registers in an exaggerated way: it has a lot of whistling and seems very artificial. Those reading these lines with a smile know deep down that this is the gospel truth. For reasons that would be too difficult to explain in an article of the present length, certain sounds make a greater impression when they are mechanically recorded. Right before our eyes, for example, they had to moisten a piece of paper before it was torn on camera because when dry it produces the same noise as an old tree branch when it is broken in real life. Many words have to be pronounced differently, because their syllables don't have the same smoothness as others when they are emitted in front of the discs that carry sounds to the "sound chamber," where a "monitor" is tasked with finding and correcting these defects.

But even aside from these circumstances, we still believe that Castilian (the "pure Castilian" that has been planted in the heads of producers by actors still living in the seventeenth century) should be used only by Spaniards with the modifications required by mechanical reproduction and in films whose story takes place in Spain. For the rest, whether they are adaptations of American scripts or reflections of our life on this continent, it seems more logical to speak pure Spanish in terms of grammar, eradicating regional idioms that could cause confusion among diverse audiences, but without the artificial pronunciation that would cause laughter during the most serious moments in the plot, for all the reasons expressed above.

Will there be films made for the Hispano American public? Then they should speak the same language as this public; there is nothing more rational. That is at least what we believe, without the pretension of being dogmatic and aware that our opinion will conflict with others expressed and published by individuals who either are blinded by anti-American prejudice or have not taken the trouble to study, even superficially, the question that we have so briefly dealt with in this article, which will hopefully not be the last of its kind about such an interesting topic.

THE SCREEN—THE RESURRECTION OF DOLORES DEL RIO

OUR REVIEW OF OUR FELLOW MEXICAN IN
THE BAD ONE; AN ARTISTIC PARALLEL WITH LUPE VELEZ

"La pantalla—La resurrección de Dolores del Río,"
published in *La Opinión*, May 9, 1930, page 8

Dolores Del Rio has stumbled a bit in her first talking picture, affirming the opinion we have expressed on other occasions that she should dedicate herself entirely to films in Spanish for linguistic reasons, among others. Far from what has happened to other screen luminaries whose voices have the effect of a splash of cold water when they reach an enthusiastic audience, extinguishing any spark of interest, her personality is further highlighted and accentuated by hearing her speak English. Furthermore, her interpretive faculties are not as rusty as one might think after a long period of inactivity. That is the opinion we formed upon leaving the United Artists Theater last night after the premiere of *The Bad One*, a film in which the central male role—and a very central one, at that—was played by the actor Edmund Lowe.[244]

The film script has a weak plot, as hackneyed and trivial as one would expect from a theme that has been so thoroughly exploited by filmmakers: a girl working in a café cantante, after her body has been submerged in the flames of every possible lust, gives her soul, which remains pure, to a man who awakens true love within her; a tragedy leads to a trial, a sentence of ten years in prison, and then a series of coincidences that precipitate a plausible conclusion, as the US audience prefers. If exhibited in Latin America, *The Bad One* would not do very well.

But story isn't everything in modern filmmaking. We have already seen that in many cases a masterful performance saves the most miserable stories seen on screen; in other cases, a weak plot is only a pretext to squander money on special effects that audiences receive with crazed jubilation; in still other cases, the director's treatment allows us to peer into the abyss of two souls, revealing a treasure of human psychology within a shoddy package. *The Bad One* belongs to the first of these categories: Dolores Del Rio and Edmund Lowe are the entire film. Sometimes he more than she; sometimes our compatriot more than he. We believe that the performances of both compensate for the defects of the film, which was directed by George Fitzmaurice at United Artists Studios.

Del Rio particularly triumphs in the scenes of high dramatic tension. Her best moments in the film come during the judgment against her lover, who later becomes her husband. Among them we would pick the "close-up" when she is about to swear but overcomes that urge and the moment in which she throws herself upon the door through which her lover has disappeared, escorted by stern policemen. When she is acting frivolous, mischievous, and flirtatious, however, we have rarely found the star from Durango convincing. And this film is hardly an exception to the rule. In the first scenes, despite the undeniable attraction of her undulating and half-naked body, she seems notably artificial. Producers have tried to make her into something that should not be permitted: an imitation of Lupe Velez. And that almost makes for a failure, in the opinion of this author. Because the souls of our two favorite stars are distinct. Lupe's resides in those parts that reflect her true personality; Dolores's is greater and more intense than that. Lupe exudes happiness, as she does in her own life, while Dolores vibrates with pain, as in hers. The former intoxicates us with the strong perfume of "whoopee," while the latter makes us feel, think, and suffer more deeply.

Edmund Lowe's performance is naturally commendable. It has the flaw of being the same character type he has played in *What Price Glory* and other films, but we figure that he is not at fault.[245] The person paying the bills has the final say. And in this case it is the public, that fine public to which Lope de Vega so cruelly referred, that must be pleased . . .[246]

THE REVIVAL OF ANTONIO MORENO

THE OLD IDOL OF THE SERIALS STUDIES DAY AND NIGHT TO MASTER THE LANGUAGE OF HIS HISPANO ANCESTORS, WHICH HE HAD SOMEWHAT FORGOTTEN

"El resurgimiento de Don Antonio Moreno," published
in *La Opinión*, June 15, 1930, page 14

It was many years ago—and the past is always a better place—when I first saw the dashing figure of Antonio Moreno on the perpendicular screen, playing opposite the blonde beauty Pearl White. He was a daring young man back then, deftly avoiding danger with the assistance of cinematic "tricks" and always coming out on top. When the film's villain, typically a Mongolian type, was on the verge of consummating his betrayal, Moreno would appear as if sprouting from the earth, revolver in hand, to prevent his efforts. And the Mexican public applauded, not only for the satisfying conclusion but also because they felt pride that Moreno was representing his people in the United States. Just seeing his Spanish name in the credits was enough to make hearts skip a beat; Antonio's popularity in our countries rested on the solid foundation of his nationality more than on his performances, making him more successful than William Desmond, [William] Duncan, and Eddie Polo, the Greek . . .

The resentment against this Iberian, the result of work by impassioned historians, did not yet exist, or at least it wasn't as harsh. In Mexico, as much as in Chile, Argentina, Venezuela, and Uruguay, Moreno was seen as a representative of our culture, a figure that symbolized an undeniable Hispano nobility. Little was known about him aside from what was published in newspapers that took their instructions from the publicity offices at Vitagraph, but his brilliant personality attracted the multitudes to the box office. This attraction was evident in Hollywood, where he received thousands of cards from passionate admirers, notes of congratulation from heads of state, and declarations of love from that eternal romantic who has by turn adored Valentino, Novarro, John Gilbert, and [George] Bancroft.

AN ARTISTIC HIATUS

Before long, the star who illuminated the nights of marriage-minded young women had been eclipsed. With the increasing disappearance of serials, Moreno steered his activity down other paths; he duly prepared for the production of more serious films and became united in matrimony with a woman of a very prominent American lineage. From that day forward, now that he had become one of the richest screen talents, Antonio lived more for his family than he had before, although with no less publicity. No Spaniard or Hispano American who arrived at the palatial residence of Moreno Highlands in search of help left empty-handed. In many cases, the nobility of this "star" was exploited by professional opportunists; in others the money he earned at the studios helped sustain a deprived family, whether or not they could properly pronounce the "c" or "z." He then felt the call of his distant homeland and, accompanied by the woman who carries his name, he visited the sunny land of Spain, always working silently as a philanthropist, always offering others a refuge from their troubles in his big heart. It was upon his return from this trip that the aristocratic residence of the Highlands was donated to a religious charitable institution. The actor and his family moved into an apartment house, paying rent when they used to receive it, sacrificing their well-being for the benefit of the hungry and thirsty . . . not exactly for justice, but for something more concrete and effective. In this instance, the poor were not just those who, according to the poet, "pray to Jesus Christ and speak Spanish," but the children of the earth who in years past provided him refuge against adversity.[247]

THE ARRIVAL OF "TALKIES"

When the intrusion of talking films made the exhibition of American pho-todramas in Hispano America impossible, producers remembered Moreno, the "drawing card" of the old days, and tried to divert his attention away from the lucrative real estate business to drag him back to the sound film stages. An actor may be a millionaire, a politician, or in the military, but he never stops feeling an attraction toward that which has always been everything to him; the spiritual sustenance of art tore Paderewski away from

CRITICISM

the presidency of Poland and Ruth Roland away from capitalist luxury to throw them back into the whirlwind of the interpretive arts.[248] Something similar happened to Antonio Moreno, who, although preserving his qualities as an actor, now found himself forced to speak Spanish after practically living the rest of his life "in English." And that's how they made *El cuerpo del delito*, *La canción del beso*, and later on *El hombre malo*.[249]

His diction in the first of these films left much to be desired; but a timely suggestion made precisely in our newspapers convinced him to study day and night the language still spoken by his elderly mother in Algeciras. We found him to be better in *La canción del beso*, while in *El hombre malo* he regained his status as a star after undergoing a surprising transformation. Not only did his accent cease to have that North American lilt that hurt his previous productions, but he spoke like Mexicans along the border. This was faithful to the interpretation of the part of Pancho López, the classic generous bandit, a type that extends from José María "el Tempranillo" to the modern bandits of legend.[250] In *El hombre malo*, Antonio re-creates as faithfully as possible—given the circumstances—the character imagined by the author of a work that made Holbrook Blinn famous not so long ago.[251] Under the supervision of Daniel Ferreiro Rea and Roberto Guzmán, a new Antonio Moreno emerged before the eyes of the moviegoing public: a Moreno who is decisive and generous, kind and grateful, just as he is in real life. Even the costuming, which belonged to Filemón Lepe, the horseman from Jalisco, gives a touch of true Mexican color to the film; from the charro hat trimmed with braiding and the flamboyant yellow shoes to his gestures, expressions, and lines that have a truly Mexican flavor, everything is correct. It could be that the film has the defects that detract from any product of human effort. But one must take into account the tremendous work of Mexicanizing a Spaniard who only knew Mexico from its border, and who in addition has lived for more than thirty years among Americans. The night before last at his apartment in the Jonathan Club, in front of a series of photographs representing a graphic history of his artistic life, Antonio himself told me: "It has been a Herculean effort. I have seen how critics have received my work, and I consider it unfortunate that they have been somewhat flippant. In some cases the roles on which they have commented so unfavorably have been done under special circumstances that critics, much less audiences, could hardly imagine. It's easy to criticize that way, without realizing the work required to play a part that we have been given two or three days to learn before shooting begins. But those who are aware of this are surely more lenient toward my work . . .

"I believe," he continued after lighting a Cuban cigar, "that *El hombre malo* is my first serious effort as a star in talking pictures. When they called me about the part, I flatly refused, arguing that only a true Mexican could interpret this character. And it was only when they demonstrated to me that there was one and only one actor who could play the role—at least in Hollywood—that I dared to ride that 'bull.' Later on they wanted me dressed up in some monstrosity of a costume to take some long shots, and I responded by ripping up my contract in front of producers. The matter of costuming is very delicate and it wasn't until I had Lepe's charro outfit in hand that I decided to act in the film. Daniel Rea did all the rest, instructing me how to speak like Mexicans. Now that all of this has passed, I can assure you that people will like the film. At least I hope so . . ."

Speaking as the author, I also hope so, because I continue to believe that Antonio Moreno is an important representative of our people within the studios: the oldest, with solid prestige, a screen veteran who works more to satisfy his artistic thirst than to earn a fistful of money, the majority of which he will distribute to those less fortunate. This film also marks the revival of one of our "stars"; of a talent who blazed trails in Hollywood, setting a path for others to later follow, including Luis Alonso, Ernesto Guillén, and that man from Durango who was destined to reach the summit after one of the longest and most tenacious struggles ever witnessed in Hollywood's orbit of intrigue and misery: Ramón Samaniego.[252]

CONCERNING THE WORDS OF MR. WILL HAYS, CINEMA CZAR

WE WILL HAVE TO SEE IF SUCH LOVELY WORDS HOLD TRUTH; WILL THINGS CONTINUE AS THEY ARE, OR WILL OUR SPIRIT AND TRADITIONS FINALLY BE RESPECTED?

"En torno de las palabras de Mr. Will Hays, czar del cine,"
published in *La Opinión*, January 11, 1931, page 5

Three days ago the Supreme Dictator of cinema, Will Hays, made some statements of great significance to our people, as they concern sound film production in Spanish. Speaking with Genaro Estrada, Secretary of Foreign Relations in the cabinet of [Pascual] Ortiz Rubio, he said the following:

"I very solemnly promise that the Film Industry *will continue* to proceed with the greatest care, ensuring that our talking pictures respect both the spirit and traditions of Mexico and other Spanish-speaking countries in the Western Hemisphere . . ."

We do not know how Mr. Estrada responded to these words; he is visiting Los Angeles on his honeymoon, and under these circumstances we have little or no time to strike up a conversation with him. Mr. Hays's promise to "continue" respecting, etc., implies that they indeed currently do respect this spirit and these traditions. But do they really?

It doesn't happen in Spanish productions, in which we are offered a mere translation of English films—a literary, artistic, and even psychological translation; characters from our lands are not represented by the major studios in any film that we are aware of, aside from *El hombre malo*. Unless we are greatly mistaken, this is also the case with English-language production. And here are three pieces of evidence:

There are films out there like the one titled *So This Is Mexico*, in which the old traditions and spirit are certainly shown in a bad light; films like *In*

Old Arizona, in which the evil female character sells out the bandit who had showered her with silks and jewels, only because he had found a "new love," presumably in the form of a Mexican woman; films like *Wings*, in which we see the social and political situation of Nicaragua painted in the most shameful manner possible.[253] And we could cite hundreds more films like these, both short and feature length, in which the parts of the "villain" or the "vamp" are embodied by people of our race, with characteristics that are unmistakably Hispano American. The men have black mustaches, abundant hair, and broken accents; the women have their hair parted down the middle and it appears oily, with a mantilla or decorative comb clearly testifying to the character's intended origins. Now it is worth asking the question: Does Mr. Hays promise to "respect" our spirit and traditions in the future or to "continue respecting" them? This is a point that remains to be clarified.

And it is not the case that we are overly sensitive. It's not that we are resentful about sometimes being portrayed as bad guys, with our customs and sensibilities distorted; rather, what wounds us is that they *always* portray us this way. We are human and thus not exempt from a natural self-love . . .

The illustrious Mr. Hays also said in his meeting with Mr. Estrada that "the industry that I represent will continue searching for and hiring the most significant talent from Latin America in the capacity of consultants, writers, and actors to make films dedicated to the Hispano American market." Here again appears the "will continue" that implies an affirmation of existing practice and demonstrates how poorly informed he is about the matters that directly concern him. Mr. Hays, the Cinema Czar, is involved in the production of films. There's not much more we can say about that.

Hopefully the promise of respect referred to by Mr. Estrada's prominent interlocutor in his remarks will begin to produce clear effects. We wouldn't want to see our homegrown characters wearing wings and strumming a celestial harp, but they should at least appear in a logical way: at times as the embodiment of evil, at times with nobility, as there is a little bit of everything in the Lord's Vineyard. Until now the only one of our characters that has been conceded a relatively picturesque nobility is Pancho López in *The Bad Man*. But even in this case, there is a notable effort to offer the public a "Mexican"; even if he dispenses justice effectively and equitably, he is still a thief, a cattle rustler, and a man outside the Law, generally speaking.

Once Mr. Estrada returns from his honeymoon and has some time, it will behoove him to ruminate on the promise of Mr. Hays and examine its fruits to determine whether or not these lovely words hold any truth . . .

A Surprise from the Anonymous Masses

Lost among the "Extras," Tito Davison Rose to Stardom after a Long Wait; His Work in *El Presidio* Has Established Him as a Powerful Actor

"Una sorpresa del montón anónimo," published in
La Magazín de la Opinión, January 18, 1931, pages 5–6

"Where did this actor come from? His popularity is growing so quickly that you heard his name from one day to the next, as if he had suddenly sprouted from the earth; he is undoubtedly a fortunate man or someone with connections good enough to get him into the studios. After all, becoming a star is all just a question of influence and good luck . . ."

These or similar comments constitute the general opinion of the unanointed every time a new figure shines in Hollywood's firmament. Those who struggle in vain to make headway, those who fall asleep every night dreaming of a stardom that never arrives, look enviously upon those caressed by the public's adulation; and in the depths of their bitter hearts they continue to hold a silent resentment.

But the name of a screen actor or actress does not manage to command the public's attention until it begins to shine with its own light. Everyone was surprised by the sudden fame of Valentino, and more than a few were dumbfounded when an unknown name stood out from the cast of *The Prisoner of Zenda*: Ramón Samaniego. And nonetheless . . .[254]

Before cinephiles memorize a name and carve a face into the stone tablet of their minds, many things happen of which they are unaware. It's as if a theater curtain rises and the spectators admire an actor's interpretation of a role; they receive an already finished product without knowing anything about the laborious rehearsals, the reprimands of the director, or the difficulties overcome by the actor to immerse himself in the character's personality, moment by moment, hour after hour, and then day after day . . .

Something very similar has happened with Tito Davison. The public gave him an ovation after his nearly masterful work in *El presidio*, and even those with a better memory only barely remember having seen his face before, without knowing exactly where.[255] The general impression, nonetheless, was that this was a discovery, a fortunate coincidence, or a case of good luck. But those who have known Tito for a while smiled to themselves about the naivete of his new admirers; they knew what was behind the curtain before the finished product was presented to the public. And the person writing these lines was one of them.

Because Tito Davison is not an accidental flash in the pan. Despite his young age, he has gone on to earn, one by one, the imaginary laurels that adorn his dreamer's forehead; but this labor has been silent and almost disregarded. He is the only one who knows the bitterness of his long preparation. There where you see the romantic girls, in love with his naive and almost childlike image, Tito has been struggling constantly through three years of disappointments and setbacks that would have forced many to retreat. The first time he stepped onto the "sets" of a film studio was September 1927.

Who Plays the Role of Kent?

The second youngest of five children from the Herman marriage, Tito Davison was born in the modestly sized town of Chillán, Chile, on November 14, 1911. He is the son of Herr Julius Herman and Mrs. Amanda Davison Morgan de Herman, which gives a clear and direct sense of his European heritage. His father is German and his mother English; they were drawn together in the far-off Republic of the South at the beginning of the current century.

Mr. Herman was, and still is, a business broker linked with a Packard automobile distributorship in the extreme south of Latin America. The family has always been of modest means, but fortune smiled upon them to a certain extent, allowing them to provide their children with a proper education. When the young actor came into the world, he was baptized with the name Oscar. From there we deduce that "Tito Davison" is, in reality,

Oscar Herman, son of foreigners but, by his own declaration, Chilean on all four sides: by birth, by custom, by heart, and by inclination.

As in many cases with actors who have scaled these heights, Oscar harbored the theatrical vocation in his soul since he was little. At the age of five he was already singing for benefit shows, calling attention to his precocity and constituting a source of pride for his mother in particular. It was precisely at one of these functions, where he performed during the first glimmers of his life, that one of the photographs illustrating this article was taken. You can already see the embryonic actor in it, if you will, but with clear indications of maturity.

Oscar Herman's childhood unfolded in the same way as for many of his contemporaries: nursery school first, then humanities studies, and then seminary school, where he spent only two years. His education began in Chillán and continued in Santiago de Chile, where he made his first friends and perhaps found his childish heart disquieted by the fantasy of romantic love. Even then he demonstrated a strange inclination toward the theater, and his dream at the time was to become an opera singer. The hand of Destiny would later guide him in other directions, with the results that we are now beginning to see.

One of his cousins, Carlos Francisco Borcosque, began to stand out as a cineaste in 1923, starting with the production of *Novedades*, brief cinematic reviews that showed the events of the day on screen.[256] He later had the opportunity to direct a silent film, giving him a name down there so far from Hollywood, but where the influence of the United States' richest industry can now be felt.

Restless like every other Latino spirit, Borcosque always nurtured the dream of coming to Hollywood, becoming established within the arena of silent film, and returning after a while to produce films in his own country. Carlos Francisco's hard work ended up drawing the attention of the government, and they subsidized his journey to North America to "study the technical procedures of Cinema" with a sort of modest grant that was sufficient to fulfill his basic needs for the moment. This happened in the middle of 1927.

OSCAR HEADED TO NORTH AMERICA

Like all of Borcosque's friends and family, Oscar knew about his relative's journey, and he began to entertain hopes of coming to these foreign lands, which, based on the information from magazines and films, struck him as a promised land. The boy's parents took an interest in his future, and given that he felt an inclination toward adventure, they had no problem letting him come here under the guardianship of his cousin to try his fortune in Hollywood, despite his tender years.

Finally, on August 20, 1927, the *Bokuyo Maru*, a Japanese merchant vessel, disembarked from the Valparaíso pier, carrying on board the two young men with their heads full of dreams, leaving the Herman family behind on the dock with their eyes full of tears. The crossing was long and arduous. A few days later the same boat docked at the port of San Pedro, California, depositing the two dreamers on land. They were thirsty for adventure and had the hope of success rooted in their hearts like never before.

Everything above passed before our eyes during a series of intimate conversations at a table at the Café Metro, which was at that hour brimming with Film actors, some of them established, others in decline; the others were aspirants hoping that in time people would turn their heads toward them in admiration. Wallace Beery was at a nearby table with an undershirt and robe thrown on, laughing loudly, his outfit signaling that he was acting in a new film. Behind us a group of Italians—Hector Sarno and Francisco Marán, two gentlemen who seemed to be torn from the pages of Murger's *La Vie Bohème*—were devouring mountains of spaghetti and conversing between mouthfuls with Fred Malatesta about something that happened in their far-off homeland. And we overheard the frequent use of words like "Il Duce," "I fascisti," and every once in a while a "Sporca M . . ." that made our hair stand up on end.[257]

María Ladrón de Guevara, dressed for her scenes in *La mujer X* and invariably followed by her husband, Carlos Navarro, was chatting with a pretty blonde and Giovanni Martino, born Juan Martínez.[258] Speaking loudly, they passed near us while we were savoring our chat more than we were the steaming dishes that had just been placed before our eyes by a waitress with little inclination to smile. Luis Díaz Flores, a new young screen actor, joined us for lunch and settled in to listen.

THE TRIALS OF THOSE FIRST DAYS

"I confess that at first," said Tito Davison, "I felt disheartened and there was one day that I seriously considered asking my parents for money to survive. It's true that I was living with 'Pancho'"—that's what he calls the director Borcosque—"but spending thirty cents each way on the bus to get to the studios every day, only to come back without any hope, was not at all satisfying. A bit of self-love and the shame of saddening my mother and father gave me the resolve to continue my daily pilgrimage in search of an important Film role. I wasn't content with the idea of being an 'extra,' not even temporarily, although I was soon convinced that there is no better path to getting a 'part' than joining the anonymous ranks of extras. An education like that is indispensable for a cinematic career, so that you gain more and more confidence until you feel capable of acting . . ."

"Did that state of affairs last long?"

"Not very long, fortunately. I can remember just as if it were today the afternoon when they used me as an extra in the anonymous crowd in *The Divine Lady* with Corinne Griffith at First National Studios.[259] I felt like my heart was racing; it seemed that the director was going to notice me, call me aside, and very seriously entrust me with an important role. I even mentally rehearsed the words I would use in response, because I had learned a bit of English in high school in Santiago de Chile, although only in passing. The occasion never arrived . . . but it was about to . . . !"

The waitress came to ask if we would like anything to drink with our lunch. Someone asked for a glass of milk and the rest ordered coffee. Once she left, Tito continued:

"Where were we? Ah, yes! In *The Divine Lady*, a version of the Lady Hamilton story, we were a little more than a thousand extras and I was the last in line because I was new, inexperienced, and perhaps a bit younger. And that arrangement lasted until it was time to get paid; I was the last to cash my five-dollar check, the total earnings for the day. And I'm telling you, I got home at three in the morning . . . !"

AN INTENSE MOMENT OF EMOTION

Tito Davison laughed like a child. He has a bit of Lew Ayres in him and a lot of the long-forgotten Gareth Hughes; the soul of a thinker was enclosed behind the adolescent exterior . . .

"I suppose you worked for a very long time . . ."

"The same story as always. A day of work, and then a month of idleness. During this time I went around to all the studios, was rejected for every part, and was discouraged by those who had been in Hollywood longer than me. But I was determined and prepared to go down fighting, if necessary. Finally, one night, when I was part of the extras for an Alice White film, director Mervyn LeRoy, who is now a great friend, needed a young man to complete a group that would be dancing around the restless blonde, who was the rival of Clara Bow. He stepped onto a chair and looked over the entire group, and we experienced a moment of anticipation. I raised my head as high as I could, with the hope of drawing his interest. He looked at me for an instant, and I felt the blood rush to my face.

"'Hey, you, young man!' he said. 'Come to the front! . . .'

"I asked him if it was me, afraid that I was mistaken. I think my voice even came out choked with emotion.

"'Yes, you . . . !,' he shouted.

"And he got down from the chair. The rest made way for me to pass; the distance seemed eternal. I felt like I was walking on wool and that everyone else was looking at me with envy. They probably didn't even notice me, but that was the impression I received. I arrived at the front, they put me with Alice White, and she smiled at me. I didn't know what else to do but smile back, but I think I probably had a dumb look on my face at that moment because one of the girls in the group said:

"'Isn't he silly?'[260]

"I still don't know if she was referring to me or not, but under those circumstances anyone would have believed it . . ."

THE OPPORTUNITY: *SOMBRAS DE GLORIA*

The Metro dining room seemed like a giant human beehive at that moment. José Polonsky's bald head passed between the groups in search of a seat he never found. Women and men of all nationalities were milling around the door in hopes of finding a vacant seat. The waitress arrived with coffee.

"That was the beginning of something good, I assume . . ."

Tito Davison again smiled like a little boy and shook his head.

"They never remembered me again. At that time the commotion of talking pictures was beginning, and since my English isn't perfect, I lost hope of getting an important part. I continued being an extra, although they were gradually getting to know me at the studios. I worked with Leatrice Joy on *A Most Immoral Lady* and other important productions, but without speaking a word. An opportunity emerged with *Sombras de gloria*, the first film made in Spanish.[261]

"When they were casting, I went to see José Bohr, who gave me a test. It must have turned out satisfactorily because instead of the one scene in which I was originally slated to appear, I was in several of them. For the first time in my life I made fifteen dollars a day . . ."

We finished our lunch. The telling gazes of those who had not yet had the opportunity to sit down made us decamp, and we continued the conversation in the alleyways that divide the different "stages." Tito walked by my side with his hands inside the pockets of his roomy golf pants. He was not wearing a hat, and a plaid tie broke up the harmony of his gray suit. I recall making an observation about his sport pants.

"Have you just come from playing golf . . . ?"

He responded with another jovial question:

"Are you pulling my leg?"

Tito Davison, like all men his age, has an excellent sense of humor. He's a romantic at heart, not the kind of sickly romanticism of languished gazes that gives his followers the look of wet rats, but rather something more reminiscent of springtime. For him, a career in Cinema is a strict school and nocturnal debauchery has no place in that.

"When I arrive—if I arrive—I will have time for everything; for now, what good does it do me to give satisfaction to those who say that 'Tito is a seducer' or 'There goes a man who's lucky with the ladies,' if at the end of the day it ends up damaging my talent? I need all my energy for the struggle that is harder now than ever; letting all that go to waste on 'parties' and other nonsense would be both dangerous and stupid. That's why I live exclusively dedicated to my work, to studying, to concentration . . ."

Tito Davison's work in *Sombras de gloria* was so satisfactory that it gave him the opportunity for a role in *Así es la vida*, in which he was notably bad.[262] This was a useful experience for him, as he became convinced that comedy did not agree with his personality. So he focused exclusively on performing roles like those we have seen in *La fuerza del querer*, in *Pájaros de cuenta*, and finally in *El presidio*, which has done nothing less than establish him as a star.[263] As these lines were being written, Universal was planning to use him opposite Blanca de Castejón in a comedy about high society, playing the role performed by Lew Ayres in English.[264]

Tito is opposed to the idea that our actors should imitate American performers when they make Spanish versions of those films. He believes that an actor should place himself in the situation of the character with whose life he has been temporarily entrusted and should speak, gesticulate, and move according to his feelings, rather than the way directors want him to do it. And he might be right on this count, as he played his role in *El presidio* in a way that was distinct from Robert Montgomery's performance, resulting in a success. He is also an advocate of placing action over words in talking Film, and he is certain that's how filmmaking will be in the near future: action, life, and a few monosyllables to accentuate facial expressions, banishing long literary tirades that, while tolerable in theater, are nearly disastrous for Cinema.

And . . . here you have all that can be written about this young man for the moment. He is barely on the verge of turning nineteen and he has his entire future ahead of him, provided he does not stray from the road that he has followed thus far: study, don't become easily conceited, and be human, eminently human.

LA LLAMA SAGRADA IS AN INTENSELY HUMAN PHOTODRAMA

ITS PREMISE, HOWEVER, IS BASED ON A COLD, EGOTISTICAL, AND CRUEL MORALITY; OUR REVIEW OF THE FILM

"Un fotodrama intensamente humano, *La llama sagrada*,"
published in *La Opinión*, February 3, 1931, page 4

Critics and audiences alike have been anxiously anticipating the exhibition of the First National film *La llama sagrada*, which was already rumored to be one of the best examples of sound film produced in Spanish.[265] There were compelling reasons for this: Elvira Morla, who left us so satisfied in *Olimpia*, would be taking the lead role; W. Somerset Maugham's signature on the story ensured a strong dramatic foundation; and the adaptation by Guillermo Prieto Yeme, a well-known Mexican literary figure, also provoked curiosity.[266] With this film, First National was also initiating the production of films in Spanish with "no expense spared," and the sets constructed for the film were a strong indication of this determination.

But then came the screening of *La llama sagrada*. Lest he be accused of taking this lightly, the author of this article saw the film twice, with an interval of time passing between the two screenings; he strove to go into the theater divested of all prejudice . . . here is the conclusion he reached:

AN INTENSELY HUMAN WORK

La llama sagrada is an intensely human story. You would never expect less from the author who staged *Outward Bound*.[267] There is nothing illogical or "casual" about this fable, aside from the fact that the tragedy at the heart of the wedding drives the entire story. Much could have been done with good direction, and good performances would have produced a perfect work. Unfortunately, the film had neither, in the opinion of the person writing these lines.

William McGann's direction is barely adequate, but this dictator of the megaphone missed out on so many opportunities that he had to establish himself as a master of sound film dramatization.[268] That's why Somerset Maugham's drama just glides along without shame or glory, just as if someone were reading a manuscript correctly but without any interpretive soul for the benefit of an indifferent audience. A work of this potential in the hands of Erich von Stroheim or even Edwin Carewe would have had the audience on their feet . . .

We have described *La llama sagrada* as intensely human, but we must also caution that its premise is based on a cold and cruel Saxon morality, to put it bluntly. For this reason we fear that audiences in our countries will not receive it well. We shall see what the critics of Mexico, Spain, Cuba, and Argentina have to say.

FOR THOSE WHO HAVE NOT SEEN IT . . .

In a few words, here is the story: A young English colonel is joined in matrimony with a girl he is in love with. Their names are Mauricio and Estela. After the marriage, and just at the moment that they are about to board a plane to embark on their honeymoon, an accident occurs that breaks Mauricio's spinal cord. A skilled doctor saves his life, but the unlucky man is stuck there, an invalid tied forever to a wheelchair. His beautiful wife is within his reach but he is unable to be anything but a patient to her. Both live in the mansion belonging to his mother, who, according to her own lovely words at the wedding ceremony, "is not losing a son, but gaining a daughter."

Three years go by. Mauricio's brother, young and handsome, returns from distant lands and falls in love with Estela. For her part, Estela returns his affection and they plan to run away together. The mother suspects this, and . . . here is the problem that Somerset resolves in the cruelest, most cold and inhumane way imaginable. Mauricio's mother poisons him so that her other son and her daughter-in-law can love each other freely!

This resolution, which English and American critics may applaud, will probably not be received the same way by our critics, who think and write for the world in which they live. In that environment—Spanish and Hispano American, generally speaking—we are certain that there is not a single mother, as cultured as she may be, who would dare take a step of this nature. It is true that Estela, being young, attractive, and full of joie de vivre, would certainly feel raging urges of the flesh; that she would suffer terribly by being tied down to this human dishrag whom she nonetheless once loved with a burning passion. But is this woman then nothing but a female in heat seeking carnal pleasures, thirsting for sensuality and lust? Did she not swear before an altar that she would accept her partner in life "for better or worse"?

THE LATINO POINT OF VIEW

If such a misfortune were to befall one of our women, she would consider it her inescapable duty to remain faithful to the man who made her his wife. And if infidelity alone is repugnant, what can you say about being unfaithful to a defenseless being who can't even move from the chair to which he is affixed by Destiny? What about infidelity that makes an accomplice of the husband's brother, flesh of his flesh, blood of his blood? Is a woman's purpose only to be an irrational female, to have a sexual purpose without any hint of spirituality?

Now let's talk about the mother. To any woman whose beautiful eyes are now scanning these lines: place your hand on your heart, reflect for a moment, and then answer. If one of your sons suffered a misfortune of this magnitude, would you kill him so that his unfaithful wife—the ingrate who now prostitutes the home that sheltered her in good times—could enjoy the love of one of your other sons? Would you justify the attitude of that woman who, certain that her husband could not move from his sickbed, isn't even risking her life by giving herself over to his own brother, no less? Seriously, come on . . .

That's why we say that the premise of *La llama sagrada* is based on a selfish morality that lacks basic compassion. Estela loved Mauricio when she married him and would have been incapable of giving herself to any other man. Did she ever love him for himself, or just because he was a man? That seems to be the work's premise, and we very openly disagree with it. As we have said before, Woman is more than just a female trembling with desire. That is why we would venture to predict that audiences in our countries will reject *La llama sagrada*, unless we have it all backward and the spirit of our perpetually self-sacrificial women is undergoing a regression to pagan times.

THE PHOTODRAMA'S PERFORMANCES

The actors playing the parts in Somerset's work, executed in Spanish by Mr. Prieto Yeme (Alvaro Gimeno), still leave much to be desired. Elvira Morla, whom we saw perform in an exquisitely natural way in *Olimpia*, strikes us as too theatrical and affected: she recites instead of "speaking," as if she were on stage instead of in front of the cameras. She is nonetheless the best of the cast, and there must have been a good reason for her to abandon her usual effortless charm.

[Martín] Garralaga is positively cold, falling on the extreme opposite side of the spectrum. And Luana Alcañiz, although very promising, has not yet made that promise crystallize. There is still hope: she has youth, beauty, and the raw material of an actor; she only lacks a bit of versatility. Spanish actor Guillermo del Rincón—if you can believe this—speaks with a disagreeable English accent in a Spanish-language film! Carmen Rodríguez has two or three successful moments. And the rest of the cast is sincerely bad . . . at least in this film. If we weren't afraid of hurting sensitive feelings, we would indicate the reasons for this opinion point by point, detail by detail. But with things as they are, it's best that we remain silent.

THE WORK OF MR. PRIETO YEME

This journalist is ignorant of how much restraint was placed on the activities of the work's translator, because it could be that his decisions were unilateral. The language is correct, with one or two exceptions in which a coarse word was placed in the mouth of a refined English character. We also believe that the dialogue suffered from excessive length. But we repeat: this could be because Mr. Prieto Yeme did not have the complete liberty to "dramatize," focusing instead on translating as closely as possible.

The last scene is especially well written, although it is too theatrical for Cinema, which aspires to be a faithful reflection of life. Our opinion, after evenly weighing the defects and virtues, is that the balance tips in favor of the Mexican man of letters, who is making his debut as a cinematic writer with this film.

A short comedy from Fox titled *Entre platos y notas* was screened during the same program.[269] The only person in it worth mentioning is Delia Magaña, with her immense artistic soul and a grace that captivates from her first moments on screen. The rest of the cast lacked either the will or the opportunity to demonstrate their talents.

That is our opinion of both works, an opinion, as with every other opinion we deliver, that may or may not be fair. But it has the indisputable merit of being sincere and dispassionate.

The Opportunity to Fail in Cinema

The Studios' Tricks for Ending the Careers of Promising Aspirants Who "Don't Make a Good Impression"

"La oportunidad de fracasar en el cine," published in
La Magazín de la Opinión, February 8, 1931, pages 5–6

The employment of Spanish-speaking actors by the Cinema Studios is not a matter of nationality, or of pronunciation, or of accents: it is a question of quality. Those actors who possess all the fundamental requirements are not and cannot be rejected. It behooves the studios to hire this kind of talent; how foolish would they be to decide to turn them down?

These words, my dear readers, were not produced by the author of this article. They were pronounced on a certain memorable occasion by one of the most prominent representatives of the Hollywood film studios and in the presence of Hispano American actors.

Considering such declarations objectively, it's worth verifying whether these lovely words are true or not. And before moving forward, we assure you that we will not discuss or even try to debate those who for one reason or another harbor animosity toward actors who are not from the Iberian Peninsula when it comes to casting films at production companies that are shooting in Spanish.

We only think it appropriate to present the facts without deliberately embellishing them with commentary. The actors who fail before the cameras are of different nationalities, and we don't believe—at least for the moment—that a silent campaign is being directed toward those who were born on this side of the Atlantic, even though many of those who came from "over there" may be directly or indirectly responsible for the fact that the public, which is always eager for scandal, so readily adopts accounts that are critical of these very individuals.

FLEETING STARS IN THE CINEMATIC FIRMAMENT

Just as one actor is given the opportunity to succeed, we have seen that others are given the most direct, ample, and firm opportunity to fail before the camera and the microphone. Is it intentional? We won't debate that here. The fact exists, and that's enough.

How many of those aspiring to Cinematic glory have seen their castle of illusions demolished after that first test on which their entrance into or banishment from the studios almost always depends? Those disillusioned by Hollywood, even in the terrain of Spanish films alone, could form a division robust enough to start and win a revolution in any one of our turbulent Indo-Hispanic republics. The public knows about those who have triumphed after a long struggle in certain cases, or those who have found the most success. But those who fall—and fall on a daily basis—are known only to their friends and family, and to those pessimistic naysayers who are always ready to tell us after a setback, with their eyes fixed on the rearview mirror and a tone of sadness that sounds sincere:

"Didn't I tell you so?"

On more than a few occasions we have seen a name printed in large letters on programs or posters as if it belonged to the "star" of a production. We become halfway familiar with their photograph, and then, after the film is released, it's as if they had been swallowed up by the earth. No one remembers them: not the audience, not the producers, no one. What could be the best explanation for such cases?

In the majority of cases, the actor or aspirant has been given the most ample opportunity to fail, intentionally or not, and always with the same result. Their performance is dreadful, their makeup is so mediocre that it would cause outrage if it weren't so tragic; they are the victims of "miscasting," and there are thousands of them in Hollywood.

THE CASE OF THOSE CONSECRATED

Because it's undeniable that Cinema, even now that it makes use of the spoken word, is primarily a matter of character types. Valentino lived in anonymity while he played a "heavy," then triumphed overwhelmingly when he became the passionate and dominant leading man that we know so well from his silent performances; no one would be at all interested in Lon Chaney in the role of a seductive beau, or in Lillian Gish as a "vampire" brimming with evil. Having Gloria Swanson start out in Peter Pan would have killed her artistic career the day the film premiered. And Lupe Velez, if appearing for the first time as an ingenue or grande dame, would be back dancing at the Lírico or some other second-rate theater, her cinematic career completely ruined. No one can seriously deny what has been expressed in this paragraph.

The Lupe Velez that we saw in *The Gaucho*, the point of departure for her undeniably successful career, was not the "Güerita" in love with the generous bandit as depicted in the script: it was, clearly and simply, Lupe Velez herself carried to the screen, with her same mannerisms, with her same turbulent and slightly uncouth personality, endearing in her audacity and captivating in her tendency to break with all social conventions.[270] That was the secret of her initial success. Once producers started paying attention to her, it was the beginning of what we would call her "training" as an actor and the improvement of her makeup. In one word: opportunity. Even if Lupe may be a disagreeable woman, no one could reasonably deny our view that she was truly beautiful in *Lady of the Pavements*, thanks to special lighting, appropriate makeup, and the clear investment of the director in presenting her as a beauty . . .[271]

THE "TRICKS" OF THE "TEST"

But let us now talk about the little "tricks" that the Industry uses to outright destroy the effectiveness of an actor with a single stroke of the pen. One of them is the "test" undertaken without the necessary preparation.

Any actor gifted with certain qualities and with a commendable artistic track record arrives in Hollywood in search of a part that will open the door through which to breach the guarded walls of the talking picture studios. After a laborious process, during which he resorts to any recourse imaginable—opportunity is almost always a question of influence—he is called to the studio and informed that he will be subjected to a test. He heads to the appointment with a heart racing at 120 beats per minute.

Once on the sound stage, the actor is dressed in one way or another, his makeup done in haste and in most cases badly, and he is handed a sheet of paper from which to learn a part from memory. An hour later, and without any preparation, he is placed in front of a camera and a portion of dialogue he was given to learn is randomly selected. In the majority of cases it is exactly the part that the candidate is most uncertain about, and his anxiety grows into delirium.

Anyone who has stood before a camera or microphone for the first time knows the kind of sensation you feel in those circumstances. There is a hostile group facing the actor—a director, assistants, a supervisor, etc.—whose eyes fix upon the individual with a curiosity that holds no small amount of judgment, and in that way the impassive eye of the camera acquires for him the contours of a machine gun barrel ready to fire. A general silence arrives, which only aggravates the situation, and then the actor is invited to perform a role about which he still knows very little. The camera begins rolling and two minutes later the action is cut. There is no encouraging comment, nor a single sentence that conveys any hope. The result is that when the processed celluloid is exhibited for a group of harsh critics, the actor or actress—who had earned great displays of approval from theater audiences—has been transformed into a mess. You can see their figure on screen, trembling nervously; their voice is guttural, horrible, and their gestures uncertain. In their eyes you can perceive anguish, the effort to remember the "lines" they've been made to memorize. The aspirant almost never sees the test, and the silence of the producer or director regarding the results clearly conveys just how painful the failure has been.

ANOTHER WAY TO FAIL

On some occasions the test is done with two actors between whom a short dialogue unfolds: one is the aspiring actor, the other an actor or actress who has been tested and accepted and is therefore sure of getting the part. They do a little rehearsal before the short scene, and the director, raising his voice and relying on all the famous lexicon of the Chicago "gangs," assures them that they should use a different voice, that their intonation is too low, or that this, that, or the other movement is too forced. The figure of the interlocutor is outside the camera's radius and only his voice can be heard during the test. In many cases, said interlocutor is perfectly prepared and is reading what he recites, while the unfortunate individual who is being tested must speak from memory. And when both individuals are photographed—which sometimes happens—the result is even worse. One can see clearly one person's composed command of the scene, while the aspirant is noticeably nervous about the unfavorable conditions he is facing compared to the other actor. This is one way that actors are given the opportunity to fail.

Naturally, when the aspiring actor or his agent seeks a role in an upcoming production, the producer or his representative responds with a tone of trembling pity:

"*Who? That guy? Come on, man: he's no good! He was given a chance and still!* . . ."

So now tell me that it's a question of quality!

There are other ways of causing an aspiring actor to fail, even when the test has turned out moderately satisfactory. The aspirant may be offered a film contract and given a part to study two or three days before the first scene. But the part itself is the antithesis of what the actor's personality reveals. If he is a juvenile type, full of natural joie de vivre, they "cast" him in the role of a villain, they give him a mustache reminiscent of Zapata's disciples, and during the shooting of scenes the director is constantly complaining about his performance. When the film is released on the market, the public is convinced that the new actor is a "dud" and they calmly turn their backs on him. For him, the doors of the studio are definitively closed unless there is an urgent necessity for his services. But this does not happen very often, especially now that in Hollywood the laws of supply and demand are broken, with the former overtaking the latter in a proportion of 200 percent . . .

ANOTHER ASPECT OF THE TEST

When there is someone invested in the success of an actor or actress, the situation is different. They prepare the aspirant, surrounding him with a supportive environment, calming him with every means at their disposal; he is given ample time to learn his "lines" from memory and to adapt his personality type to the one the author has developed in the script. During these rehearsals, which are much more extensive than in the cases mentioned above, there is always a little pat on the back, a word of encouragement either sincere or feigned, and a desire to make sure the aspirant stands out. And almost always, if the actor or actress has the cooperation of the director, the role is performed well. Rescued from The First Obstacle, a contract arrives . . . and we are now out of danger.

You must take into account that the influence of valuable friends, personal relationships, and other details are decisive factors in the test in question. And that influence has to extend to makeup artists as it does to the producer and then naturally to the director, who is the "factotum" of a cinematic career. Today, casts are decided in studios amid a mystery that rivals those of the departed Conan Doyle. The most profound secrecy surrounds the selection of roles until the cast is revealed and they begin to work. But the fact that external influences exert great power over the majority of these cases is as certain as the light of the sun. With one or two exceptions, we don't know of a single case that disproves this rule, which is acknowledged by everyone in the always buzzing beehive of Hollywood, the triumphant and the defeated alike.

SOME OF THE VICTIMS

Manuel Sánchez Navarro, who was on the verge of taking a role in *Resurrección*; the beautiful Cora Montes, who even played the lead role in *Monsieur Le Fox* for two weeks before being cut and replaced by another actress; María Conesa and many other actors now left out of talking pictures: all are living examples whose experiences prove what has been established in previous paragraphs.[272] In every case, it was said they had the "raw material," and many of them frankly and decidedly had histrionic talent. But the tests were unfavorable and their careers were cut short. And we won't even talk about Ernesto Vilches, who has always been a great actor on stage but who has turned out to be a shameful mediocrity in talking pictures . . .

Then there are those who successfully pass the test but still do not see their stock go up in the eyes of producers. Elvira Morla masterfully played a lead role in *Olimpia* but was nonetheless rejected for a part that would have launched her career because she lacked "sex appeal," according to one expert; María Teresa Renner also very admirably played a role in *Pájaros de cuenta*, but no one has remembered her since. Nelly Fernández "stole" scenes in her first part in *Del mismo barro* and reached great heights in *El barbero de Napoleón*.[273] But shortly thereafter she had difficulties, including not being allowed entry into the secure confines of one company's film studios.

We've restricted ourselves here to cases involving Hispano actors, because if we extended the discussion to others we'd have thousands of examples. We would even say that the temporary eclipse of José Bohr was due to casting him in a part that did not fit his personality. After his triumph in *Así es la vida*, they gave him a starring role in *The Rogue of the Rio Grande*, and the public, his public, which has always loved him, did not recognize him in this production.[274] Instead of playing a lighthearted part in keeping with his personality, he was obligated to inhabit the character of a Cinematic "Bad-Man," and the result was instantly clear.

Raquel Torres, who was enchanting in *White Shadows in the South Seas*, was overshadowed in *The Bridge of San Luis Rey* thanks to bad photography and a selection of scenes that, if intentional, deserves reproach. In this film they photographed her in profile, her worst angle, and made her cry near the camera, resulting in a performance that was grotesque rather than tenderly painful. In *Aloha* it was necessary to create a part for her that was an exact fit with her talents to achieve a vindication that almost arrived too late.[275]

A similar case occurred with Rosita Ballesteros. As she was poorly directed in her first film, *El hombre malo*, and disoriented in *Monsieur Le Fox*, everyone was certain that she had failed when Ramon Novarro chose her to play "Lola" in *Sevilla de mis amores*.[276] Those who have seen the film know how it turned out: Rosita became a leading actor thanks to the special circumstances that surrounded her.

We have written the lines above full steam ahead, without stopping to seek out all appropriate cases and only citing from memory the first ones that came to mind.

The problem of Hispano Cinema is not a question of "quality" but instead of opportunity, of circumstances, of influences and sacrifices.

We repeat: we don't consider it a matter of systematically repudiating Hispano Americans, since there are already important figures working in talking Cinema.

NOVARRO'S NEW RIVAL HAS MADE HIS ENTRANCE INTO CINEMA

JOSÉ MOJICA IS POISED TO DETHRONE THE MEXICAN PUBLIC'S FAVORITE STAR

"Un nuevo rival de Novarro ha hecho su entrada al cinema,"
published in *La Opinión*, July 26, 1931, page 5

Just this week two local theaters are exhibiting films in which Ramon Novarro and José Mojica have starring roles, provoking comparisons between the two Mexican talking-picture stars. Having seen both films and mulled them over carefully, we consider that the artistic prestige of Mr. Novarro is seriously imperiled by the still-ascending career of the sensational tenor from Jalisco, who gave life to the operetta *Hay que casar al príncipe*.[277]

Until now Novarro has been the indisputable favorite among our people. Since his triumph in *Ben-Hur*, which was as spectacular as the film itself, he has become a national hero.[278] Single girls openly swooned over him, and cinephiles would go into a theater solely on the assurance that one of his films was being projected. His name, his undeniable talent, and his continuous successes have consecrated him as a continental hero. From the Mexican border to the theaters of Tierra del Fuego, any of his films was received without discussion or debate, crowning him with that storybook prestige so beloved by the dreaming spirit of Hispano Americans.

THE ARRIVAL OF MOJICA

Then came the talking pictures. A new opportunity for Ramon came with them, because he had always dreamed that his voice, which has a pleasant tone and rich texture, would carry him to unreachable heights. He made *The Pagan* under these circumstances, the first film comedy in which he appears singing.[279]

But a few months later a powerful rival appeared on the cinematic horizon. José Mojica was ripped from the opera stage and transplanted to the studios in a strikingly defiant gesture. A famous American writer sounded the first clarion call with an article titled "Watch This Hombre!"[280] And fans of Mojica as an opera singer readily stood in line at the movie theater.

From the first film in which we saw José, *El precio de un beso*, we realized what the near future could have in store for him.[281] His voice, especially that splendid voice that seems to be made for recording technology, captivated audiences just as rapidly as Valentino's kisses captivated cinephiles in 1921. It also occurred to us then that "in the near future Ramon Novarro will need to guard his laurels against the threat of Mojica." The moment has arrived, and the star from Durango has a formidable competitor in this young man with a lovely smile, considerable personal charm, and, above all, a voice with a resonant and impressive timbre.

THE COMPARISON OF THE MOMENT

We do not mean to insinuate that while Mojica is rapidly climbing the staircase to Glory, Novarro is in decline. That day has not yet arrived, and the memory of *Sevilla de mis amores* will live on in the hearts of Hispanos for a long time. Nonetheless, circumstances have been favorable for the former and adverse for the latter. Comparing the public's enthusiasm for *Hay que casar al príncipe* with its reception of the more conventional scenes in *Son of India*, we can only conclude that the competition has become increasingly fierce.[282] The public is fickle and quickly forgets. It often tears down its idols to erect statues of new heroes over the ruins of those pedestals. Hopefully this is not the case, but . . . there is plenty of reason to be concerned.

Of course, by limiting himself to films in English, Novarro has lost contact with our public. Mojica, to the contrary, has secured his popularity with English-speaking cinephiles and gains new fans every day among those who only understand Spanish. This is a very serious symptom not in the financial sphere, where Navarro already has his problems perfectly resolved, but rather in artistic and especially in racial terms.

José Mojica's prestige is becoming even more undeniable. He seems to study carefully for each new film and to improve until he achieves perfection, something that could not be said about Mr. Novarro. Proof of this assertion has come in the past year: every one of Mojica's films has been better than the last, while the productions in which Novarro appears have become worse.

AN ASSESSMENT OF *SON OF INDIA*

Son of India has a story that strikes us as artificial, childish, and absurd, even considering what we would expect from the art of "make believe." It is practically an Elinor Glyn novel coated in Hindustani varnish, and even the most generous viewers would find the ending dismal.

It is true that Novarro valiantly holds his own, but in our opinion that is all he does: hold his own. We found him convincing in *Call of the Flesh*, but then came *Daybreak*, a painfully mediocre film.[283] And now that the public is anxiously awaiting the arrival of this new production, they have been let down by the studio that produced it for the screen. A marked decline and a lack of enthusiasm are apparent, something that places Ramon a hundred leagues below his stupendous role in *Ben-Hur*. Madge Evans is a mistake in her feminine role; even Marjorie Rambeau, a famous theater actor, seems mediocre. Conrad Nagel, once a favorite of cinephiles, is reduced here to his most minimal expression. Given these surroundings, it's no wonder that Ramon would feel disheartened.

JOSÉ MOJICA'S GOOD POINTS

We have already said that Mojica is improving every day. He now has in his favor his elegant bearing and youthful good looks, the way he knows how to wear both a military uniform and the outfits of Spanish bandoleros from past centuries, a charming self-confidence, and a smile that women find captivating. In addition, he has another resource that places him far above Novarro: the quality of his voice, his unique way of using it, and the interpretation of his songs. There is hence reason to believe that he will be a successful substitute. If Novarro does not return to Spanish-language pictures, or returns too late, his place in the public's heart may already be occupied by the star of *Hay que casar al príncipe*.

This, at least, is the sincere and disinterested impression of the person writing this piece.

OUR PUBLIC WANTS THEIR OWN MOVIES, REFLECTIONS OF THEIR LIVES

THE MISSION OF NEW PRODUCTION COMPANIES IN LATINO COUNTRIES; WHY MOVIES IN SPANISH HAVE FAILED UNTIL NOW

"Cine suyo, reflejos de su vida, es lo que pide nuestro público,"
published in *La Opinión*, August 23, 1931, page 5

This time there seems to be official news that Mexico has established film studios for the purpose of producing works of this type in Spanish, at least initially for the Mexican market and then with an eye toward extending the scope of distribution across Hispano America. The company should have solid foundations and should not just be an enormous "bluff," as it was in past instances. Otherwise, the President of the Republic should not have had his portrait taken at their laboratories wearing headphones and then allowed that photograph to be cast to the four winds, suggesting this new enterprise be taken more seriously.

Those who have read our Sunday pages have already been informed that in Mexico there is a Compañía Nacional Productora de Películas, S.A., a company resolved to elevate the prestige of Spanish-language film, which Hollywood studios have allowed to fall into a regrettable decline.[284] It remains to be seen whether the company possesses, along with the natural enthusiasm of a noble endeavor, economic support sufficient to allow them to avoid wasting time on experiments and instead to directly and vigorously tackle an undertaking of such transcendence.

Because in the future, films in Spanish should come from Spanish-speaking countries. It is necessary. It is imperative if they want to have a product worthy of the public, one that is faithful to historical, geographic, and social truth. But for this to happen it is also absolutely necessary to have enthusiasm, money, and, above all, the indispensable spirit of sacrifice that should accompany any new artistic endeavor.

Mexico City, Buenos Aires, Barcelona, and Madrid are the centers called upon to bring this idea to fruition, because they are the beacons that radiate, or at least should, a truly Hispano artistic culture that is faithful to our traditions and our sensibilities, in keeping with our own ideology and the elevated level of our postulated morals. If the example set forth by the Compañía Nacional Productora de Películas, S.A. de México, provokes a healthy desire for emulation on the part of other countries, we are on the verge of a movement of great significance to our race.

THE DECLINE OF HOLLYWOOD

In Hollywood, unfortunately, enthusiasm for Hispano production is in full decline. Fox Studios, central to the hopes of actors, directors, and screenwriters of our race, has begun to downsize after a valiant artistic effort. Columbia is struggling along, although it produces better films than any other studio. As proof we have *Carne de cabaret*, *El código penal*, and now *El pasado acusa*, which critics have justifiably showered with praise.[285]

Paramount continues its production in Paris, increasing its output bit by bit, but always moving forward cautiously, like someone still unsure of the ground on which they tread; at this point Metro-Goldwyn-Mayer, Warner Bros., RKO, and Universal are not giving any signs of life.

Of the films now coming out of the studios, perhaps Paramount's are the most firmly rooted in our sensibility and our particular way of seeing things and dealing with subject matter, since the personnel there are far from the influence of the standard American film.[286] So we see that *Su noche de bodas*, although it is a version of *Her Wedding Night*, presents us with something distinct from what we saw in Clara Bow's performance.[287] They have not done a literal translation of the script, but rather a version that allows for truly Hispano touches, wordplay in our tongue that is untranslatable to another language, and a general environment that very much resembles the one in which Hispano Americans live, even within foreign countries.

SLICES OF OUR OWN LIVES

It is logical to assume that when they begin producing Spanish-language movies in our home countries, the stories themselves will develop more in keeping with our lives than those presented until now by studios in the United States. The social problems of the Saxons are completely foreign to us, while ours seem absurd from the perspective of the decadent Anglo-American civilization. So in a film made by the studios of this country, a woman could become a heroine despite trampling on tradition and the social norms of our people. In our Spanish-speaking countries, we may admire the more or less successful performance of this or that actor, but we would never see in that film a reflection of our own lives, which are so multifarious and distinct from those that govern the actions of the inhabitants of a country like the United States. For that audience, the one we must nurture and whose tastes we must satisfy, movies made under these circumstances seem lovely, with excellent photography and sound that approximates reality more and more all the time, but they are absolutely lacking in Latino ambience and ideology.

The Spanish-speaking public living in the United States will undoubtedly find the movies made down there a little antiquated; the technical procedures will seem inferior, but they will understand that from any perspective the films will be more human and closer to our particular sensibility. This audience comprises some one or two million people, the majority of whom live their lives in English, while there are still at least 100 million whose tastes must be satisfied and who are fortunate enough to live far from the influence of jazz, divorce, and what many would consider feminine impertinence. The Yankee production companies don't seem to realize this . . . unless they are deliberately attempting to conquer the Latino spirit, to invade our intimate lives with their particular ideology and customs, preparing a new generation of Filipinos and Puerto Ricans to be something that is neither Latin nor Saxon, but an unstable mix of the most objectionable aspects of both civilizations. However, the combination of particular characteristics that constitute our immutable idiosyncrasies is too firmly rooted for that to happen. These companies run the risk of suffering the same fate as the Romans, who in another era used their powers to conquer Greece, but whose own spirit was conquered by the very people they vanquished.

TRANSLATIONS IN EVERY SENSE

Until now every talking picture in Spanish has been nothing but a long translation from the English. They have translated the words, the situations, and the character types, but the ideological center remains in place. Aside from *Sevilla de mis amores*, the ambience in all of them is strictly Saxon. We still remember the absurd and cruel ethos of *La llama sagrada*, which was applauded and considered reasonable by those with the Yankee mindset. But it could not be so for our people, since it conflicted with all of our traditions and with the concept of love toward both mothers and society that we hold dear in our countries.

One can't deny that the enthusiasm of Hispano Americans for a film spoken in their own language has visibly declined. But from our perspective the reason resides not only in the poor quality of acting and directing but also in the fact that the very substance of these films has not managed to convince them. They tolerate North American stories when performed by artists who are foreigners, because they see the whole thing as exotic and distant; but when these same stories are presented in Spanish, their artificiality becomes apparent. In the mouth of a North American speaking English, for example, we accept a concept that openly conflicts with our sensibility; in the mouth of a Spaniard speaking his own language, it becomes something absurd and even scandalous.

What's missing, then, is for Cinema to bring slices of life to audiences of Spanish-speaking nations, plausible stories in keeping with their traditions and customs, so that they remain interested. Let's suppose that a company presented, in English, a film in which the characters moved, behaved, and spoke like us; that they presented the eternal love triangle that culminated at the height of tragedy; that there is a son who sacrifices everything for his parents and respects them in their advanced age as much as he did when he was a little boy. The result would leave a North American audience with a frankly disastrous, absurd, and ridiculous impression. Although its artistic execution may have been impeccable, they would not understand and consequently would not be interested in the particular manner in which Hispanos resolve their problems. When American films are translated into Spanish, the same thing happens to the enthusiasm of millions of Central and South Americans, not counting those from the Iberian Peninsula, for whom tradition is perhaps even more firmly rooted than it is for our own people.

A HISTORICAL COMMENTARY

As we write these lines we are reminded of a commentary penned by a recognized authority regarding the exhibition of *The Passion Flower*, the

English adaptation of [Jacinto] Benavente's *La malquerida*.[288] A writer who enjoys prestige among American cinephiles declared in print that the conclusion was perfectly absurd and illogical. "Raymunda should have filed for divorce upon learning that her husband Esteban and her daughter Acacia were carrying on, since everything was in place," she said. "Why would a woman become a criminal when with a little reflection and common sense she could have happily continued on living to enjoy the full expanse of her golden years?"

Nonetheless, *La malquerida* is an intensely human work from our point of view. The idea that a young woman would fall in love with her stepfather is nothing less than sacrilegious; the tragedy in this case is inevitable, and this character survives because she does what any of our women would do in such circumstances, with love and dignity.

If production companies in our countries manage to successfully release three well-made films to the market, the competition will be serious. All that remains is for them to begin working more seriously and, following American technology—which is perfect considering what is humanly possible—to rely on Latino ideology. This is something that production companies in and around Hollywood have either failed or refused to do.

THERE ARE NO HISPANIC STARS!

WHY DO WE LACK THIS ATTRACTION SO CHARACTERISTIC OF AMERICAN FILM? THE PARTICULAR CASE OF CARLOS VILLARÍAS; HOW TWO PRODUCTION COMPANIES WASTED GOLDEN OPPORTUNITIES; LOOKING AHEAD TO THE FUTURE

"No hay estrellas hispanas!," published in *La Opinión*, September 20, 1931, page 5

Those with a fondness for Spanish-language cinema—which has continued to gradually develop from the unfortunate *Sombras habaneras* to the current day—couldn't help but agree that Hispano Cinema lacks a decisive element for the marketing of its films: it has no stars.[289]

It's worth mentioning that if our Cinema effectively lacks the appeal that might defend it against American films, it's because production in Spanish is still in its infancy, because it has not allowed its public to choose its favorite actors, and, finally, because the studios themselves have placed restrictions and obstacles on the development of potential stars for the Hispanic screen. These circumstances have various causes and are produced by a combination of small details. We will not specifically address them in this piece, whose only purpose is to comment from the margins of Cinema spoken in our language, which is now in definitive danger of disappearing.

In effect: we have no stars. In the silent Cinema we had Dolores Del Rio, Ramon Novarro, and Lupe Velez, not to mention other Mexican actors. When it comes to actors speaking Spanish in talking pictures, we have encountered an extraordinary democracy that has leveled out all of our artistic talent by transforming actors into cogs in the machinery of production. No one stands out; there are no opportunities for them to do so. Producers are determined to rely on the film's name to drum up business or on the promises made by publicity sheets about the film's story. And this, which in many cases they wouldn't dare do with English films, cannot produce the fantastic results that they initially expected from Hispano American films.

THE IMPORTANCE OF STARS

Stars are highly important for a public as impressionable as ours. Almost all of us—including you, dear reader—file into a Movie theater when we see a name like . . . John Barrymore advertised at the top of a poster, to take one example, although this actor with the Apollonian profile is not worshipped by many. We know in advance that we'll be seeing a film that won't ultimately surprise us because it ends with an obligatory kiss, if not with the chords of an accompanying march by Mendelssohn Bartholdy.[290] We don't care if the setting is Hispanic, French, Arabic, or clearly American. We don't even notice the beauty or erotic appeal of the leading actress. We go simply to see and hear Barrymore, and we focus our mind entirely on his performance when the projection begins. An actor's splendid performance—or what we regard as such in our state of infatuation—is all that attracts us. And if in many cases we don't clearly recall the story, the memory of that marvelous performance continues to resonate in our minds like the ringing of a bell.

Producers count on the psychology of audiences in advance, and they choose their stars based on box office figures, the only standard that elevates film actors to that status. After they have featured their "star" in a successful work and the audience has willingly swallowed the hook, they worry less about the setting through which their "vehicle of human life" travels. They know that the audience will tolerate anything in exchange for savoring the star's artistic interpretation. When they notice that there is less demand for tickets, the actor returns to his former status or takes refuge at an inferior studio.

SOME SPECIFIC CASES

We repeat: Spanish-language cinema has produced no stars. The name of a single actor is not sufficient for our people, although it is an important factor. If they know that Carmen Larrabeiti, to take one example, is appearing in a film, they still verify beforehand whether the story is good or not and carefully scrutinize the rest of the cast. At first it was the novelty of hearing actors speak Spanish that pulled them into the theater; then it was interest in the stories, until that interest was exhausted. That was the opportunity to have a star emerge, but producers either found no viable candidates, or they unwittingly let the moment pass by when they should have been taking action instead.

The memory of a specific case comes to mind when talking about this issue. There is a film actor named Carlos Villarías, whose situation unfolded about a year ago and grabbed our attention. He was contracted by Fox for a period of time, and they began to use him in Spanish versions being made by Hollywood studios.

Sometime later Universal planned to make *Dracula* in Spanish.[291] They chose Villarías for the central role, had him loaned from Fox for a high price, and began shooting. The result surprised even skeptics. Villarías managed to embody the bizarre and supernatural role of the vampire count, and his name instantly acquired great popularity.

This was the moment for Fox to create a star. What did it do with this kind of opportunity? They gave Villarías a secondary role in one of the studio's films and gave his name fourth or fifth billing in a cast that he easily could have led.

WASTED OPPORTUNITIES

When Columbia began trying its luck with Spanish-language cinema, its producers recalled the work of Villarías in *Dracula*, and they had him loaned out for *El código penal*. The result revealed that *Dracula* had not been a fluke, but Villarías returned to Fox to now do "bit parts" instead of secondary roles; in other words, something barely more important than being an extra. Then Columbia had him loaned out for *El pasado acusa*, a work in which, we sincerely believed, Villarías had performed the best role of his career, revealing himself as a consummate actor. And Fox once again cast him in insignificant roles until his obligations to them expired. The contract, which had an optional clause for the producers, was not renewed.

The studio had the chance to create a star and didn't do it. Something similar happened with Paramount in the case of María Calvo, who triumphed as a comedic character actor. After her work in *Estrellados*, she was specifically chosen for roles that were completely mismatched with her talent.[292] As a star of comic theater, she could have earned the studio a ton of money. There are many such cases if we decided to remember them one by one.

VILCHES AND VIRGINIA FÁBREGAS

As we were recently told by an executive at MGM, whose words were once printed in these very columns, "The problem with Hispano Cinema is that it hasn't figured out how to create audience favorites. Our business is stars and not the film in and of itself. Greta Garbo, Norma Shearer, and Joan Crawford all earn money with any cast and any script . . ."

It's true. But it's also true that when audiences designate favorites by insisting on seeing films with one actor or another, it is the producers that must be attentive to this demand. MGM itself has had opportunities to take control of the Hispano American market and has not done so, as a result of either mistrust or the lack of serious advice. They could have retained [Ernesto] Vilches, whose star qualities we won't discuss here and whose name is instant money in Hispano American theaters, but they did not. They argued that Mr. Vilches was impossible to deal with, that he had strange demands and a very bad temperament. But even if this were true, is any Greta Garbo docile, manageable, or normal? What would they say about the "temperament" of John Gilbert? And nonetheless, since their films earn money, they are retained come rain or shine.

Then they had a brilliant opportunity with Virginia Fábregas.[293] Setting aside national pride, one would think that Virginia's name could sell one, two, ten films in the theaters of Spanish America. With her cast in starring roles appropriate for her character, temperament, and age, the production company could undoubtedly have made money, because the veteran actress not only carried her talent and artist's soul to the screen but had a track record of theatrical triumph across the [American] continent. She has built her prestige bit by bit, year by year, season after season. And the studios had this at their disposal . . .

Cinema, like theater in Spanish, is a business of stars. There is absolutely no doubt about this. We have seen how a theater sometimes casts a mediocre star, as in the tragedy *Wu Li Chang*, whose central role was played by Manuel Sánchez Navarro; then a few months later, the same play broke records when the role was played by Ernesto Vilches. The play was the same, the authenticity of the set design almost identical; the audience was the same and the condition of the theaters was almost equal. What could the explanation be? It comes to mind that the appeal resides in WHO had the starring role.

THE MOST VIABLE CANDIDATES

Within the scarce Hispano production at the Studios, three actors stand out as destined for stardom . . . when the studio that employs them finds it opportune to consider them as such. In France it is Imperio Argentina who took the audience by storm with *Su noche de bodas*. Here it is José Mojica, perhaps the most powerful actor of all, and Carmen Larrabeiti. Even with all their abilities, other actors have not had the opportunity to play important roles or to develop their talent in a comprehensive or noteworthy way.

Lupita Tovar's career is also up in the air. La Compañía Nacional Productora de Películas de México has her under contract for the filming of *Santa*.[294] But we still don't know if they will feature her as a star—which she deserves when it comes to Mexican audiences—or make her secondary to the film's title, which would after all be the most fair and correct thing to do.

In terms of our stars in English-language films, there's not much to say at the moment. Ramon Novarro is no longer a star or is about to stop being one, so that he can play a major role opposite Greta Garbo. Dolores Del Rio no longer belongs to us. It was predicted that she would act in Spanish-language cinema, but she has abandoned it to give herself entirely to English-language roles. Lupe Velez has done the same, and Raquel Torres has already embraced a theatrical career and retired from the screen. She also declared to us not so long ago that she would not act in Spanish-language films because they were very difficult and producers didn't even give actors time to understand the characters they were playing.

At any rate, for the moment we don't have any stars. How long will this situation last?

IT'S TIME TO INNOVATE!

INGENIOUS SUGGESTIONS FOR THE SOLUTION TO OUR THEATRICAL PROBLEM; WHAT COULD BE DONE WITH HISPANO ACTORS FROM HOLLYWOOD; A TOTAL CHANGE IS NECESSARY

"¡Hay que renovarse!," published in *La Opinión*, January 18, 1931, page 5

Some days ago we published an article commenting on the Depression, which has made its effects felt in the theater business of late, especially relative to entertainment in Spanish. We made conjectures about the factors contributing to this Depression that has now assumed threatening proportions. The last two successes at the Teatro México during special functions have fortunately come to support our theory that a complete overhaul is necessary in order to keep the public interested. We must at least defend what we have, now that it is no longer possible to do lucrative business on the basis of a single actor or company, as it was in times past.

Properly speaking, there are three theaters whose activities are dedicated to satisfying the Spanish-speaking community. From south to north we have the California International, the México, and the Hidalgo. They are all within a perfectly defined urban zone and could stand in for one another, since their enterprises have always figured out how to understand the conditions necessary for success.

EL TEATRO CALIFORNIA

The first theater mentioned only exhibits films spoken in Spanish, all of them premieres, following the American system of changing the program on a weekly basis. Due to the level of its amenities, this theater is patronized in particular by that part of our community that lives far from Main

Street. That's how it is able to stay open, since it is located in a place that our people aren't obliged to walk by.

Business at the California is not going badly, although earnings aren't as fantastic as the owners would like. An average of three thousand people pass through this entertainment venue every week, leaving behind a sum that is never less than $1,500 in terms of admissions. The overhead is modest, and "one way or another" there is never a large deficit at the end of each week. The California survives through constant and systematic newspaper advertisements, handbills, and ads on Spanish-language radio programs. Unlike its competitors, it can't rely on its marquee since, as we said before, our pedestrians rarely walk past.

The system of weekly program changes is typically American; our public is accustomed to even more frequent changes, but they are slowly getting used to this state of affairs. Furthermore, if films are now shown for shorter runs than usual at the California, film production in Spanish will not be able to keep up with the demand.

About Teatro "México"

This theater enjoys the best location, although it does not have the amenities of the one described above. Hundreds of Mexicans walk by it every day, and on its corner is a trolley stop that links downtown to our neighborhoods: line "P" in particular connects Belvedere to the city.

What's more, the México holds more than a thousand spectators; it has comfortable seats and a stage with enough space to mount major shows. Its condition has been maintained in accordance with the law, and there's no reason that it wouldn't make a brilliant business for any company that is truly interested. It's worth mentioning in passing that it is the only venue that presents live theater, representing an advantage over its competitors. Nonetheless, judging by what you see at first glance, business is not necessarily that wonderful.

What could account for this anomaly?

Our humble opinion is that innovation is necessary. There remains no doubt that the public responds when truly attractive entertainment is presented, as the functions held last night and last Wednesday demonstrate. For the latter, the public filled three-quarters of the auditorium despite a torrential rain; for the former, which did not encounter this difficulty, the box office was frankly very good. Our readers know that once these actors have already appeared on more than one occasion, there is no reason to repeat the same attractions.

By contrast, a "gala" function was organized last week and the results were less than satisfactory. Was the play being premiered good or bad? The public never found out. What it did know, based on the profuse advertisements, was that there was not a moment of entertainment to be found in this function (in terms of novelty, that is); that was the source of its failure. If the spectators left the show satisfied, this fact was of little benefit to the theater. They read programs and newspaper advertisements—cheaply produced, no doubt—and heard about the show in advance on their radios. Nonetheless, very few people attended. From our perspective, this proves our previous assertion: that the public wants novelty, entertainment, and something that provokes curiosity.

There was a curious case last Friday. As the California premiered a film in Spanish that day, attracting the public, one would expect that the México would do something to thwart the competition, a competition all the more acute since it was the day before a big production at the México itself. Nonetheless, on that Friday they didn't hand out programs or place a single advertisement in the local press. Why the lack of interest in attracting spectators? Every day generates costs for a business, so it is incomprehensible that they would not do something to offset this. Friday night's program was filled by an insignificant *sainete*, so the small company on stage ended up acting "among family."[295]

We are convinced that if the entertainment at this theater—what it puts on the stage and screen—was reorganized, things would change for the better. Why not give it a try? It wouldn't be impossible with a little work . . .

Speaking with someone connected to the México about our previous article on this subject, we were told that "there is no way to bring new entertainment; there are not enough actors in Los Angeles or along the Mexican border." This is simply a misguided assessment.

Attracted by the prestige of the movie studios, there is now in Los Angeles more theatrical talent than there is in the capital of our Republic or those of the major countries of Spanish America. We have two or three famous, top-billed actresses here; a number of leading men; and a serious number of young actors and some young actresses, all of them suited for so-called shows in verse. Then there is a select group of singers: first-rate sopranos, tenors, baritones, basses, as well as orchestra conductors, dancers, variety artists, magicians, ventriloquists, comedians, etc. Believe it or not, all of this exists in Hollywood. One could choose from among this assortment to form an attractive ensemble, pay that ensemble well, keep them on the bill for one or two weeks, and then continue by organizing another show.

The fact that all this talent is busy making Cinema is not a serious counterargument, not in the least. There are studios constantly producing films in Spanish, employing a total of twenty actors, the majority of them under contract to these studios. There are more than a hundred unemployed actors who could easily work for a week without losing occasional opportunities in Cinema; it all depends on paying them handsomely. The money for these salaries will come from the public, who would happily go see a comedy that featured, for instance, Elvira Morla, Luisa Llaneza, María Calvo, Pablo Alvarez Rubio, Manuel Sánchez Navarro, José Soriano Viosca, and Amelia Soler. We are also certain that they would likewise attend a zarzuela in which they could hear the singing of Alma Real, Rodolfo Hoyos, or Luis Alvarez, accompanied by Carmita Tarrazo or Juan Aristi Eulate and under the artistic direction of, for example, maestro Eduardo Arozamena and the musical direction of maestro Giuseppe Miceli or maestro Fernando López Cabello. They would also go to see a revista with sets designed by Tarazona, music by Rafael Gama, Félix Loera, Miceli, or others, a libretto by proven and well-known local authors, and comedies starring tiples Celia Montalván and Delia Magaña, Cora Montes in a serious role, Luana Alcañiz dancing, character actor María Calvo, and many comic actors we won't cite here so as not to offend your sensibilities.[296] With the talent that exists, one could form seven different companies, all of them of high caliber. Why not give it a try? The public wants something new, and the theater will be back on the right track if it offers it to them . . .

In the Teatro Hidalgo

The Hidalgo has recently been renovated and exhibits interesting films. If its box office has decreased—and we don't know this with scientific certainty—it could be because the newspapers say nothing about its existence. Its projection and sound reproduction equipment are pretty good; its system of management is also good, and is based on the American model. Its small space perhaps doesn't work in its favor, but balancing the budget makes it a good business. If that is indeed the case . . . !

The person writing these lines is not claiming to give a lecture about putting on a theatrical show, something that is beyond his expertise. But it seems that the advice above, as technically defective as it may be, is also as logical as taking a drink when you are thirsty and have water in your hand. Theatrical talent is already a known quantity, and the public's interest in these actors has worn out after having seen them perform for so many years, playing the same roles, making the same gestures, and striking the same poses. Actor X, for example, comes on stage and stands very seriously before the footlights to say:

"I am Don Alvarado de Menda . . . !"

And the audience has the crazy urge to yell back:

"Whatever! You're X. We already know who you are . . ."

And for this reason no performance is taken seriously by the respectable spectator . . .

A complete overhaul is thus necessary. We can all agree that the economic situation of our people is precarious in this day and age, but the Lord always provides. Do you want proof? We saw proof just last night and in functions of equal caliber the Saturday before. Everything, even the strain of this situation, is relative. And if not, hopefully someone dares give it a try and the results will be superior . . .

A COMPETITOR TO HOLLYWOOD HAS EMERGED

MEXICO HAS A GREAT FUTURE AS A NATION THAT PRODUCES TALKING FILMS; ALL CIRCUMSTANCES SEEM TO FAVOR OUR PRODUCTIONS

"Ha surgido ya un competidor de Hollywood,"
published in *La Opinión*, April 3, 1932, page 5

Mexico is turning out to be the logical center of production for films in Spanish, and Hollywood's most formidable rival as an entertainment factory for Latin America and even for Spanish possessions, although not for the peninsula due to questions of national pride. With *Santa* already made although not yet exhibited, the studios are already preparing to produce *Aguilas frente al sol*. Carlos Noriega Hope is busy at work on the script for *Clemencia*, the unforgettable and unique novel by maestro [Ignacio Manuel] Altamirano.[297] This proves that the outlook is not cloudy: to the contrary, there is determination, enthusiasm, and even rarer, the energy sufficient to crystallize what very well could have remained sickly and passive lyricism.

Perhaps Mexican producers have unintentionally placed their fingers in the wound. Hollywood could not have a more powerful Latin American rival in the future. Conditions in Mexico are clearly ideal in terms of atmosphere; the country boasts millions of unexploited landscapes that could serve as exteriors: the construction of sets or other structures in the "Studios" turns out to be cheaper than in Hollywood because of monetary exchange rates. What would cost a million dollars to erect here could be underway for a million Mexican pesos over there, if someone wanted to waste that kind of money. After all, fantastic buildings, squandering money on luxury or architectural style, are not necessary for an artistic production.

Didn't [Jesse L.] Lasky and his friends make films—and good films—in a horse stable just a quarter century ago? All you need is a good camera and good sound-recording equipment. It would seem that Compañía Nacional has them.

Mexico's proximity to Hollywood is another advantage with which no other Spanish-speaking country could compete. A competent director, a famous actor, a good cinematographer, respectable equipment, and pieces of machinery, etc. could be in Chapultepec twenty-four hours after they are ordered. But most important of all is the low cost of production, which will always be easy to maintain, contrary to what happens in Hollywood, where the most miserable picture never costs less than fifteen or twenty thousand dollars. We believe—unless we are entirely mistaken—that a superior production in Mexico could be made at a total cost of fifty to sixty thousand Mexican pesos, if production managers are well versed in the one thousand and one twists and turns of sound film economics.

There is also a wide market for Mexican film. We have not only the hundred million possible spectators from Spanish America but also a non-negligible population of one million cinephiles in the United States who pay in dollars and who are thirsty for films that deal with our issues in a Latin spirit. A premiere of any of our films in Los Angeles, El Paso, or San Antonio would yield at least a thousand dollars; in a Mexican theater it might be a formidable hit, but ticket sales would not reach a third of that amount. Subsequent ticket sales in the United States theaters patronized by the Spanish-speaking community would pay for almost three-fourths of production costs. So the market on this side of the Rio Grande is one that can't be underestimated.

Here we are waiting with a certain curiosity and more than a little interest for the premiere of *Santa*. If it turns out to be what we know it will, there will be nothing to do but correct notable defects moving forward so that the next production is an improvement. With an open market, facilities at the ready, and those that the Mexican government will undoubtedly provide given its interest in the advance of production, the fifth film will be able to compete with those made abroad in every sense. That's what we desire, at the very least for the good of our language and the preservation of our customs that are now more than ever in danger of being replaced by those of the United States. As good as these may be, they aren't grounded in our particular sensibility.

WHY THE HIDALGO HAS MADE A COMEBACK AS THE "RENDEZVOUS" OF THE COMMUNITY

IT IS THE ONLY PLACE WHERE A GROUP OF ACTORS CAN MAKE A LIVING, AND IT IS TRYING TO REKINDLE THE FLAME OF ENTHUSIASM FOR HISPANIC PRESENTATIONS

"Porque resurgió el Hidalgo como 'rendezvous' de la colonia,"
published in *La Opinión*, May 1, 1932, page 7

The Spanish-speaking public has lately been attending the Teatro Hidalgo, which until just recently was considered an insignificant venue in our community, and applauding actors whom they had once only seen as images on the perpendicular screen. They are rubbing elbows with Film stars who just last year would have refused an invitation from this theater, even though they might have slipped furtively into its portico, eager to see some movie or other that was already outdated. The regular audience at the Hidalgo is finally sitting alongside people from the "West" or Hollywood, many of whom, despite their lengthy residence in Los Angeles, had never ventured to North Main, much less to enjoy themselves in a venue that offers such modest productions.

This has naturally prompted curiosity. What could explain this phenomenon? How is it that the unwritten, ironclad rules of etiquette have been broken to allow artistically and socially "decent" people to visit places reserved for the more modest social classes?

It is self-evident that "the actor makes the theater and not the other way around." We might add to this ancient dictum that "the audience makes the show," or, better yet, that it completely dignifies the proceedings with its approving presence. From these notions we can at least deduce the explanation for the phenomenon that we mentioned in the first lines of this article.

WHY WERE THEY NOT ATTENDING BEFORE?

Let's consider the audience. The Teatro Hidalgo has been a part of our world for many years, practically without shutting its doors for even a day. Why wasn't the public going?

The most logical answer that comes to mind is that there were other theaters open to the public in the southern part of Los Angeles whose capacity and stages offered better conditions. First was the México, which is now dedicated to American shows of a salacious nature. Then there was the California; every film in Spanish paraded across its screen and every local celebrity set foot on its stage within a brief period of time. Ramon Novarro, Dolores Del Rio, José Mojica, Lupe Velez, Mimí Aguglia . . . all of them stood before the footlights of the California time and again, not to mention those who have yet to earn that kind of immense popularity. But the California closed its doors after a rapid decline in the material available for shows, leaving the Hidalgo as the only refuge of the community. It may be modest and everything, but it is the only venue in which you hear Spanish spoken on and off the stage. The Spanish-speaking public first began gathering there timidly and with some hesitation. The owners realized the opportunity this presented and improved their shows. Day after day, different people came, some out of curiosity, others excited about entertainment offered in Spanish. That's how "Hidalgo Mondays" were born, each of them featuring a benefit event, a premiere, or a gala held for one reason or another. The result was that the best of our community began attending, attracted by the shows that were advertised, without being aware of past prejudices toward the theater.

THE ATTITUDE OF THE ARTISTS

Another reason that a certain category of the public once abstained from attending the Hidalgo was the poor quality of the shows. For the same price one could see something better in American theaters even if it wasn't exactly in our language. Now, without raising prices—and we say this without any promotional intention—the Hidalgo has managed to present on their stage the most prominent of our talent working in Hollywood. Rodolfo Hoyos, [Fortunio] Bonanova, and Samuel Pedraza have recently sung there; María Calvo and Eduardo Arozamena have acted; artists have danced there who had previously done so only at the Hollywood studios. Prestigious personalities have been attending lately, including consuls of our nations and Film stars working in both Spanish and English. This seems to have inspired the confidence of the public in general.

This rebirth, which is in large part a product of circumstance—and the lack of other theaters in particular—also has its basis in the attitude of the artists themselves, who have broken a rule about categories that they themselves established. Their contingent has not hesitated to offer entertainment on a stage that is more modest than the ones they are accustomed to. It is a commendable attitude from any perspective, even taking into account the amount of money they may or may not make for their work. And it is commendable because by breaking with that absurd established etiquette, they have served as an example for the audience to do the same, which at the end of the day means success. That's the way we see things . . .

THE HIDALGO IS ONLY A SYMBOL

Artists, journalists, and spectators in general have contributed to this effort, convinced that at least for now the Hidalgo is the last stronghold of our bruised and battered interpretive arts, the only venue in Los Angeles where they act and perform in Spanish. And it is right to rekindle this dying flame so that it will not be extinguished, leaving us in the dark as far as Hispano entertainment is concerned. In addition, it is a means of subsistence for many: actors, actresses, dancers, singers, painters, stagehands, ticket sellers, and even the simple and humble people who sweep the house, all of them Mexican. If it were any other theater instead of the Hidalgo, we are inclined to believe that the attitude of our artistic and social element would be the same. At the end of the day, the Hidalgo is nothing more than a symbol: a symbol of the performing arts and the preservation of our culture. What could be more unfortunate than letting it disappear?

ENTERTAINMENT—OUR REVIEW OF AN ADVANCE SCREENING OF THE FILM *THUNDER OVER MEXICO*

EISENSTEIN'S WORK JUDGED FROM FOUR DIFFERENT PERSPECTIVES

"Espectáculos—Como vimos la película 'Thunder over Mexico' en su exhibición previa," published in *La Opinión*, May 12, 1933, page 4

Last Wednesday night revolutionary Russian director Sergei Eisenstein presented his film *Thunder over Mexico* to a large audience of invited special guests. The film was made entirely in our country over the course of fourteen months and was previously christened with the name *Viva México*, which was replaced with the above-mentioned title. The advance screening was held at the Carthay Circle and was preceded by explanatory comments read by socialist author Upton Sinclair.[298]

The change of name made good sense. Because a film like this one hardly justifies the title *Viva México*, even taking into account the good intentions of that portion of the public that knows or claims to know our country. Overall, the film is a hymn to the Revolution, and aside from the typically Mexican costuming, it could pass for an episode from pre-Soviet Russia, in whose spirit the director Eisenstein seems to be so immersed.

There are four aspects by which one might judge this film whose expressive aspects were achieved with uncommon success: artistic, political, social, and historical. We will endeavor to offer our evenhanded opinion on each of them, attending to our initial impression, as we figure an audience of spectators might have, without attempting a proper journalistic critique. Here is our opinion of this work:

THE ARTISTIC POINT OF VIEW

Seen through the eyes of an art lover, *Thunder Over Mexico* seems to us, as we said above, a rare expressive and aesthetic accomplishment. The photography is admirable and novel. The effects achieved by the direction are elegant in their simplicity; through them each of the characters is marked by a stamp of tragedy, desolation, and misfortune, which we also perceive in individuals living in Russia before Lenin.

More than 100,000 feet of raw film stock was needed to obtain these results, of which only a total of 9,000 was used. The editing and assembly of the film therefore must have been easy, as the entire film reveals an extraordinary spontaneity. The landscapes are marvelous, if stereotypical (volcanoes are the camera's central focus), and the Toltec and Mayan ruins—not Aztec, as the titles suggest—have been captured from extraordinary angles, compensating for the subject's lack of novelty, generally speaking.

Without the formidable assistance of the music, however, the splendid photography would have left something to be desired. The dramatic landscapes are brought to life by the rhythm of the score, from the solemn serenity of the millenary volcanoes to the boisterous ambience of the fleeting bullfight. The music is an original composition by Mexicans whose names will someday be illustrious: Francisco Camacho Vega and Juan Aguilar Adame. Some parts of the score lack originality and suffer from an unfortunate lack of inspiration, but they are in some respects bolstered by a fortress of harmony that pushes its resources to the limit, producing a grandiose impression. What we might call the prelude of the score sounded the best to us, as we perceived in it the influence of contemporary Russian masters in its frequent movement through tonal scale and the skillful use of brass instruments.

Seen without any historical prejudice whatsoever, the film is a true masterpiece: a profound lament, emotion carried to the screen and hitting the audience in the face with all of its original brutality. Cinematic art has rarely been taken to such heights as it is in *Thunder over Mexico*.

THE POLITICAL ASPECT OF THE WORK

We said before that the film exhibited last Wednesday at Carthay Circle is a resounding hymn to Revolution. And not the Mexican Revolution, which is touched on incidentally, but rather political revolution around the world. The conclusion of the work symbolically presents us with a Mexico that is

in tune with modern advancements: a Mexico of machinery and powerful boilers; an athletic and military Mexico, healthy in mind and spirit in
keeping with revolutionary standards. This is why a film that raises serious
objections for us has actually been sanctioned by our nation's government
as a powerful aid in propaganda efforts directed at new generations, at the
cost of partially sacrificing the truth.

As an ode to the movement of 1910, it could not resist the temptation to throw veritable buckets of mud at the figure of Porfirio Díaz.
Ideologically speaking, he is blamed for the misfortune of the peons who
are dependent on the whims of their masters. At one daring moment
in the narrative, when the Indian maiden is forcibly seduced by a rich
creole behind closed doors, the camera pans toward a large oil painting
portraying the dictator, as if to reveal him as the sole cause of this tragedy,
which could honestly occur under any political banner despite current
revolutionary advances.

All of this is very unfair. Looking back objectively at this period (1906),
the film could just as well show both sides of the coin. That is, the film
could also reveal, alongside the state of peasant life, the highest ranks of
Mexican society during that time. It was not only rapes that were committed under the hand of the dictator; railroads were also constructed, the
national treasury grew considerably, and Mexico as a nation was elevated
to a new level of respectability. It would later experience a decline from
which it is now, however, slowly but surely recovering. The sin consequently
resides not in what the film shows but in what it excludes. Why does it
conceal these things? Could any jury arrive at a verdict when it has only
been presented with the allegations of the prosecution, without hearing a
single word from the defense?

There is a moment at the end of the work that could pass by unnoticed, since Eisenstein apparently accorded it little significance. After the
"Revuelta" section (the subtitle says "Revolt") and as proof of Mexico's
rebirth, the audience is presented with a symbol of militarism: parading
troops, the deafening sound of drums and bugles filling the air, showy
uniforms, and heads raised to attention. And this ostentatious display of
militarism is exactly the same one that tried to destroy the Revolution of
1910 . . . !

In addition, there is an involuntary note of irony based on the fact
that all of this symbolism of war takes as its backdrop the elegant monu-
ment to independence, the architectural pride of América, constructed and

inaugurated . . . during the time of General Díaz, when his administration was at the height of its splendor.

FROM A SOCIAL PERSPECTIVE

If the film aspires to be a reflection of social conditions during the first decade of the current century, it also suffers from unfortunate errors. On this point, at least from our perspective, *Thunder over Mexico* is one of the films we would consider denigrating toward us. This is not only because of its one-sided nature but also because it is destined for exhibition abroad, as the English-language narration, titles, and publicity reveal. We can at the very least say that this is unjust, because it will create the impression beyond our borders that Mexico is a half-savage country before the "Revuelta" section, without considering how foreign audiences may continue to wonder whether or not this is still the case, despite the struggle that fortunately brought an end to all of that. Mexico has fared better than what Mr. Eisenstein presents to us: it has a social environment on a par with more civilized nations, an honorable army, and an educated civil service. These three things are currently no better than they were before. It's not a secret to anyone that the privileged caste of the past has been replaced by another instead of being completely exterminated. Any level-headed and sincere person living in Mexico will confirm that we are right in this respect.

It is as if a filmmaker were to make a propaganda film about the United States by exclusively showing scenes that demonstrate the cruelty of plantation owners during the period of black slavery. Or if, when making a film that extolled the progress of the new France, he relied on showing squalid, miserable scenes from the reign of the Louis kings without a single reassuring note amid that painful situation.

HOW A HISTORIAN WOULD VIEW THE FILM

If historians were inspired by this film to trace the contours of Mexican history, we would be lost. There are unfortunate exaggerations in the film that, in keeping with the propagandistic nature of the work, would instead confuse anyone studying the conditions of Mexico at the beginning of the century. The federation's rural troops were never, as far as we know, under the control of any hacienda owner. But director Eisenstein portrays them as subservient to the creole's chaotic thirst for pleasure during that period, without any basis in fact. On the other hand, they paint the daughter of the hacienda owner as a heartless woman with the temperament of an Amazon who joins the pursuit of the pulque makers and fires on the peons. At no moment does her soul show an echo of pain for the dishonored Indian virgin. Mexican women have never been like this. The "aristocratic woman" of Porfirian times was generally demure, devoted, and gifted with a noble and generous heart that often contrasted with the brusqueness of her masculine counterparts. Above all, she was eminently feminine, a woman guided by affection and sweetness. What else could this hybrid character be other than a general insult to the Mexican woman? To top it all off, she is the cause of three unfortunate sacrifices.

The person writing these lines is descended from Mexico's most humble classes. As such, he lived in that environment and can sincerely confess that he never saw workers on the haciendas treated inhumanely. It's not as if the hacienda owners were magnanimous. They were cruel, with the cruelty that comes with the pride and social position forged by money. But criminal acts were punished by law. It may have been a law bribed with the gold of the privileged, but it was law just the same. On the other hand, the "punishment by horse" could have existed during Spanish domination, but in post-independence history there is no single archive that could serve as the basis of such a barbaric assumption.

In summary, the film *Thunder over Mexico* receives very high marks as a work of art, although it most certainly has debatable value as a glorification of the movement that overthrew the Porfirian dictatorship. But it also neither represents nor elevates our country. Exhibited abroad, it will be an inexhaustible source of confusion for those who would like to penetrate the true soul of Mexico. And this is not good for anyone, for either revolutionaries or reactionaries.

It was thus very sensible for the title *Viva México* to be erased from the first reel.

That's the least that could be done . . .

THE FIRST OBSTACLE

MEXICO WILL BE OBLIGATED FOR THE MOMENT TO PRODUCE FILMS FOR MEXICANS WITHIN AND BEYOND ITS BORDERS; A PREJUDICE; OURS IS THE COUNTRY WITH "OPEN ARMS"; BUT OUR BROTHERS IN LATIN AMERICA DO NOT FEEL SO INCLINED . . .

"El primer obstáculo," published in *La Opinión*, June 5, 1932, page 5

Bit by bit, but apparently in a firm and assured manner, sound film production in Spanish seems to be headed exclusively in the direction of free companies, which are referred to as such because they do not belong to the New York–Hollywood Trust that controls the American market. The first was *Santa*, which has already been seen in Los Angeles. Now comes *Aguilas frente al sol*, a film by Sáenz de Sicilia featuring Jorge Lewis and Hilda Moreno, ready to be released in Spanish America. Every effort is closer to perfection, each instance seems to make the most of the impartial teachings of experience. And it seems that Mexicans are those most inclined to fully enter into this venture, which, like any other undertaking of the sort, poses infinite challenges in return for benefits that can only be absolutely and definitively clarified by the future.

These independent companies have broad and daring plans. They now hope to take advantage of the opportunity presented them to acquire control of theaters equipped for sound in our América; to bring to each Hispano American city and town the entertainment that their public has been asking for since characters were gifted with the spoken word, thanks to the efforts of Warner Bros. in Hollywood. The market indeed exists, but one of the greatest obstacles is unifying continental opinion and erasing the thousand and one prejudices that exist in the minds of different populations that, despite speaking the same language and belonging to the same family, continue to fight like "cats and dogs" at every turn, as Teodoro Torres tells us in his entertaining book about Mexican democracy.[299]

"PLEASE, GENTLEMEN: NO MORE MEXICANS!"

Let's take *Santa* as an example, the first Mexican production to be shown on the screens of our theaters. It was the product of a Mexican mind, adapted from [Federico] Gamboa's novel under our own flag and performed almost entirely by Mexicans; therein lie its principal drawbacks. In Mexico everyone has forgiven its defects: Mexicans in the United States have treated it with leniency, with that air of kindness with which we overlook the imperfection of our children as they begin to speak, to take their first faltering steps, to gradually understand everything that surrounds them on their march toward a vigorous youth. But . . . can we expect the same from audiences in countries that, although ethnically similar, are saturated with an antagonistic prejudice toward everything that comes from the North?

We know all too well that Cuba grudgingly tolerates us and that we will not now nor probably ever be worshipped as saints in Argentina. In Venezuela they look at us sideways and in Colombia there are only a few people who grant us some artistic or literary competence. Chilenos are exclusively and fiercely patriotic. In the sphere of theater, this tidbit is enough proof:

A publication of that sister country praised the work of a certain revista company that dared to invade its theaters with undeniable success. But at the end of an encomiastic review, we find these words, or something similar to them:

"The works of Company X have brought us moments of true enter-tainment and we have applauded them without reservation. But . . . please, no more Mexicans; in Chile we have very competent talent worthy of consideration . . ."

OUR CALCULATIONS ARE BASED ON THE MEXICAN PUBLIC

As far as we know, *Santa* has still not been shown in those countries. But we bet double to nothing—and we'd love to be wrong, of course—that the film will not be well received by our "little brothers" to the South. Stripped of patriotic sentiment, the South American public will see the defects through a magnifying glass, comparing them to works that come from the insurmount-able crucible of Hollywood. It is enough for it to be a Mexican script made by Mexicans for it to have the usual prejudices directed against it. They will talk about "supremely childish efforts," about "vain boasts," and about "an absurd eagerness to impose." And if not, they will with Time.

Mexican production then has to be calculated for audiences in our country, within and beyond its borders. If the product can pay for itself with the box office from our theaters, the business will have wind in its sails. If not, it's perhaps best not to embark on that journey. Unless we manage to produce something marvelous, impeccable, something that everyone considers the epitome of perfection. And even then, there is so much to criticize in all that is human, which must necessarily be imperfect!

There is also another factor working against us: the characteristic self-love among South Americans that is so exaggerated, so intransigent, so exclusive.

"Why," they will ask, "is Mexico coming to us with talking pictures? Are we going to tolerate this imposition when we have talent in our own country that could surpass Mexicans in sound film production? We have accepted Hollywood films because they come from a great and powerful nation; because they are well made, although we understand neither their language nor their spirit. But from Mexico . . . what for?"

THE COUNTRY OF OPEN ARMS

We know that all of this is unfair, but . . . the world is how it is, not as we would like it to be. "Mexico," a prominent screen actor recently told us, "is a country of open arms." Everything that comes from abroad must necessarily be better than what is ours; Spanish actors have been idolized in Mexico; peninsular writers almost always find us inexplicably kneeling before them. From Salvador Rueda to Luis Araquistáin, all the way to the questionable Francisco Villaespesa and Blasco Ibáñez, every poet and novelist who has visited us has always encountered a reception worthy of those given to a conquering king by a subservient people.[300] Then in the arena of civilizational progress, there are thousands of cases. North American engineers are always superior to ours. German doctors come to pontificate, and lecturers from Spain, France, South America, and even Syria-Lebanon make us believe truths that we doubt when they come from the mouths of Antonio Caso or José Vasconcelos . . . [301]

By contrast, our people are received with mistrust everywhere. In Colombia they assure us that we don't know how to speak Spanish; in

Cuba they think we're a joke, and our exiled Mexican journalists have had to make an enormous effort to partially overcome that prejudice during the time when they were obliged to make a living from the press in the Pearl of the Antilles.

WE MUST ALWAYS BE CERTAIN

We fear that the same thing will happen to our films to the extent that we produce them and release them on the market. Hopefully we are incorrect or are guided by isolated observations, which in the case of seeing a solitary swallow "does not mean it's summer." But we have to be certain, above anything else. Mexico should produce its films with the Mexican market as its primary province, understanding that the results in other countries may be gradual or nebulous and in any case should never be relied upon.

Of course, by criticizing those who pontificate in other countries, we are not ourselves aspiring to pontificate. We are merely expressing our mistrust, which is very well founded, with the hope of being totally wrong. Only when our productions have been shown in countries like Cuba, Argentina, Chile, and Colombia can we say the last word about this. Hopefully that word will be satisfactory. We need it very much, even if only as a gesture of reciprocation toward the "country of open arms," for which everything that comes from abroad is always better than what it has, regardless of the merit inherent in its artists, its literary figures, and its thinkers . . .

Fleeting Impressions

Chinas Poblanas Wearing Sequins and Beads; Yes, We Are "Spanish"; Why Do We Feel So Hurt by the Representative Types of Our Race?

"Impresiones fugaces," published in *La Opinión*, July 10, 1932, page 7

We frequently complain that Mexican costuming in American film and theater is painfully adulterated. In productions called "Spanish," they present character types dressed as if they came from the epoch of Su Alteza Serenísima Don López de Santa Anna, with the addition of a cummerbund identical to those worn by our military in the Porfirian era and a little hat with tiny woolen pom-poms hanging from the brim.

"That's not Mexican," we say. "These people reveal a complete ignorance of our customs and clothing . . ."

Nonetheless, we cannot cast the first stone. In shows that call themselves "truly Mexican," there is naturally always a china poblana and a charro from Jalisco. And the "beaver skin" jackets of our chinas are studded with sequins; their heads are wrapped in a tricolor ribbon, and the breasts of their shirts are embroidered with an eagle devouring a serpent . . . !

The truth is that we have also never seen our people wearing sequins, embroidered eagles, or tricolor ribbons as clothing. It's simply a matter of theatricality. Then why don't we understand that our American cousins are just putting in their two cents by adulterating our clothing? In the end, "we are all guilty . . ."

Seen this way, we have no reason to feel insulted when they call us "Spanish" instead of "Mexican" in any English-language newspaper. In many cases, we have witnessed protests from one actor or another billed as "Spanish" who interrupts to rectify the error: "Mexican, please; I am a Mexican." The correction is made and all is well, with the exception of the Mexican whose self-esteem is wounded because their true origin was not cited.

Nonetheless, by considering us Spanish they do not have the least intention of confusing us with our brothers from the Iberian Peninsula. North Americans refer to those from Spain as "Spaniards" and use the distinction "Spanish" for everything Hispanic, in other words, everything of Spanish origin. That word encompasses our twenty republics and the country now under the control of Don Niceto Alcalá Zamora.[302] Accordingly, although the dictionary definition may be different, we are indeed "Spanish," at least in the minds of Yankees, who tend to simplify everything. For them it is too complicated to differentiate between Argentines, Mexicans, Chileans, Paraguayans, Colombians, etc., etc. That's how we have to understand it . . . In many of our countries don't we call all foreigners "gringo"?

Another of our peculiarities is that we are offended when we see certain figures portrayed in magazine illustrations, Cinema, or theater: the pelado, the tamal vendor, the peasant in white shorts, or any other of our humble Indian women grinding away over a stone metate in the commendable labor of making tortillas.[303]

"Why," we say in an angry tone, "don't these people represent Mexicans dressed in tailcoats at a dinner party, on the streets in an impeccable American suit, or our women at elegant 'soirees' dressed as they would be in real life? That isn't Mexico. Or at least, it's not ALL of Mexico . . ."

It's true that we Mexicans dress in tailcoats on certain occasions and that we eat with the aid of forks and spoons; that we also use automobiles and dance "jazz" in dance halls. But in the eyes of foreigners, these are all just passed on from European civilization. The typical, the original, that which is distinctively ours, is the costume with the wide hat, Indian women making tortillas, street vendors selling tamales, sheep menudo, and pig's feet. To see people in modern dress, you don't even have to travel: Americans have all of that at home.

Would it perhaps not be a terrible disappointment for us to see photographs of the Chinese and Japanese dressed like Europeans? We always expect to see types dressed in the clothing of the Oriental people; a Japanese woman playing piano lacks interest for us, while one of them sitting before a koto and drawing strange sounds from its strings offers the ideal satisfaction. What is more distressing than photographs of the King of Siam wearing a "jacket" and topped with a silk hat? What is a moor without a turban, without his robe and musket, or without the restless Arabian horse bucking beneath his body that is agile as a tiger?

The Europeanized Mexican interests no one except perhaps Mexicans themselves, and only out of snobbery. Our capacity to adapt to foreign influences is one of the most powerful enemies we have because they are destroying our own personality, the customs and traditions that are, in the final analysis, the true soul of the people . . .

Let's Make Cinema "in Spanish" and Not Cinema "Translated into Spanish"

In Hollywood They Are Starting to "See the Light" When It Comes to Movies in Our Language; What Will Be the Future of Our Cinema, Now That It Has Begun?

"Hacemos cine 'en español' y no 'cine traducido al español,'" published in *La Opinión*, illustrated supplement, December 25, 1932, page 3

We now have Cinema in Mexico. Making Mexican Cinema is also just as important and necessary. We should use the more general term "Hispano American Cinema," but the ideological difference is essentially minimal. Our culture could be just as perfectly understood in a cultivated Colombia as it is in the racial melting pot of Argentina. Mexican film, if it is well conceived, will have a market from the swampy lands of Central America to the distant corners of Tierra del Fuego. What we need is Cinema in Spanish and not Cinema "translated into Spanish."

The gratifying news about film production in the Aztec capital is reaching us even here in Hollywood, igniting a spark of enthusiasm in the spirit of Latinos who, for one reason or another, find themselves tied to this old center of production. But if things continue along these lines in Mexico, Hollywood will soon be a thing of the Past. The facts show, with the incontrovertible certainty of Truth, that Mexico has taken its first steps toward independence from Hollywood. Hopefully these steps take us toward our desired goal; hopefully what is now just starting to crystallize will very soon become an irrefutable reality.

Here we have only seen *Santa* and *Aguilas frente al sol*; the defects of the first can be excused because it was a trial by fire for talent full of laudable intentions; the second was amateurish and artificial to the point that it inspired a little bitterness in us. But the press has told us about the clamor of enthusiasm that has greeted *Una vida por otra*, *Mano a mano*, and *El anónimo*, in addition to announcing the upcoming exhibition of works like *Sobre las olas* and *Revolución*.[304] In terms of title, essence, and atmosphere, both of these are as Mexican as the eagle and the serpent. *Chucho el Roto* and *La llorona*, José Bohr's next productions, are also a welcome promise of a better future.[305]

From all of this we can deduce a simple, concrete fact: that the Twilight of Hollywood is coming near in our countries, despite the splendid quality of their productions, despite the sumptuous scenery paid for by the gold of the multitudes, despite the established names that the masses have learned to adore like so many gods in a brand-new, transitory Olympus. Because we now have Cinema in Mexico . . .

When something starts off well, it is a shame to ruin it on the second try. In order for our cinema to be effectively ours, it must not depart from the ideological line of the Latino spirit. Anything less would not pass for more than an absurd obfuscation, a crude imitation that will confuse the public, leaving us in a worse place than the one we are now fighting to abandon. As a result of inevitable comparison, the masses will end up turning their backs on our cinema with the same snobbery that has driven them to dress in imported suits because they consider their materials superior to national products. This is what we must avoid. To achieve it, the best path forward is a strict vigilance over the stories chosen, the progression of scenes, the endings of films, and even the gestures and poses of the actors. Everything should be exclusively Latino, even the technical aspects. From Hollywood we should only take advantage of the equipment, since we can't construct it ourselves; the manufacture of film is not yet within our reach and our technical capacity is also very limited. In essence, the spirit of our films should be truly ours and should reveal pieces of our lives, reflecting our sensibility as individuals and as a people.

The so-called happy endings should exist only in comedies and filmic opera. The bitterness that is inherent in the Latino soul, this tendency toward the tragic that pulls at the heartstrings, is part of our racial distinctiveness. Although we all share the same life, it flows into different streams for the Saxon race and for people of Latino origin. In the former, there is something logical in its artificiality, a by-product of childhood upbringing. In the latter, life is something helplessly fatal whose progression finds tragedy waiting behind every corner; at certain moments it is stricken with a sentimentality incomprehensible to the Saxon spirit.

Cinema, just like the novel or drama, should faithfully reflect the sensibility of the people who produce it. A film's scenes will clash with our established character if they are not experienced the way we ourselves experience these moments in our short journey. The public will initially receive it with curiosity, but will then turn its back as it does toward everything it misunderstands because it is outside of its own ideology. We are certain that there still remains—despite the slow yet relentless Saxon invasion of our people's spirit—a reserve of our own sensibility that will never disappear from our race, as it is our traditional patrimony.

So Mexican cineastes, understood here as those who are working to build the new Industry in our country, have the responsibility to make Cinema that is human, true to life, and a faithful reflection of the soul of our nations if they want to capture the support of the public from the Rio Grande to Punta Arenas. They cannot compete with the great laboratory of emotions that is Hollywood, because they would instantly be crushed by the high quality of production and because people here are immersed in the atmosphere that their films portray with more or less fidelity. The salvation of Mexican cinema will therefore lie in being sincere and simple, but intensely human.

And this can be achieved effortlessly by simply casting off the North American influence before it ends up absorbing even the very spiritual life of the Latino Race, relegating its traditions, its ideology, its special sensibility to the old storage closet, to the trunk perfumed with lavender that holds the belongings of our grandparents from a past that may or may not have been better . . .

The Scene—We Must Foster a Love of Amateur Theater among the Spanish-Speaking Communities of California

Incalculable Advantages

"La escena—Urge estimular el amor por el teatro de aficionados
en las colonias de habla española de California," published in
La Opinión, August 26, 1934, section II, pages 3, 8

With theater bankrupted as a means of support for artists and almost nullified as a lucrative profession for playwrights, it is necessary to resort to clever means so that it does not die out completely, so that we at least save this source of artistic satisfaction in the Hispano life of California. Under these circumstances it is advisable to foster amateur theater to the greatest extent possible.

Many of our local youth have a vocation for the stage. But in the case of women, their families always cry to the heavens when someone mentions the possibility of their daughter participating in a theatrical company; and for men, it may be that the need to become established in some profession is greater than the desire to embark on a venture that may or may not provide a future. The former can't dedicate themselves to theater because of the moral order, while the latter are likewise incapacitated by a material order.

But an amateur company—or several of them—is different than a group of professionals. In the first place, that which terrifies protective mothers automatically ceases to exist, as their daughter could be among trustworthy individuals, those whom their families consider to be of the same social standing; and second, the ambition for success is centered exclusively on artistic terrain. At the same time, amateur theater offers incalculable advantages, to say nothing of making art just for the satisfaction of doing so.

One of these advantages is the strengthening of friendships among youth, erasing prejudices and solidifying social ties. Those who have ever been part of an amateur theater company, even by accident, feel a strange emptiness the day after the show when the group disperses and the rehearsals that kept them under the same roof come to a halt. Within a few days they have become accustomed to one another; in many cases, they grow to consider each other family. And more than one happy marriage has had its origins in the rehearsals for a comedy that was later staged as a benefit . . .

Another advantage is the constant cultivation of the Spanish language in an environment like the one in which we live, where it is gradually taken away from us to be replaced by the hard inflections of English. Practice perfects diction, awakens curiosity to know the meaning of certain words, familiarizes us with the art of conversation, and transforms what were previously only decorative figures at social functions into interesting young people. With the constant exercise of language skills, a desire is born in our spirits to read, and we all know that reading is one of the shortest paths to culture in general.

Then comes the natural ambition to show off, the desire to stand out, the intoxication of applause that for many is worth more than money. When determination is applied to a good rehearsal, it puts existing talents on display that have not yet had the opportunity to rise to the surface. For women, demonstrating these talents at the very least constitutes a way to attract men who prefer healthy interests over frivolity. For men it may mean the start of a cinematic career, now that Cinema has almost completely absorbed theater.

For all of these reasons, and others that would take too much space to relate, it is advisable to support amateur theater among the Mexican communities of California. At bookstores there are easy, short works with small casts that could be put to use. Periodically—every month, for example—one or another group of amateurs could organize a show as a benefit or only as a means of practicing, which would offer the advantages of providing families with wholesome entertainment, encourage the love of a career among youthful spirits, and every once in a while inject an artistic expression into the monotony of urban life, not to mention providing some help to the needy in special cases of philanthropic events.

In Los Angeles there are a number of social clubs formed by educated and ambitious youth. We believe that if each of these clubs were to form its own theatrical company under competent direction, we would soon have at least two or three companies presenting works in rotation. They could easily offer a monthly show, accomplishing everything that we have taken time to mention in the previous paragraphs.

We believe that theater owners would provide facilities to these groups for their presentations; that because they have a solely recreational and social purpose, the press and radio stations could offer their services for free when it comes to publicity.

Why not give it a try?

That's Hollywood!—We Need to Make Cinema for the Masses, the Ones Who Pay for It

Hollywood Producers' Great Mistake; If Only Directors Emerged from Mexico . . . !

"Este Hollywood! Hay que hacer cine para las masas, que son las quo lo pagan," published in *La Opinión*, June 23, 1935, section II, page 6

We have always maintained in these columns that Cinema should be made for the popular masses, prioritizing this over any other kind of entertainment that might appear on screen. We have already expressed the reasons for this, and they can be summed up in one statement, which will simplify everything: it is the gente del pueblo, the middle class, that is handing over its money at the movie theater box office. Intellectuals and those who consider themselves "aristocracy" only go with a free pass or on special occasions. Now that this has been settled, what could be more logical than to dedicate production efforts to entertaining those who spend their own money to support the functioning of thousands of movie theaters in countries where Spanish is spoken and understood?

The principal defect of Cinema made in Hollywood for the Hispanic market—with notable exceptions—is the choice of subject matter, that palpable desire to invade intellectual territory. As a result, these productions have an undefined quality, so that they remain far below the interest of the upper class and far above the comprehension of the lower class. It's up in the air, we might say. Some are theatrical works with a markedly European flavor, those that are transplanted to "sets" in order to take advantage of the talents of a Catalina Bárcena, for example; others, whose events apparently unfold in a fable, take place in lands very distant from our own with the corresponding displacement of customs, situations, and overall atmosphere. We believe that in one instance after another, producers have thrown handfuls of money out the window. Given that our public has narrow cultural horizons, what do they care about a script that takes place in Russia, the Balkans, the Costa Azul of the Mediterranean, or the faltering courts of Europe? Forgetting all of this is probably why producers of this or that film are astonished when production costs aren't covered, attributing their failure to the most fantastic speculations.

On the other hand, the audience for cinema goes to the movie theater for excitement, with the desire to laugh, cry, or simply have fun but never to wrap their heads around the complicated social problems of the upper class. In a democratic atmosphere, dukes, marquises, counts, and princes make them yawn once a minute. Long and flowery literary discourses, which have a decisively surprising effect in the theater, lose their force in Cinema, an art that demands actions over words. As characters on the screen are as close to the spectator as they would be in real life, a gesture, a facial expression, or a meaningful look is worth more than a declaration of love that is full of verbal gymnastics that are both empty and bland. It is curious how these things can produce a gratifying sensation when read; but when spoken on the screen they seem stilted, tacky, and worthy of ridicule. The explanation could be that literature has a deliciously subjective quality, while cinematic action can only be part of an objective art that borders on the edge of reality.

The public, in other words, demands Cinema open to rapid comprehension. The visual impression plays a primary role in this modern entertainment, and the spoken word is only complementary; the tradition of Cinema, with its origins in pantomime, requires us to give secondary importance to the word. If you add to a visual impression the progression of an intensely interesting story that reflects our very lives, our own struggles, our own problems—provided they are not too complicated—this film would make money at the box office and earn 65 percent of its production budget in its "first run."

For Hispano Cinema to take off as popular entertainment, it's indispensable for it to be a productive business. This can only happen if it is taken to the very heart of the people, the great force that sustains this industry in countries where other languages are spoken. It's not enough for the dialogue to be in a more or less "authentic" Spanish; the very atmosphere, the spirit of the work, and the situations that emerge from the subject matter must be truly Hispano. Our public, whether in terms of film, theater, or literature, merely tolerates works translated into their language, applauding masterpieces only on occasion. Between a common, mediocre script executed in Spanish with limitations imposed on it by gentlemen who know little to nothing about our culture, and one originally conceived by a Hispanic mind, there is no doubt which would be favored by our public's taste, although the latter may be as mediocre as the former. This is what Hollywood producers have not understood or even shown signs of understanding. This blindness accounts for the constant failure of films coming out of the California studios. They are impeccable in mechanical execution, blessed with magnificent photographic and sound technology, and beautifully presented like the fruits produced by that state's soil. But just like these fruits, they lack a certain something that is truly ours, something that can't be substituted by chemical extracts and is impossible to replace with any kind of ostentatious "presentation."

Hollywood producers should be grateful that our Cinema is still in inexperienced hands. Because the moment that a company in Mexico, Spain, or Argentina makes use of directors and technicians as capable as those in Hollywood, there will be the sound of "Miserere" for the production it calls Hispanic based on language alone.[306] On the other hand, once these same producers awaken to the reality of the situation and manage to stamp their productions with a truly Hispanic seal, the entire market will be theirs. Hispano Americans are eager to see Cinema; with theater in decline, the multitudes have taken refuge in projection halls, dedicating their time to rest and recreation. But they want Cinema that touches their souls, Cinema that interests them, that entertains them, that reflects their own lives, and that serves as spiritual nourishment for their own sensibility that is fertilized, we might say, with their own ideology.

Cinema that is Hispanic in its form and foundation; Cinema in which words are only a complement to the action; Cinema for the people who buy the tickets: this is what more than a hundred million potential Spanish-speaking spectators in América and Spain have been waiting for in vain for the past six years. The producer who breaks with all the pernicious influences of ignorant consultants, dispensing with the belief that he is infallible, leaving aside the stubborn presumption of knowing everything—even that which is racially foreign to him—could finally offer this Cinema to the Spanish-speaking world, in addition to doing priceless good for our Latin sensibility; he will have found the legendary Philosopher's Stone.

Hollywood's New Failure

Why the Production of Films in Spanish Has Turned Out to Be Counterproductive at the California Studios; A Yankee Dressed Up as a Charro; The Largest Production Companies Are Shutting the Doors of Their Spanish Departments

"Un nuevo fracaso de Hollywood," published
in *La Opinión,* July 2, 1935, section II, page 6

Just a few days ago, in a publication dedicated entirely to matters of Cinema, we read certain declarations from an official at Fox Studios, which until recently had a department dedicated to the production of films in our language. The spirit of these declarations was more or less as follows:

"To tell the truth, we do not understand the tastes of the Hispano American public when it comes to cinematic entertainment. We have struggled for several years to bring them films in their own language and the results have been frankly negative. Now, the competition initiated by centers of production in Mexico, Spain, and other countries has compelled us to cease production. Unless something unforeseen happens, we will not release another film with a story and dialogue in the Spanish language . . ."

Of course we are reciting this from memory. The words, originally dictated in English, may or may not be the same, but the essence of these statements remains untouched, in all of their lamentable childishness. Fox Studios has been releasing dull films for some time now, films that are technically polished but hollow in terms of their Latin sensibility. If "nothing unforeseen happens"—something so common in Hollywood, the land of surprises—they will not resume production activities in November as they said they would. The closure is now definitive, irrevocable. The failure of this venture has left them disillusioned. Competition from our productions is apparently affecting the studio directly. On the doors of what was once Fox's Spanish Department—unless that aforementioned unforeseen something happens—they could write "The End," just as it is written on the last foot of their films.

THE PARADOX OF COMPETITION

Let's take this in parts. The author of these declarations talks about the fierce competition from Hispano American producers that have studios in our countries, compelling us to analyze the product released on the market by Fox and those produced by our incipient, homegrown enterprises. We will try to establish an approximate parallel so that we may then reason logically about the facts.

In terms of its polish, a Fox film in Spanish is almost as perfect as the English-language films produced by the same studio. The photography is admirable, the sound is perfect considering what one would expect from advances in the science of reproduction, and the direction leaves little to be desired in terms of correctness. The scripts, cinematically speaking, are prepared using the same formulas as American films, which have been so widely accepted in the nations of our continent. The direction is acceptable and at times even entrusted to an expert in this area. There is little that deserves criticism in terms of what we would call the editing of the film. And finally, the publicity for exhibition is of a quality only possible with the enormous resources of the North American studios. The distribution channels available to the companies are the best in the world, and hundreds of theaters are controlled by the New York office. Accordingly, it's not difficult to find a place for their product once it is released on the Spanish-speaking market.

Let us now analyze Mexican production, which differs only slightly from that of other countries of Spanish descent. The technical quality of our films is highly defective. The cameras used are antiquated, many of them discarded by Hollywood; sound-recording equipment is made clandestinely, or at least far from the great Western Electric laboratories because our producers can't pay the exorbitant sums required to rent that company's product. Properly speaking, we don't have directors worthy of the name. The majority of our screenwriters have learned through experience, relying more on intuition than on academic training. And then the editing of our films is painfully mediocre, revealing a lack of resources and the ignorance of those tasked with preparing films for exhibition. Furthermore, our publicity is deplorably mediocre, done by unskilled individuals who believe they are highly effective. And to top it all off, Hispano Americans lack channels of distribution, finding themselves forced to do it on a small scale, relegated to filling out the programs rented by exhibitors from large firms in Hollywood and New York.

WHERE THE MAIN DIFFERENCE LIES

After comparing the American product with those of our national companies on these terms, we can now ask: Why do the latter represent such strong competition for those who by all appearances have superior technical polish and execution? How could it be that a technically inferior product compels Hollywood companies to cease their efforts after years of struggle and failure?

The answer, in all of its harsh sincerity and potentially detrimental to our own interests, is that the blame for this defeat resides with the very production companies in California. Our people are victorious in this struggle despite their own mediocrity and their ignorance of the technical aspects of production, while the former fail despite their brilliant personnel, their enormous budgets, and their formidable publicity machine. Hollywood knows how to make movies in English, but they don't know how to make them in Spanish. That is, they are clueless about a host of details because they can't be bothered to learn about them, blinded as they are by the exaggerated perception of their own superiority. Ingenuity itself and the crude quality of our films place them above those released by Hollywood in Hispano markets.

The secret lies not in the production per se, but in what we might call the flavor of the film. We possess this secret naturally, without even having to seek it out. They could also possess it, but only if they pursued it with determination and care. In the final analysis, the difference resides in the sincerity of our modest productions, compared with the insincerity of those that come out of Hollywood.

LIKE A YANKEE DRESSED AS A CHARRO . . .

To put the issue "in a nutshell," as they say, North Americans apply their own spirit to movies filmed in a language completely unknown to them. That is, they make Hispano cinema with a Saxon perspective. The result might be compared to a Connecticut Yankee who shows up to one of our parties dressed as a Mexican charro and shouting "Viva México" in a markedly foreign accent: movingly absurd, ridiculous in a ridiculously pitiful way, a grotesque attempt at sincerity, and more worthy of shame than reproach. The naive Yankee tried to show his love for our culture, trading his urban apparel for the costume of national character types, but he has only attended to the exterior. He is missing the most important thing: the spirit. While he remains silent, his appearance doesn't draw attention; but when he opens his mouth the deception is apparent, the desire to please without knowing how, the involuntary nonsense that is his Saxon soul in a Latin package.

That is exactly why, if an elegant charro appeared at this same imaginary party—shouting with an accent, irreproachably dressed in a leather jacket, sporting a hat with braided trim, and wearing an authentic Saltillo blanket over his shoulder—none of that lavishness would prevent any upstanding charro wearing a guayabera and straw hat from defeating him in a competition for the applause of those gathered. The former has blue eyes and blond hair, while the latter has dark eyes and a head of jet-black hair; the former speaks with a Saxon accent while the latter speaks with the authentic inflections of our common lexicon.

THE CORRUPTION OF ACTORS

The same thing happens with Hispano films edited in Hollywood. Producers have preoccupied themselves too much with external aspects and completely neglected internal sentiment. Guided by this inexorable perspective, their actors and actresses feel obligated to emote in English; confronted with the haughty stubbornness of someone who knows they are rich and powerful, actors who earn their keep by working for this person end up shrugging their shoulders and doing what he orders them to do. And this attitude is so common that it ends up coming naturally to actors who then adopt an American perspective, forgetting that south of the border, in the places where these films will be exhibited, the Latin sensibility has remained intact.

And then, when our public prefers their own products—not necessarily for being good, but through the inalienable circumstance of being theirs—producers declare that they "do not understand the taste of the Hispano American audience" and marvel at the fact that something they consider inferior is creating such merciless competition for what they release on the market. If these millionaire producers had muted the voice of their own pride to hear what has been proposed by those living the same lives as the audiences that will come and judge their films, the studios would probably be booming, even partially taking control of the American market south of the Rio Grande.

It Is Not Enough to Understand Spanish

Taken as a lesson, what has just occurred can be advantageous. If producers decide to reconsider their agreement to once again attempt the production of films in a language foreign to them, designed for an ideology that likewise has nothing in common with their own, they should put themselves completely in the hands of someone who can produce film in accordance with our particular way of feeling. But even then, those individuals should nonetheless be scrutinized carefully instead of giving them a production only because "they have been" to Spain—probably just to visit—and they butcher the language of Latin America. It is not enough to speak Spanish: it is also necessary to think and feel in Spanish. We would like to know what the American public would say about a film made by Mexicans visiting the United States if that film had a Saxon story, was spoken in English, and was destined for distribution in New York, Chicago, Detroit, or Los Angeles . . . ! It would surely be a blunder the size of a cathedral, and we would be the first to recognize that in advance.

On the other hand, if the American studios completely cease production in other languages, they will have won on two counts. For themselves, they will have saved plenty of money that they can then risk elsewhere; for us, it will truly leave the field open for genuine Hispano cinema, which although technically inferior has the merit of being undeniably sincere, wholly reflecting the lives of the people who will go to those movies to have fun, to enjoy themselves, or to be moved.

We have written tirelessly about this subject in the past. They have never taken the opinion of the Mexican press seriously, and probably won't do so in the future. Producers are too busy riding on their high horses to descend for even a moment. But after all, as they themselves say, "It's their own funeral . . ."

LET'S BRING DIGNITY TO MEXICAN CINEMA

MEXICAN CINEMA IS CRYING OUT FOR BETTER SCRIPTS, AN EDUCATIONAL AND MORAL TENDENCY IN ITS FILMS, AND ABOVE ALL, THE ABOLITION OF "CHARRO" FILMS; HOPEFULLY IT HAPPENS SOON

"Dignifiquemos al cinema mexicano," published in
La Opinión, June 26, 1936, section II, page 6

Now that the public has developed a solid and definitive fondness for Hispano Cinema, we believe it must begin to fulfill the role that this Industry should play in contemporary social life as it aspires to become Art. Films should always be the bearers of an uplifting message for our multitudes. They should be a source of education, not the dry or annoying sort of education designed for superficial spirits, but rather an education that delights as it instructs. In order to achieve this, those that make Cinema need to understand their responsibility toward today's generation.

To begin with, the careful selection of cinephonic stories is imperative. In the case of our Cinema in particular, this matter is more important than the question of actors. Since we don't have stars, properly speaking—fascinating personalities who draw multitudes with their name alone—we need to center interest on the subject matter: topical subjects with a wholesome approach; subjects that uplift instead of depress; subjects with a strong moral foundation—not the vulgar morality of insincere preachers, but a constructive morality that inspires the desire for improvement, for progress, for culture. This can be done so easily that it's amazing that filmmakers have only occasionally attempted it and probably without even meaning to.

Our opinion is that the tendency to cater to the multitudes, corrupting their artistic tastes in the process, should end once and for all. Until now, and with few exceptions, films have been subordinated to the rhythm of a more or less insipid melody, taking advantage of a song's popularity to draw the audience to the box office. When we do manage to find educational value in a scene, it is presented in a glaringly tacky way that provokes laughter in people of average intelligence. Films alternate between turn-of-the-century melodrama and vacuous comedy without dwelling on the space between them. One would think that the intellect of Cinema writers is hopelessly corrupted; that they don't know how to make anything aside from horrifying tragedies or insubstantial "jokes." You can count on one hand the photodramas that make you both think and feel. Films are dedicated either to making cooks burst into tears or to provoking the laughter of idiots. The foundations of a film are often subordinated to form. And this form is so cheap that at times it inspires hopelessness in those of us who have dreamed of a Cinema that is tendentious, uplifting, and about ideas and emotions at the same time. One has to remember that in Cinema, as in all artistic endeavors—and Cinema aspires to be an art form—truth and beauty should go hand in hand. The same holds true in the theater, which is a schoolhouse of customs and a vehicle of culture.

Until now the majority of our films have been merely "charrerías" that are exhausting the attention of spectators. Of every three films they send us from Mexico, two come wrapped in a Saltillo blanket and wearing a big sombrero. In these films a guitar is as inevitable as street slang. One would imagine that in Mexico there are only men riding horses and women wrapped in shawls; that every individual is a vernacular songbook and every woman a soldadera. The plague of these films has reached such an extreme that it seems as if we're watching the same movie as last week, but with a different title. This should not be the case. Mexico has incomparable beauty in its countryside and its haciendas; the charro is one of the most virile types to be found on this continent; the guitar is the national instrument and song is a beautiful means of expression for the popular classes. But everything has its limits. Abusing these beautiful things is the same as feeding a man sopes, tamales, and enchiladas every day; as delicious as they may be, the moment arrives when he is eager to have a cup of hot chocolate or a grilled steak, if only for the sake of variety.

It's necessary to get out in front of this situation, before the public itself repudiates our vernacular films. Producers should take into account that there is a moment when a change of direction becomes necessary so that they are not carelessly risking the money required to produce sound films. From our perspective, the moment has arrived. And if not, it's almost here.

Courage is necessary to remake our Cinema. From our point of view, we believe that it is the duty of those releasing films to the market to elevate the public toward the screen instead of lowering films to the level of the masses. It's not that every comedy or drama film should be an irritating sermon, but they should all carry an uplifting message and an educational purpose. Dignity must be brought to our Cinema. It has barely entered its youth in our countries but has already followed the path of least resistance, with a focus on catering to questionable tastes. If it aspires to be Art, it has to be noble and set its sights on an unwavering course of action. At least this is our sincere opinion.

MAKE YOUR OWN MOVIE (PART I)

HOW A GROUP OF YOUNG ENTHUSIASTS—OR ANY ENTHUSIASTS—CAN START A CAREER IN CINEMA, WHILE PROVIDING SOCIETY WITH HEALTHY ENTERTAINMENT

"Haga usted una película," published in *La Opinión*, July 10, 1938, section II, page 6

Cinema is currently the most popular entertainment in the entire world. Former vehicles of expression like books and theater have in many cases been replaced by films, which are simultaneously an objective education and a source of recreation. You, our reader, who marvels before the cinematic performances on screen, have stopped attending theater that is merely scenic in nature. And we would bet that you read fewer books since your love of Cinema has been ignited. Now you like to watch movies. The next step is to make them yourself.

This undertaking, which may at first seem like a fantasy, is relatively easy if you have resolute willpower and a bit of artistic preparation. The cost of a cinematic work is not too high—we're naturally referring to amateur films that are silent and intended to be screened among family, in a manner of speaking. A half hour of entertainment would not cost you more than twenty-five dollars, as incredible as it may sound. And along the way you can get started in a career that might translate into a brilliant future down the road. Who knows? The majority of film actors and directors began as mere amateurs . . .

WHAT YOU NEED TO MAKE A MOVIE

Obtaining an eight millimeter film camera, a projector of the same gauge, and the film stock for 400 feet of entertainment—including developing and printing the film—requires a total cost of twenty dollars. You can expect to spend an additional five dollars on titles. There you have the fixed amount we mentioned in the previous paragraph. The equipment to make titles is also not expensive. Together with the cost of acquiring a camera and projector, the expenses can be handled by forming Cinema clubs whose members each contribute a nominal amount for membership dues.

The easiest process for amateurs could be the following:

Organize a "Cinema Club" among a group of enthusiast friends with dues, for example, of a dollar a month. Supposing that you can gather forty members, you will then have the necessary amount available for an initial down payment on the camera, the projector, and the equipment for titles. The monthly payments, which are usually moderate in these cases, will come from the same dues. By the second month of the club's existence, you will have the funds necessary to buy the film and your cinematic production can get underway.

How much does the production equipment cost? Thinking modestly, the total amount comprises the following costs:

A good eight millimeter camera $30.00

A good eight millimeter projector . . . $36.00

Equipment to make titles $15.00

A screen for exhibition (of better quality) . . . $10.00

Total . . . $91.00

Your "entrée" would not be more than twenty dollars and the monthly payments would not be higher than eight dollars. As you can see, the budget is more economical than those unfamiliar with the "ins and outs" of amateur Film might suppose. The films that result from this activity will be clearly photographed and can be projected on a screen of reasonable size in a room that holds more than fifty people.

THE FORMATION OF AN ARTISTIC "COMPANY"

We now have the necessary information about the purchase of equipment and film material. Next we need to form the company that will act in front of the camera, whether in a comedy or drama. There are plenty of amateurs around to do this. There are young men with a strong presence and cinematic ambitions and young, photogenic women with acting talent. In silent Cinema, anyone can be an actor because the character type is of the utmost importance. The director, in charge of the film's action, is an individual whose essential qualities should include a certain artistic sensibility, a little creative talent, and a good amount of common sense. Nothing more is required to make an amateur film.

In our next article, we will try to give some advice for those aspiring to direct films at this level. If you, our reader, are truly interested in this career, you will surely understand these suggestions, which we will try to publish in very simple language. In this same article, we will also try to put forth other suggestions that will undoubtedly prove useful, including what you, the amateur producer, will need to bring any story to the screen.

Meanwhile, it seems appropriate to insist on the recreational and social value of "Little Cinema," which we will call this activity that has yet to be fully exploited by the Spanish-speaking population. Narrative films—whether comedies or dramas—or simply informative ones that serve as a vehicle of education hold a delightful treasure for young and old alike. And their "shooting" will in the process serve to create healthy social bonds among our young Cinema enthusiasts.

MAKE YOUR OWN MOVIE (PART 2)

THE "RHYTHM" OF SILENT FILMS; YOU
SHOULD LIVE IN FRONT OF THE CAMERA, NOT
ACT; EDITING AND PRODUCTION TITLES

"Haga usted una película," published in *La Opinión*, July 31, 1938, section II, page 6

In this, the last article in our recent series on amateur Film, we refer briefly to the progression of production, incidents that could happen during the process, and finishing the film. The director should always be mindful that Cinema is a matter of character types, not actors. When a person with good judgment and directorial talent turns a script into a film, it is sufficient to find individuals who look like the characters he has imagined so that he can make the most of them. And in Cinema you don't act; you live. It is not like theater, where exaggerated gestures and movements are necessary for the audience to understand the situations presented. On screen a facial expression is enough to reveal a mood; movements have to be slower and more measured, because the camera is more precise than the human eye. One should avoid too much gesticulation, otherwise the result will seem extremely ridiculous. Naturalness, naturalness, and more naturalness are the key ingredients for achieving a good production.

As you continue shooting scenes for the film, it's necessary to mark them properly. This is done by placing a chalkboard with the corresponding number from the script in front of the camera before the scene begins, so that you don't end up with a mess on your hands. If you do this carefully, it should be sufficient for perfect "continuity" in the film you are making.

Developing the film is something always done by the company that sells the raw film stock. Then you take a look at it to determine what should go where and proceed with the editing and assembly, which are the most delicate parts of cinematic production. There are few people qualified to edit when it comes to professional films. In the case of amateur films that don't pretend to be major productions, the director can do this work by using equipment made for this purpose, which is sold in stores that deal in cameras, lenses, and film accessories. It is advisable to consult with such businesses.

In cinematic jargon, "rhythm" is what they call the equilibrium of the action. Scenes should not be too long nor all filmed from the same angle. To give a scene life, it is necessary to take some "Close ups" while shooting, which can be opportunely inserted to provide emphasis to any expression. We won't talk here about the "Fade in" or "Fade out," because their execution requires professional skill. You have to remember that we're talking about amateur films, which are made as a pastime and to entertain spectators, the majority of whom will be the actors themselves.

With the film edited and assembled, all that's left are the titles. These should be minimal, reducing action to simple pantomime to the extent possible. There is also equipment to photograph these titles; the film with titles included is printed and developed by the businesses we previously mentioned. You must be careful to make the titles short. An intelligently written sentence is enough to explain a scene's action. You should use them for dialogue only when it comes to something important, making sure that the words are inventive: they should make the audience either laugh or think. That would be sufficient.

The author of this column is always available for consultation or to offer suggestions to the producer during difficult moments. If you are making an amateur film and have been following these articles, don't hesitate to ask for suggestions by writing to us at this newspaper's address. We are in the best position to help you through these difficult steps.

The formation of Cinema clubs would be beneficial for several reasons. First, because it facilitates the economic dimension of cinema and the selection of a crew. And then because the existing relationships between those involved will become stronger, creating healthy friendships and keeping young people away from more dangerous forms of entertainment. But this is just a suggestion, and we will do everything in our power to support you within the modest means available to us.

TIJUANA, PRODUCTION CENTER FOR SOUND CINEMA

THE CITY BRINGS TOGETHER THE CONDITIONS NECESSARY TO ESTABLISH AN EMPORIUM OF CINEPHONIC ACTIVITY; THE FIRST FILMS

"Tijuana, centro productor de cine hablado," published in
La Opinión, March 5, 1939, section II, page 6

Almost without fanfare, as if someone wants to hide something instead of publicizing it, two Spanish-language films have recently been produced in the northern territory of Baja California. The first of them has a military theme, the other a more sentimental one. The actors in both are almost exclusively Mexicans. Louis Gasnier, the veteran French director, handled the megaphone for one of them; on the other, Carlos Gómez Fournier, known better to the public as "Don Chema," took his first shot at directing. The titles chosen were *Juan Soldado* and *Perdón, madre*.[307] The financing was entirely Mexican.

We won't be talking about the films themselves in this column but instead about the limitless possibilities of Tijuana as a production center for Cinema, something that visionaries of the past have noted without ever seeing their dreams realized. Tijuana has more of the necessary conditions than Mexico City and, believe it or not, more than Hollywood. We're going to try to explain why in some of the following paragraphs.

FILM "PIONEERS" IN ZARAGOZA

Some years ago a group of Film enthusiasts, overcoming great difficulties, produced a Spanish-language film with negative results in Zaragoza, a town that everyone insists on calling Tijuana. The work was called *Contrabando*, and it featured Ramón Pereda, Don Alvarado, Virginia Ruiz, and some amateur talent.[308] The production company, which included people with great aspirations but who knew almost nothing about Cinema, could not make the situation work to their advantage. Its members were Alberto Méndez Bernal, Fernando Méndez, and Enrique Martínez, the last of whom was also a theatrical impresario in the region. As one would expect, the venture was a complete failure and none of the founders ever thought about cinema again. The film turned out to be poorly made for a number of reasons, the first being the producers' unfortunate ignorance of the film industry.

Then came Roberto Farfán, another dreamer and visionary, with a fantastic project to establish Imperio Azteca Studios in the same sinful border city. This time it was a more serious effort. An engineer drew up plans for the construction of stages; Farfán opened an office in Hollywood, established connections with some actors and aspiring talent, and, as in all other such cases, solicited help from the Mexican government. Having obtained magnificent promises from them, he put his plans in a tin tube, had stock certificates printed, and headed to the capital. But he didn't have any luck. While en route, he heard the shocking news that the Calles administration had fallen, and all his dreams along with it. He returned to Hollywood disheartened but still fighting, waiting for a better opportunity that never arrived.

A Long Period of Inactivity

An unfortunate period of inactivity followed. The proximity of Hollywood seemed dangerous to businessmen, who didn't dare invest money in building studios. Farfán kept struggling for some time and then opted to abandon his projects, taking refuge in the management of a Mexican theater in San Diego. Meanwhile, film production in the capital of the republic was undergoing enviable growth. After the *Santa* venture came *Aguilas frente al sol* and *La llorona*, among others, each one more successful than the last. Cinephonic talent began to emerge in Mexico, directors began to gather, and the country's capitalists began to show interest. Tijuana remained unaffected. In cantinas, among the ranks of the unemployed, there was still talk about vague possibilities, but no one took the matter of Cinema seriously. With things in this state, a theatrical variety company headed by "Don Chema" came to Los Angeles. The company met its demise in California and its director had to take refuge in Tijuana, still not knowing what he would do for the winter. That's when the old enthusiasm was reborn and some theatrical impresarios partnered with the actor for the production of *Juan Soldado*. From Mexico they hired María Luisa Zea and Emilio Tuero, and they obtained the cooperation of the district governor. The results remain unknown to the world. We know they made a movie, but no one has spoken of it since . . .

THE NATIONAL LOTTERY GRAND PRIZE

At the end of last year the National Lottery grand prize was won in Tijuana, showering riches upon some families, including that of Silverio Romero. "Don Chema" took advantage of this opportunity and managed to get Romero and the Ibarra brothers, who own a garage, interested in resuscitating sound cinema. With great difficulty they organized the production of the second film, *Perdón, madre*, a popular melodrama that gave Estelita Zarco the opportunity to act in the leading role of the young woman and that relies on Barry Norton as a box office attraction. The film is now in the process of being cut and edited without us knowing the artistic results. It may be that the film is good; or maybe not. But with this third venture it has been proven that movies can be made cheaply in Tijuana. A cinephonic work can't be made in Hollywood for under forty thousand dollars; in Tijuana they have shown that you can make one for a third of that amount.

ORGANIZED EFFORT IS LACKING

But the efforts made to support cinema in the northern territory of Baja California have been only temporary ventures lacking in solid organization and undertaken almost as a hobby, as if they weren't giving the matter the gravity it deserves. And I honestly know that the region offers a veritable gold mine for those brave enough to exploit it with serious investments. To begin with, the proximity of Hollywood, far from being an obstacle, is an enormous advantage. In a matter of a few hours one could transport from here a technical crew, recording equipment, cameras, and even actors. On the other hand, the distance from Mexico City means that union associations in the capital don't intervene as they do in the Federal District, causing enormous and certain harm. All that remains is to ensure that these are serious efforts rather than passing ventures: that a first-class technical crew is hired, which can be contracted at a modest cost from California; that the matter is put in expert hands; and that care is taken with the production so that the hen laying golden eggs is not killed with a single blow.

Without claiming to be prophets, we can say that Tijuana has a brilliant future ahead of it as a center of filmmaking in Spanish. A little bit of vision, formal organization, and a desire to do things as God commands is all that's needed. As time goes on, with the construction of a modest "studio" and taking advantage of government facilities, films can be produced in the northern territory of Baja California at low cost and under generally favorable conditions—not only Mexican films but also movies in English that they call "quickies." When they are needed, laboratories are here, just four hours away. Hiring extras is not a problem. In expert hands, a production can be completed in ten days. What are businessmen waiting for? You have to remember that opportunity only knocks once upon our door, and if you don't eventually answer, it will never return . . .

NOTES

1.   Classic accounts of the formation of Mexican immigrant enclaves, or barrios, include Ricardo Romo, *East Los Angeles: History of a Barrio* (Austin: University of Texas Press, 1983); George J. Sánchez, *Becoming Mexican American: Ethnicity, Culture, and Identity in Chicano Los Angeles, 1900–1945* (New York: Oxford University Press, 1993); and Douglas Monroy, *Rebirth: Mexican Los Angeles from the Great Migration to the Great Depression* (Berkeley: University of California Press, 1999).

2.   See, for instance, Francisco E. Balderrama, *In Defense of La Raza: The Los Angeles Mexican Consulate and the Mexican Community, 1929 to 1936* (Tucson: University of Arizona Press, 1982).

3.   In early accounts of Mexican migration to the United States, as George Sánchez has pointed out, both countries were framed as possessing distinct, even static, cultures, with people's adherence to one or the other often dependent on generation or gender. Sánchez himself offered a more nuanced account of how "a collective identity . . . emerged from daily experience in the United States." George Sánchez, *Becoming Mexican American*, 6, 11.

4.   See, for example, Monroy, *Rebirth*, 168–81; Mario T. García, *Desert Immigrants: The Mexicans of El Paso, 1880–1920* (New Haven, CT: Yale University Press, 1981), 197–232; Vicki Ruiz, *From Out of the Shadows: Mexican Women in Twentieth-Century America* (New York: Oxford University Press, 1998), 51–70; and Sánchez, *Becoming Mexican American*, 171–87. On audience agency, see José Limon, "Stereotyping and Chicano Resistance," in *Chicanos and Film: Representation and Resistance*, ed. Chon A. Noriega (Minneapolis: University of Minnesota Press, 1992), 3–17; Rosa Linda Fregoso, *MeXicana Encounters: The Making of Social Identities on the Borderlands* (Berkeley: University of California Press, 2003), 148–68; and Curtis Marez, "Subaltern Soundtracks: Mexican Immigrants and the Making of Hollywood Cinema," *Aztlán: A Journal of Chicano Studies* 29, no. 1 (2004): 57–82.

5.   Colin Gunckel, *Mexico on Main Street: Transnational Film Culture in Los Angeles before World War II* (New Brunswick, NJ: Rutgers University Press, 2015); and Laura Isabel Serna, *Making Cinelandia: American Films and Mexican Film Culture before the Golden Age* (Durham, NC: Duke University Press, 2014).

6.   On the term "ethnic Mexican" and its use, see David G. Gutiérrez, *Walls and Mirrors: Mexican Americans, Mexican Immigrants, and the Politics of Ethnicity* (Berkeley: University of California Press, 1995), 218n3.

7.   See Serna, *Making Cinelandia*, 180–214; and Colin Gunckel, Jan-Christopher Horak, and Lisa Jarvinen, introduction to *Cinema between Latin*

America and Los Angeles: Origins to 1960, ed. Colin Gunckel, Jan-Christopher Horak, and Lisa Jarvinen (New Brunswick, NJ: Rutgers University Press, 2019), 1–30.

8. Jan-Christopher Horak, "Cantabria Films and the L.A. Film Market, 1938–1940," in Gunckel, Horak, and Jarvinen, *Cinema between Latin America and Los Angeles*, 108–14.

9. For more on the history of these movie theaters, see Rogelio Agrasánchez Jr., *Mexican Movies in the United States: A History of the Films, Theaters, and Audiences, 1920–1960* (Jefferson, NC: McFarland, 2006).

10. Foundational work in this area includes two anthologies edited by Daniel Bernardi: *The Birth of Whiteness: Race and the Emergence of U.S. Cinema* (New Brunswick, NJ: Rutgers University Press, 1996) and *Classic Hollywood, Classic Whiteness* (Minneapolis: University of Minnesota Press, 2001).

11. The ambitious and influential volume *Global Hollywood* introduced readers to the complex landscape in which contemporary Hollywood extended its reach via practices of coproduction, shifting intellectual and copyright regimes, new distribution and marketing strategies, and the cultivation of global audiences. Toby Miller, Nitin Govil, John McMurria, and Richard Maxwell, *Global Hollywood* (Berkeley: University of California Press, 2002). Today the number of film studies books with "transnational" in the title is astounding. Useful starting points for understanding the term's application to contemporary cinema include Steven Rawle, *Transnational Cinema: An Introduction* (London: Palgrave, 2018); Elizabeth Ezra and Terry Rowden, eds., *Transnational Cinema: The Film Reader* (New York: Routledge, 2006); and the offerings of the journal *Transnational Screens* (previously *Transnational Cinemas*), founded in 2009.

12. Jasmine Nadua Trice's work on cinema in the Philippines complicates the national by studying various sectors' claims on film culture. See Jasmine Nadua Trice, *City of Screens: Imagining Audiences in Manila's Alternative Film Culture* (Durham, NC: Duke University Press, 2021).

13. Key works on so-called race film include Pearl Bowser and Louise Spence, *Writing Himself into History: Oscar Micheaux, His Silent Films, and His Audiences* (New Brunswick, NJ: Rutgers University Press, 2000); Cara Caddoo, *Envisioning Freedom: Cinema and the Building of Modern Black Life* (Cambridge, MA: Harvard University Press, 2014); Allyson Nadia Field, *Uplift Cinema: The Emergence of African American Film and the Possibility of Black Modernity* (Durham, NC: Duke University Press, 2015); Jane M. Gaines, *Fire and Desire: Mixed-Race Movies in the Silent Era* (Chicago: University of Chicago Press, 2001); and Miriam J. Petty, *Stealing the Show: African American Performers and Audiences in 1930s Hollywood* (Berkeley: University of California Press, 2016). Key works on ethnic film cultures include Denise Khor, *Transpacific Convergences: Race, Migration, and Japanese American Film Culture before World War II* (Chapel Hill: University of North Carolina Press, 2022), as well as a number of essays in Melvyn Stokes and Richard Maltby, eds., *American Movie Audiences: From the Turn of the Century to the Early Sound Era* (London: BFI, 1999).

14. We borrow the quoted phrase from Jon Lewis and Eric Smoodin, eds., *Looking Past the Screen: Case Studies in American Film History and Method* (Durham, NC: Duke University Press, 2007).

15. Deborah Cohen and Maura O'Connor, "Comparative History, Cross-National History, Transnational History—Definitions," in *Comparison and History: Europe in Cross-National Perspective*, ed. Deborah Cohen and Maura O'Connor (Abingdon, Oxon, UK: Routledge, 2004), xiii. On the distinction between transnational and international, see Seth Fein, "Culture across Borders in the Americas," *History Compass* 1, no. 1 (2003): 1–6.

16. *Histoire croisée* has been most fully developed as a methodological approach by European historians. See Michael Werner and Bénédicte Zimmermann, "Beyond Comparison: *Histoire Croisée* and the Challenge of Reflexivity," *History and Theory* 45, no. 1 (2006): 30–50.

17. See the forum "Entangled Empires in the Atlantic World," *American Historical Review* 112, no. 3 (2007): 710–99. It presents three essays that use this framework and a response that questions the distinction between entangled histories and borderlands histories.

18. Examples of this scholarship include explorations of Jewish communities in medieval Europe, postcolonial approaches toward early modern Eurasian history, and the history of science in the Southern Cone. See, for example, Elisheva Baumgarten, Ruth Mazo Karras, and Katelyn Mesler, eds., *Entangled Histories: Knowledge, Authority, and Jewish Culture in the Thirteenth Century* (Philadelphia: University of Pennsylvania Press, 2017); Sanjay Subrahmanyam, "Connected Histories: Notes towards a Reconfiguration of Early Modern Eurasia," *Modern Asian Studies* 31, no. 3 (1997): 735–62; and Julia Rodriguez, "South Atlantic Crossings: Fingerprints, Science, and the State in Turn-of-the-Century Argentina," *American Historical Review* 109, no. 2 (2004): 387–416.

19. Marie Cronqvist and Christoph Hilgert, "Entangled Media Histories: The Value of Transnational and Transmedial Approaches in Media Historiography," *Media History* 23, no. 1 (2017): 130–41.

20. See Michele Hilmes, "Entangled Media Histories: A Response," *Media History* 23, no. 1 (2017): 142.

21. G. Cristina Mora, *Making Hispanics: How Activists, Bureaucrats, and Media Constructed a New American* (Chicago: University of Chicago Press, 2014).

22. A notable exception to these trends was the way that Douglas Monroy situated film culture alongside other elements of mass culture such as fashion, and cultural institutions such as public schools, as a point of tension for the American-born or -raised children of Mexican immigrants. It's notable that sociological studies form his base of primary sources, giving him insight into how cinemagoing and film culture fit into the lives of Mexican youth in early twentieth-century Los Angeles. See chapter 4 of Monroy's *Rebirth*.

23. For more about these filmmakers, see Rogelio Agrasánchez Jr., *Guillermo Calles: A Biography of the Actor and Mexican Cinema Pioneer* (Jefferson, NC: McFarland, 2010); Alejandra Espasande Bouza, "Romualdo Tirado and the Pioneers of Spanish-Language Cinema in Los Angeles," in *Hollywood Goes Latin: Spanish-Language Cinema in Los Angeles*, ed. María Elena de las Carreras and

Jan-Christopher Horak (Brussels: Fédération Internationale des Archives du Film, 2019), 113–25; and Horak, "Cantabria Films and the L.A. Film Market," 97–118.

24. See Gunckel, *Mexico on Main Street*, 55.

25. On film magazines as "intermedial" points of contact, see Daniel Biltereyst and Lies Van de Vijver, "Introduction: Movie Magazines, Digitization and New Cinema History," in *Mapping Movie Magazines: Digitization, Periodicals and Cinema History*, ed. Daniel Biltereyst and Lies Van de Vijver (Cham, Switzerland: Palgrave Macmillan, 2020), 2.

26. This reimagining of what we mean when we talk about cinema began in the 1990s when scholars began to examine the place of historical rather than theoretical spectators and the social and cultural formations that emerged around and with film. Eric Smoodin advocated this type of broad historical inquiry as a way of reframing the history of cinema as a history not only of film texts but also of the social and cultural space of cinema "beyond the screen." See Eric Smoodin, "Introduction: The History of Film History," in Lewis and Smoodin, *Looking Past the Screen*, 1–34. Other important early studies of film culture, the social and cultural complex that emerged around film, include Kathryn H. Fuller, *At the Picture Show: Small-Town Audiences and the Creation of Movie Fan Culture* (Charlottesville: University of Virginia Press, 2001); Shelley Stamp, *Movie-Struck Girls: Women and Motion Picture Culture after the Nickelodeon* (Princeton, NJ: Princeton University Press, 2000); Jacqueline Najuma Stewart, *Migrating to the Movies: Cinema and Black Urban Modernity* (Berkeley: University of California Press, 2005), especially chapters 4 and 5; and Lynn Spigel, *Make Room for Television: Television and the Family Ideal in Postwar America* (Chicago: University of Chicago Press, 1992), an early influential intervention in the scholarship on the social dimensions of media. Scholarship focused on audiences, exhibition sites, and other cultural and social dimensions of cinema has been reintroduced as a component of "new cinema history." See Daniel Biltereyst, Richard Maltby, and Philippe Meers, "Introduction: The Scope of New Cinema History," in *The Routledge Companion to New Cinema History*, ed. Daniel Biltereyst, Richard Maltby, and Philippe Meers (New York: Routledge, 2019), 1–12.

27. Mainstream accounts—that is, those by mainly white critics writing in major outlets—include analyses of film criticism as a part of cinema's broader infrastructure, such as Huw Walmsley-Evans, *Film Criticism as a Cultural Institution* (New York: Routledge, 2018), and Mattias Frey and Cecilia Sayad, eds., *Film Criticism in the Digital Age* (New Brunswick, NJ: Rutgers University Press, 2015); broad historical accounts such as Mattias Frey, *The Permanent Crisis of Film Criticism: The Anxiety of Authority* (Amsterdam: Amsterdam University Press, 2015); and monographs focused on specific time periods or political contexts, including Jeff Smith, *Film Criticism, the Cold War, and the Blacklist: Reading the Hollywood Reds* (Berkeley: University of California Press, 2014), and Hector Amaya, *Screening Cuba: Film Criticism as Political Performance during the Cold War* (Urbana: University of Illinois Press, 2010). The gendered and racialized dimensions of film criticism have begun to be explored. See, for example, Melanie Bell, "Film Criticism as 'Women's Work': The Gendered Economy of Film Criticism in Britain, 1945–65," *Historical Journal of Film, Radio, and Television* 31, no. 2 (2011): 191–209; and Anna Everett,

Returning the Gaze: A Genealogy of Black Film Criticism, 1909–1949 (Durham, NC: Duke University Press; 2001).

28. Victor Valle contends that, with respect to nonfiction literary production in Los Angeles, the canon has been constructed out of "monolingual literature circumscribed by a strict genre hierarchy and national borders." Victor Valle, "LA's Latina/o Phantom Nonfiction and the Technologies of Literary Secrecy," in *Latinx Writing Los Angeles: Nonfiction Dispatches from a Decolonial Rebellion*, ed. Ignacio López-Calvo and Victor Valle (Lincoln: University of Nebraska Press, 2018), 5. In their efforts to resurface the United States' multilingual literary heritage, Marc Shell and Werner Sollors emphasize how literary history marginalizes most writing in other languages. Marc Shell and Werner Sollors, eds., *The Multilingual Anthology of American Literature: A Reader of Original Texts with English Translations* (New York: New York University Press, 2000).

29. More information about the Recovering the US Hispanic Literary Heritage project is available on the Arte Público Press website at https://artepublico press.com.

30. Sean Latham and Robert Scholes, "The Rise of Periodical Studies," *PMLA* 121, no. 2 (2006): 528.

31. Kirsten Silva Gruesz, "Mexican/American: The Making of Borderlands Print Culture," in *The Oxford History of Popular Print Culture*, vol. 6, *US Popular Print Culture, 1860–1920*, ed. Christine Bold (New York: Oxford University Press, 2011), 457–76.

32. For the type of advocacy most common during the silent period, namely letters or articles in local Spanish-language newspapers, see Limon, "Stereotyping and Chicano Resistance." See also Serna, *Making Cinelandia*, 174–77, on letters written by immigrants to consulates or other government bodies. On media activism in the late 1960s and 1970s, see Chon A. Noriega, *Shot in America: Television, the State, and the Rise of Chicano Cinema* (Minneapolis: University of Minnesota Press, 2000).

33. See Arcelia Gutiérrez, "No More Prostitutes, Pimps, and Pushers: Deploying Hispanic Panethnicity in Media Advocacy," *Critical Studies in Media Communication* 36, no. 4 (2019): 309–22.

34. On the Treaty of Guadalupe Hidalgo, its provisions, and its lack of protection for former Mexican citizens, see Richard Griswold del Castillo, *The Treaty of Guadalupe Hidalgo: A Legacy of Conflict* (Norman: University of Oklahoma Press, 1990). On tenuous citizenship, see Rosaura Sánchez, *Telling Identities: The Californio Testimonios* (Minneapolis: University of Minnesota Press, 1995); and Laura E. Gómez, *Manifest Destinies: The Making of the Mexican American Race* (New York: New York University Press, 2007).

35. On the development of the citrus industry in greater Southern California, see Matt Garcia, *A World of Its Own: Race, Labor, and Citrus in the Making of Greater Los Angeles, 1900–1970* (Chapel Hill: University of North Carolina Press, 2001), especially chapters 1 and 2. On the role of rail transportation, see Douglas Cazaux Sackman, *Orange Empire: California and the Fruits of Eden* (Berkeley: University of California Press, 2005), 31–39.

36. On the late nineteenth-century copper boom in New Mexico and Arizona, see Charles K. Hyde, *Copper for America: The United States Copper Industry from Colonial Times to the 1990s* (Tucson: University of Arizona Press, 1998), 127–39.

37. While some sources claim that 10 percent of Mexico's population, or almost one million people, entered the United States between 1910 and 1920, more recent demographic analyses put this figure at a more modest 350,000 to 400,000 after accounting for returning migrants. See Robert McCaa, "Missing Millions: The Demographic Costs of the Mexican Revolution," *Mexican Studies / Estudios Mexicanos* 19, no. 2 (2003): 367–400.

38. Douglas Monroy notes that this turn of phrase was used by some in the railroad industry in the 1920s. See Monroy, *Rebirth*, 110.

39. Sánchez, *Becoming Mexican American*, 63–83.

40. The activities of the Liga are described in Jose Amaro Hernandez, *Mutual Aid for Survival: The Case of the Mexican American* (Malabar, FL: Robert E. Krieger, 1983), 79–82.

41. For example, the Comité de Defensa de Ventura Rodriguez was formed to support a Mexican woman accused of killing a Jewish merchant in Los Angeles in 1918; see "Continúan los trabajos de defensa de Ventura Rodriguez," *El Heraldo de México*, June 23, 1918, 7. Another example was the committee formed to raise funds for people affected by the Xalapa earthquake in 1920. See "Dignamente Secundados por nuestros compatriotas, continuamos firmes en nuestra humilde obra de filantropía y patriotismo," *El Heraldo de México*, February 4, 1920, 1.

42. Sánchez, *Becoming Mexican American*, 181–84.

43. For more on Pedro J. González and other early Spanish-language pioneers, see Dolores Inés Casillas, *Sounds of Belonging: U.S. Spanish-Language Radio and Public Advocacy* (New York: New York University Press, 2014), 21–50; and Sánchez, *Becoming Mexican American*, 171–87.

44. Navarro reported his year of entry into the United States as 1917 in the 1930 census. Some published sources claim that he arrived in 1922 as part of a touring company, but archival evidence suggests that he arrived sometime between 1918 and 1919. Though his young son's death was registered in Mexico City in June 1918, he might have already gone on to the United States. See Department of Commerce, Bureau of the Census, Fifteenth Census of the United States, 1930, Los Angeles, California, Sheet 14A, Enumeration District: 0312, FHL microfilm 2339879, National Archives and Records Administration.

45. Gabriel "Hap" Navarro (1919–2014) would become an important fixture in Los Angeles's boxing world. He served as matchmaker at the Hollywood Legion Stadium from 1953 to 1955. See Gene Aguilar, *Lost Stories of West Coast Latino Boxing* (Charleston, SC: Arcadia, 2021), 17–19.

46. See "Latin Notables Await Musicale," *Los Angeles Times*, May 5, 1941, A12. The article refers to Navarro, who served as guest orchestra conductor for the evening, as the former director of President Carranza's National Artillery Band. His service in the revolutionary forces is mentioned in Eugenio de Zarraga, "Gabriel Navarro: Paladín Mexicano en Los Ángeles," *Revista de Revistas*, no. 1272,

September 30, 1934. It's unclear how much schooling Navarro had, but he was clearly literate.

47. "La Obertura 'Tally's,'" *El Heraldo de México*, May 21, 1920, 7.

48. Gabriel Navarro, "El amo nuevo," *El Heraldo de México*, June 12, 1920, 6; "La hora del retorno," *El Heraldo de México*, June 16, 1929, 6; and "Laboremos," *El Heraldo de México*, August 17, 1920, 4.

49. On this ideological diversity, see John H. Flores, *The Mexican Revolution in Chicago: Immigration Politics from the Early Twentieth Century to the Cold War* (Champaign: University of Illinois Press, 2018). Indeed, the editor of *El Heraldo de Mexico*, D. Juan de Heras, had come to Los Angeles in 1914 after the failed coup of Victoriano Huerta. Heras was described in an obituary as belonging "always, because of his political opinions and his conservative spirit, to that element [of society] that valued order." "Ayer por la mañana falleció en Los Ángeles el periodista mexicano, Sr. Juan de Heras," *El Tucsonense* (Tucson), February 2, 1924, 1.

50. For examples of Navarro's poetry and romantic prose, see "Reconciliación," *El Heraldo de México*, August 28, 1921, 5; "Todavía me quieres," *El Heraldo de México*, July 28, 1921, 5; "Lilia," *El Heraldo de México*, August 18, 1921, 7; and his historical meditation "Los mártires: Cuento de la Guerra de Independencia," *El Heraldo de México*, September 16, 1920, 2.

51. "Una velada en la liga protectora Latina," *El Heraldo de México*, June 25, 1921, 3. On his active participation, see "La sesión de esta noche en la 'Liga Protectora Latina,'" *El Heraldo de México*, August 4, 1921, 3; "Una noche de arte la ultima sesión de la 'Liga Protectora Latina,'" *El Heraldo de México*, August 13, 1921, 4; "Una iniciativa para celebrar las fiestas del centenario en Los Ángeles," *El Heraldo de México*, August 12, 1921, 7; "Poco a poco crece el fondo del centenario," *El Heraldo de México*, August 18, 1921, 1; and "Animada sesión en la sucursal 30 de la Liga," *El Heraldo de México*, October 9, 1921, 7.

52. Navarro's name appears in accounts of weddings and baptisms that were high profile enough to be written about in *El Heraldo*. See, for example, "La colonia Mexicana en Los Ángeles registró una hermosa nota nupcial dos jóvenes distinguidos Maria Luisa Castilla y Leopoldo," *El Heraldo de México*, January 26, 1921, 1, 3; and "El advenimiento de una nueva Cristiana, fue recibido con una entusiasta fiesta, *El Heraldo de México*, July 19, 1922, 6. *El Heraldo's* social page commented on his health and that of his family, and when he moved to San Diego his periodic visits to Los Angeles were noted. See, for example, "Viajeros," *El Heraldo de México*, June 28, 1917, 6; "Viajeros," *El Heraldo de México*, May 24, 1927, 6; "La semana social," *El Heraldo de México*, October 16, 1927, 6; "El 'club recreativo Olimpia' despidió al 1927," *El Heraldo de México*, January 6, 1928; and "Fue operada la Señora Luisa María Alvarez de Navarro," *El Heraldo de México*, January 19, 1928, 6.

53. They appear to have participated in the same event in September 1924, he as one of the masters of ceremonies and she as a performer. See "Una verdadera noche de gala fue la del lunes anterior en el Teatro Hidalgo, con motivo de la función de la U[nion] Mexicana de Periodistas," *El Heraldo de México*, September 3, 1924, 1–2. He interviewed Reyes early on during her stay in Los Angeles and,

under the pseudonym "Fidelio," published "Maria de la Luz Reyes" in *El Heraldo de México*, January 11, 1925, 8.

54. In her dissertation, Antonia Garcia-Orozco writes that she believes the two had a common law marriage, as she, like us, could not find any documentation of a marriage or divorce. Antonia Garcia-Orozco, "Cucurrucucu Palomas: The Estilo Bravío of Lucha Reyes and the Creation of Feminist Consciousness via the Canción Ranchera" (PhD diss., Claremont Graduate University, 2005), 116. See also Marie Sarita Gaytán and Sergio de la Mora, "Queening/Queering Mexicanidad: Lucha Reyes and the *Canción Ranchera*," *Feminist Formations* 28, no. 3 (2016): 200–2.

55. De Zarraga, "Gabriel Navarro."

56. Their wedding was announced in *La Opinion*'s society section: "El matrimonio Flores-Navarro, Ayer," October 3, 1929, 6. The announcement was reprinted in *El Tucsonense*, October 5, 1929, 1. Earlier, Navarro was briefly married to a woman named Luisa Maria Alvarez, who was the daughter of a Mexican general, Francisco de P. Alvarez. Their marriage was noted in the newspaper and later in 1930 was registered in Mexico City. "Contrajeron matrimonio la Srita. Luisa María Alvarez y el Sr. Gabriel Navarro," *El Heraldo de México*, November 15, 1927, 4.

57. Born Francisco Daniel, Daniel Navarro (1931–2022) worked for Los Angeles County and published his own book on silent cinema, *Navarro's Silent Film Guide: A Comprehensive Look at American Silent Cinema* (Los Angeles: New University Press, 2013). Mike (b. 1934) is a successful advertising executive.

58. Navarro is named as the editor of *El Pueblo* in the caption of a photograph of him with members of the Council for Civic Unity published in the *Mississippi Enterprise*, April 22, 1944, 1. We have been unable to find any extant issues of the publication.

59. Manuel Ibo Alfaro wrote *Malditas sean las mujeres* (1858), which was well received, especially in Latin America. It was reedited by Lezcano Comendador, who used the title to launch his own collection, under the pseudonym IA, of popular romantic novels with similar titles. See Immaculada Benito Argaiz, "Una aclaración necesaria en la bibliografía del escritor cerverano Manuel Ibo Alfaro (1828–1885)," *Berceo* 132 (1997): 7–28.

60. See Gunckel, *Mexico on Main Street*, 51–88.

61. "Ernie Smith Leaves Beaten Paths to Make Travelogue of Old Mexico," *International Photographer*, July 1932, 6; and Agrasánchez, *Guillermo Calles*, 95–99.

62. Lisa Jarvinen, *The Rise of Spanish-language Filmmaking: Out from Hollywood's Shadow, 1929–1939* (New Brunswick, NJ: Rutgers University Press, 2012); "Scripters," *Box Office*, November 26, 1938, 40; and "Trovador Spanish Treat," *Hollywood Reporter*, November 30, 1938, 3.

63. "Velada de la Sociedad Filarmónica Mutualista Mexicana de Los Angeles," *El Heraldo de México*, November 9, 1927, 6; and "Hoy sería la velada literario-musical de la Sociedad Filarmónica," November 15, 1927, 6.

64. "Stars to Aid in Benefit," *Los Angeles Times*, October 19, 1933; and "Storm Victims Benefit Billed: Mexican Artists and Other Live Entertainment," *Los Angeles Times*, October 20, 1933, A2.

65. Isabel Morse Jones, "Two Musical Events Win Attention," *Los Angeles Times*, May 8, 1941, 17; and "Padilla Opens Mexican Casa at Belvedere," *Los Angeles Times*, May 6, 1945, A2.

66. For more on the Sleepy Lagoon case and the Defense Committee, see Edward J. Escobar, *Race, Police, and the Making of a Political Identity, 1900–1945* (Berkeley: University of California Press, 1999); and Eduardo Obregón Pagán, *Murder at the Sleepy Lagoon: Zoot Suits, Race, and Riot in Wartime L.A.* (Chapel Hill: University of North Carolina Press, 2003).

67. See Joint Fact-Finding Committee on Un-American Activities in California, *Un-American Activities in California* (Sacramento: California State Senate, 1943), 203–17. Navarro joined the executive committee of the Sleepy Lagoon Defense Committee in January 1944 after having supported the group's work. See *Appeal News* 2, no. 4, January 17, 1944. His name can be found in the documentation of the Special Committee on Un-American Activities chaired by Congressman Martin Dies Jr., the conservative Democrat from Texas. Special Committe on Un-American Activities, *Investigation of Un-American Propaganda Activities in the United States: Hearings before a Special Committee on Un-American Activities, House of Representatives, Seventy-eighth Congress, Second Session on H. Res. 282, Appendix Part 9, Vol. 2.* (Washington, DC: Government Printing Office, 1944), 1566.

68. Though he does not mention Navarro by name, Kevin Allen Leonard writes extensively about the council in his book *The Battle for Los Angeles: Racial Ideology and World War II* (Albuquerque: University of New Mexico Press, 2006); see page 193. Navarro's involvement is documented in the caption of an untitled photograph published in the *Mississippi Enterprise*, April 22, 1944, 1.

69. Edmund Roybal represented the multiracial Ninth District, which in 1950 stretched from Boyle Heights to the Central Avenue District in south-central Los Angeles. For more on the impact of Roybal's election to the city council, see Katherine Underwood, "Pioneering Minority Representation: Edward Roybal and the Los Angeles City Council, 1949–1962," *Pacific Historical Review* 66, no. 3 (1997): 399–425.

70. "In Memoriam: Gabriel Navarro," Resolution, City Council of Los Angeles, December 12, 1950. Courtesy of Mike Navarro.

71. "Independent Theater Guide," *Los Angeles Times*, December 21, 1950, A6. Nina Hoechtl presents an overview of this rebirth and of the theater's subsequent declines and revivals in "On the *Nuevo Teatro Máximo de la Raza*: Still Thinking, Feeling, and Speaking Spanish On- and Offscreen," in Gunckel, Horak, and Jarvinen, *Cinema between Latin America and Los Angeles*, 138–58.

72. Steven Loza, *Barrio Rhythm: Mexican American Music in Los Angeles* (Urbana: University of Illinois Press, 1993), 64.

73. "Se construye la Ciudad Presidente Alemán," *El Sol* (Phoenix, AZ), January 26, 1951.

74. "Pioneer Latin Newsman Dies," *Los Angeles Times*, December 9, 1950, 14.

75. Nicolás Kanellos uses the term "exilic" to refer to the many Spanish-language publications helmed by political exiles that emerged in the late nineteenth

and early twentieth centuries. See Nicolás Kanellos, *Hispanic Immigrant Literature: El sueño del retorno* (Austin: University of Texas Press, 2011), 21.

76. For more on the history of the Spanish-language press in the United States during the early twentieth century, see Kirsten Silva Gruesz, "Mexican/American"; Juan Bruce-Novoa, "*La Prensa* and the Chicano Community," *Americas Review* 17, nos. 3–4 (1989): 150–56; Ramón D. Chacón, "The Chicano Immigrant Press in Los Angeles: The Case of 'El Heraldo de México,' 1916–1920," *Journalism History* 4, no. 2 (1977): 48–64; Nicolás Kanellos and Helvetia Martell, eds., *Hispanic Periodicals in the United States: Origins to 1960* (Houston: Arte Público, 2000); and Francine Medeiros, "*La Opinión*, a Mexican Exile Newspaper: A Content Analysis of Its First Years, 1926–1929," *Aztlán: A Journal of Chicano Studies* 11, no. 1 (1980): 65–87.

77. Nicolás Kanellos, "A Brief History of Hispanic Periodicals in the United States," in Kanellos and Martell, *Hispanic Periodicals in the United States*, 37–43.

78. Evelyn Brooks Higginbotham, *Righteous Discontent: The Women's Movement in the Black Baptist Church, 1880–1920* (Cambridge, MA: Harvard University Press, 1993), 7.

79. Nancy Fraser, "Rethinking the Public Sphere: A Contribution to the Critique of Actually Existing Democracy," in *Habermas and the Public Sphere*, ed. Craig Calhoun (Cambridge, MA: MIT Press, 1992), 123. For more on the role of Spanish-language radio during this period, see Casillas, *Sounds of Belonging*, 35–50; and Félix F. Gutiérrez and Jorge Reina Shement, *Spanish-Language Radio in the Southwestern United States* (Austin: Center for Mexican American Studies, University of Texas, 1979), 5–12.

80. Flores, *Mexican Revolution in Chicago*, 4. For more on the ideological diversity and tension within the Mexican-descent population of the United States during the period, see Julia G. Young, *Mexican Exodus: Emigrants, Exiles, and Refugees of the Cristero War* (New York: Oxford University Press, 2015), 61–100.

81. John Pluecker has labeled this general attitude as the "ideology of return" that existed alongside the "México de afuera" discourse. See Pluecker, "'One More Texas-Mexican': Under the Texas Sun and Conflicts of Nation," in *Under the Texas Sun / El sol de Texas*, ed. Conrado Espinoza (Houston: Arte Público, 2007), 114. See also Kanellos, *Hispanic Immigrant Literature*, 52–79.

82. For more on the concept of "México de afuera," see Kanellos, "Brief History of Hispanic Periodicals," 37–43.

83. Ruiz, *From Out of the Shadows*, 51–70.

84. On migrant authors as symbols of the nation, see Kanellos, *Hispanic Immigrant Literature*, 123–45. A number of Mexican authors working in the United States penned literary works warning of the costs and dangers of immigration, including the loss of cultural integrity and traditional gender norms. Translated editions of such books include Facundo Bernal, *A Stab in the Dark* (Los Angeles: Los Angeles Review of Books, 2018); Espinoza, *Under the Texas Sun / El sol de Texas*; and Daniel Venegas, *The Adventures of Don Chipote, or, When Parrots Breast-Feed* (Houston: Arte Público, 2000). These themes were also taken up by Mexican authors writing in Mexico, including film critic Carlos Noriega Hope and statesman and author Genaro Estrada, who explicitly thematized film culture

in their work. See Jason Borge, *Latin American Writers and the Rise of Hollywood Cinema* (New York: Routledge, 2008); and Laura Isabel Serna, "Popular Mexican Masculinity and American Culture in the 1920s: Migrants and Fifis," *Latin American Research Review*, 57, no. 2 (2022): 422–39.

85. Gabriel Navarro, "The City of No Return," *La Prensa*, April 8, 1927, in this volume. (Citations denoted "in this volume" refer to the translated essays in the present work, and the English-language titles are used in the citations. In other citations to Navarro's writing, the original Spanish titles are used.) Also in this volume, see Navarro, "Why the Hidalgo Has Made a Comeback as the 'Rendezvous' of the Community," *La Opinión*, May 1, 1932, 7.

86. See in this volume, for example, Gabriel Navarro, "Fleeting Impressions," *La Opinión*, July 10, 1932, 7.

87. For more on the politics of multiracial Los Angeles before World War II, see Scott Kurashige, *The Shifting Grounds of Race: Black and Japanese Americans in the Making of Multiethnic Los Angeles* (Princeton, NJ: Princeton University Press, 2008), 1–90; Josh Sides, *L.A. City Limits: African American Los Angeles from the Great Depression to the Present* (Berkeley: University of California Press, 2003), 11–35; and Mark Wild, *Street Meeting: Multiethnic Neighborhoods in Early Twentieth-Century Los Angeles* (Berkeley: University of California Press, 2005).

88. For a discussion of these distinctions within the cultural debate of the period, see Joan Shelley Rubin, *The Making of Middlebrow Culture* (Chapel Hill: University of North Carolina Press, 1992), 1–33.

89. Richard deCordova, *Picture Personalities: The Emergence of the Star System in America* (Champaign: University of Illinois Press, 2001).

90. Richard Abel and Amy Rodgers, "Early Motion Pictures and Popular Print Culture," in *The Oxford History of Popular Print Culture*, vol. 6, *US Popular Print Culture, 1860–1920*, ed. Christine Bold (New York: Oxford University Press, 2011), 196.

91. Gabriel Navarro, *Barbara La Marr: Una historia de placer y dolor* (San Antonio: Casa Editorial Lozano, 1926), 23, 6.

92. Navarro, *Barbara La Marr*, 2.

93. For an exhaustive account of La Marr's life, see Sherri Snyder, *Barbara La Marr: The Girl Who Was Too Beautiful for Hollywood* (Lexington: University Press of Kentucky, 2017). She addresses La Marr's own mythification of her ethnic identity on page 7.

94. Navarro, *Barbara La Marr*, 7.

95. Navarro, *Barbara La Marr*, 115.

96. Denise McKenna, "The Photoplay or the Pickaxe: Extras, Gender, and Labour in Early Hollywood," *Film History* 23, no. 1 (2011): 5.

97. See Hilary A. Hallett, *Go West, Young Women! The Rise of Early Hollywood* (Berkeley: University of California Press, 2013), 17–25. See also Heidi Kenaga, "Making the 'Studio Girl': The Hollywood Studio Club and Industry Regulation of Female Labour," *Film History* 18, no. 2 (2006): 129–39; and McKenna, "Photoplay or the Pickaxe." For an example of this discourse in fan magazines, see Ruth Waterbury, "Don't Go to Hollywood!," *Photoplay*, March 1927, 50–51, 125.

98. See Kate Fortmueller, *Below the Stars: How the Labor of Working Actors and Extras Shapes Media Production* (Austin: University of Texas Press, 2021), 24–25.

99. On the conditions of ethnic Mexican extra work in silent-era Hollywood, see Laura Isabel Serna, "Atmosphere: Mexican Extras and Race Making in Silent Hollywood," *Journal of Cinema and Media Studies* 63, no. 2 (forthcoming). For more on the links between Navarro's criticism and *La Ciudad,*, see Colin Gunckel, "Ambivalent Si(gh)tings: Stardom and Silent Film in Mexican America," *Film History* 27, no. 1 (2017): 110–39.

100. See, for instance, Gutiérrez, "No More Prostitutes, Pimps, and Pushers," 309–22; Noriega, *Shot in America*; and Allison Perlman and Hector Amaya, "Owning a Voice: Broadcasting Policy, Spanish Language Media, and Latina/o Speech Rights," *Communication, Culture and Critique* 6, no. 1 (2013): 142–60.

101. For an account of this incident in 1922, see Laura Isabel Serna, "'As a Mexican I Feel It's My Duty': Citizenship, Censorship, and the Campaign against Derogatory Films in Mexico," *Americas* 63, no. 2 (2006): 225–44. See also Gabriela F. Arredondo, *Mexican Chicago: Race, Identity, and Nation, 1916–1939* (Urbana: University of Illinois Press, 2008), 143; Serna, *Making Cinelandia*; and Ruth Vasey, *The World According to Hollywood, 1918–1939* (Madison: University of Wisconsin Press, 1997).

102. Caddoo, *Envisioning Freedom*, 139–70.

103. Lori Kido Lopez, *Asian American Media Activism: Fighting for Cultural Citizenship* (New York: New York University Press, 2016), 24.

104. For more on the concept of "de-Mexicanization" and its relation to popular culture, see Monroy, *Rebirth*, 165–207.

105. Laura Isabel Serna explores the production of transnational Mexican fandom and the production of a distinctly Mexican iteration of Hollywood, "Cinelandia," in Serna, *Making Cinelandia*.

106. For more on this distinction, see Gunckel, "Ambivalent Si(gh)tings."

107. Joanne Hershfield, *The Invention of Dolores del Río* (Minneapolis: University of Minnesota Press, 2000), 16.

108. In this volume, see Gabriel Navarro, "The Infancy of a Giant," *La Opinión*, January 6, 1929, 14, and "Concerning the Words of Mr. Will Hays, Cinema Czar," *La Opinión*, January 11, 1931, 5.

109. Gabriel Navarro, "The City of No Return," *La Prensa*, February 6, 1927, in this volume.

110. In this volume see Gabriel Navarro, "Enriqueta's Voyage to the Old World," *La Prensa*, December 6, 1925, 17. See also The Crystal Ball (column), *La Prensa*, February 8, 1925, 12.

111. In his coverage of La Marr's death (and promotion of his forthcoming book), Navarro likewise attributes her decision to pursue a theatrical career to her "Latin blood." See "Los últimos momentos de Barbara La Marr," *La Prensa*, February 7, 1926.

112. In this volume, see Gabriel Navarro, "Mexican Extras without Work," *La Opinión*, September 2, 1928.

113. In this volume, see Gabriel Navarro, "Let's Make Cinema 'in Spanish' and Not Cinema 'Translated into Spanish,'" *La Opinión* (suplemento ilustrado), December 25, 1932, 3.

114. Navarro, "Let's Make Cinema 'in Spanish,'" 3.

115. See, for example, in this volume, Gabriel Navarro, "Hollywood's New Failure," *La Opinión*, July 2, 1935, II-6.

116. América Rodríguez, "Creating an Audience and Remapping a Nation: A Brief History of US Spanish Language Broadcasting, 1930–1980," *Quarterly Review of Film and Video* 16, nos. 3–4 (1999): 357–74.

117. In this volume, see Navarro, "Concerning the Words of Mr. Will Hays." Regarding stereotypes and the representation of Mexico, see also Gabriel Navarro, "Entertainment—Our Review of an Advance Screening of the Film *Thunder over Mexico*," *La Opinión*, May 12, 1933, 4, in this volume, and "Una película denigrante para México, a punto de ser lanzada a la distribución," *La Opinión*, January 20, 1929, 14.

118. For recent works that document the rather dismal representation of minorities within the media industries, see Frances Negrón-Muntaner et al., *The Latino Media Gap: A Report on the State of Latinos in U.S. Media* (Los Angeles: National Association of Latino Independent Producers; Washington, DC: National Hispanic Foundation of the Arts; New York: Columbia University Center for the Study of Ethnicity and Race, 2014); and Nancy Wang Yuen, *Reel Inequality: Hollywood Actors and Racism* (Newark, NJ: Rutgers University Press, 2016).

119. Gabriel Navarro, "Por que el público de Hispano América está condenado a ver solamente películas mediocres," *La Opinión*, July 13, 1930, 14.

120. See de las Carreras and Horak, *Hollywood Goes Latin*; Gunckel, *Mexico on Main Street*; J. B. Heinink and Robert G. Dickson, *Cita en Hollywood: Antología de las películas norteamericanas habladas en castellano* (Bilbao, Spain: Mensajero, 1990); and Jarvinen, *Rise of Spanish-Language Filmmaking*.

121. In this volume, see Gabriel Navarro, "The Screen—Opportunities that Spanish-Speaking Cinema Offers to Our Actors," *La Opinión*, January 30, 1930, 6.

122. Among the articles Navarro wrote on this topic are "Con la producción cinematográfica muerta, hay solo un camino que seguir," *La Opinión*, October 15, 1931, 5; "¿Qué sucede con la cinefonía española?," *La Opinión*, July 6, 1932, 4; "Este Hollywood!," *La Opinión*, May 26, 1935, II-6; "Hollywood's New Failure," *La Opinión*, July 2, 1935, II-6; "¿Por qué han fracasado los 'films' en español?," *La Opinión*, February 15, 1931, 5; "Por qué la película Española es inferior a la 'americana,'" *La Opinión*, August 14, 1932, II-5; "Por qué no se hacen más películas en español," *La Opinión*, August 16, 1931, 5; "La revolución del cine hispano," *La Opinión*, September 27, 1931, 5; "Sangre nueva, Hollywood!," *La Opinión*, December 25, 1938, II-6; and "Una sugestión," *La Opinión*, January 1, 1939, II-6. In this volume, see "The Screen—Opportunities that Spanish-Speaking Cinema Offers to Our Actors," *La Opinión*, January 30, 1930, 6; "Our Public Wants Their Own Movies, Reflections of Their Lives," *La Opinión*, August 23, 1931, 5; "There Are No Hispanic Stars!," *La Opinión*, September 20, 1931, 5; and "That's Hollywood!—We Need to Make Cinema for the Masses, the Ones Who Pay for It," *La Opinión*, June 23, 1935, II-6.

123. See, for instance, in this volume, Gabriel Navarro, "*La llama sagrada* Is an Intensely Human Photodrama," *La Opinión*, February 3, 1931, 4.

124. Articles by Navarro on this issue include "Un peligroso 'boomerang,'" *La Opinión*, October 4, 1931, 5; "Nuevamente se nos culpa del fracaso del cinema hispano," *La Opinión*, November 1, 1931, 5; and "El culpable es el mismo público hispano, dice un funcionario del cinema," *La Opinión*, August 16, 1931, 5.

125. Gabriel Navarro, "'El futuro del cinema en nuestras manos," *La Opinión*, January 24, 1932, 5.

126. See Arlene Dávila, *Latinos, Inc.: The Marketing and Making of a People* (Berkeley: University of California Press, 2001).

127. See Navarro, "That's Hollywood!"

128. Navarro, "Hollywood's New Failure."

129. See Lisa Jarvinen, "A Mass Market for Spanish-Language Films: Los Angeles, Hybridity, and the Emergence of Latino Audiovisual Media," in Gunckel, Horak, and Jarvinen, *Cinema between Latin America and Los Angeles*, 83–84.

130. For more on Tirado's career, see Espasande Bouza, "Romualdo Tirado," 113–25.

131. See in this volume, Gabriel Navarro, "Tijuana, Production Center for Sound Cinema," *La Opinión*, March 5, 1939.

132. The articles Navarro wrote about this controversy include "Tempestad en un vaso de agua," *La Opinión*, January 8, 1939, II-6, and "La embajada artística mexicana en Hollywood," *La Opinión*, January 22, 1939, II-6.

133. Navarro, "Let's Make Cinema 'in Spanish.'" See also in this volume, "Let's Bring Dignity to Mexican Cinema," *La Opinión*, June 26, 1936, II-6.

134. Jarvinen, "Mass Market for Spanish-Language Films," 92.

135. Navarro's profiles of such stars in this volume include "A 'Cinderella' from the Pearl of Humaya," *La Opinión*, December 9, 1928, 14; "The Revival of Antonio Moreno," *La Opinión*, June 15, 1930, 14; and "A Surprise from the Anonymous Masses," *La Magazín de la Opinión*, January 18, 1931, 5–6.

136. See, for instance, Hye Seung Chung, *Hollywood Asian: Philip Ahn and the Politics of Cross-Ethnic Performance* (Philadelphia: Temple University Press, 2006), 33–56; Peter X. Feng, "Recuperating Suzie Wong: A Fan's Nancy Kwan-dary," in *Countervisions: Asian American Film Criticism*, ed. Darrell Y. Hamamoto and Sandra Liu (Philadelphia: Temple University Press, 2000), 40–56; Paula J. Massood, "African American Stardom Inside and Outside of Hollywood: Ernest Morrison, Noble Johnson, Evelyn Preer, and Lincoln Perry," in *Idols of Modernity: Movie Stars of the 1920s*, ed. Patrice Petro (New Brunswick, NJ: Rutgers University Press, 2010), 227–49; and Petty, *Stealing the Show*, 1–26.

137. See Navarro, "There Are No Hispanic Stars!"

138. For example, Navarro defends Lupe Velez's role in *Wolf Song* (1929, dir. Victor Fleming) in "Una película denigrante para México."

139. See Navarro, "Mexican Extras without Work" and "The Opportunity to Fail in Cinema," *La Magazín de la Opinión*, February 8, 1931, 5–6, in this volume.

140. Articles by Navarro addressing these issues include "Cunde un verdadero pánico entre los artistas de habla Española en Hollywood," *La Opinión*, March 15, 1931, 5, and "De la crítica 'benévola,'" *La Opinión*, December 7, 1930, 5.

141. See Navarro, "Mexican Extras without Work," 12.

142. Gabriel Navarro, "Es terrible la situación de los artistas en Los Angeles," *La Opinión*, July 1, 1932, 6.

143. See, for instance, Gabriel Navarro, "La casa Fox ha anunciado la reanudación de sus actividades hispánicas," *La Opinión*, June 19, 1932, 5. In this volume see also "It's Time to Innovate!," *La Opinión*, November 18, 1931, 5.

144. Gabriel Navarro, "El primer triunfo," *La Opinión*, October 15, 1933, II-3.

145. Navarro, "Por que el público de Hispano América." See also Navarro, "The Opportunity to Fail in Cinema."

146. See Navarro, "It's Time to Innovate!" Other articles by Navarro on this topic include "La reapertura del teatro 'México,'" *La Opinión*, July 17, 1932, 7; "¿Qué pasa con el teatro español en Los Angeles?," *La Opinión*, December 1, 1928, 4; and "Teatrales," *La Opinión*, August 11, 1933, 4.

147. Navarro, "It's Time to Innovate!" See also Navarro, "¿Qué pasa con el teatro español en Los Angeles?"

148. Gabriel Navarro, "La reapertura del Teatro 'México,'" *La Opinión*, July 17, 1932, 7.

149. Navarro, "Teatrales."

150. See, for instance, "Los primeros frutos de la labor del club 'Mitla,'" *La Opinión*, March 22, 1930, 4.

151. In this volume, see "Make Your Own Movie," *La Opinión*, July 10, 1938, II-6, and "Make Your Own Movie," *La Opinión*, July 31, 1938, II-6.

152. See Field, *Uplift Cinema*; and Lary May, *Screening Out the Past: The Birth of Mass Culture and the Motion Picture Industry* (New York: Oxford University Press, 1980), 43–59.

153. Navarro refers here to Father Miguel Hidalgo y Costilla (1753–1811), a priest who sparked the movement for independence from Spain by calling for revolution on September 16, 1810.

154. The song "Ojos tapatíos" (Jaliscan eyes) is a likely reference to Navarro's own upbringing in the Mexican state of Jalisco, a background that the two characters here presumably share. The song was composed by Fernando Méndez Velázquez and was recorded on Victor as early as 1917. It would later be a staple of Mexican *comedia ranchera* films and would be associated in particular with Jorge Negrete, one of the genre's biggest stars.

155. This line of the Mexican national anthem, composed in 1853 by Francisco González Bocanegra, refers to cannons at the Battle of Tampico, when Mexican forces successfully defended that city from a Spanish invasion in 1829. The battle is regarded as a decisive moment in Mexico's struggle for independence.

156. Because the Mexican revolution was marked by numerous revolutions and counterrevolutions, it is likely that Navarro is referring here to the first uprising against Porfirio Díaz, in November 1910.

157. Rafael Reyes Spíndola is largely regarded as the father of the modern press in Mexico. In 1896 he founded the newspaper *El Imparcial*. The paper cost a penny, focused on broad circulation, and relied on advertising revenue rather than political patronage. See Jerry W. Knudson, "Periodization of the Mexican Press," in *Contemporary Mexico: Papers of the IV International Congress of Mexican History*,

ed. James W. Wilkie, Michael C. Meyer, and Edna Monzón de Wilkie (Berkeley: University of California Press, 1976), 747–50.

158. British adventurer Charles La Trobe used the phrase City of Palaces (Ciudad de los Palacios), commonly misattributed to German naturalist and explorer Alexander von Humboldt, to describe Mexico City in his 1836 book *The Rambler in Mexico* (New York: Harper Brothers, 84). The roller coaster (*montaña rusa*) that Murillo remembers here was one of the attractions at the city's Parque Luna, a recreational center located approximately where Chapultepec Park is today. Aimed at the city's upper classes, it featured, in addition to the roller coaster, a skating rink, a vaudeville stage, musical performances, and boliche, among other diversions. See Heriberto Martínez Brígido, "Juegos y diversiones en la ciudad de México, 1910–1920" (thesis, Universidad Autónoma Metropolitana, Unidad Iztapala, 2002).

159. Many young Mexican women during this period would have been chaperoned in public places by a family member. Doing otherwise would have violated norms of propriety and thrown the young woman's reputation into question. On chaperonage as a cultural practice in Southern California immigrant communities, see Vicki Ruiz, "The Flapper and the Chaperone," chap. 3 in *From Out of the Shadows*, 51–71. Navarro likely intends the presence of Estela's chaperone to contrast with the more carefree attitude of Betty and her seemingly absent parents.

160. In this poem, Murillo likens Estela to the Mater Dolorosa, or sorrowful mother, one of three artistic representations of the Virgin of Sorrows.

161. Navarro uses an Italian expression that translates roughly as "to die for" and that was used in Spanish at the time.

162. Messalina, the third wife of Roman emperor Claudius, had a reputation (deserved or not) of being power hungry and sexually promiscuous.

163. Navarro here refers to the lead character in *Manon*, an opera written in 1884 by Jules Massenet based on a novel by Abbé Prévost. Its story centers on Manon Lescaut, a young woman arriving in Paris from the countryside to enter a convent. Seduced by the pleasures and luxuries she encounters in the city, she is soon torn between the love of a young student and marriage to a wealthy tax collector. As might be expected, this tale ends in tragedy.

164. A charanga is a small musical ensemble that performs traditional Cuban music.

165. Here Navarro refers to the remote territory in the southern part of the Mexican state of Sonora occupied by members of the Yaqui Indigenous group.

166. "La Sultana de Occidente" was a common nickname for the city of Guadalajara.

167. Navarro added a footnote here that reads, "La muerte de Safo.— Lamartine." This verse is Navarro's relatively loose translation of a stanza from the poem "Sapho" by Alphonse de Lamartine, which appears in *Nouvelles méditations poétiques* (Paris: Hachette, 1924), 17–22.

168. Navarro here refers to Rex Ingram's 1922 film *Trifling Women*, which was a remake of his 1917 film *Black Orchids*.

169. *The Three Musketeers* (1921) was directed by Fred Niblo; *The Prisoner of Zenda* (1922) by Rex Ingram.

170. *Black Orchids*, a 1922 remake of the 1917 film of the same name, was released as *Trifling Women*. *Thy Name Is Woman* (1924) was directed by Fred Niblo.

171. The Abbasid caliph Harun al-Rashid, whose reign was fictionalized in various parts of *One Thousand and One Nights*, was known to walk the streets of Baghdad in disguise, gathering information from his subjects about their living conditions and the state of the kingdom.

172. In the 1910s, the Princess Theater (formerly Fischer's Theatre) on First Street hosted vaudeville and live theater, including musical comedy. Rechristened the Teatro Princesa in the early 1920s, it alternated between cinema and Spanish-language variety shows that catered to a largely Mexican audience. By 1928 the theater had been demolished to make way for civic construction.

173. Pobre Valbuena is the lead character in a Spanish *sainete* (a humorous one-act play usually based on customs or types and performed during a theatrical intermission) written by Carlos Arniches and Enrique García Alvarez. It premiered in Madrid in 1904 and was adapted for film twice, in 1910 and 1923. The character feigns injury in order to attract the attention of women.

174. It is unclear to which film the character is referring here, but it is most likely *The Burning Trail* (1925, dir. Arthur Rossen; Universal Pictures Corp.), in which Daugherty's character rescues a woman from a burning house.

175. Elinor Glyn was a British novelist and scriptwriter who was known for her romantic fiction. Considered scandalous for its time, her work was relatively tame by modern standards. Her novels and stories were the basis of many films during the silent period, including the Clara Bow vehicle *It* (1927, dir. Clarence G. Badger). For more on Glyn, see Hilary A. Hallett, *Inventing the It Girl: How Elinor Glyn Created the Modern Romance and Conquered Early Hollywood* (New York: Liveright, 2022).

176. *The Eternal City* (1923) was directed by George Fitzmaurice.

177. Navarro added a footnote here that reads, "Here we've substituted another name for the true name of the owner of this letter, who is a famous Hollywood actress, on her own recommendation. A copy of the letter is still in my desk."

178. This is a reference to La Marr's 1924 film *The White Moth*, which was produced and directed by Maurice Tourneur; La Marr cowrote the screen story. Throughout Navarro refers to it as *La falena* (The moth), which was most likely its release title in Spanish.

179. *Sandra* (1924) was directed by Arthur H. Sawyer; *The White Monkey* (1925), by Phil Rosen.

180. *The Girl from Montmartre* (1926) was directed by Alfred E. Green.

181. Tuberculosis was often referred to as the "white plague."

182. This is indeed an excerpt from a poem by Barbara La Marr titled "The Savage." For the entire poem, see Snyder, *Barbara La Marr*, 307–8. Navarro's punctuation of the lines differs from Snyder's.

183. Torres refers here to the poem "La cama de la novia" (The bride's bed) by Spanish modernist poet Cristóbal de Castro. See Cristóbal de Castro, *Poesía lírica* (Córdoba: Ayuntamiento de Iznájar and Diputación Provincial de Córdoba, 1995), 146–48.

184. This is likely a reference to Saint Margaret, a martyr renowned for her remarkable beauty. When she refused to renounce Christianity, Roman officials subjected her to multiple tortures from which she emerged unscathed until she was finally beheaded. As was the case with Barbara La Marr, Saint Margaret was raised by adoptive parents.

185. Duque Job was one of several pseudonyms of the Mexican writer Manuel Gutiérrez Nájera. One of his most popular poems was "La Duquesa Job," about a working-class woman who is the object of the narrator's affections.

186. These lines were taken from Echegaray's play *El gran Galeoto*. See José Echegaray, *El gran Galeoto: En el puño de la espada* (Barcelona: Orbis, 1983).

187. For example, *Don Quixote*, to which Torres refers earlier.

188. This is a reference to Fairbanks's role in the film *Don Q, Son of Zorro* (1925, dir. Donald Crisp).

189. This is a reference to Casto Méndez Núñez, a Spanish naval officer who commanded the Spanish fleet in the Pacific in the nineteenth century. Images of Méndez Núñez invariably featured his large mutton chop sideburns.

190. The costumes Navarro describes correspond to roles that each of these actors played in 1925 and 1926: Antonio Moreno as Ulysses Ferragut in *Mare Nostrum* (1926, dir. Rex Ingram); John Gilbert as Marquis Bardelys in *Bardelys the Magnificent* (1926, dir. King Vidor); and Ramon Novarro as Judah Ben-Hur in *Ben-Hur: A Tale of the Christ* (1925, dir. Fred Niblo).

191. This is a reference to Guadalajara, Laura Cañedo's (and Navarro's) hometown.

192. This is a reference to Gloria Swanson, whose third husband was the French aristocrat Henry de La Falaise, Marquis de La Coudraye. The couple married in 1925; their divorce was finalized in 1931.

193. Celis was Navarro's maternal family name. His father's first name was Valente.

194. Criolla has the connotation of a mixed-race (mestizo) person, but one primarily if not exclusively of Spanish descent.

195. This is a reference to a painting by Rembrandt, *Belshazzar's Feast* (1635–38; oil on canvas), which was based on an episode from the biblical book of Daniel in which the destruction of Belshazzar's reign is prophesied in writing on the wall created by the hand of God.

196. It is possible that Navarro is referring here to Madame Lefresne, a character portrayed by silent film vamp Theda Bara in *The Light* (1919, dir. J. Gordon Edwards).

197. Marquise de La Falaise is again a reference to Gloria Swanson.

198. Navarro is here invoking poet Amado Nervo, whose works were full of allusions to mysticism. Nervo was born in Tepic, Nayarit, in 1870. "Bueno, ¡y qué!" is the title of the twenty-first chapter of Nervo's book *Plenitud*, in which he advises readers to confront "a misgiving, a fear, an apprehension" with a resounding "so what?" Amado Nervo, *Plenitud* (Mexico: Salesiana, 1919), 73–74.

199. Negri's first, short-lived marriage was to Count Eugeniusz Dąmbski. The couple's 1919 marriage was annulled in 1922.

200. The flowery phrase Navarro uses is "hope hunters."

201. As the reader will learn later on, Raymundo's mother makes an appearance toward the end of this tale. Apparently Navarro forgot he had killed her in this installment. This hints at the pace at which he wrote the serial.

202. Charlotte M. Brame (1836–84) was a nineteenth-century English novelist whose work appeared in popular weekly publications. Her serialized novels took up themes of love and honor in the English countryside and were known for their rich descriptions of the life of the gentry. José María de la Concepción Apolinar Vargas Vila Bonilla (1860–1933), better known as José María Vargas Vila, was a Colombian writer and public intellectual. A controversial author, he took on social institutions such as the Roman Catholic Church and traditional concepts of family and society. Some of his books were banned, and he was excommunicated by the Church in 1900 after the publication of his novel *Ibis*.

203. The "Court of Miracles" refers to the slum areas of Paris that were thought to have inspired Victor Hugo's *Hunchback of Notre Dame* (1831) and *Les Misérables* (1862). The name derives from the common belief that beggars faked disabilities to appeal to people's sense of compassion. Once they returned to the slum, those disabilities miraculously disappeared.

204. Pierre Alexis Ponson du Terrail was a prolific mid-nineteenth-century French author. His first novels traded in the supernatural, including vampires. He became extremely well known for his adventure series featuring the protagonist Rocambole, which was first published as a serialized novel in the daily newspaper *La Patrie*. The popularity of that effort led to nine more novels featuring the modern adventure character.

205. When Sharkey speaks to her at this point, he switches from the formal *usted* to the familiar *tú*, indicating a presumption of intimacy, and maintains that form of address throughout his further dialogue with her.

206. This is another reference to the biblical story of the Feast of Belshazzar.

207. Navarro reminds his readers of Theda Bara, who played Cleopatra in the 1917 film *Cleopatra*, directed by J. Gordon Edwards. Although he invokes Sarah Bernhardt's name, the 1926 film *Nell Gwyn* (dir. Herbert Wilcox) starred Dorothy Gish. This could be a product of the speed at which Navarro was writing to meet the demand for regular installments.

208. The French is in the original. It translates to "without a fuss" or "without a care."

209. In his writing as a journalist, Navarro occasionally scolded theater owners who lured unsuspecting audiences with false promises of celebrity appearances or presented talent with inflated or false credentials. See Navarro, "Teatrales."

210. In Greek mythology, Silenus is a follower of Dionysus and is associated with dance and drunken revelry.

211. Here he addresses her using the informal *tú*.

212. The *cuple* was a risqué theatrical song that became popular in Spain in the nineteenth century. Sung by women, this genre was associated with lowbrow, male-only theaters. The form spread to the Americas, including Mexico and ethnic Mexican communities in the United States.

213. Navarro uses the adjective *litris* to describe these girls. A somewhat old-fashioned term, it can mean pedantic, pretentious, or affected.

214. Here Navarro refers to renowned composer and bandleader John Philip Sousa (1854–1932). Mercator likely refers to a Belgian brass band founded in 1863 that has reformed in recent decades as the Mercator Brass Band.

215. Velino M. Preza was a composer and director of the Police Band of Mexico. His was among the first of such Mexican orchestras to record for the Edison Company in 1905. See John Koegel and José Juan Tablada, "Compositores mexicanos y cubanos en Nueva York, c. 1880–1920," *Historia Mexicana* 56, no. 2 (2006): 565–66.

216. *El Heraldo de México* announced that the Police Band would be performing at Grauman's Theater. The paper expressed particular excitement because the band had never appeared on the West Coast despite touring the United States on multiple occasions. "La Banda de Policía viene a Los Ángeles," *El Heraldo de México*, May 4, 1921, 1.

217. Julián Carrillo, Arnulfo Miramontes, and Manuel Ponce were active in the twentieth century. See Yolanda Moreno Rivas, *La composición en México en el siglo XX* (Mexico City: Dirección General de Publicaciones del Consejo Nacional para la Cultura y las Artes, 1995); and Eduardo Soto Millán, *Diccionario de compositores mexicanos de música de concierto, siglo XX* (Mexico City: Sociedad de Autores y Compositores de Música; Fondo de Cultura Económica, 1996–98). Felipe Villanueva, Melesio Morales, and Ricardo Castro were active in the nineteenth century. See Yolanda Moreno Rivas, *Rostros del nacionalismo en la música mexicana: Un ensayo de interpretación* (Mexico City: Universidad Nacional de México; Escuela Nacional de Música, 1995).

218. Felipe de Jesús Villanueva Gutiérrez (1862–93) was a violinist, pianist, and composer. It is unclear who Berger may be in this context, but both Abundio Martínez (1875–1914) and Velino M. Preza (1866–1944) were musicians and composers who wrote popular music. Preza, as described above, was the director of the Banda de Música de la Policía de la Ciudad de México in 1904–14 and 1920–43.

219. While it is unclear who Calderón is in this context, the other names mentioned in this paragraph were well-known composers of waltzes and other forms of popular music in the late nineteenth century. They are José Pomar (1880–1961), composer, pianist, and orquesta director; Chucho Martínez (1880–1916), composer; Rodolfo Campodónico (1866–1926), composer; and Alfredo M. Garza (1877–1928), composer.

220. Given his romantic relationship with Lucha Reyes, we assume that Crispín is a pseudonym for Gabriel Navarro, one that does not appear elsewhere in the newspaper.

221. María de la Luz, better known as Lucha Reyes, would become famous for her forceful and emotive interpretation of ranchera songs that continues to influence the genre into the present. While living in Los Angeles, she supposedly had a tumultuous relationship with Navarro, about which rumors and speculation abound. See Garcia-Orozco, "Cucurrucucu Palomas," 135–36; and Alma Velasco, *Me llaman La Tequilera* (Mexico City: Suma de Letras, 2012), 94–112.

222. *Forbidden Paradise* (1924) was directed by Ernst Lubitsch; *A Woman of Paris* (1923) by Charles Chaplin. Lubitsch (1892–1947) was a German film director

who became well known in his native country for his escapist comedies and large-scale historical dramas. In 1922 he came to the United States, where he worked until his death, under contract with silent film star Mary Pickford, who hired him to direct the film *Rosita* (1923).

223. Marion Morgan (1881–1971) was a choreographer and screenwriter and the longtime companion of film director Dorothy Arzner. Her dance troupe, the Marion Morgan Dancers, performed on the vaudeville circuit in the 1910s and 1920s and later, when she began to focus on motion pictures, performed in numerous films.

224. Universum-Film Aktiengesellschaft was a Berlin-based film production company founded in 1917. Under the direction of Erich Pommer, the company's films, including comedies and historical epics, were considered Hollywood's competition in international markets.

225. *Where the Pavement Ends* (1923) was directed by Rex Ingram.

226. *Forbidden Paradise* (1924) was directed by Ernst Lubitsch.

227. *Ben-Hur* (1925) was directed by Fred Niblo.

228. Given the language, style, and perspectives on gender present in this article, we suspect that Rosa María is a pseudonym for Navarro himself.

229. *Love* (1927, dir. Edmund Golding) is the silent adaptation of Tolstoy's *Anna Karenina* starring Greta Garbo and John Gilbert. *Red Hair* (1928, dir. Clarence G. Badger) stars Clara Bow.

230. Here Navarro is likely referring to Spanish poet Juan Nepomuceno González de León, author of *El poeta filósofo, o poesías filosóficas en verso pentámetro* [The philosopher poet, or philosophical poetry in pentametric verse] (Seville: Manuel Nicolás Vásquez y Compañía, 1775).

231. Via Crucis, or Stations of the Cross, is a set of images with accompanying prayers that depict Jesus on the day of his crucifixion. The concept would have been familiar to Navarro's predominantly Catholic readership.

232. *The Woman Disputed* (1928) was directed by Henry King.

233. *Eternal Love* (1929) was directed by Ernst Lubitsch.

234. This role apparently never came to fruition for Rico.

235. Significantly, both of these productions were elaborate pantomimes staged without dialogue. Not coincidentally, both would be adapted as silent films. *Sumurun* (1920) was directed by Ernst Lubitsch, who also appeared in the film alongside Pola Negri. Two competing versions of *The Miracle* were released in 1912, a year after the play's premiere in London. For more on the adaptation of Reinhardt's pantomime productions, see Karl Teopfer, *Pantomime: The History and Metamorphosis of a Theatrical Ideology* (San Francisco: Vosuri Media, 2019), 774–96.

236. *In Old Arizona* (1928) was directed by Irving Cummings.

237. *The Singing Fool* (1928, dir. Lloyd Bacon), starring Al Jolson, is the follow-up to *The Jazz Singer* (1927, dir. Alan Crosland). The tremendous success of both films has been credited with inspiring the film industry to transition to all-sound production, hence Navarro's comparison here. *In Old Arizona* is an adaptation of the 1907 O. Henry short story "The Caballero's Way" (it is not a novel as Navarro suggests). This story would also introduce readers to the Cisco Kid, who would for decades be a staple of westerns set in the US-Mexico borderlands.

238. Notably, *The Red Dance* (1928, dir. Raoul Walsh) also starred Dolores Del Rio as a Russian peasant.

239. *The Dove* (1927, dir. Roland West), set in a fictional Latin American nation to prevent provoking offense to Mexico, stars Norma Talmadge as the "Mexican" dancer Dolores. *The Girl of the Golden West* was first staged by Belasco in 1905 and adapted to the screen multiple times. The 1923 version, in fact, was produced and directed by Edwin Carewe, two years before he "discovered" Dolores Del Rio and began managing her career.

240. It is likely that this was one segment of *Gus Edwards' International Colortune Revue* (1929), which showcased musical performances of various songs from around the world.

241. The capital that Navarro references here is Mexico City.

242. This is clearly a reference to Navarro's serialized novel of the same name.

243. James Ramsay MacDonald served as prime minister of the United Kingdom, the first who belonged to the Labour Party. He led minority Labour governments for nine months in 1924 and again between 1929 and 1931.

244. *The Bad One* (1930) was directed by George Fitzmaurice.

245. *What Price Glory* (1926) was directed by Raoul Walsh.

246. In an address to the Academy at Madrid titled "The New Art of Making Plays in This Age," noted Spanish playwright Lope de Vega (1562–1635) advocated for the production of three-act comedies despite their violation of Aristotelian precepts and their reputed lack of artistic respectability. In defending his position and the embrace of popular taste, he explained, "I write in accordance with that art which they devised who aspired to the applause of the crowd; for, since the crowd pays for the comedies, it is fitting to talk foolishly to it to satisfy its taste." The speech is reprinted in Lope de Vega, *The New Art of Writing Plays*, translated by William T. Brewster (New York: Dramatic Museum of Columbia University, 1914), 24–25.

247. This quotation, referring to residents of Latin America, is taken from the poem "To Roosevelt" by modernist Nicaraguan poet Rubén Darío (1867–1916). The poem is a searing rebuke of the Roosevelt administration's interventionist approach toward Latin American nations. In his rejection of these policies, the poet postulates a common, long-standing history of resistance across the continent: "You are the United States, / future invader of our naïve America / with its Indian blood, an America / that still prays to Christ and still speaks Spanish." *Selected Poems of Rubén Darío*, translated by Lysander Kemp (Austin: University of Texas Press, 1965), 69.

248. Navarro here refers to composer and pianist Ignacy Jan Paderewski, who resumed his musical career in 1922 after serving as prime minister of Poland.

249. *El cuerpo del delito* (1930, dir. Cyril Gardner and A. Washington Pezet) is the Spanish-language version of Paramount's *The Benson Murder Case* (1930, dir. Frank Tuttle). *La canción del beso* (1930, dir. James Tinling and Marcel Silver) is the alternate title of Fox's *El precio de un beso*, the Spanish-language version of *One Mad Kiss* (1930, dir. Silver Tinling). *El hombre malo* (1930, dir. William McGann) is the Spanish-language version of the Warner Bros./First National film *The Bad Man* (1930, dir. Clarence Badger).

250. José María Hinojosa Cabacho, "El Tempranillo," was a notorious bandit active in the Andalusia region of Spain in the early nineteenth century. His life would become the focus of the Spanish film *El rey de Sierra Morena* (1950, dir. Adolfo Aznar).

251. Holbrook Blinn starred in both the original theater play *The Bad Man* and the silent film adaptation released in 1923, which was produced and directed by Edwin Carewe. The film was remade by First National in the early sound period, starring Walter Huston as Pancho López.

252. Luis Alonso is better known by his stage name, Gilbert Roland. Ramón Samaniego is the given name of silent film star Ramon Novarro.

253. *So This Is Mexico* (1926, dir. Noel M. Smith), produced by and starring Richard Talmadge, was also released under the title *The Blue Streak*. *Wings* (1927), was directed by William A. Wellman.

254. *The Prisoner of Zenda* (1922) was directed by Rex Ingram.

255. *El presidio* (1930, dir. Ward Wing) is the Spanish-language version of MGM's prison drama *The Big House* (1930, dir. George W. Hill).

256. Carlos Borcosque directed a number of Spanish-language Hollywood films before eventually returning to South America. He went on to have a prolific career in Argentina, where he directed films into the 1960s. For more on his early career, see María Elena de las Carreras, "Carlos Borcosque: Learning the Ropes in Hollywood (1927–1938)," in de las Carreras and Horak, *Hollywood Goes Latin*, 83–94.

257. All are references to Mussolini. The Italian *sporco* or *sporca* means *dirty*.

258. *La mujer X* (1931, dir. Carlos F. Borcosque) is the Spanish-language version of MGM's *Madame X* (1929, dir. Lionel Barrymore).

259. *The Divine Lady* (1928) was directed by Frank Lloyd.

260. Navarro here used the original English for the quote and translated it for his readers in a parenthetical that reads "¿No tiene cara de tonto?"

261. *A Most Immoral Lady* (1929) was directed by John Griffith Wray. *Sombras de gloria* (1930, dir. Andrew L. Stone) is the Spanish-language version of *Blaze o' Glory* (1929, dir. Renaud Hoffman and George J. Crone), from Sono Art. It is widely regarded as one of the first Spanish-language features ever produced and distributed.

262. *Así es la vida* (1930, dir. George J. Crone) is the Spanish-language version of Sono Art's *What a Man* (1930, dir. George J. Crone).

263. *La fuerza del querer* (1930, dir. Ralph Ince) is the Spanish-language version of *The Big Fight* (1930, dir. Walter Lang). Also distributed under the title *Los que danzan*, *Pájaros de cuenta* (1930, dir. William McGann) is the Spanish-language version of the Warner Bros./First National film *Those Who Dance* (1930, dir. William Beaudine).

264. It is possible that Navarro is referring here to *Del mismo barro* (1930, dir. David Howard), although neither Castejón nor Davison appears in that film, the Spanish-language version of Fox's *Common Clay* (1930, dir. Victor Fleming).

265. *La llama sagrada* (1931, dir. William McGann) is the Spanish-language version of *The Sacred Flame* (1929, dir. Archie L. Mayo).

266. *Olimpia* (1930, dir. Chester M. Franklin) is the Spanish-language version of the MGM film *His Glorious Night* (1929, dir. Lionel Barrymore).

267. It is somewhat unclear what Navarro means by this reference. Based on a 1924 play by Sutton Vane, *Outward Bound* was adapted by Warner Bros. in 1930 and directed by Robert Milton, who had also staged its original Broadway run. Milton, however, was not involved in the production of *La llama sagrada* or of the English-language original. Indeed, as *Outward Bound* was produced by another studio, none of the directorial or writing credits listed in the *AFI Catalog* overlap with either version of *The Sacred Flame*.

268. Here Navarro refers to film directors' use of a megaphone to shout orders on set.

269. *Entre platos y notas* (1930) was directed by Jack Wagner.

270. *The Gaucho* (1927, dir. F. Richard Jones) was a Douglas Fairbanks vehicle that marked Lupe Velez's Hollywood feature film debut.

271. *Lady of the Pavements* (1929) was directed by D. W. Griffith.

272. The Universal film *Resurrección* (1931, dir. Edwin Carewe) is the Spanish-language version of *Resurrection* (1931, dir. Edwin Carewe). Both versions starred Lupe Velez. *Monsieur Le Fox* (1930, dir. Hal Roach) is the Spanish-language version of the MGM film *Men of the North* (1930, dir. Hal Roach). Gilbert Roland was the lead in both the Spanish and English versions.

273. *Del mismo barro* (1930) was directed by David Howard. *El barbero de Napoleón* (1930, dir. Sidney Lanfield) is Fox's Spanish-language version of *Napoleon's Barber* (1928, dir. John Ford).

274. *The Rogue of the Rio Grande* (1930) was directed by Spencer Gordon Bennet.

275. *White Shadows in the South Seas* (1928) was directed by W. S. Van Dyke; *The Bridge of San Luis Rey* (1929) by Charles Brabin; and *Aloha* (1931) by Albert S. Rogell.

276. *Sevilla de mis amores* (1930), directed by Ramon Novarro, is the Spanish-language version of *Call of the Flesh* (1930, dir. Charles Brabin). In addition to directing the French version, Navarro starred in the English, French, and Spanish versions.

277. *Hay que casar al príncipe* (1931, dir. Lewis Seiler) is the Spanish-language version of *Paid to Love* (1927, dir. Howard Hawks).

278. *Ben-Hur* (1925) was directed by Fred Niblo.

279. *The Pagan* (1929) was directed by W. S. Van Dyke.

280. The article in question is Katherine Albert, "Watch This Hombre! Is He the New Valentino, Who Will Sing His Way into Millions of Hearts?," *Photoplay* 37, no. 2 (January 1930): 31. In this piece, Albert offers comparisons similar to those made by Navarro: "Jose has everything—the refinement and sweetness of Ramon Novarro and Buddy Rogers, and that old-fashioned lure copyrighted by Jack Gilbert and Rudolph Valentino."

281. *El precio de un beso* (1930) was directed by James Tinling and Marcel Silver.

282. *Son of India* (1931) was directed by Jacques Feyder.

283. *Daybreak* (1931) was directed by Jacques Feyder.

284. This company would indeed go on to produce what most consider the first Mexican feature film with recorded sound: *Santa* (1931, dir. Antonio Moreno).

285. *Carne de cabaret* (1931), directed by Christy Cabanne, is the Spanish-language version of *Ten Cents a Dance* (1931), directed by Lionel Barrymore. *El código penal* (1931), directed by Phil Rosen, is the Spanish-language version of *The Criminal Code* (1931, dir. Howard Hawks). *El pasado acusa* (1931), directed by David Selman, is the Spanish-language version of *The Good Bad Girl* (1931), directed by Roy William Neill.

286. Navarro here refers to Paramount's production facility at Joinville, France (outside Paris), where the studio produced films in over a dozen languages.

287. *Su noche de bodas* (1931) was directed by Louis Mercanton; *Her Wedding Night* (1930) by Frank Tuttle.

288. *The Passion Flower* (1930) was directed by William C. de Mille.

289. *Sombras habaneras* (1929), directed by Cliff Wheeler, was initially heralded as the first Spanish-language sound feature, but its production was hampered by multiple difficulties, including the loss of original negatives in a fire. A postponed premiere, technical problems, and poor dubbing led many critics at the time to ultimately challenge its status as the first film produced in Spanish. See Heinink and Dickson, *Cita en Hollywood*, 26–27.

290. Felix Mendelssohn Bartholdy was a German composer, pianist, organist, and conductor active in the first half of the nineteenth century.

291. Tod Browning directed the English-language version (1931) for Universal. The 1931 Spanish-language version of *Dracula*, starring Mexican actress Lupita Tovar, was directed by George Melford and Enrique Tovar Avalos.

292. *Estrellados* (1930, dir. Edward Sedgwick) is the Spanish-language version of the Buster Keaton film *Free and Easy* (1930, dir. Edward Sedgwick). Curiously, Keaton was the lead in both versions. Like Laurel and Hardy in their foreign-language versions, he learned and recited his Spanish dialogue phonetically.

293. Virginia Fábregas (1871–1950) was perhaps Mexico's most prominent theatrical talent during this period. Her company's stint in Los Angeles during the late 1920s was transformative for the city's Spanish-language theater scene. She appeared only in one Hollywood film in the 1930s: *La fruta amarga* (1931, dir. Arthur Gregor). In this Spanish-language version of *Min and Bill* (1930, dir. George Hill), Fábregas played the lead role originated by Marie Dressler.

294. *Santa* (1932) was directed by Antonio Moreno.

295. A *sainete* is a form of one-act operatic comedy that gained popularity in Spain during the eighteenth century.

296. Tiples were stage actresses who worked primarily in Mexico during the 1910s and 1920s. Saúl Iván Hernández Suárez defines them as performers who "alternated between comedic acting and song, distinguished by their high-pitched voices, which were between mezzo-soprano and contralto." They were associated with theaters patronized by the working class and were known for their ribald sense of humor and suggestive clothing. See Saúl Iván Hernández Suárez, "Como violetas entre pavoreales: Las tiples, del cine mudo al sonoro," *Alter: Enfoques Críticos* 9, no. 18 (July–December 2018): 15–19.

297. *Aguilas frente al sol* (1932) was directed by Antonio Moreno; *Clemencia* (1935) by Chano Urueta.

298. Upton Sinclair is most widely known today for his expose of Chicago's meatpacking industry, *The Jungle* (1906). He was one of the film's primary financial backers, although he eventually withdrew support when the film went over budget and over schedule. *Thunder over Mexico* is a version of Eisenstein's film, edited without the director's input, that Sinclair helped release as a way of recouping his investment. The film would later be restored, re-edited according to Eisenstein's notes, and released as *Que Viva México!* For insight into the film's production and the relationship between Eisenstein and Sinclair, see Harry M. Geduld and Ronald Gottesman, eds., *Sergei Eisenstein and Upton Sinclair: The Making and Unmaking of 'Que Viva México!'* (Bloomington: Indiana University Press, 1970).

299. Navarro is here referring to the satirical novel about the Mexican Revolution penned by fellow expatriate journalist Teodoro Torres, which, like *La Opinión* and Navarro's own novels, was published by Casa Editorial Lozano. Teodoro Torres, *Como perros y gatos, o, las aventuras de la seña democracia en México: Historia cómica de la revolución mexicana* (San Antonio: Casa Editorial Lozano, 1924).

300. Salvador Rueda (1857–1933) was a Spanish journalist and poet; Luis Araquistáin (1886–1959) was a socialist politician and writer; Francisco Villaespesa (1877–1936) was a modernist poet, dramaturge, and writer. Blasco Ibáñez was a radical journalist, politician, and novelist, many of whose works were adapted for film by Hollywood studios in the late teens and twenties. For example, his novel *Los cuatro jinetes del Apocalipsis*, first published in 1916, was the basis for the 1921 World War I epic starring Ramon Novarro and directed by Rex Ingram. All of these authors were popular in Mexico during the early twentieth century.

301. Antonio Caso and José Vasconcelos were founders of the Ateneo de la Juventud, a group of intellectuals who promoted the humanities in general and the arts and culture in particular as an antidote to the positivist bent of the Porfirian regime, which had mobilized scientific racism to shape public policy. Both served as rectors of the Universidad Nacional de México (now the Universidad Nacional Autónoma de México) in the 1920s. Vasconcelos, who also served as secretary of public education, is most widely known for his 1925 book-length essay *La raza cósmica*. Long considered a key text of indigenismo, which in Mexico sought to incorporate the country's Indigenous past into contemporary Mexican nationalism, *La raza cósmica* has been reevaluated by scholars who have pointed out Vasconcelos's own reliance on the biological racism he decried in building his theory of mestizaje. See José Vasconcelos, *The Cosmic Race: A Bilingual Edition*, trans. Didier T. Jaén (Baltimore: Johns Hopkins University Press, 1997).

302. Alcalá Zamora was the prime minister of Spain at the time.

303. The pelado was a caricature of the urban underclass, popular in both theater and cinema.

304. *Revolución* (1933, dir. Raméon Peón) was eventually released as *La sombra de Pancho Villa* (*Shadow of Pancho Villa*). Other films mentioned here: *Una vida por otra* (1932, dir. John H. Auer), *Mano a mano* (1932, dir. Arcady Boytler), *El anónimo* (1932, dir. Fernando de Fuentes), and *Sobre las olas* (1933, dir. Miguel Zacarías).

305. *Chucho el Roto* (1934) was directed by Gabriel Soria; *La llorona* (1933) by Ramón Peón.

306. "Miserere" may refer specifically to Psalm 51, in which the speaker asks for God's mercy, or to its musical arrangement by Italian composer Gregorio Allegri, during the 1630s.

307. *Juan Soldado* (1939) was directed by Louis J. Gasnier. Although it does not appear in extant filmographies and databases, *Perdón, madre* (1939, dir. Carlos Gómez) was reviewed in San Antonio's *La Prensa* newspaper. See J. Angel Torres, "Dos nuevas películas en español," *La Prensa*, April 23, 1939. Given its low-budget, independent production, the film was probably not distributed widely and is in all likelihood lost.

308. *Contrabando* (1932) was directed by Alberto Méndez Bernal. For more on the production of this film, see Eduardo de la Vega Alfaro, "Competing against Hollywood: A Case Study, *Contrabando*," in de las Carreras and Horak, *Hollywood Goes Latin*, 171–77.

SELECTED BIBLIOGRAPHY

Newspapers and Periodicals
The Appeal News
Box Office
El Heraldo de México (Los Angeles, CA)
The Hollywood Reporter
The International Photographer
Los Angeles Times (Los Angeles, CA)
La Magazín de la Opinión (Los Angeles, CA)
The Mississippi Enterprise (Jackson, MS)
La Opinión (Los Angeles, CA)
Photoplay
La Prensa (San Antonio, TX)
Revista de Revistas (Mexico City)
El Sol (Phoenix, AZ)
El Tucsonense (Tucson, AZ)

Books and Articles

Abel, Richard, and Amy Rodgers. "Early Motion Pictures and Popular Print Culture: A Web of Ephemera." In *The Oxford History of Popular Print Culture*, vol. 6, *US Popular Print Culture, 1860–1920*, edited by Christine Bold, 191–210. New York: Oxford University Press, 2011.

Agrasánchez, Rogelio, Jr. *Guillermo Calles: A Biography of the Actor and Mexican Cinema Pioneer.* Jefferson, NC: McFarland, 2010.

———. *Mexican Movies in the United States: A History of the Films, Theaters, and Audiences, 1920–1960.* Jefferson, NC: McFarland, 2006.

Aguilar, Gene. *Lost Stories of West Coast Latino Boxing.* Charleston, SC: Arcadia, 2021.

"AHR Forum: Entangled Empires in the Atlantic World." *American Historical Review* 112, no. 3 (2007): 710–99.

Amaya, Hector. *Screening Cuba: Film Criticism as Political Performance during the Cold War.* Urbana: University of Illinois Press, 2010.

Arredondo, Gabriela F. *Mexican Chicago: Race, Identity, and Nation, 1916–1939.* Urbana: University of Illinois Press, 2008.

Balderrama, Francisco E. *In Defense of La Raza: The Los Angeles Mexican Consulate and the Mexican Community, 1929 to 1936.* Tucson: University of Arizona Press, 1982.

Baumgarten, Elisheva, Ruth Mazo Karras, and Katelyn Mesler, eds. *Entangled Histories: Knowledge, Authority, and Jewish Culture in the Thirteenth Century.* Philadelphia: University of Pennsylvania Press, 2017.

Bell, Melanie. "Film Criticism as 'Women's Work': The Gendered Economy of Film Criticism in Britain, 1945 –65." *Historical Journal of Film, Radio, and Television* 31, no. 2 (June 2011): 191–209.

Benito Argaiz, Immaculada. "Una aclaración necesaria en la bibliografía del escritor cerverano Manuel Ibo Alfaro (1828 –1885)." *Berceo* 132 (1997): 7 –28.

Bernal, Facundo. *A Stab in the Dark*. Los Angeles: Los Angeles Review of Books, 2018.

Bernardi, Daniel, ed. *The Birth of Whiteness: Race and the Emergence of U.S. Cinema*. New Brunswick, NJ: Rutgers University Press, 1996.

———, ed. *Classic Hollywood, Classic Whiteness*. Minneapolis: University of Minnesota Press, 2001.

Biltereyst, Daniel, Richard Maltby, and Philippe Meers. "Introduction: The Scope of New Cinema History." In *The Routledge Companion to New Cinema History*, edited by Daniel Biltereyst, Richard Maltby, and Philippe Meers, 1–12. New York: Routledge, 2019.

Biltereyst, Daniel, and Lies Van de Vijver. "Introduction: Movie Magazines, Digitization, and New Cinema History." In *Mapping Movie Magazines: Digitization, Periodicals and Cinema History*, edited by Daniel Biltereyst and Lies Van de Vijver, 1–13. Cham, Switzerland: Palgrave Macmillan, 2020.

Bold, Christine, ed. *The Oxford History of Popular Print Culture*, vol. 6, *US Popular Print Culture, 1860 –1920*. New York: Oxford University Press, 2011.

Borge, Jason. *Latin American Writers and the Rise of Hollywood Cinema*. New York: Routledge, 2008.

Bowser, Pearl, and Louise Spence, eds. *Writing Himself into History: Oscar Micheaux, His Silent Films, and His Audiences*. New Brunswick, NJ: Rutgers University Press, 2000.

Bruce-Novoa, Juan. "*La Prensa* and the Chicano Community." *Americas Review* 17, nos. 3 –4 (1989): 150 –56.

Caddoo, Cara. *Envisioning Freedom: Cinema and the Building of Modern Black Life*. Cambridge, MA: Harvard University Press, 2014.

Casillas, Dolores Inés. *Sounds of Belonging: U.S. Spanish-Language Radio and Public Advocacy*. New York: New York University Press, 2014.

Chacón, Ramón D. "The Chicano Immigrant Press in Los Angeles: The Case of 'El Heraldo de México,' 1916 –1920." *Journalism History* 4, no. 2 (1977): 48 –64.

Chung, Hye Seung. *Hollywood Asian: Philip Ahn and the Politics of Cross-Ethnic Performance*. Philadelphia: Temple University Press, 2006.

Cohen, Deborah, and Maura O'Connor. "Comparative History, Cross-National History, Transnational History—Definitions." In *Comparison and History: Europe in Cross-National Perspective*, edited by Deborah Cohen and Maura O'Connor, ix –xxiv. Abingdon, Oxon, UK: Routledge, 2004.

Cronqvist, Marie, and Christoph Hilgert. "Entangled Media Histories: The Value of Transnational and Transmedial Approaches in Media Historiography." *Media History* 23, no. 1 (2017): 130 –41.

Dávila, Arlene. *Latinos, Inc.: The Marketing and Making of a People*. Berkeley: University of California Press, 2001.

deCordova, Richard. *Picture Personalities: The Emergence of the Star System in America*. Champaign: University of Illinois Press, 2001.

de las Carreras, María Elena, and Jan-Christopher Horak, eds. *Hollywood Goes Latin: Spanish-Language Cinema in Los Angeles.* Brussels: Fédération Internationale des Archives du Film, 2019.

Escobar, Edward J. *Race, Police, and the Making of a Political Identity, 1900–1945.* Berkeley: University of California Press, 1999.

Espasande Bouza, Alejandra. "Romualdo Tirado and the Pioneers of Spanish-Language Cinema in Los Angeles." In *Hollywood Goes Latin: Spanish-Language Cinema in Los Angeles*, edited by María Elena de las Carreras and Jan-Christopher Horak, 113–25. Brussels: Fédération Internationale des Archives du Film, 2019.

Espinoza, Conrado. *Under the Texas Sun / El sol de Texas.* Houston: Arte Público, 2007.

Everett, Anna. *Returning the Gaze: A Genealogy of Black Film Criticism, 1909–1949.* Durham, NC: Duke University Press, 2001.

Ezra, Elizabeth, and Terry Rowden, eds. *Transnational Cinema: The Film Reader.* New York: Routledge, 2006.

Fein, Seth. "Culture across Borders in the Americas." *History Compass* 1, no. 1 (2003): 1–6.

Feng, Peter X. "Recuperating Suzie Wong: A Fan's Nancy Kwan-dary." In *Countervisions: Asian American Film Criticism*, edited by Darrell Y. Hamamoto and Sandra Liu, 40–56. Philadelphia: Temple University Press, 2000.

Field, Allyson Nadia. *Uplift Cinema: The Emergence of African American Film and the Possibility of Black Modernity.* Durham, NC: Duke University Press, 2015.

Flores, John H. *The Mexican Revolution in Chicago: Immigration Politics from the Early Twentieth Century to the Cold War.* Champaign: University of Illinois Press, 2018.

Fortmueller, Kate. *Below the Stars: How the Labor of Working Actors and Extras Shapes Media Production.* Austin: University of Texas Press, 2021.

Fraser, Nancy. "Rethinking the Public Sphere: A Contribution to the Critique of Actually Existing Democracy." In *Habermas and the Public Sphere*, edited by Craig Calhoun, 109–42. Cambridge, MA: MIT Press, 1992.

Fregoso, Rosa Linda. *MeXicana Encounters: The Making of Social Identities on the Borderlands.* Berkeley: University of California Press, 2003.

Frey, Mattias. *The Permanent Crisis of Film Criticism: The Anxiety of Authority.* Amsterdam: Amsterdam University Press, 2015.

Frey, Mattias, and Cecilia Sayad, eds. *Film Criticism in the Digital Age.* New Brunswick, NJ: Rutgers University Press, 2015.

Fuller, Kathryn H. *At the Picture Show: Small-Town Audiences and the Creation of Movie Fan Culture.* Charlottesville: University of Virginia Press, 2001.

Gaines, Jane M. *Fire and Desire: Mixed-Race Movies in the Silent Era.* Chicago: University of Chicago Press, 2001.

García, Mario T. *Desert Immigrants: The Mexicans of El Paso, 1880–1920.* New Haven, CT: Yale University Press, 1981.

Garcia, Matt. *A World of Its Own: Race, Labor, and Citrus in the Making of Greater Los Angeles, 1900–1970.* Chapel Hill: University of North Carolina Press, 2001.

Garcia-Orozco, Antonia. "Cucurrucucu Palomas: The *Estilo Bravío* of Lucha Reyes and the Creation of Feminist Consciousness via the *Canción Ranchera*." PhD diss., Claremont Graduate University, 2005.

Gaytán, Marie Sarita, and Sergio de la Mora. "Queening/Queering *Mexicanidad*: Lucha Reyes and the *Canción Ranchera*." *Feminist Formations* 28, no. 3 (2016): 196–221.

Gómez, Laura E. *Manifest Destinies: The Making of the Mexican American Race*. New York: New York University Press, 2007.

Griswold del Castillo, Richard. *The Treaty of Guadalupe Hidalgo: A Legacy of Conflict*. Norman: University of Oklahoma Press, 1990.

Gruesz, Kirsten Silva. "Mexican/American: The Making of Borderlands Print Culture." In *The Oxford History of Popular Print Culture*, vol. 6, *U.S. Popular Print Culture, 1860–1920*, edited by Christine Bold, 457–76. New York: Oxford University Press, 2011.

Gunckel, Colin. "Ambivalent Si(gh)tings: Stardom and Silent Film in Mexican America." *Film History* 27, no. 1 (2017): 110–39.

———. *Mexico on Main Street: Transnational Film Culture in Los Angeles before World War II*. New Brunswick, NJ: Rutgers University Press, 2015.

Gunckel, Colin, Jan-Christopher Horak, and Lisa Jarvinen, eds. *Cinema between Latin America and Los Angeles: Origins to 1960*. New Brunswick, NJ: Rutgers University Press, 2019.

Gunckel, Colin, Jan-Christopher Horak, and Lisa Jarvinen. Introduction to *Cinema between Latin America and Los Angeles: Origins to 1960*, edited by Colin Gunckel, Jan-Christopher Horak, and Lisa Jarvinen, 1–30. New Brunswick, NJ: Rutgers University Press, 2019.

Gutiérrez, Arcelia. "No More Prostitutes, Pimps, and Pushers: Deploying Hispanic Panethnicity in Media Advocacy." *Critical Studies in Media Communication* 36, no. 4 (2019): 309–22.

Gutiérrez, David G. *Walls and Mirrors: Mexican Americans, Mexican Immigrants, and the Politics of Ethnicity*. Berkeley: University of California Press, 1995.

Gutiérrez, Félix F., and Jorge Reina Shement. *Spanish-Language Radio in the Southwestern United States*. Austin: Center for Mexican American Studies, University of Texas, 1979.

Hallett, Hilary A. *Go West, Young Women! The Rise of Early Hollywood*. Berkeley: University of California Press, 2013.

Heinink, J. B., and Robert G. Dickson. *Cita en Hollywood: Antología de las películas norteamericanas habladas en castellano*. Bilbao, Spain: Mensajero, 1990.

Hernandez, Jose Amaro. *Mutual Aid for Survival: The Case of the Mexican American*. Malabar, FL: Robert E. Krieger, 1983.

Hershfield, Joanne. *The Invention of Dolores del Río*. Minneapolis: University of Minnesota Press, 2000.

Higginbotham, Evelyn Brooks. *Righteous Discontent: The Women's Movement in the Black Baptist Church, 1880–1920*. Cambridge, MA: Harvard University Press, 1993.

Hilmes, Michele. "Entangled Media Histories: A Response." *Media History* 23, no. 1 (2017): 142–44.

Hoechtl, Nina. "On the *Nuevo Teatro Máximo de la Raza*: Still Thinking, Feeling, and Speaking Spanish On- and Offscreen." In *Cinema between Latin America and Los Angeles: Origins to 1960*, edited by Colin Gunckel, Jan-Christopher Horak, and Lisa Jarvinen, 138–58. New Brunswick, NJ: Rutgers University Press, 2019.

Horak, Jan-Christopher. "Cantabria Films and the L.A. Film Market, 1938 –1940." In *Cinema between Latin America and Los Angeles: Origins to 1960*, edited by Colin Gunckel, Jan-Christopher Horak, and Lisa Jarvinen, 108 –14. New Brunswick, NJ: Rutgers University Press, 2019.

Hyde, Charles K. *Copper for America: The United States Copper Industry from Colonial Times to the 1990s*. Tucson: University of Arizona Press, 1998.

Jarvinen, Lisa. "A Mass Market for Spanish-Language Films: Los Angeles, Hybridity, and the Emergence of Latino Audiovisual Media." In *Cinema between Latin America and Los Angeles: Origins to 1960*, edited by Colin Gunckel, Jan-Christopher Horak, and Lisa Jarvinen, 80 –96. New Brunswick, NJ: Rutgers University Press, 2019.

———. *The Rise of Spanish-language Filmmaking: Out from Hollywood's Shadow, 1929–1939*. New Brunswick, NJ: Rutgers University Press, 2012.

Joint Fact-Finding Committee on Un-American Activities in California. *Un-American Activities in California*. Sacramento: California State Senate, 1943.

Kanellos, Nicolás. "A Brief History of Hispanic Periodicals in the United States." In *Hispanic Periodicals in the United States: Origins to 1960: A Brief History and Comprehensive Bibliography*, edited by Nicolás Kanellos and Helvetia Martell, 8 –136. Houston: Arte Público, 2000.

———. *Hispanic Immigrant Literature: El Sueño del Retorno*. Austin: University of Texas Press, 2011.

Kanellos, Nicolás, and Helvetia Martell, eds. *Hispanic Periodicals in the United States, Origins to 1960: A Brief History and Comprehensive Bibliography*. Houston: Arte Público, 2000.z

Kenaga, Heidi. "Making the 'Studio Girl': The Hollywood Studio Club and Industry Regulation of Female Labour." *Film History* 18, no. 2 (2006): 129 –39.

Khor, Denise. *Transpacific Convergences: Race, Migration, and Japanese American Film Culture before World War II*. Chapel Hill: University of North Carolina Press, 2022.

Kurashige, Scott. *The Shifting Grounds of Race: Black and Japanese Americans in the Making of Multiethnic Los Angeles*. Princeton, NJ: Princeton University Press, 2008.

Latham, Sean, and Robert Scholes. "The Rise of Periodical Studies." *PMLA* 121, no. 2 (2006): 517 –31.

Leonard, Kevin Allen. *The Battle for Los Angeles: Racial Ideology and World War II*. Albuquerque: University of New Mexico Press, 2006.

Lewis, Jon, and Eric Smoodin, eds. *Looking Past the Screen: Case Studies in American Film History and Method*. Durham, NC: Duke University Press, 2007.

Limon, José E. "Stereotyping and Chicano Resistance." In *Chicanos and Film: Representation and Resistance*, edited by Chon A. Noriega, 3 –17. Minneapolis: University of Minnesota Press, 1992.

Lopez, Lori Kido. *Asian American Media Activism: Fighting for Cultural Citizenship*. New York: New York University Press, 2016.

Marez, Curtis. "Subaltern Soundtracks: Mexican Immigrants and the Making of Hollywood Cinema." *Aztlán: A Journal of Chicano Studies* 29, no. 1 (2004): 57 –82.

Massood, Paula J. "African American Stardom Inside and Outside of Hollywood: Ernest Morrison, Noble Johnson, Evelyn Preer, and Lincoln Perry." In *Idols of Modernity: Movie Stars of the 1920s*, edited by Patrice Petro, 227–49. New Brunswick, NJ: Rutgers University Press, 2010.

McCaa, Robert. "Missing Millions: The Demographic Costs of the Mexican Revolution." *Mexican Studies/Estudios Mexicanos* 19, no. 2 (2003): 367–400.

McKenna, Denise. "The Photoplay or the Pickaxe: Extras, Gender, and Labour in Early Hollywood." *Film History* 23, no. 1 (2011): 5–19.

Medeiros, Francine. "*La Opinión*, a Mexican Exile Newspaper: A Content Analysis of Its First Years, 1926–1929." *Aztlán: A Journal of Chicano Studies* 11, no. 1 (1980): 65–87.

Miller, Toby, Nitin Govil, John McMurria, and Richard Maxwell. *Global Hollywood*. Berkeley: University of California Press, 2002.

Monroy, Douglas. *Rebirth: Mexican Los Angeles from the Great Migration to the Great Depression*. Berkeley: University of California Press, 1999.

Mora, G. Cristina. *Making Hispanics: How Activists, Bureaucrats, and Media Constructed a New American*. Chicago: University of Chicago Press, 2014.

Navarro, Daniel. *Navarro's Silent Film Guide: A Comprehensive Look at American Silent Cinema*. Los Angeles: New University Press, 2013.

Navarro, Gabriel. *Barbara La Marr: Una historia de placer y dolor*. San Antonio: Casa Editorial Lozano, 1926.

Negrón-Muntaner, Frances, Chelsea Abbas, Luis Figueroa, and Samuel Robson. *The Latino Media Gap: A Report on the State of Latinos in U.S. Media*. Los Angeles: National Association of Latino Independent Producers (NALIP); Washington, DC: National Hispanic Foundation of the Arts; New York: Columbia University Center for the Study of Ethnicity and Race, 2014.

Noriega, Chon A. *Shot in America: Television, the State, and the Rise of Chicano Cinema*. Minneapolis: University of Minnesota Press, 2000.

Pagán, Eduardo Obregón. *Murder at the Sleepy Lagoon: Zoot Suits, Race, and Riot in Wartime L.A.* Chapel Hill: University of North Carolina Press, 2003.

Perlman, Allison, and Hector Amaya. "Owning a Voice: Broadcasting Policy, Spanish Language Media, and Latina/o Speech Rights." *Communication, Culture and Critique* 6, no. 1 (2013): 142–60.

Petty, Miriam J. *Stealing the Show: African American Performers and Audiences in 1930s Hollywood*. Berkeley: University of California Press, 2016.

Pluecker, John. "'One More Texas-Mexican': Under the Texas Sun and Conflicts of Nation." Introduction to *Under the Texas Sun / El sol de Texas*, edited by Conrado Espinoza, 113–38. Houston: Arte Público, 2007.

Rawle, Steven. *Transnational Cinema: An Introduction*. London: Palgrave, 2018.

Rodríguez, América. "Creating an Audience and Remapping a Nation: A Brief History of US Spanish Language Broadcasting, 1930–1980." *Quarterly Review of Film and Video* 16, nos. 3–4 (1999): 357–74.

Rodriguez, Julia. "South Atlantic Crossings: Fingerprints, Science, and the State in Turn-of-the-Century Argentina." *American Historical Review* 109, no. 2 (2004): 387–416.

Romo, Ricardo. *East Los Angeles: History of a Barrio*. Austin: University of Texas Press, 1983.

Rubin, Joan Shelley. *The Making of Middlebrow Culture*. Chapel Hill: University of North Carolina Press, 1992.

Ruiz, Vicki. *From Out of the Shadows: Mexican Women in Twentieth-Century America*. New York: Oxford University Press, 1998.

Sackman, Douglas Cazaux. *Orange Empire: California and the Fruits of Eden*. Berkeley: University of California Press, 2005.

Sánchez, George J. *Becoming Mexican American: Ethnicity, Culture, and Identity in Chicano Los Angeles, 1900–1945*. New York: Oxford University Press, 1993.

Sánchez, Rosaura. *Telling Identities: The Californio Testimonios*. Minneapolis: University of Minnesota Press, 1995.

Serna, Laura Isabel. "'As a Mexican I Feel It's My Duty': Citizenship, Censorship, and the Campaign against Derogatory Films in Mexico." *Americas* 63, no. 2 (2006): 225–44.

———. "Atmosphere: Mexican Extras and Race Making in Silent Hollywood." *Journal of Cinema and Media Studies* 63, no. 2 (forthcoming).

———. *Making Cinelandia: American Films and Mexican Film Culture before the Golden Age*. Durham, NC: Duke University Press, 2014.

———. "Popular Mexican Masculinity and American Culture in the 1920s: Migrants and Fifís." *Latin American Research Review* 57, no. 2 (2022): 422–39.

Shell, Marc, and Werner Sollors, eds. *The Multilingual Anthology of American Literature: A Reader of Original Texts with English Translations*. New York: New York University Press, 2000.

Sides, Josh. *L.A. City Limits: African American Los Angeles from the Great Depression to the Present*. Berkeley: University of California Press, 2003.

Smith, Jeff. *Film Criticism, the Cold War, and the Blacklist: Reading the Hollywood Reds*. Berkeley: University of California Press, 2014.

Smoodin, Eric. "Introduction: The History of Film History." In *Looking Past the Screen: Case Studies in American Film History and Method*, edited by Jon Lewis and Eric Smoodin, 1–34. Durham, NC: Duke University Press, 2007.

Snyder, Sherri. *Barbara La Marr: The Girl Who Was Too Beautiful for Hollywood*. Lexington: University Press of Kentucky, 2017.

Special Committee on Un-American Activities. *Investigation of Un-American Propaganda Activities in the United States: Hearings before a Special Committee on Un-American Activities, House of Representatives, Seventy-eighth Congress, Second Session on H. Res. 282, Appendix Part 9, Vol. 2*. Washington, DC: Government Printing Office, 1944.

Spigel, Lynn. *Make Room for Television: Television and the Family Ideal in Postwar America*. Chicago: University of Chicago Press, 1992.

Stamp, Shelley. *Movie-Struck Girls: Women and Motion Picture Culture after the Nickelodeon*. Princeton, NJ: Princeton University Press, 2000.

Stewart, Jacqueline Najuma. *Migrating to the Movies: Cinema and Black Urban Modernity*. Berkeley: University of California Press, 2005.

Stokes, Melvyn, and Richard Maltby, eds. *American Movie Audiences: From the Turn of the Century to the Early Sound Era*. London: BFI, 1999.

Subrahmanyam, Sanjay. "Connected Histories: Notes towards a Reconfiguration of Early Modern Eurasia." *Modern Asian Studies* 31, no. 3 (1997): 735–62.

Trice, Jasmine Nadua. *City of Screens: Imagining Audiences in Manila's Alternative Film Culture*. Durham, NC: Duke University Press, 2021.

Underwood, Katherine. "Pioneering Minority Representation: Edward Roybal and the Los Angeles City Council, 1949–1962." *Pacific Historical Review* 66, no. 3 (1997): 399–425.

Valle, Victor. "LA's Latina/o Phantom Nonfiction and the Technologies of Literary Secrecy." In *Latinx Writing Los Angeles: Nonfiction Dispatches from a Decolonial Rebellion*, edited by Ignacio López-Calvo and Victor Valle, 1–32. Lincoln: University of Nebraska Press, 2018.

Vasey, Ruth. *The World According to Hollywood, 1918–1939*. Madison: University of Wisconsin Press, 1997.

Venegas, Daniel. *The Adventures of Don Chipote, or, When Parrots Breast-Feed*. Houston: Arte Público, 2000.

Walmsley-Evans, Huw. *Film Criticism as a Cultural Institution*. New York: Routledge, 2018.

Werner, Michael, and Bénédicte Zimmermann. "Beyond Comparison: *Histoire Croisée* and the Challenge of Reflexivity." *History and Theory* 45, no. 1 (2006): 30–50.

Wild, Mark. *Street Meeting: Multiethnic Neighborhoods in Early Twentieth-Century Los Angeles*. Berkeley: University of California Press, 2005.

Young, Julia G. *Mexican Exodus: Emigrants, Exiles, and Refugees of the Cristero War*. New York: Oxford University Press, 2015.

Yuen, Nancy Wang. *Reel Inequality: Hollywood Actors and Racism*. Newark, NJ: Rutgers University Press, 2016.

ABOUT THE EDITORS

COLIN GUNCKEL is an associate professor of film, television, and media, American culture and Latina/o studies at the University of Michigan and the author of *Mexico on Main Street: Transnational Film Culture in Los Angeles before World War II* (Rutgers University Press, 2015). He has published essays in *American Quarterly, Aztlán: A Journal of Chicano Studies, Film History, Journal of Popular Music Studies, Social Justice,* and *Velvet Light Trap,* in addition to editing and contributing to multiple edited collections and exhibition catalogs, including the award-winning *La Raza* (UCLA Chicano Studies Research Center Press, 2020). He also serves as associate editor of the A Ver: Revisioning Art History monograph series on individual Latina/o artists.

LAURA ISABEL SERNA is an associate professor of cinema and media studies and history at the University of Southern California. She is the author of *Making Cinelandia: American Films and Mexican Film Culture before the Golden Age* (Duke Univerrsity Press, 2014). Her work has appeared in edited collections and journals including *Latin American Research Review, Film History, Journal of Cinema and Media Studies,* and *Aztlán: A Journal of Chicano Studies.*

INDEX

Barbara La Marr (*continued*)
characters:
—Barbara La Marr: adoptive family
of, 113, 115, 133, 144–47, 149–51;
in *Black Orchids*, 115–17; career of,
124–25; children of, 123–24, 125,
133, 134, 145, 150; desire for fame,
113–14, 122, 126, 134–35, 136;
illness and death, 142–52; image
of, 116, 117–18, 122, 126, 134–35,
141; marriages of, 113–15, 123;
movies of, 118, 124, 128, 133,
135, 141; changes name, 249,
251, 269–70; scandals of, 122; as
"White Moth," 141, 143
—Fidel Murillo, 138, 139
—Jack Daugherty, 115–16, 119–23,
125, 126, 128–33, 135–40
barbero de Napoleón, El (film), 285,
371n283
Bárcena, Catalina, 328
Bardelys the Magnificent (film), 365n190
Barrymore, John, 251, 252, 296,
Barrymore, Lionel, 370n258, 371n266,
372n285; in *Barbara La Marr*, 133
Battle of Tampico, 362n155
Baxter, Warner, 254, 255
Beery, Wallace, 234, 271
Belasco, David, 255, 369n239
Belshazzar/Balthasar, 365n195,
366n206; in *City of No Return*, 161
Ben-Hur (film, theatrical production),
241, 256, 287, 289, 365n190,
368n227
Bennett, Richard, in *Barbara La Marr*,
133
Bernhardt, Sarah, 366n207; in *City of
No Return*, 198
Birth of a Nation, The (film), 34
Black Orchids (film), 363n168, 364n170;
in *Barbara La Marr*, 115, 117, 118,
124

Blinn, Holbrook, 264, 370n251
Blue Streak, The (film), 370n253
Bohr, José, 257, 274, 285, 323
Bonanova, Fortunio, 308
Borcosque, Carlos Francisco, 270, 272,
370n256, 370n258
Bow, Clara, 273, 291, 364n175,
368n229
Brame, Charlotte M., 366n202
Bridge of San Luis Rey, The (film), 286,
371n275
Bronnen, Arnolt, 28
Browning, Tod, 372n291
Burgess, Dorothy, 254–55
Burning Trail, The, 364n174

"Caballero's Way, The" (Henry),
368n237
Café Montmartre, in *Barbara La Marr*,
120; in *City of No Return*, 194
Calderón, Mauricio, 11
California International Theater, 300–1,
302
Calles, Guillermo, 7, 15
Calvo, María, 297, 303, 309
Campillo, Anita, 45
Campodónico, Rodolfo, 230, 367n219
cancion del beso, La (film), 264, 369n249
Carewe, Edwin, 227, 369n239,
370n251, 371n272
Carne de cabaret (film), 291, 372n285
Carranza, Venustiano, 11–12, 353n46
Carrillo, Eduardo A., 14
Carrillo, Julián, 229, 367n217
Carville, Robert (Bob), in *Barbara La
Marr*, 114, 142
Casa del Artista, 45
Casa Editorial Lozano, 22, 110, 373n299
Caso, Antonio, 317, 373n301
casting: in *City of No Return*, 178, 179;
discriminatory, 280; exploitive,
45; of extras, 246, 248; miscasting,

Mexican National Band, 227–28. *See also* Banda de Música de la Policía
Mexican Revolution, 1, 26, 258, 311, 362n156, 373n299
Mexican War of Independence, 12
Mexico: border region of, 3; as civilized nation, 313; Hollywood boycott by, 33–34; music of, 227–30; political situation of, 12, 249; portrayals of, 44, 311–14, 320; publications from, 22; in transnational culturescape, 21. *See also* Mexican film production; Mexican Revolution; Mexican War of Independence
Mexico City, 20, 21, 291, 344, 363n158, 369n241
México de afuera, 23, 33, 38, 357n81
MGM (Metro-Goldwyn-Mayer), 39, 298; in *Barbara La Marr*, 115; in *City of No Return*, 177, 179, 180, 181; films of, 291, 370n255, 370n258, 371n266, 371n272
Miceli, Giuseppe, 303
Miller, Patsy Ruth, in *Barbara La Marr*, 138, 140
Milton, Robert, 371n267
Miracle, The (play), 253, 256, 368n235
Miramontes, Arnulfo, 229, 367n217
miscasting, 42, 45, 281, 280–86, 297, 298
Mojica, José, 45, 287–89, 308
Monroy, Douglas, 350n22
Monsieur Le Fox (film), 285, 286, 371n272
Montalván, Celia, 303
Montenegro, Conchita, 16, 44
Montes, Cora, 285, 303
Mora, G. Cristina, 6
Morales, Melesio, 229, 367n217
morality. *See* gender norms; sexual norms; social norms

Moreno, Antonio, 238, 239, 241, 262–65, 365n190; 372n284; 373n297; in *Barbara La Marr*, 137; in *City of No Return*, 156
Moreno, Hilda, 315
Morgan, Marion, 238, 368n223
Morla, Elvira, 276, 278–79, 285, 303
Most Immoral Lady, A (film), 273, 370n261
Motion Picture Producers and Distributors of America, 41
mujer X, La (film), 271
Murillo, Fidel, avatar for Navarro, 25, 26–27, 28, 30, 33. See also *Barbara La Marr; Señorita Estela*
Murray, Mae, 240; in *City of No Return*, 156
music, types of: charangas, 363n164; in *Señorita Estela*, 54, 83, 87; marches, 229, 296; movie scores, 204, 230, 261; musicals, 14; operas, 363n163; songs, 228, 229, 230, 288, 362n154, 369n240; waltzes, 367n219
musical performance/programs, 3, 11, 16, 227–30, 362n154, 362n154, 363n158, 364n172, 369n240. *See also* theater/theatrical productions
mutual aid societies, 8, 10, 15

Nagel, Conrad, 289
Naldi, Nita, in *Barbara La Marr*, 120–21
Navarro, Carlos, 271
Navarro, Francisco Daniel (Dan), 14, *14*, 355n57
Navarro, Gabriel
—biographical information: as author-journalist, 6; awards/honors for, 19–20; career and legacy of, 1–2, 34; children of, 14, *14*; as columnist, 15, 24, 33, 35, 37, 39, 40; community involvement of,

Villanueva Gutiérrez, Felipe de Jesús
  (Felipe Villanueva), 229, 367n217,
  367n218; in *Señorita Estela*, 72
Villarías, Carlos, 297
Viva México (film), 310, 314

Warner Bros., 14, 291, 315, 369n249,
  370n263, 371n267
"Watch This Hombre!" (Albert), 288,
  371n280
Welles, Orson, xxvi, *xxvii*
West, Roland, 369n239
What Price Glory (film), 261, 369n245
Where the Pavement Ends (film), 240,
  368n225
White, Alice, 273,

White Monkey, The (film), 364n179; in
  Barbara La Marr, 141
White Moth, The (film), 364n178; in
  Barbara La Marr, 141
White Shadows in the South Seas (film),
  286, 370n261
Wings (film), 370n253; in *City of No
  Return*, 217
Woman Disputed, The (film), 267,
  370n253
Woman of Paris, A (film), 234, 367n222
Wray, John Griffith, 370n261
Wu Li Chang (film), 298

Zarco, Estelita, 346
Zea, María Luisa, 346